THE NEOCONSERVATIVE PERSUASION

The Neoconservative Persuasion

Selected Essays, 1942–2009

IRVING KRISTOL

Edited by
Gertrude Himmelfarb

Foreword by
William Kristol

BASIC BOOKS
A Member of the Perseus Books Group
New York

Published by Basic Books,
A Member of the Perseus Books Group

Books published by Basic Books are available at special discounts for bulk purchases in
the United States by corporations, institutions, and other organizations. For more
information, please contact the Special Markets Department at the Perseus Books
Group, 2300 Chestnut Street, Suite 200, Philadelphia, PA 19103, or call
(800) 810-4145, ext. 5000, or e-mail special.markets@perseusbooks.com.

Designed by Brent Wilcox

The Library of Congress has catalogued the print edition of this book as follows:
Kristol, Irving.
   The neoconservative persuasion : selected essays, 1942–2009 / by Irving Kristol ;
edited by Gertrude Himmelfarb ; foreword by William Kristol.
      p.   cm.
   Includes bibliographical references.
   ISBN 978-0-465-02223-6 (alk. paper)
   1. Conservatism.   2. Conservatism—United States.   I. Himmelfarb, Gertrude.
II. Title.
   JC573.K6658 2010
   320.520973—dc22

                                                                    2010038251

E-book ISBN: 978-0-465-02333-2

10 9 8 7 6 5 4 3 2 1

CONTENTS

FOREWORD: IN MEMORIAM: IRVING KRISTOL, 1920–2009

In 1994 my father wrote a piece for the *Wall Street Journal* titled "Life Without Father." It dealt with the subject of the family and poverty and welfare—with my father drawing for his argument, as he so often did, on a combination of social science, common sense, history, and personal experience. In the course of the article, my father briefly discussed his father, Joseph Kristol, who, he wrote, "was thought by all our relatives and his fellow workers to be wise, and fair, and good. I thought so too."

So have Liz and I always thought about our father. To us, he was wise, and fair, and good. I honestly don't think it ever occurred to us that we could have had a better father. So as we enter the rest of our life—a life without our father—we are overwhelmed not by a sense of loss or grief, though of course we feel both, but by a sense of gratitude: Having Irving Kristol as our dad was our great good fortune.

Now, my father would often speak of his own great good fortune. That was meeting my mother. Shortly after graduating from City College, my father—a diligent if already somewhat heterodox Trotskyist—was assigned to attend the meetings of a Brooklyn branch of the young Trotskyists. As my father later wrote, the meetings were farcical and pointless, as they were intended to recruit the proletarian youths of Bensonhurst to a cause they were much too sensible to take seriously. But the meetings turned out not to be entirely pointless, because my father met my mother there. They were married, and they remained happily married—truly happily married, thoroughly happily married—for the next sixty-seven years.

Dan Bell, who knew my parents for that whole span, called my parents' marriage "the best marriage of [his] generation." I only knew my parents for fifty-six years, so I can't speak with Dan's authority—and my first couple of years with my parents are something of a blur. But I know enough confidently to endorse his judgment.

During the 1960s and 1970s, when Liz and I were growing up, everything is supposed to have become complicated and conflicted and ambiguous. Not so with respect to my parents' love for each other. Or with respect to the love and admiration that Liz and I—and later, Caleb and Susan—had for my father. Our love for him was always straightforward, unambivalent, and unconditional.

As was the love of his five grandchildren for him. And as was his love for them. Almost seven years ago, my father was scheduled for lung surgery. As we were talking the night before, my father matter-of-factly acknowledged the possibility he might not survive. And, he said, he could have no complaints if that were to happen. "I've had such a lucky life," he remarked. (Actually, I'm editing a bit since we're in a house of worship. He said, "I've had such a goddamn lucky life.")

But, he said, it would be just great to get another five years—in order to see the grandchildren grow up. That wish of his was granted. He got almost seven years. So he was able to see Rebecca and Anne and Joe graduate from college. He was able to attend Rebecca and Elliot's wedding. He—a staff sergeant in the army in World War II—developed a renewed interest in things military as Joe trained to be, and then was commissioned as, a second lieutenant in the Marine Corps.

And he was able to see Liz's children grow up too, to watch Max and Katy become poised and impressive teenagers—it turns out that's not a contradiction in terms. My father was able to get to know them, and to talk with them, in a way you can't with much younger kids. So that too was a great source of happiness.

Everyone knows of my father's good nature and good humor. He kept that to the end. In the last couple of years, his hearing loss—and the limitations of even the most modern hearing aid technology—sometimes made it difficult for him to understand everything that was being said in a noisy restaurant or a busy place. But he compensated. A few months ago, my parents were out for brunch with the Stelzers and the Krauthammers. After a stretch where he couldn't quite pick up some exchanges between Irwin and Charles, my dad said to the two of them: "I can't hear what you're saying. So I make it up. And," he added, smiling, "sometimes you disappoint me."

But my father was in general not the disappointed sort. It's true that he loved dogs and never had one. But he made up for that by doting on his two granddogs—Liz and Caleb's Sandy, and of course Patches, whom he saw more of because of our proximity. Patches really loved my father—and as many of you know, Patches is choosy in his affections.

Just a day or so before he slipped from consciousness last week, my father was greeted by one of those well-trained dogs that visit hospitals, in this case a big golden retriever. He patted it and communed with it for a while. Then, as the owner led the dog away, my father commented to us, as if for the ages—"dogs are noble creatures."

My father liked humans too—though I'm not sure he thought they quite rose to the level of dogs as noble creatures. Still, as I look around today, I do wish my father could be here, because he would have so enjoyed seeing and talking with all of you.

In one of the many, many e-mails and notes I've gotten in the last few days, a friend commented, "When I'd stop by the *Public Interest* office in the 1980s, your dad would always start a conversation with, 'How's the family?' I suppose that was his standard opener. But I noticed in the last few years, when I'd see him at AEI or somewhere else in D.C., he'd ask about 'the family' and then 'how's everyone?' If I mentioned some former *PI* editor or writer, he'd beam—as if it were news of his own extended family."

My father's extended family ended up being pretty large. In politics and law and business and journalism, in New York and Washington and elsewhere, even in the strange outposts of modern academe, there are scores, legions—hordes they must seem to those who disapprove of them—who have been influenced, and not just casually, by my father.

How did he do it? I do think that in my father was found an unusual combination of traits—confidence without arrogance; worldly wisdom along with intellectual curiosity; a wry wit and a kindly disposition; and a clear-eyed realism about the world along with a great generosity of spirit. He very much enjoyed his last two decades in Washington, but he had none of the self-importance that afflicts us here. He loved intellectual pursuits, but always shunned intellectual pretension. For example, I don't think I ever heard him use the phrase "the life of the mind," though my father lived a life of the mind.

Beneath the confident wit and the intellectual bravado, my father had a deep modesty. My father spoke with gratitude of his good fortune in life. He wouldn't have claimed to deserve the honors that came his way—though he did deserve them.

Perhaps in part because he was a man who was marked by such a deep sense of gratitude, he was the recipient of much deeply felt gratitude. Even I've been surprised, judging by the e-mails and phone calls since his death, by the sheer number of those befriended by my father, by the range of those affected by him, by the diversity of those who admired him. I expected the appropriate remarks from distinguished political leaders and professors, and we were moved by eloquent testimonials from people who've known my father well, in some cases for many decades. But what struck all of us in the family were the e-mails from individuals who met my father only once or twice, but who remembered his kindness or benefited from his counsel—or from people who had never met him, but who were still very much influenced by his writing or other enterprises he was involved in.

For example, this, from a young Capitol Hill aide: "Your father was one of the first people I met, totally by accident, when I went to work at AEI a few years ago. And I will always remember how incredibly gracious and kind he was toward me, an utterly clueless research assistant." Or this, an e-mail forwarded by one of our kids: "Sorry to hear about your grandfather. He was ahead of his time and provided the intellectual underpinnings for the only conservative kid in his Jewish youth group in Tulsa, Oklahoma." Of all the communications my mother and my sister and I have received, I suspect my father might have gotten a particular kick out of that one.

Leon Kass said to me last week, after a final visit to my father, "It's hard to imagine a world without Irving Kristol." So it is. But as Leon would be the first to say, we're not left simply with a world without Irving Kristol. It's true that his death leaves the world a poorer place. But it's a world made richer by the life he lived and the legacy he leaves.

William Kristol
Funeral service
Congregation Adas Israel
Washington, D.C.
September 22, 2009

INTRODUCTION

The memoir by my husband introducing his last volume of essays in 1995, *Neoconservatism: The Autobiography of an Idea*, opens with a typical Irving Kristol quip.

> Is there such a thing as a "neo" gene? I ask that question because, looking back over a lifetime of my opinions, I am struck by the fact that they all qualify as "neo." I have been a neo-Marxist, a neo-Trotskyist, a neo-socialist, a neoliberal, and finally a neoconservative. It seems that no ideology or philosophy has ever been able to encompass all of reality to my satisfaction. There was always a degree of detachment qualifying my commitment.

That memoir does not mention the earliest manifestation in print of that "neo" gene. Rummaging among old files shortly after his death in September 2009, I came upon a couple of small tattered magazines entitled *Enquiry: A Journal of Independent Radical Thought*. Started by my husband and some of our fellow-exiles from Trotskyism, this was the first of several magazines he helped found; it lasted little more than two years, for a total of eight issues, by which time he and most of the other contributors were in the army. (Later, when an enthusiastic young person came to him with an idea, he was likely to say, "Start a magazine.") My penciled note on the cover of my copy of the first issue, dated November 1942, identified the author of one of the articles, William Ferry, as Irving Kristol. (William Ferry was his "party name" in his brief Trotskyist period in college). The other issue, dated April 1944, required no such identification; here the author was Irving Kristol.

Rereading those articles now is illuminating, both for what they tell us about his thinking in those early years and for what they portend about neoconservatism itself. "The Quality of Doubt" in the first issue is a review of W. H. Auden's book of poetry *The Double Man*. It opens with the now-famous quotation from the poem, written on the eve of the war, about the thirties, that "low dishonest decade," and goes on to describe the "growing doubts" and "undercurrent of questioning uncertainty" in Auden's later poetry. Those doubts and uncertainty had an obvious political source, Auden's disillusionment with Stalinism. But it is the poet's pervasive moral tone, his sense of the "moral vacancy" of that troubled age, that impresses the reviewer—a "moral subtlety, receptivity, and sensitivity [that] is close to brilliant."

"The Moral Critic" in a later issue of *Enquiry*, a review of Lionel Trilling's book about E. M. Forster, is almost entirely on Trilling, Forster entering late in the review almost as an afterthought. It is also less about Trilling's book on Forster than about an earlier essay by him on T. S. Eliot's *Idea of a Christian Society*, and more particularly about the critique of radicalism and liberalism that Trilling found in that essay—a critique that he (and the reviewer) entirely shared. Abandoning their traditional moral vision by permitting means to prevail over ends and having a simplistic faith in their ability to change human nature, the radicals betrayed, Trilling wrote, "a kind of disgust with humanity as it is and a perfect faith in humanity as it is to be." That attitude, he said, derived from a liberalism that was smug and self-righteous, preferring not to know that "the good will generates its own problems, that the love of humanity has its own vices and the love of truth its own insensibilities." For the reviewer, this was the characteristic, and altogether commendable, mode of all of Trilling's work, a "moral realism" that amounted to nothing less than a "brilliant and sustained, if sometimes impatient, exploration of the complexities of moral perfection and of the paths thereto."

In 1942, when my husband wrote the first of these articles, he was all of twenty-two and two years out of college where he had majored in history (after a brief foray in mathematics) and minored, so to speak (in the Trotskyist alcove at City College), in Marxism, post-Marxism, and anti-Marxism. He was now working as a machinist in the Brooklyn Navy Yard awaiting his induction into the army—altogether an unlikely initiation, one might think, into the world of poetry and literary criticism. Yet even as a neo-Trotskyist, he had been more "neo" than most of his comrades, for while he was engaging in disputes about the Marxist dialectic or the prospects of international revolution, he was also reading the fashionable "modernist" writers—his memoir mentions D. H. Lawrence, T. S. Eliot, W. B. Yeats, Franz Kafka—and was entering the New York intellectual world by way of *Partisan Review*, the preeminent "little magazine" of the time. It was in *PR*, in 1940, that he read Trilling's essay on Eliot, the first of many of Trilling's essays that, he later recalled, "hit me with the force of a revelation."

It is against this background that the founding of *Enquiry* (which may have been inspired, on a very much smaller scale, by *Partisan Review*) may be understood. Yet even then, and in that congenial circle, Kristol was conspicuously a "neo." The subtitle of *Enquiry*, "A Journal of Independent Radical Thought," does not capture how "independent" he was, not only in regard to the writers he chose to write about (his were the only pieces in *Enquiry* on literary subjects) but also in his appreciation of the moral sensibility and complexity he found in them. Half a century later, in the preface to *Neoconservatism*, he expressed his surprise upon finding, in essays on a wide variety of subjects and written over a long span of time (the first essay in that volume dates from 1949), the "homogeneity of approach, the consistency of a certain cast of mind." He would have been even more surprised had he reread those still earlier *Enquiry* articles, which might have been written, with perhaps only the smallest emendations, at any point in his career.

His memoir emphasizes another aspect of the neo gene—his abiding interest in and respect for religion. This too is evident in those early articles, in his praise of the "religiosity of tone" in Auden's poems and, in the Trilling essay, of the "religio-ethical tone" of such other critics of radicalism as Jacques Maritain, Reinhold Niebuhr, and Christopher Dawson. Another essay, "A Christian Experiment," is a sympathetic although not uncritical account of a novel by Ignazio Silone about the hero's evolution from "revolutionary Marxian politics to a libertarian revolutionary Christianity." And "Other People's Nerve" is, among other things, a rebuke to Sidney Hook for dismissing too cavalierly the religious "heretics" who were defecting from the supposedly "scientific" irreligion of the Left.

That religious neo gene emerged most conspicuously in *Commentary* a few years later. Kristol's first article, in September 1947 (the very month he came on the staff), "The Myth of the Supra-Human Jew," is a learned exploration of the idea, for good and bad, of "the chosen people," quoting not only from Jacques Maritain but also from Raïssa Maritain and such other French theologians as Léon Bloy, Ernest Renan, and Charles Péguy—not the usual authorities cited in *Commentary* (or even *Partisan Review*). His next article, four months later, was on more familiar terrain. "How Basic Is 'Basic Judaism'" is a critique of a conception of Judaism so "basic" as to deny, he thought, the very essence of Judaism. Other essays followed, on Christianity as well as Judaism. Because he was the only editor interested in religion—this in a Jewish magazine—he became the *de facto* religious editor. But here

too, as his memoir testifies, his neo gene prevailed, for he was then, as he remained, "a nonobservant Jew, but not a nonreligious one"—indeed, a "neo-
orthodox" Jew.

It was in *Commentary* that yet another neo-ism revealed itself. As Trilling,
the "skeptical liberal," was the dominant influence upon Kristol in the 1940s,
so Leo Strauss, the "skeptical conservative," was in the 1950s. And as Trilling's
essays had struck him as a "revelation," so Strauss's *Persecution and the Art of
Writing*, in 1952, produced "the kind of intellectual shock that is a once-in-a-
lifetime experience." In both cases what impressed him was not so much their
political views (which were more implicit than overt), but the mind-set that informed their views of culture, religion, society, philosophy, and politics alike.
His review of *Persecution and the Art of Writing* focuses on Maimonides as the
exemplar of Strauss's major themes: the relation of the esoteric and the exoteric,
of reason and revelation, of philosophy and the polity. It concludes by com-
mending Strauss for accomplishing "nothing less than a revolution in intellectual history" by recalling us to the "wisdom of the past."

The English journal *Encounter*, founded with Stephen Spender the following year, displayed a breadth of interest and receptivity to ideas that transcended party, class, and national lines. An important intellectual and political
force in the Cold War period—an antidote to the communism that was still attracting many liberals as well as radicals—it served as a model for similar magazines on the Continent and abroad. It was also an education for Kristol,
introducing him to a culture and polity different from but wonderfully congruent with that of America. He returned to the States in 1958, first as the
editor of *The Reporter* and then at the publishing house Basic Books, with an
enriched sense of the Anglo-American tradition and historic "relationship."

The "neo" disposition took on a more political and economic character
with the founding in 1965 of *The Public Interest*, co-edited first with Daniel
Bell and then with Nathan Glazer. The "quality of doubt," the "questioning,"
"uncertainty," and "sharp, cynical analysis" that had been so provocative in
Auden's poetry reappear, more prosaically, in a journal that was ever doubting,
questioning, and sharply, even cynically, analytic of social policies and reformers. So, too, Trilling's observations about the simplistic, self-righteous liberals, who do not know that "good will" and "love of humanity" generate their
own problems and vices, are echoed in *The Public Interest*'s repeated invocation
of the principle of unanticipated consequences. And Trilling's critique of the
liberal reformers of his generation was all too applicable to a later generation
of reformers, chastised in *The Public Interest*, who were intent upon waging a
"War on Poverty" in the name of "the Great Society."

For Kristol, this mode of thought—questioning, skeptical, ironic, yet "cheerfully pessimistic," as he said—soon evolved into "neoconservatism," a label invented by others as a pejorative term that he happily adopted for himself. Again, there were reminiscences of the past, as in the title he gave *Two Cheers for Capitalism* in 1978, recalling Forster's "two cheers for democracy," which he had cited in his essay on Trilling. He now made this a defining principle of neoconservatism, three cheers being too utopian for any human venture, including capitalism. So, too, the "moral realism" he had admired in Trilling (and in Forster as well) was now identified, by himself and others, with neoconservatism, and not only with respect to domestic affairs but foreign affairs as well—as exhibited in yet another journal founded (but not edited) by him in 1985, *The National Interest*. Ten years later, an essay in the Festschrift dedicated to him was entitled "Irving Kristol's Moral Realism." It is fitting that that essay should have been written by the co-founder of *Enquiry*, Philip Selznick, although it is unlikely that Selznick recalled the provenance of that phrase half a century earlier.

In Kristol's later years, he wrote less about literature, religion, and philosophy and more about politics, economics, and foreign affairs, not as separate disciplines but as parts of a whole, imbued by a common purpose and disposition. Thus he reminded economists of the political and ethical dimensions of their subject—"political economy," as Adam Smith (himself a professor of Moral Philosophy) had termed it. He urged politicians to embrace a "new economics," supply-side economics, which would invigorate the polity and society as well as the economy. He cautioned statesmen and foreign policy experts to be wary of the simplicities and ideologies that pervert the best-intentioned policies and subvert the national interest. And he advised all of them that the success of their endeavors depends upon an ethos, a culture, and—that enduring token of "American exceptionalism"—a religious disposition that make for a stable and decent society.

Yet even as the focus of his writings shifted, his old interests persisted. In 1984, in a symposium in *Partisan Review* on the question of how his cultural and political views had changed in the past decades, he recalled the problem that had always vexed that journal: how to reconcile its radical or liberal politics with an admiration for modernist literature that was often politically reactionary (most notably in the case of T. S. Eliot and Ezra Pound). He himself had no such problem. His cultural views, he assured his old friends, had evolved in happy congruence with his political views.

Meanwhile, for myself, I have reached certain conclusions: that Jane Austen is a greater novelist than Proust or Joyce; that Raphael is a greater painter than Picasso; that T. S. Eliot's later, Christian poetry is much superior to his earlier; that C. S. Lewis is a finer literary and cultural critic than Edmund Wilson; that Aristotle is more worthy of careful study than Marx; that we have more to learn from Tocqueville than from Max Weber; that Adam Smith makes a lot more economic sense than any economist since; that the Founding Fathers had a better understanding of democracy than any political scientist since; that. . . . Well, enough. As I said at the outset, I have become conservative, and whatever ambiguities attach to that term, it should be obvious what it does *not* mean.

He might have recalled, as he did in his memoir, a remark by Leo Strauss: that a young man might think Dostoyevsky the greatest novelist, but in maturity he should give that plaudit to Jane Austen.

***

The title of this volume, *The Neoconservative Persuasion*, comes with the authority of the author, who used it as the title of his last essay on the subject in 2003. He then referred in passing to a book he had reviewed almost half a century earlier, *The Jacksonian Persuasion*, by the historian (and his good friend) Marvin Meyers. The final paragraph of that review has a special pertinence to his own work.

> The word "persuasion," which he [Meyers] defines as "a half-formulated moral perspective involving emotional commitment," hits off exactly the strange destiny of ideas in American politics. Parties do not have anything so formal as an ideology, but they do—and must—profess something more explicit than a general ethos. "Persuasion" is a most apt term for what in fact issues from this predicament.

"Persuasion" is also a "most apt term" for neoconservatism. If neoconservatism is not, as Kristol repeatedly insisted, a movement or an ideology, let alone a party, it is something more—a "moral perspective" deriving from a broad spectrum of ideas, beliefs, and sentiments that inform politics, to be sure, but also culture, religion, economics, and much else. (The cover of a pamphlet of his much-reprinted essay "Adam Smith and the Spirit of Capitalism" bears his handwritten notation, "The Bourgeois Persuasion," an allusion to the ethical as well as economic dimension of Smith's political economy.) Over the years he used other terms to characterize neoconservatism: "imagination," "disposition," "tendency," "impulse," "cast of mind," "spirit," even "instinct." The Festschrift published in 1995 on the occasion of his seventy-fifth birthday bears the title *The Neoconservative Imagination*. But finally he himself settled on "persuasion."

Much has been made of the consistency of tone in his writings—bold and speculative but never dogmatic or academic, always personal, witty, ironic. That tone is not only a matter of style; it suggests a distinctive intellectual sensibility—skeptical, commonsensible, eclectic, and at the same time strong-minded and hard-headed. It is a double-edged scalpel that he wielded against the "terrible simplifiers" of his generation, the utopians of the Left and the dogmatists of the Right, both of whom failed to appreciate the complicated realities of human nature and social action—realities, he insisted, that had to be confronted honestly and boldly.

From the many hundreds of uncollected essays by Irving Kristol, I have selected about fifty. (The only one that has previously appeared is "An Autobiographical Memoir" from his last volume.) Divided topically, they reflect the many subjects that engaged him in his long and productive career. They also reflect the free-flowing quality of his mind, one theme suggesting another, so that some of the essays could have been assigned to more than one category. Within each category, the essays are in chronological order, showing the evolution of his thought—or, as often as not, the consistency of his thought over so long a period of time.

The essays speak for themselves. If anything more needs saying, by way of background or explication, he himself has said it in the memoirs reprinted in this volume. (The only changes are in punctuation, capitalization, and paragraphing, which often depended upon the whim of the editors of the journals in which the essays appeared.) The bibliography provides further documentation of his range of interests and vitality of mind. And the eulogy prefacing this volume, delivered at the funeral service by our son, William Kristol, expresses the sentiments of so many after his death who paid tribute to a man whose influence in the lives of young people was as memorable as his contribution to the political and intellectual life of his times.

Gertrude Himmelfarb
December 2010

ENQUIRY

A Journal of Independent Radical Thought

NOVEMBER, 1942

Vol. I, No. 1   Ten Cents

 88

I

IN THE BEGINNING...

Enquiry

Auden

The Quality of Doubt

The Double Man has been treated with consideration by the majority of re-viewers. These registered their approval of the expressed religiosity of tone, the inward searching doubts concerning the viability of a humane revolutionary program, the bursting bubble of "clever hopes" expiring at the end of a "low, dishonest decade." A congenial attitude was evident toward the feeling that

All our reflections turn about
A common meditative norm,
Retrenchment, Sacrifice, Reform.

Be that as it may; we leave their motives and motivations unquestioned, de-siring, rather, to explore certain political problems, incidental to the poetry as such yet relevant to the attitudes expressed therein.

Auden is certainly one of those "whose works are in better taste than their lives." His early verse, ideologically viewed, was brashly positive, didactic, clever, facile, and possessed of a nasty Stalinist bent. The undercurrent of ques-tioning uncertainty, often stilled but always there, became dominant only late in the decade. A "New Year's Letter" (1941), a part of this latest volume [*The Double Man*], is the organized end product of these growing doubts, and its moral subtlety, receptivity, and sensitivity is close to brilliant. The bitterly ac-quired political wisdom of a generation seems to flourish in the pen and stag-nate in the poet. Of course, being poetry, the problem is only stated; but a good statement is half a solution.

It is not the need for specific moral decisions by the poet which so troubles the verse, as it is the feeling that the basic issues of morality itself are undefined, immediate, and pressing—a common enough revelation of the age's moral vacancy. Combined with this is the guilt-fear of the individual for the crimes committed around him, the responsibility of even passive contribution, the warping of ideals by greed and egoism, which leads Auden to say:

Our million individual deeds
Omissions, vanities, and creeds,
Put through the statistician's hoop
The gross behavior of a group.

To put the issue more bluntly than the poetry permits, what is being advanced is a working concept of original sin, a concept which gives the conditions of idealism and forces to the fore unremittingly a sharp, cynical analysis of self and others, ends and means. Rather than hypostasizing goodness as a quality which by hypothesis some men must possess, let it be remembered that men in all ways seem better than they are. Those who see the world of the future making tremendous forward leaps through the agency of technology and the applied social sciences, or who believe in a complete spiritual regeneration of a majority of men, are deceiving themselves. The permeating fact of evil, both past and present, speaks differently.

Scientists and nonscientists alike live on an inclined plane of credulity, and it is given to no one type of mind to discern the totality of truth. The science of politics, consistent with the nature of science as such, is a process of abstraction, simplification, and logical exclusion. It strives for the quantitative and minimizes the qualitative. The partial efficacy of all this brooks no denial, but its partiality must be insisted upon. A systematic rationality of action is encouraged which is often a false rationality of unity, simplicity, and generality. As a counterweight to this exists the insight of ontology (to borrow a term made current by John Crowe Ransom), which attempts to see things wholly, qualitatively, in their full particularity. It is contemplative, not utilitarian, and its medium is the arts, not the sciences. The three main weapons of the ontological view are tragedy, irony, and comedy. Tragedy offers a realism of its own against ingenuous enterprise, warning against "excessive expectations as to the prosperity of structures." Irony exists when the spectator is given an insight superior to that of the actor. When spectator and actor are one, this insight is that of the "double man," inducing humility and possibly a certain measure of self-contempt. The comic corrective ("sense of humor") is a reaction against human acts being determined by abstract principles and is essentially critical of programs. It is these constituents of the double or ontological view which engender the quality of doubt, respect the headlines and loss of balance as the tax which all action must pay, and force a constant reference of means (abstract political principles) to ends (concrete colorful humanity).

The juxtaposition of personal and impersonal, private existence and public politics, its ensuing dialectic self-analysis with its confession that truth is equivocal—all of this is a vitiation of animal confidence and vigor, a symptom of approaching age. It cannot be erased by a repetitive moral earnestness which serves only to blur the perception of the actual. The crisis in conscience is deep and enduring and any renewal of heart will have to accept it as a fellow-traveler. On the other hand, to elevate doubt into a political program is distinctly impracticable, having the common consequences of accepting the status quo as a sure good contrasted to all kinds of future imaginable evils. Many have advanced from doubt to negation, decrying political movements *in toto* as destined to fall short of their ends. Even though these prophesies bear fruit, they are irrelevant to an individual's participation, which is based primarily upon moral considerations. Whether a man lives or dies in vain can never be measured by the collective activity of his fellows. It is only seen in the way he faces his problems, in the way he resolves his inner conflicts, in his deliberate exercise of choice. And the integrity of the intellect will always add its admonition in the face of chaos:

But ideas can be true although men die.

1942

A Christian Experiment

To Thomas Mann's dictum: "In our time the destiny of man presents its meaning in political terms," we may add the observation, drawn from current intellectual trends, that our political destiny is on the way to being formulated in religious terms. Which may be a more or less natural reversion. It is a comparatively recent phenomenon, perhaps peculiar to our modern Western civilization, that masses of men should work, think, and agitate for a reconstruction of society according to some ideal of social perfection. It belongs to the order of religion rather than politics, as this latter was previously understood. It finds its parallel in extremist religious movements such as the Anabaptists in Luther's Germany and the Levellers in Cromwell's England. With the estrangement of religion from crucial social activities political ethics becomes secular in origin and intent. The revolutionists are driven by the recognition that actual society is an embodiment of force and fraud, organized for no ideal end. As remedy after remedy fails, the deeper grows the dissatisfaction. When disillusionment becomes complete, all that is most vital in the moral life of the time alienates itself from the political life of society and from the service of the state as something unworthy and unclean. Piecemeal reconstruction is deemed hopeless, and men return to the more enduring vision of universal pervasive principles which absorb all problems and solutions into a single expanded perspective.

If this general analysis were to be applied point by point to Mr. Silone, it would be found to be accurate and even indispensable to understanding, but insufficient. For we are not dealing with a man who bends to a pattern but with one of singular gifts, the outstanding of which is integrity. Integrity signifies an honest, thorough, and capable analysis of one's own views, a prerequisite for which is a sufficient sum of intellectual distinction, so that it would be presumptuous to dismiss his theories as mere reflection. Rather are they positive contributions to policy, to be distilled and evaluated. And of course there is the novel qua novel.

The Seed Beneath the Snow completes the intellectual evolution of Pietro Spina from revolutionary Marxian politics to a libertarian revolutionary Christianity, begun in *Bread and Wine*. There is little narrative since the novel is demonstrative in purpose, contrasting Spina's way of life with that of the others, elaborating the doctrinal meanings in innumerable dialogues, and with a few simple images proposing the silent ideas. The philosophy is not new and was stated succinctly by Thoreau when he said: "Action from principle, the perception and performance of right, changes things and relations; it is essentially revolutionary, and does not consist wholly with anything which was." Action is to be based solely on principles, without adaptation or compromise. The basic principles are the maxim "Do unto others as you would have them do to you," the regenerative power of love, humility, sacrifice of worldly vanities, and a devotion to the poor and oppressed. The central symbol is taken to be Christ's sacrifice, an act of "madness," seditious to law and order. The portrayal of Spina in this latest novel is supposed to indicate what such a life would look like in practice.

As a novel it is a poor performance, and since a substantial amount of his previous stylistic vigor is present, the dominating orientation seems to be to blame. A passionate approach to ethical behavior lacking a set of rigid categories (such as Dostoyevsky often possessed) is diffused into romantic sentiment. Much of what Spina says and does is, by the universal canons of experience, downright silly, i.e., reveals an incongruity of cause and effect, an irrelevancy in act and feeling. In a "naturalistic" portrait this defect is fatal. His relations with the deaf-mute Infante possess all the sentimentality of Steinbeck's *Of Mice and Men* without the dramatic force; the same is even more true of the ending. Silone's desire to pierce the hard shell which separates men is to be appreciated. But in actual life the "inner man" always turns out to have a shell of his own. When transparent purity is attained, as is the case with Spina, genuine human personality is extinguished. The failure of the image of Spina, the saint, may be contrasted with the convincing and impressive presentation of Don Severino, the saint "manqué," the latter being a more universal, poignant, and significant condition.

There is, too, a vitiating "anti-theoretical" bias, revealed plainly in the repeated scorn of political rhetoric as a technique of obfuscation. The goods of life, especially love between all living creatures, are seen as immediately present in existence, yearning to be grasped in action. Discourse and dialectic are idle, and only emotional affirmatives are justified. Contrasting this Silone with the earlier Malraux is suggestive. In Silone, confusion commences in the concrete, in Malraux, in the abstract. Silone insists that love and sacrifice are only fruitful if applied to living creatures and denied to symbols and programs, which, because of their abstract nature, have a somewhat Satanic power. Malraux's characters are driven into a fury of action by the overriding power of some symbolic view of man's fate. While Malraux's characters can never develop because of the bounds within which they were conceived, Silone's cannot be created but reside somewhere within the supposed intrinsic gravitational force of his superb intentions.

The fundamental flaw is an excess of pride, a confidence in one's own revolutionary innocence. Silone would have us "build on a new foundation, start with simple hay and clear water and then feel our way forward." But it is not so easy; there are few in our time who have sufficient naïveté of spirit to play innocent. We are born with a heritage, a long task assigned, a character imposed. It is when life is understood to be a process of redemption that its various phases are taken up in turn, without undue haste. The image of Pietro Spina fails because such a vision cannot be conceived willfully and hurriedly, no matter how provocative the stimulus. There is no simple formula that can be employed in the contravention of corruption and "provisional living"; the adaptation to the nausea of daily life, sustained by some vague anticipation, is not merely a mistaken notion which can be dissipated by adherence to principles. Proud, too, is the blinding illumination of the Good. In this novel of intense moral feeling we do not find what we would most expect, an acute awareness of subsistent evil. The characters and images are either representations of the Good or background for such representations. Even Dona Faustina, at first a seemingly careless woman, concludes with a radiance of virginal purity.

Towards the end of the novel there is a dialogue between Faustina and Spina:

"These are the rules, Pietro; we must have patience; we didn't invent the game, but we must play it, as hounds or hares, one or the other."

"And what if a man should refuse to be either a hound or a hare, Faustina?"

"Then he is no part of civilized society and he must run away; in short he must be a hare."

Mr. Silone is attempting an experiment in a Christian morality which avoids these disjunctives. The experiment will fail. In the meantime we must wait upon the course of events, till hares become hounds, and integrity may assume its rightful political forms.

1943

Other People's Nerve

The January-February and March-April issues of *Partisan Review* have featured a discussion of the "New Failure of Nerve." It has been interesting, provocative reading, as could have been expected given such substantial contributors as Sidney Hook, John Dewey, Ernest Nagel, Ruth Benedict, and others. Yet it seems to me to have missed the mark somewhat, and in the case of Sidney Hook's polemic against the failure of the Left, to have committed gross and significant errors.

The trend under criticism is identified with "a rise of asceticism, of mysticism, in a sense, of pessimism; a loss of self-confidence, of hope in this life and faith in normal human efforts. . . ." It signifies a disillusionment with the method of science as a curative for human ills, and a reversion to principles of social organization and individual attitude that have usually been considered religious—the principles of myth, dogma, and prayer. This movement seems to have had a decided influence in academic circles, and insofar as it has been weakened by the *Partisan Review* counterattack all is to the good. The pietistic revival among the professors is too loudly colored with Catholic prejudices and absolutes not to have reactionary political consequences. But the deviation that is witnessed in the cases of men like Eliseo Vivas and Charles W. Morris is not amenable to such simple denunciation. And it is here that the mark is missed, for Messrs. Hook and Nagel seem to possess their own version of "original sin," the locus of which is the willful perversity of intellectuals who recalcitrantly gravitate toward nonscientific philosophies. The facile explanation, that the origin lies in the current disorganization of beliefs and institutions, contains a truth but explains nothing. Why this turning to religion by these people, who have in the past been associated with progressive ideas and movements, at this time?

It should be recognized that, whatever the status of their special theories, these "heretics" pose problems that have more than a representative psychological significance; they demonstrate an awareness of actual deficiencies and crises. They are a tribute-in-reverse to the paucity of ideals and to the synthetic idealism which has characterized the socialist movement. Their defection highlights the neglect which scientific thought has meted out to those who insist upon a larger view, a dramatic integration, of one's character, activities, and goal. Professor Nagel's logical objections to the various propositions on religion appear, from this point of view, a tour de force. Since they presuppose criteria of validity unacceptable to any religion, their cogency depends upon prior conviction. More important, the literal interpretation that such an analysis employs cannot do justice to the *import* of such ideas; to talk of "supernaturalism" is to attempt to state the moral and intellectual questions of the twentieth century in nineteenth-century categories. There are good reasons these days for pessimism and lack of confidence in human effort, and they cannot be exorcised glibly by admonishing against a "flight from responsibility." And as far as "nerve" goes, Aldous Huxley in his thoroughgoing mysticism demonstrates greater integrity than does Ruth Benedict in her fluent Stalinized liberalism.

Professor Hook's article on the "Failure of the Left" is really a separate argument in itself, having little relevance to the recrudescence of religiosity and the reaction against science. (Unless he would assert that his political views are the only scientific ones, all others suffering from a metaphysical bias somewhere along the line; but the evidence for such an imputation of arrogance is hardly sufficient.) All left-wing groups are castigated severely; indeed so burning is Professor Hook's indignation that he extends his attacks to certain groups which no one else seems to have thought of as being leftist. It does seem a bit silly to criticize *The Nation*, *New Leader*, and the American Labor Party for lacking socialist militancy; he might as well charge the night with being dark. However, it is when he inveighs against "Platonic Revolutionists" that he is most vitriolic, and it is explicit that the source of his anger is their views on World War II.

The "Platonic Revolutionists" (i.e., those with Marxian-Leninist convictions) stand indicted because their political program, which deems this war just another imperialistic conflict, is a stubbornly stupid repetition of fetishized slogans. Instead of an empirical analysis of the consequences of action, they insist upon reasoning deductively from fixed categories containing such essences as Capitalism, Socialism, Fascism, etc., all immutable and non-overlapping. In their union of fanaticism and metaphysics, they have become in Professor Hook's eyes "Lenin's Witnesses." Now, few thinkers are as admirably equipped as Professor Hook to investigate the philosophical and political distortions occasioned by Leninist dogma; most of his past criticisms of these precepts possess knowledge and insight. But it should be evident that in this case he has allowed a general theory, guided by sentiment, to substitute for an analysis of the fact, a characteristic, ironically, of the Platonic fallacy. Any just and honest appraisal of the position of this group will reveal the following:

1. In large measure, their position is based on empirical grounds, upon the actualities of the war situation. Among these are the pronounced and implicit war aims of the contestants, the strengthening of the control of social institutions by reactionary forces, and the inability of the victory of either group to solve the decisive economic, political, and moral problems of which Fascism was a direct product.

2. As a basis for validating perspectives, they have available an invaluable fund of historical experience, and this experience includes estimates of the consequences of certain types of action for the goal of socialism. This background indicates the vulnerability of ruling classes when faced with a bloody collapse of their organization of society and the revelation of the hypocrisy of their verbal ideas. It also suggests that wars fought for selfish motives receive, in time, due recognition from the peoples, and that it is political suicide for any opposition group to identify itself, even conditionally, with such an eventual object of disgust and disillusion.

3. Inflexible dogmas need not lead to inflexible tactics. In their policy of the United Front, especially as it was applied during the Spanish Civil War, the Leninists have demonstrated great adaptability to the conditions of the fight. To present them as ideological purists in their position on war, pursuing an abstentionist path out of sheer petulance with events, is to misrepresent them. They do have a program for positive action which, whatever sense it may possess or lack in the eyes of any single person, does fulfill the requirements for a set of meaningful proposals.

4. Fanaticism is an evil-sounding word. If, however, it is realized that this is what its defenders deem a moral attitude of intransigent socialist internationalism, one's reaction is not so easily channelized.

"But what," Professor Hook would ask, "does this have to do with licking Hitler?" In this near-hysterical insistence upon the pressing military danger and in the complaint, "mere theoretical carping," we recognize not only a common academic reaction to events, but also an ominously familiar ideological weapon. It is the exact technique of the Communist-Liberal coalition during the days of the Popular Front and collective security. One element in the situation is seized from its context as the receptacle of all political significance, and crucial political disagreements based on a broader perspective than "licking the villain" are condemned as malicious and irresponsible criticism. The following, by Professor Hook, is an example of this method: "If Hitler wins, democratic socialism has no future. But at least [with an Allied victory] it has a chance! It is the failure to grasp this simple piece of wisdom which marks the political insanity of infantile leftism." Yet if this is wisdom in 1943, why did Professor Hook brand it as stupidity in 1939? Any real alternative in terms of international working-class solidarity was as firmly excluded then as it is presumed to be now. What is involved here is more than a programmatic difference of opinion. There is revealed more nearly a change in moral attitude ("nerve") than an understandable intellectual disagreement. When the attainment of an ideal is conceived as a product of day-to-day pressures, as among the Stalinists and social-democrats, rather than as a planned relation between an end-in-view and the conditions of action, then idealism becomes identical with opportunism. This is not only morally undesirable but also politically futile, for the consequences of Professor Hook's program for the defeat of Hitler would be such as to vitiate his ultimate socialist goal.

His program is avowedly an acceptance from the Left of the "Clemenceau thesis," i.e., urging unsparing prosecution of the war and denouncing the ineptness and ineffectiveness of the war effort as currently managed. The labor organizations should be the organizers of victory. In the very interest of a military victory over Hitler, the war must be fought in a total democratic fashion, regardless of the restrictions of capitalist property relations. It is a program of critical political support along with complete military participation.

In selecting the "Clemenceau thesis" as his key strategic insight, Professor Hook has committed a blunder; it holds water neither as a historical analogy nor as a practicable method. The "Clemenceau thesis" was the result of a struggle *within a class*, a dispute over method, not over goal. The war aims of its proponents and opponents were identical, and one of the dominant aims was the preservation of capitalist property rights. If the labor movement were to adopt Professor Hook's convictions, it would have one of two possible results, both totally contrary to original intentions: there would be open civil war, or complete capitulation on the part of labor. (Peaceful capitulation by business interests is inconceivable.) When political criticism insists upon any fundamental change in the economic system, the military effort is bound to be adversely affected. Such demands would bring to the point of crisis latent class antagonisms. It is certain that the conservatives, possessing, on the whole, more guts and wisdom than the Hook variety of socialist, will be adamant in resisting concessions, despite probable ruinous effects at the fronts (viz., Churchill's treatment of India). They are not committed to *any* war against Hitler, but solely to one controlled by them in their own interests. So the socialist critics will retreat in the interests of "unity," and the final scene will have Professor Hook mimicking Harold J. Laski in public bewailing and prayer, and still dreaming of an honest-to-goodness war against Hitler, while the forces of reaction consolidate their grip.

The one glaring omission in the article that gives the show away is—Japan. There is no mention of the war in the Far East, only the battle against Hitler! This incredible state of affairs demonstrates that Platonism, or acting on the basis of hypostatized abstractions, is not solely a sectarian malady. The war in Asia clarifies brutally the activating war aims of the United States, Britain, and the Netherlands as far as the vital questions of empire and freedom are concerned. Professor Hook busies himself with an abstract war against Hitler rather than handle the less attractive reality of a completely reactionary crusade against "those yellow b——s."

It's always the other fellow's nerve.

1943

James Burnham's
The Machiavellians

He would have men prepared to encounter the worst of men: and therefore he resembles him to a man driving a flock of sheep, into a corner, and did there take out their teeth, and instead, gave each of them a set of wolves teeth so that, whereas one shepherd was able to drive a whole flock, now each sheep had need of a particular shepherd, and all little enough.

**"The Vindication of That Hero of Political Learning,
Nicholas Machiavel" by James Boevey
(quoted in Wyndham Lewis, *The Art of Being Ruled*)**

The atmosphere, these days, contains a good deal more of what is called "realism" than is usually considered desirable for healthy progress. In some measure this is a natural symptom of the ebb of insurgent liberal-socialist thought. The prospects of large-scale reform having been largely dissipated in the past two decades, a new starting point, with a more stringent perspective, is sought. The war, too, is taking its toll, withering at contact all attractive formulations as to its ultimate purpose, so that alternatives are constantly being narrowed between greater evils and slightly lesser ones. The Union for Democratic Action has now progressed to that point where the delineation of the future balance of power in Europe is a prime programmatic concern, while Ely Culbertson's "practical" nonsense is mouthed by leftist politicos, prelude to a new Congress of Vienna. Illusions are discarded, political self-consciousness prevails, or so it seems. But where do political illusions begin, and where end? What is the locus of realism, and what are its lessons?

James Burnham has worked out a cogent argument which has this in its favor. It states in general form the conditions of all effective social action, rather than being circumscribed within a particular dilemma. That he has been so vigorously denounced by the liberal press indicates that they do not feel at ease within such an inclusive structure, preferring to "stick to the facts." The more sophisticated critics say that problems of power are always specific, which is true; and that there is no general problem of power, which is false and a non sequitur. What in another context might be welcomed as a cautious disavowal of sweeping generalizations is clearly in this case an unwillingness to discuss the premises of their program. For Burnham deals in "fundamentals," and only those who have given no hostages to the powers-that-be can take a hand in such a radical game. (This applies to the Marxian groups too. Here, loyalty to an *a priori* system, the cultivation of which has taken a century of strenuous effort, performs the same role that the political commitments of the past ten years do for the New Dealers.)

The Machiavellians summarizes the relevant writings of Machiavelli, Mosca, Sorel, Michels, and Pareto, and from their points of tangency sets up a theory of political behavior that has provocative implications for current discussion. It is to be feared, however, that the substantial contribution of the book will be neglected because of certain shortcomings in method and tone. They are limitations of a glib, schematic, intemperate intellect, with an inexplicable Marxian bias towards history. To dub the Machiavellians "defenders of freedom" for erecting valid hypotheses concerning social conduct is to give to truth a partisan flavor of which it is innocent; a moral concern must be demonstrated. Even John Calhoun could write, while defending slavocracy: "Power can only be resisted by power and tendency by tendency. . . . Those who exercise power and those subject to its exercise—the rulers and the ruled—stand in antagonistic relations to each other." There is a naïve positivism at work, and an easy misuse of science, in the sheer contradiction established between blunt truth and dishonest myth, which ignores the symbolic quality of ideals as they find expression in myths. Myths need not lie (though some do), nor are all myths equally meaningful, nor do all myths deceive rather than enlighten. Myth is a mode of expression, not a constituent of that which is expressed. Again, Burnham reduces goals to immediately ascertainable possibilities presented spontaneously by the situation. A more careful statement would recognize that the selection of specific ends is vitally influenced by more distant and less articulate ends, in the absence of which evidence is but brute data.

From an extended analysis of Dante's *De Monarchia*, Burnham draws a crucial distinction between the formal and real meaning of a political philosophy or program. The purpose is to raise to the level of academic thought the dearly bought insight of ordinary men that the words of politicians are not to be taken at their face value. The formal is the literal, dictionary meaning; the real meaning, which is the theory in action, is discovered only in the context of social life. Secretary of State Hull, for instance, preaches concord among nations (after the war). When the words are translated into the workings of the State Department they signify American commercial and political dominance in world affairs. Even if this latter were not Mr. Hull's intent at all, it is the objective, operational import of his program, for where intent is not translated into effect its existence is conjectural, and conversely, it is only in overt demeanor that intent can be evaluated. A more obvious case is the Soviet Constitution, which guarantees freedom of speech and assembly, and means saleable propaganda to the gullible. The British Labor Party has agreed to an electoral truce to ensure a united effective struggle against Hitlerism; the meaning of this tactic is the presence in the cabinet of labor leaders enforcing a conservative program in domestic, foreign, and military affairs. The manner in which the formal program distorts and disguises the real program not only inspires self-deception (the opposition is rarely misled), but also renders the real meaning recalcitrant to deliberate control. The Bolshevik theory of the dictatorship of the working class turned out to mean the dictatorship of the central committee, to the surprise and horror of many adherents. By the time the discovery was made the situation had already been determined.

Burnham's handling of this question is such as to invite a speedy objection. He insists that the theories of the Machiavellians are scientific in that the formal and real meanings coincide. That is to say, the literal meaning of their propositions exemplifies the concrete workings of their subject matter; the world of words does not pervert the world of things. But since his test case, Dante's tract, is a gaudy metaphysical apologia for a self-centered politics, Burnham seems to permit himself the liberty of imputing Dante's motives. At which point his censors are prompt to point to the supposed personal fascistic leanings of Sorel, Mosca, and Pareto, while rejecting their theories as a reactionary cloak. Now it should be evident that to raise such a psychological issue is both unwarranted and undesirable. The relations between men and their words can be amazingly complex, as the social sciences have only recently begun to appreciate in their study of semantics and ideology. Moreover, assertions about motivation are not open to the same rigors of proof as is the case of an inferred meaning constructed by juxtaposing word against fact. Broadly speaking, the hypotheses of, say, Michels are scientific, while those of Dante are not, for the same considerations that would apply to conflicting formulas in chemistry and physics: when subject to observation and experiment they fulfill the conditions of true statements.

The distinction between formal and real meaning once having been made, its function in Machiavellian theory becomes clear. The formal antitheses which set apart different parties are shown to issue from a lowest common denominator, their direction towards the achievement and retention of power. "If our interest is in man as he is on this earth, so far, as we can learn from the facts of history and experience, we must conclude that he has no natural aspiration for peace and harmony, he does not form states in order to achieve an ideally good society, nor does he accept mutual organization to secure maximum social welfare. But men, and groups of men, do, by various means, struggle among themselves for relative increases, in power and privilege." This seems to say a good deal about "human nature" and possesses a grand air of "defeatism"; as a result it has been discussed in just such terms. Readers with a more generous and less sectarian vision would have politely segregated this personal emphasis from the impersonal core of the theme, even if such generosity deprived them of an easy target. That history is a "struggle for power" is an elementary, even trite, description; all parties organized for certain ends find it imperative to wield coercive authority. But beyond this commonplace can be noted a more singular trend: power slowly takes priority over the professed goals as an end-in-itself, and the closer to the effective exercise of power one is, the higher is its priority rating. This can be explained in part by the internal consequences of organization noted below, and in part by the confidence of participants, especially leaders, in the rightness of the cause for which they have sacrificed so much, which urges them to gloss over "expedient" measures. Any less intransigent attitude would be intolerable to people of such extreme concentration and seriousness. In most cases the party must either hold power, regardless of whether or not its methods contravene the formal program, or abdicate in favor of the hated enemy. When the choice is between power at any price and political suicide, the answer can be readily imagined; even if this disjunction were fictitious, the heated conflict of extreme viewpoints would lend it an aura of reality. Struggles for principles come to mean struggles for power.

It might be well to repeat: motives propose but the exigencies of practical action dispose. It is silly to deny that there are individuals so imbued with disinterested idealism that they are willing to forgo the prerogatives of power when these negate the ideals. But it can be safely said: (1) they are few and far between, (2) they repudiate the most potent means of exerting an enduring influence, and (3) when such individuals enter into a group in order to further these ideals, the attributes of the group will not be those of the individual. The history of the Franciscan Order, surely the most ambitious attempt to break through this circle, in its evolution from complete abnegation to ruthless regimentation, is instructive on this score. Illustrative, too, is the experience of the Spanish Anarchists, who, scornful of political power, awoke one day to find themselves burdened with Anarchist ministers in the Republican cabinet. Just as the assumption of "economic man" is not necessary to explain the workings of a price economy, so any concept of "power lust" is extrinsic to the above generalizations. The question is not one of faith or lack of faith in human nature, but of which specific faiths are justified by the way men act in defined situations.

The general laws of organization expounded by Michels are too well known to require elaboration. Burnham puts it succinctly: "Social life cannot dispense with organization. The mechanical, technical, psychological, and cultural conditions of organization require leadership, and guarantee that the leaders rather than the mass shall exercise control." This "iron law of oligarchy" reinforces the pursuit of power-ends at the expense of the formal ends. The life of leadership is one of incessant effort to build the party, with a consequent identification of the interests of the leaders with those of "their" party. Through a process of self-dedication the offices of leadership become synonymous with the highest welfare of the membership, not to speak of humanity, civilization, et al. Their retention of control is vindicated as a defense of the traditional faith and an assurance of future victory. A struggle for leadership is, above all, a struggle for power between opposing elites—the "ins" and the "outs." Programmatic differences assume the role of vehicles which represent and sanction the rebellious intent. Even if the conflict were originally incited by an ideological disagreement, the need of articulating these differences would involve a campaign for organizational preeminence whose demands would take precedence.

What is the significance of this disparity between professed and operational aims in politics? Three pertinent implications may be suggested here:

1. Utopian political doctrines are to be deplored, and not only because of their unattainability; in practice they will have worse effects than those more conservative and cautious. The example which Burnham treats convincingly is the liberal aim of democracy, defined as self-government by the people. While, as an ideal, this is irreproachable, as a dependable, practicable precept it is delusive; the formula today means strengthening the trend toward Bonapartism or Caesarism. The suffrage

mechanism which realizes the principle is fetishized into an efficient guarantor, while the developed techniques of mass control warp elections into plebiscites for the confirmation of despotism. More important, the assumption of a unanimity of interest between the ruler as the representative and the ruled as the represented is grist for the totalitarian mill. The socialist ideal of a "classless society" can be judged similarly defective when one realizes that (a) its formal meaning is so vague and ambiguous that whatever steps are taken can be subsequently interpreted as consistent with it, (b) this inability to delimit means and procedures provides a convenient cloak for unscrupulous careerists, (c) it is psychologically and historically intertwined with a preference for a completely collectivized society, and (d) it supposes that the question of power can be definitively settled, which is as good an excuse as any ruling elite can wish for suppressing dissidents as disruptive and anarchic.

2. Democracy must be defined in terms like Mosca's "liberty" and "juridical defense." This means a set of impersonal restrictions upon those in power and protection by law and the courts of the familiar democratic rights. It emphasizes government by due process rather than by the unchecked rule of self-titled delegates of History or the Workers, and is summed up in the right of organized opposition and subversion.

3. But laws and constitutions may easily be violated in practice while respected in speech. Further: "No theory, no promises, no morality, no amount of good will, no religion will restrain power. Neither priests nor soldiers, neither labor leaders nor business men, neither bureaucrats nor feudal lords will differ from each other in the basic use they will seek to make of power. . . . Only power restrains power." Freedom is the product of the conflict of social forces, not of their unity and harmony. (Most socialists would agree that this holds for all societies save a socialist one, whose exceptional status is transcendentally assured.) It is only through such freedom that the maximum of self-government is achieved. Opposing elites will make promises to masses in exchange for support, and if victorious, must keep some of them. The struggle stimulates the growth of new demands among the non-elite and encourages new pretenders to rise. "The masses, blocked by the iron law of oligarchy from directly and deliberately ruling themselves, are able to limit and control, indirectly, the power of their rulers. The myth of self-government is translated into a measure of reality by the fact of freedom."

There are many, including Burnham, who feel that recognition of these aspects of group action inevitably inhibits socialist activity as we have come to understand it. I feel that this flows from a confusion of perspectives. A general sociological outlook is not relevant in the same degree to all problems. Machiavellian theory is an indispensable analytical tool, even on its present abstract and elementary level; but it modifies only in small part traditional revolutionary socialist strategy. The problems posed by a declining capitalism may now appear more intricate and complex, but this should have been expected. The immense significance of Burnham's approach is potential; we can ignore it only at the risk of being disarmed by the future course of events.

1943

The Moral Critic

It was in the *Partisan Review* of September-October 1940 that Mr. Trilling publicly announced his strategy. Discussing T. S. Eliot's "Idea of a Christian Society" in the light of Matthew Arnold's dictum that criticism "must be apt to study and praise elements that for the fullness of spiritual perfection are wanted," he subjected the liberal-socialist ideology to a vigorous and pointed chiding. His subsequent writings might be viewed as a search for those "elements which are wanted," a brilliant and moral sustained, if sometimes impatient, exploration of the complexities of perfection and of the paths thereto.

In fact, and this is our special interest, in that very same article Mr. Trilling incorporated two distinct chidings. He was angry with the Left for having surrendered its traditional moral vision, and at the same time accused it of allowing this vision to blind it to the true principles of humanism. It was all done with such noble vehemence as to blur any hint of incompatibility. (It is certain that Mr. Trilling felt none.) Yet, the two tendencies are interesting and important in themselves, and have a larger reference which makes them worthy of attention.

The distinguishing feature of modern radical thought, wrote Mr. Trilling, "is that a consideration of means has taken priority over the consideration of ends . . . immediate ends have become more important than ultimate ends." The noteworthy quality of Eliot, contrasted to Trotsky, is his belief in morality as an end, not simply as a means, as an ever-present shaping ideal, not a set of prescribed tactics. Moral politics rather than historical criteria are seen as the measure of action: "Politics is to be judged by what it does for the moral perfection rather than the physical easement of man." The sense of immanent moral revolution, so profoundly developed in the eighteenth century, the concern with the potentialities of the individual and the race, have lost their vitality. Instead of asking, "What shall man become," socialists have concentrated exclusively upon maneuvering for temporary advantages in the contest for influence and power.

"Lenin," wrote Mr. Trilling, "gave us the cue when, at the end of *The State and Revolution*, he told us that we might well postpone the problem of what man is to become until such time as he might become anything he chose." One understands how such a thing gets said; but one understands, too, that saying it does not make a suspension of choice: it is a choice already made and the making of it was what gave certain people the right to wonder whether the ethics and culture of communism were anything else than the extension of the ethics and culture of the bourgeois business world. For many years the hero of our moral myth was that Worker-and-Peasant who smiled from the covers of *Soviet Russia Today*, simple, industrious, literate—and grateful. Whether or not people like him actually existed is hard to say; one suspects not and hopes not; but he was what his leaders and the radical intellectuals were glad to propagate as a moral ideal; that probably factitious Worker was the moral maximum which the preoccupation with immediate ends could accommodate.

This critique of radicalism partakes of the normal religio-ethical tone so consistently set forth by men like Maritain, Niebuhr, Dawson. It breaks with secularized politics, with politics, as one writer has called it, as an "independent art in an imperfect world," and insists that politics is but a branch of that broad science of ethics which derives from and is orientated towards the Good. In a sweep of revulsion from the interminably sordid conflict of interests it cries for social action whose goals are dictated by the fixed ethical imagination, not the fluid criteria of expediency; whose motivation is disinterested devotion, not interested gain; whose present status reflects, however crookedly, that image which is ideal. Such an appeal cannot help but be effective in these days when an ideal is at best a momentary, individual vision, and the raw stuff of politics is so pervasive and unyielding. It offers a way of penance and justification, all the more attractive for having so few definite programmatic implications. It stimulates the more pragmatic-minded to review their deeds in relation to their ends, and revise the one to suit the other. It encourages frank self-analysis and excites the moral faculties—two very good things.

Yet there appears in the same essay another strain of thought, destined to dominate the later writings, which, while not detracting from the fierce probity of the moralist, leads in a direction more agreeable to the workaday world. It is seen in the disparagement of radical philosophers who imply that man, in his quality, in his kind, will be wholly changed by socialism in fine ways that we cannot predict: man will be good, not as some men have been good, but good in new and unspecified fashions. At the bottom of at least popular Marxism there has always been a kind of disgust with humanity as it is and a perfect faith in humanity as it is to be. It is this simplistic faith in perfectibility which cultivates the domineering arrogance of the self-righteous reformer, and which forgives in advance inhumanity disguised as humanistic zeal. The present is only a transitional (almost illusory) epoch, and living men possess value in a potential and inferential sense, never in their own right and by virtue of their present human qualities. "The ultimate man has become the end for which all temporal men are the means."

The incongruity between the two tendencies is incipient and veiled. Presented in such an eloquent and original fashion, they tend to coerce unified assent through the many truths they both contain. Radical politics has been morally barren, has sacrificed men to means. We do feel disgust with the human quality of any given moment, and carelessly sanction the sacrifice of men to Man. It is only in some of his later reviews and especially in his book on Forster that the divergence and its pertinence to the larger issues becomes evident. And it is the latter of these attitudes which permeates the literary and philosophic judgment.

Mr. Trilling's taste in style will serve as an entrée; his "official" taste, one might add. He is impatient with the modern schools of the novel and points approvingly to the tradition of Dickens and Fielding. (The fact that the moderns on whom he wreaks his wrath are always second-stringers, never including a Joyce, Kafka, or Malraux, indicates the grounds for emphasizing the formal nature of these verdicts.) The nineteenth-century novel was a form of civilized social intercourse, with a relation between author and reader that was frank and friendly. The casual camaraderie, the good-humored witticism, the clear comic contrivance, all breathed the spirit of tolerant worldliness, "a kind of healthy contentment with human nature"; even satire, with its open avowal of anger, worked within this mood. The novel of modernity, however, reveals quite a different temper. Evil and ugliness are not frontally attacked through the intent of the writer; they are seen as the inevitable product of the characters' transgressions, for which the author disclaims all responsibility. Indeed, the author is no longer human at all, but simply the Eye and Hand which traces the natural logic of character and situation.

This attitude, designated as increasingly sterile, Mr. Trilling sees as derived from "liberalism." The liberal state of mind is reformist and humanitarian; a state of mind whose basis is snobbery, self-satisfaction, unimaginativeness. (The religious mind is an aversion to liberalism yet partakes of the same spirit, substituting theological credo for social principle.)

The liberal flatters himself upon his intentions, "and prefers not to know that the good will generates its own problems, that the love of humanity has its own vices and the love of the truth its own insensibilities." He is paternal and pedagogic, smug in the knowledge of his righteousness, and sure of the adequacy of his program. He revels in the abstract goodness of the masses and in the abstract badness of Reaction; his art merely dramatizes these axiomatic convictions. Human beings are denigrated into terms for his syllogisms, which are then dressed up in fictional form. An insidious cruelty is at work, in which all men are expendable in order to make a point.

In contrast to this facile moralism, E. M. Forster's "moral realism" is extolled, for "he is one of the thinking people who were never led by thought to suppose they could be more human and who, in bad times, will not become less." Moral realism is aware of the paradoxical quirks of morality; it knows that good-and-evil are more often to be found than good versus evil. Though dissatisfied, of course, with the ways of men, it foresees no new virtues, but, at best, a healthier distribution of the old. It is non-eschatological, skeptical of proposed revisions of man's nature, interested in human beings as it finds them, content with the possibilities and limitations that are always with us. Dodging the sentimentality of both cynicism and utopianism, it is worldly, even sophisticated. It is partial to the comic manner, which dashes cold water on extremities of sentiment, and yet pursues doggedly its own modest goals. Forster's novels are in a personal, lucid style, omitting the glamorous facades of the tragic-romantic: he is always in the novel skillfully at work, never hidden behind the screens manipulating invisible pulleys. Preoccupied with moral questions, he is neither overbearing nor sententious. Too sensible and ironic to be "great," he can afford to do his subject matter justice.

If, as some think, ours is an "interregnum" period, then the Forster-Trilling perspective would seem natural and appropriate. It is a restrictive and somewhat alien focus, unwarmed by the expansive enthusiasm we have been accustomed to expending on matters of salvation. Summing up his political credo, Forster wrote: "So two cheers for Democracy; there is no reason to give three. Only Love the Beloved Republic deserves that." (Which moved one left-wing critic to remark, "Two cheers for Forster.") And so it is with politics, reform, revolution, war, social planning—what were once unquestioned goods now call forth two well-meaning cheers. It may not always be so. Perhaps one bright morning nothing but three throaty yells will be able to express a new feeling of assured destiny; or perhaps, and this is more likely, we shall become sated with moderation, insist upon all or nothing at all, and then give three cheers for the hell of it. But, for the present, two will probably suffice.

All of which has some implication for radical political thinking, having to do with the scope of politics, its choice of goals, the sphere of its competence. Aldous Huxley has written that "political action is necessary and at the same time incapable of satisfying the needs which called it into existence." The socialist movement, allied with the recent sweep of collegiate psychology, contends that political action should satisfy these spiritual and psychological needs of the individual. More and more is the libertarian goal identified with a single ideal of personality divested of frustration and complexes. The development of a democratic-cooperative, rational, and sort of well-rounded person is assumed to reveal the purpose of the political struggle. "Moral realism" would incline toward Huxley here: the aim of political action is to change men's status, not their nature; though the two necessarily interact, they do so outside of the objective intent of politics, and under the supervision of other forces. A reasonably ordered society can provide the most fertile testing ground for conflicting ideals of personality, since it will have eliminated irrelevant and distracting problems (such as the economic). But these worthwhile activities will spring from their mutual sources, the imaginative arts, not from commissarial decree. Certainly politics has a moral basis, but what does not—science, art, religion? Its distinctive feature is its subject matter, problems of statecraft, of the organization of existing forces and specified objectives into an effective union. In so doing, it must see people as they are, which, according to Messrs. Forster and Trilling, would not be at all in the nature of a calamity.

1944

II

ANCIENTS
AND
MODERNS

The Philosophers'
Hidden Truth

"But this much I can say about all those who have written and will write saying that they *know* the nature of the subject which is my most serious interest. . . . In my opinion it is impossible for any of these people to know anything about the matter. For there is *no* treatise of mine on these things nor will there ever be." So wrote Plato in his *Seventh Letter*, and the import of his words is stunning. Is there really *no* treatise by him on that which is his "most serious interest"? What, then, are we to make of his *Dialogues*, which fill so many volumes and are regarded as the original source of Western philosophy?

It is to the answering of this question, and not only with regard to Plato but also as it affects all pre-Enlightenment thinkers of significance, that Professor Leo Strauss—distinguished occupant of the Charles Merriam chair of political science at the University of Chicago and guest professor at the Jewish Theological Seminary's Institute on Theology—is devoting himself.* It is his thesis that few, if any, of the Great Books in philosophy and political philosophy written before the French Revolution inaugurated the era of journalism can simply be "read," no matter how vigorously the student (or the instructor) is exhorted to do so and no matter how earnestly he applies himself. They have to be studied, and in a special way; for if they are truly great, it is probably their intention to conceal as well as to reveal, and they do not yield their secrets easily. In other words, the Great Books contain, besides their exoteric teachings as piously summarized in textbooks, esoteric doctrines reserved only for the most intelligent and perceptive. It must be admitted that this sounds rather preposterous, but only until one has read Professor Strauss, after which it appears astonishingly plausible.

---

*This essay is based on *Persecution and the Art of Writing* by Leo Strauss.

The reason why these books were written this way is twofold, and pertains, on the one hand, to the relation of the philosopher to the ruling powers of his age, on the other, to his relation to the mass of men who were ruled. The philosopher's relation to the ruling powers of his age, before the emergence of a secular, liberal society, made it the part of wisdom for him to be exceedingly discreet on all matters pertaining to state or church, lest he experience the royal hospitality of the dungeon or the ecclesiastical favor of the stake. This is a situation which, in the totalitarian societies of our own day, is becoming increasingly familiar to us; and Professor Strauss indicates how a philosopher may operate under such conditions:

> We can easily imagine that a historian living in a totalitarian country, a generally respected and unsuspected member of the only party in existence, might be led by his investigations to doubt the soundness of the government-sponsored interpretation of the history of religion. Nobody would prevent him from publishing a passionate attack on what he would call the liberal view. He would of course have to state the liberal view before attacking it; he would make that statement in the quiet, unspectacular, and somewhat boring manner which would seem natural; he would use many technical terms, give many quotations and attach undue importance to insignificant details. . . . Only when he reached the core of the argument would he write three or four sentences in that terse and lively style which is apt to arrest the attention of young men who love to think. . . . His reasonable young reader would for the first time catch a glimpse of the forbidden fruit. The attack, the bulk of the book, would consist of virulent expansions of the most virulent utterances in the holy book or books of the ruling party.

This sort of thing is rather self-evident once it is pointed out. Even if there are inevitable disagreements over particular cases—for instance, whether or not Descartes' incorporation of the Deity in his philosophic system was a stratagem—it may still be conceded that we cannot always take at face value the words of a writer who lived, or lives, under despotism. What is far from self-evident, and this is at the heart of Professor Strauss's argument, is that, in the ages preceding the Enlightenment, the serious thinker freely and deliberately, as an act of "social responsibility," as it were, so censored his own writings that they would mislead the frivolous reader, the "common man." In those times, the man of learning had cautious, when not downright pessimistic, views about the possibility and desirability of popular education. For him, the abyss between the "wise" and the "vulgar" was an inescapable fact of human nature, and he assumed that there are truths that no decent man should pronounce in public because of their unsettling effect on the social order. Consequently, he set out quite deliberately to deceive the majority of his readers.

It would be an error to regard this practice as but the expression of aristocratic prejudice. This point of view is not even necessarily opposed to democracy (though it is definitely opposed to democratic, or liberal, ideologies); Spinoza, who was a democrat in politics, wrote *ad captum vulgi*—"according to the capacity of the vulgar." Nor is it irreconcilable with the reforming spirit, as we see in the case of Montesquieu, who, in the words of d'Alembert, "having often to present important truths whose direct and explicit statement might be injurious and without benefit, had the prudence to disguise them; and, by this innocent artifice, hid them from those who might be harmed, without their being lost to the wise." Indeed, the thinker who acted thus could and did plead a genuine, benevolent concern for humanity. Popular opinions had to be accepted in order that the unenlightened might be slowly moved toward an approximation of the truth, in the measure that they could tolerate it.

Obviously, all this implies some basic premises about the connection between philosophy and life, premises which Professor Strauss is not too shy to affirm, though he has not yet, in his written work, tried to establish them by argument. One premise is that reason is unalterably critical of, and opposed to, revelation; the philosopher cannot accept the supernatural *fiat*, but must explain all phenomena by "the nature of things." Another premise is that no civil order can be stable or enduring unless it is founded on a common assent to a revealed religion; for society needs a code of morality, and reason (that is, philosophy) cannot provide any such specific code, any detailed, spiritually coercive index of rights and wrongs. Reason, by its very essence unable to supply any categorical imperatives for the life of action, can only lay down general rules which are minimum requirements for a tolerable social existence, and one of these requirements is a "revealed" moral code such as reason itself cannot provide. A third premise is that philosophy itself, before modern times, assumes the superiority of the contemplative life of the individual to the practical life of the crowd, but it also takes it for granted that most men are not capable of ascending from the cave of the commonplace to the sunlight of the *vita contemplativa*, and therefore have need for a practical guidance that only revelation can give them.

So it is that, while philosophy is abstractly opposed to revelation, yet philosophers must support it. That this is what philosophers have thought and done is the recurrent theme of Professor Strauss's essays. But this deception by the philosophers would be self-defeating if it were known and talked about. It must be kept secret, except from a few disciples and potential disciples who can, in their turn, be trusted to dissimulate expertly. How this is accomplished Professor Strauss discovers in his investigation of "the art of writing," an investigation which is really an exercise in the art of reading. Does a close scrutiny of the Platonic dialogues discover that they are conversations between a superior man (usually Socrates) and one or more inferior men? And is it not also to be noted that even where two philosophers are present, they do not talk to one another? That, for Professor Strauss, is a significant clue to the effect that Socrates' opinions are not identical with his speech, that the conversational setting of each dialogue, and of every statement within each dialogue, must be taken into account if we would know what Socrates *really* believed. Such a textual analysis will disclose how Socrates managed the key problem of philosophy, namely, the relation between philosophy (the realm of theoretical truth) and politics (the realm of practical moral guidance), which is necessarily complex, obscure, and dangerous.

Professor Strauss came upon this problem in his studies of medieval Jewish and Islamic thought, which, in distinction from Christian thought of the time, put a greater stress on the importance of political philosophy for the whole of philosophy. For Jews and Muslims, what was revealed was not Faith but Law, no creed or dogma but a comprehensive order of social life. Whereas in Christianity sacred doctrine was theological and philosophy was needed for its study, in Judaism and Islam sacred doctrine was legal in character and philosophy was inherently subversive of it, for it interposed a question mark in the path of full and instant obedience. The Talmud recognized this fact when it said flatly: "He who reflects about four things—about what is above, what is below, what is before, what is behind—it would be better for him not to have come into the world." Philosophy, then, in the Jewish and Muslim worlds was forced to develop that discretion which it had in classical antiquity, and which Professor Strauss regards as its true mark of authenticity. It is not without interest that he has never thought it worth his while to write a single essay on a Christian thinker, preferring to limit himself to the Greeks, the medieval Jews and Muslims, and the secular moderns (Hobbes, Rousseau, etc.); and one cannot but suspect that for Professor Strauss, Christianity is an irresponsible and unstable mixture of doctrines.

The bulk of *Persecution and the Art of Writing* is devoted to three long essays on "the art of reading" Maimonides' *Guide for the Perplexed*, Judah Halevi's *Kuzari*, and Spinoza's *Tractatus Theologico-Politicus*. All three previously appeared in Jewish scholarly publications and have made a deep impression on Professor Strauss's fellow experts. They are so closely reasoned, so brilliant in their analysis of details of style and argument, that it is impossible fairly to summarize them. Nevertheless, in order to have a glimpse of Professor Strauss at work, it might be worthwhile here to give some abbreviated and simplified illustrations of his method, adapted from his essay on Maimonides.

What is the subject matter of the *Guide for the Perplexed*? When we try to answer this simple question, we run up against a paradox. On the one hand, Maimonides states that his book is a defense of Judaism against philosophy, which for him meant Aristotelianism; he expressly states that he is not writing a philosophical book, and that he has excluded all of physics and most of metaphysics from his purview. On the other hand, he gives as his intention the explanation of various biblical words, behind whose literal meaning there hides a secret meaning; and the highest secrets of the Bible, again according to Maimonides, are *ma'aseh bereshit* (the Talmudic phrase for physics—literally, the "story of the beginning") and *ma'aseh merkabah* (the Talmudic phrase for metaphysics—literally, the "story of the chariot" in Ezekiel).

It is possible, to be sure, that Maimonides was merely confused. It is also possible, however, that the conclusion is not accidental. In favor of this latter alternative are two explicit statements of Maimonides. In one he warns the reader that "the diction of this treatise has not been chosen by haphazard," and in the other he says that "you will not demand from me here anything except chapter headings, and even those headings are, in this treatise, not arranged according to any sequence whatsoever, but they are scattered and intermingled with other subjects the explanation of which is intended." The reference to "chapter headings" is a significant hint that the *Guide* is a philosophical book, after all; for the Talmud prohibits the teaching of *ma'aseh merkabah* (metaphysics) to more than one disciple, who must show promise of wisdom, and even then allows the teaching of only the "chapter headings." This hint is reinforced by the fact that the *Guide* is written in the form of letters to a favorite pupil, one Joseph.

Professor Strauss resolves the paradox by showing that the purpose of the *Guide* is to reveal the identity of the philosophy of Aristotle with the secrets of the Bible, and that Maimonides' "defense" of the Law against philosophy takes the form of proving that the "secret teaching" of the Law, from which the Commandments are derived and by which they can be justified, is exactly the same as the teaching of Aristotle. Thus, for Maimonides the Bible is an esoteric book, and the disorder of his *Guide* is a polished reflection of the intentional disorder of Scripture, whose "revealed" truths are but popular and imaginative expressions of rational truths as these were demonstrated by Aristotle.

To make one's way through the disorder of the *Guide*, one has to imitate Maimonides' way through the disorder of Scripture. That is, one has to read the *Guide* as Maimonides read the Bible, which is the way that Orthodox Jews have always read these "books"—realizing that any word has in it a world of meaning and that the composition as a whole is a vast and mysterious web of meaning. Every detail in the *Guide* is important. When Maimonides "quotes" some classifications of the Commandments, or some enumerations of opinions concerning providence or creation, which he had previously made in his codification of the Law, the *Mishneh Torah*, it may be found upon close examination that the quotation is inaccurate in a slight but significant way. Similarly, the first word of every chapter must be related to the first words of the preceding and succeeding chapters, to see if a (or rather, what kind of) pattern is being suggested. Particular attention must also be paid to contradictory statements, even if, or rather especially when, one is repeated assertively many times and the other is tossed off but once, in a casual way; when Maimonides repeatedly insists upon the necessity of observing the entire Law, and then at one point, in a few passing words, denies the obligatory character of the whole sacrificial legislation—that is no minor matter!

The fruitfulness of this procedure may be gathered from the following instances which Professor Strauss gives of Maimonides' "art of writing":

1. On four occasions, and each time with approval, Maimonides quotes an expression of Aristotle to the effect that the sense of touch is a disgrace to us. But two words are omitted from Aristotle's original expression, which, in its complete text, asserts that the sense of touch is *popularly considered* a disgrace. The instructed reader, who knew his Aristotle, would recognize that Maimonides was here uttering a conventional opinion, one that prized supersensual truths—i.e., "revelations"—over the truths of experience and reason. And this reader would observe, if he read closely, that there are other passages in the *Guide* which deny that there is any difference in dignity between the senses or that supersensual truths are possible. He would also be considerably provoked by the fact that one of these misquotations from Aristotle is contained in a passage that gives Maimonides' general definition of prophecy, and that this definition of prophecy is given in a conditional sentence, whose grammatical nature is obscured by its being very long and by its containing a lengthy parenthesis.

2. Maimonides vigorously declares that the immortality of the soul and the bodily resurrection of the dead are cardinal principles of Jewish faith. But when, in the *Guide*, he takes up the question of whether there is a Divine Providence and tries to answer the philosophical objections to it, he makes no use of either of these principles which are so crucial to

the religious point of view. In contrast, elsewhere in the *Guide* he inter-
prets the phrase in Deuteronomy 8:16, "the good at thy latter end," to
mean merely the fortitude acquired by the Jews from their desert wan-
derings. The sagacious reader would also notice that the problem of divine justice is discussed after Maimonides has completed his discourse
on physics and metaphysics, and he would infer that for the author this
was not a subject for theoretical knowledge but a practical matter, i.e., it
had to do with morals and government, with "political philosophy."

3. The potential sage will be struck by Maimonides' use of the first-person
plural and singular. When the author defends "our" opinion (i.e., the
opinion of the community of believers in the Law) against the philosophers, he expresses conventional beliefs. When he says "my" opinion, he
is pointing to his secret teaching. The fact that he calls the *Mishneh Torah*
"our great book" and the *Guide* "my treatise" is his way of distinguishing
between his exoteric and esoteric writings. Indeed, this was understood
by one of the medieval commentators on Maimonides, who interpreted
the quotation from Proverbs 22:17 at the beginning of the *Guide* to
read: "Bow down thine ear, and hearken to the words of the sages, [but]
apply thine heart unto mine opinion."

It must be emphasized that the above is only a superficial and coarsened
version of an essay on the *Guide* that is fifty-seven pages long, and whose argument requires a special effort by the reader in order to be followed. Professor
Strauss writes in a bold and masculine style; his sentences are unambiguous;
his paragraphs are lucid; but his reasoning is so close and subtle that one often
finds that the thread has been lost. In this respect, reading Professor Strauss is
not too different an experience from reading Maimonides.

No doubt, there will be scholars who will respectfully dispute Professor Strauss
on just about every point. They will find, as many already know, that he is a
most formidable opponent. And if in time the victory goes to Professor Strauss,
he will have accomplished nothing less than a revolution in intellectual history,
and most of us will, figuratively at least, have to go back to school to learn the
wisdom of the past that we thought we knew. It is fortunate for us that the lessons will be rather more exciting, and more daring in their implications, than
we remember them. And it is a consolation of sorts to know in advance that, for
those of us who fail to learn this art of reading, provision has been made.

1952

Niccolò Machiavelli

The inscription on Machiavelli's memorial, in the church of Santa Croce in Florence, reads: *Tanto Nomini Nullum Par Elogium*—"Such a name is beyond all praise." But both memorial and inscription were erected in 1787, more than 250 years after his death, and Machiavelli's bones do not rest beneath them. They had originally been laid in the family chapel in the same church; the chapel had then been taken over by a religious order, and it eventually fell into such decay that even its exact location was a matter for doubt. The imposing presence of the spirit, the obscurity that attends the body—these are appropriate signs of how Machiavelli stands with us, so intimate, so exasperatingly indefinite.

We have all learned from him, call him master. But what he had to teach is far from clear, and this despite the fact that his prose style is extolled by historians of Italian literature for its marvelous simplicity and limpidity, its ruthless abstinence, so rare in that language, from the pleasures of mere rhetoric. Jean Bodin, noting Machiavelli's affirmation (in the *Discourses on the First Ten Books of Titus Livy*) of a popular republic as the best form of government, and his call (in *The Prince*) for a new tyrant to liberate Italy from the "barbarians," complained that "*il ne sçait à quoi se tenir* [he doesn't know what to believe]." Leibniz found him "a Gordian knot," which he could not unravel and would not cut. And John Morley, at the end of the last century, was moved to cast a backward glance and exclaim: "In all the great countries all over the West, this singular shade is seen haunting men's minds, exciting, frightening, provoking, perplexing them, like some unholy necromancer, bewildering reason and conscience by riddles and paradox."

The more closely one examines Machiavelli's posthumous career—"his real life," it has even been called—the more difficult does it become to get a precise notion of his doctrine, or even to be absolutely sure that he had anything which could be called a doctrine. The Elizabethan playwrights freely identified him with the Evil One; but his books, when first published, had the approval of the Church. The Jesuits later had him placed on the Index, but boldly plagiarized his writings. Richelieu praised his wisdom, as did the left-wing republicans during the English civil war. Napoleon admired him, and when he drew up a list of books to form his portable library the "republican" *Discourses* headed the field in political philosophy. Rousseau admired him too, and claimed the "tyrannical" *Prince* as "*le livre des républicains.*" Macaulay baptized him a liberal: "We are acquainted with few writings which exhibit so much elevation of sentiment, so pure and warm a zeal for the public good, or so just a view of the duties and rights of citizens, as those of Machiavelli"—an opinion shared, for quite different reasons, by Treitschke. Mussolini esteemed him highly—as did the founder of the Italian Communist Party, Gramsci, who ended his days in Mussolini's jails. And T. S. Eliot has gravely informed us that "such a view of life as Machiavelli's implied a state of the soul which might be called a state of innocence."

His was a book of seven seals, to which his contemporaries or near-contemporaries no more had the key than we do. The group of young men in the Orti Oricellari who listened to Machiavelli read from the manuscript of his *Discourses* were so flushed with republican fervor that several of them proceeded to engage in a conspiracy against the Medici, an action from which Machiavelli most vigorously dissociated himself, and with a sincerity that cannot be questioned. If one earnestly intends a conspiracy, one does not commence with a series of public readings, and Machiavelli knew this as well as, if not better than, anyone else. The first edition of *The Prince*, five years after Machiavelli's death, had a preface by the printer in which he sought the protection of the Church from some persons who "do not know that those who instruct in the use of herbs and medicine, also instruct in poisons, in order to know how to guard against them"—an intriguingly cryptic remark which seems to indicate that *The Prince* was widely regarded as both a shameless defense of tyranny and a kind of homeopathic medicine against the disease of tyranny. Presumably it was the first sense of the book which made it so dear to Thomas Cromwell, Henry III, Henry IV, Catherine de' Medici, and to all the apologists of the new *raison d'état* which developed along with the new absolute monarchies. On the other hand, when Cardinal Pole visited Florence a few years after Machiavelli's death, he encountered the rumor, supposedly based on Machiavelli's own utterances, that *The Prince* had been written with the intention of bringing ruin upon the Medici; and when, in a famous essay (1612), Trajano Boccalini had Machiavelli accused before a divine tribunal, not of being a *sceleratum satanae organum*, as the Jesuits claimed, but of having been seen at night subversively inserting dogs' teeth into the mouths of sheep, he is giving expression to an interpretation that is as old as the Machiavelli legend itself.

> For a long time now I do not say what I believe, nor believe what I say, and if I have nevertheless sometimes said the truth, I have hid it among so many lies that it is difficult to find.

So wrote Machiavelli in a letter to Francesco Guicciardini on May 17, 1521. But this letter is, on the whole, frivolous in its temper, and it is impossible to know how seriously one should take the statement. Even when Machiavelli assures us he doesn't believe what he says, it is hard to know whether to believe him or not.

> I have not sought to adorn my work with high-flown phrases or grandiose words, or with any other superficial enticements or ornaments, the way most others decorate their things; because I desire no honor for my work but such as its variety of matter and the gravity of its subject may justly deserve.

The secret of Machiavelli must be concealed somewhere in this style, which is at once incomparably forthright and impossibly ambiguous. This doubleness immediately suggests irony, but to say that the style is ironical is already a simplification, for it leads us to think that, having perceived the irony, we have consequently got the point. In fact, we can do little more than wonder whether it is his irony or our double vision. And if we conclude that the irony is there, we must go on to try to locate it exactly and estimate its direction, which soon leaves us with the sensation of merely having moved from one riddle to another.

Even where the irony seems broad and inescapable, so that we flatter ourselves on having no trouble in recognizing it, we are soon plagued by second thoughts. "Frightfulness (*crudeltà*) may be said to be well used—if of evil it is permissible to speak well." That strikes us as an irony, face up. But is it really so clear? Is he asserting that *crudeltà* is not an evil at all, but is only sanctimoniously regarded as one? Or does he mean to say that it is indeed an evil, but it would have to be, if he intended the second.

Or take the following, from the dedication of *The Prince*, addressed to Lorenzo de' Medici:

> Nor will it, I trust, be deemed presumptuous if a man of low and obscure
> condition discusses and directs the government of princes; for as landscape
> painters go down to the plains to observe well the nature of mountains and
> other high places, and go up to the mountains to observe lowly things, so
> in order to understand the nature of the people one needs to be a prince,
> and to understand the nature of princes one has to be of the people.

If this be not presumption, what would presumption be? Yet we know from
Machiavelli's letters how eager he was to enter the Medici's service, and how
high his hopes were that the dedication would earn him some official favor.

Instances could be multiplied. Indeed, they could be multiplied so end-
lessly, and with such facility, that one inevitably becomes uneasy. Ironies breed
before our eyes, cancel each other out, are immediately reborn again, *ad in-
finitum*. Where a text is so fertile in ironies, is it not a case of artificial generation? This question finds additional justification in two quite remarkable
aspects of Machiavelli's style. The first is its consistency throughout all of his
writing—his private correspondence as well as his official legations, the "republican" *Discourses* as well as the "tyrannical" *Prince*, his trivial sketches as
well as his solemn studies. The second is its permanence throughout all his
life; there is no development, it exists fully grown when we first meet it, and
remains stonily indifferent to time and circumstance thereafter. Historians and
biographers of Machiavelli are fond of explaining him as "a man of his age." In
fact, all of the vicissitudes of his career—his success as diplomatist under the
republic, his dismissal by the triumphant Medici, his exile from Florence, his
slow and grudging return to favor of a sort—all these washed about him,
foamed and bubbled, and then subsided, leaving some debris on the beaches
but no observable mark on the general topography.

Irony usually exists by virtue of the *double entendre*, the saying one thing
and meaning another; and if Machiavelli is an ironist in this way, then he has
raised the art to such a degree as to be self-defeating, for we find it impossible
to disentangle the two strands. However, it is conceivable that such an irony
was not his intention, and that the ambiguities of his style arise not from any
difference between what he said and what he meant, but mainly from the very
effrontery with which he said what he meant.

We take it that Machiavelli was the founder of "political realism," and echo
Bacon, who was simple-minded in the fashion that only geniuses can be: "We are
much beholden to Machiavel and others that wrote what men do and not what
they ought to do." Now, Machiavelli was highly intelligent and was a man of
considerable experience in affairs of state; it is not, therefore, unexpected that

his writing should contain many striking insights. In themselves, they would not have earned him his fame; there are as many such insights, as felicitously put, in more than a few other writers whose books are hardly known to the public at large. (Machiavelli's contemporary, Francesco Guicciardini, was at least his match in this respect, even his superior, some would claim.) No, Machiavelli's fame was not due to his having had the bright idea of describing for the first time what men do, instead of what they ought to do. The princes and principalities of this world, in all the centuries before Machiavelli was born, had a fully competent knowledge of this distinction—one does not gain a kingdom, establish a dynasty without it. Nor were they particularly reticent about their knowledge: one has only to peruse such a book as Allan Gilbert's *Predecessors of Machiavelli* to see the extent to which "Machiavellianism" antedates Machiavelli. Statesmen were no more successful in their business for having read *The Prince* than Machiavelli was in his political career for having written it.

Furthermore, Machiavelli's treatises are not all wisdom. They are full of the most silly generalizations, simply because they are so wildly general (e.g., "whoever pursues this method in a besieged city will find it easy to defend the place"). He has his *idée fixes* (abjuring the use of firearms in war because the Romans did not use them), and he frequently gets so involved in his "lessons" from Roman history that he finds it impossible to draw any useful conclusion (as in Book II of *The Discourses*, where he finally ends up: "It does not matter much in what way a general behaves, provided his ability is so great that it quite makes up for how he behaves, this way or that"). His fondness for rigid alternatives goes to such lengths that he seems almost at times to be parodying the medieval scholastics. Here is a fair summary of the argument of the *Discorso sopra la cosa di Pisa*, in which Machiavelli discovers the best way for Florence to suppress a rebellion in Pisa:

Pisa can be gained either by (1) love or (2) force.
1. If by love, Pisa must either (a) voluntarily surrender or (b) be delivered
   over by its ruler.
   a. Since the city is in rebellion, it will not voluntarily surrender.
   b. Whether its ruler delivers the city to Florence depends on whether
      (1) he became ruler through love or (2) by force.
      1. If by love, he will not betray his city.
      2. If by force, then he is strong enough to hold it, having been strong
         enough to win it.
Therefore, there remains only:
2. Force.

True, this is probably a very early work by Machiavelli, and is a somewhat extreme example. But it is in no way untypical of the man. One has only to think of his hero-worship, in *The Prince*, of Caesar Borgia, a clever thug whose political career was based on little else than his being the son of Pope Alexander VI: he is remembered today only because Machiavelli admired him so extravagantly, and because he had a genuinely extraordinary sister and such a monster for a father.

And yet—the fact remains that there is something which the modern mind experiences as "realistic" in Machiavelli, and which it does not find in any earlier political thinker. There is a sense in which, as the Italian historian Prezzolini has observed, the precursors of Machiavelli are really his successors. That is to say, until Machiavelli came along they could not be seen as leading up to anything; they were merely worldly-wise men, who, like the poor, are always with us. They could not be understood (or misunderstood) as Machiavellians until after Machiavelli had demonstrated that there could be such a thing. What this "thing" is, one is hard put to say. For, if Machiavelli inserted a new element into political thinking, it was one so powerful that it dissolved the previous, casually mixed ingredients and lost its identity among them. From his contemporaries we get only vague and tantalizing hints of what he was up to. Jacopo Nardi referred to the *Discourses* only as "a work of a new kind never before (so far as I know) attempted by anyone." And Guicciardini, whom one would have thought to know everything worth knowing about the practice of politics, saw in Machiavelli an "inventor of new and unusual things"; but, though he wrote a long (and excellent) essay in criticism of Machiavelli, he never elaborated on that remark.

Searching for a clue to the meaning of Machiavelli, one returns to the original legend, born in the sixteenth century and dominant until the Enlightenment, which identified him as a servant of Satan, and sometimes as the Devil himself. Of course, this legend was fostered by Catholic and Protestant propagandists for their own purposes; and very few of those who helped keep it alive ever so much as read a line by Machiavelli. Nevertheless, the very pertinacity of the legend, and the ease with which it took root and flourished, are suggestive. For the two qualities most generally associated with Satan were acuteness of intellect and presumption of spirit; which two, when conjointly operating, carried one beyond the world of good and evil to a realm where everything was permitted. And it was precisely this journey which Machiavelli accomplished: from the kingdom of good and evil to that transhuman kingdom before whose gates is inscribed Nietzsche's motto for modern nihilism: *Alles ist erlaubt*—"All is permitted."

The horror that Machiavelli inspired for so long, and which he even now can inspire on occasion, is the horror of the void, which presents itself, at one and the same time, as the Nothing and the Ultimately Real. It is the sensation we feel when we read one of his more notorious passages, such as the following from his *Arte della Guerra*, in which he criticizes Christianity for having debilitated the military instincts:

> The present mode of life, thanks to the Christian religion, does not enforce the need for self-defense, as used to be done; for, of old, men defeated in war were either killed off or were left to spend their lives miserably in perpetual slavery; and, if a town was taken, it was either demolished or its inhabitants were hounded out, despoiled of their goods, and dispersed all over the world; with the result that those who were overcome in war, drank of misery to its dregs. This being so, out of sheer dread men kept up their military exercises. . . . But today this fear has to a large extent disappeared; for of the conquered but a few are killed and no one is kept long in prison. . . . Even if a city has rebelled a thousand times, it is not demolished, and its people are left with their property, the greatest evil they have to fear being a tax, with the result that men are no longer keen on undergoing military training and putting up constantly with its hardships in order to escape dangers of which they have but little dread.

One is impelled to object; but, upon consideration, one finds nothing specific to object to. What he has said is not obviously incorrect; it is not even immoral; it simply deals in a ruthlessly "objective" way with a matter of fact. And we realize that what was so shocking at first glance was nothing but his boldness in discussing, in a totally matter-of-fact way, what is usually regarded as a matter of morality. Moral imperatives, for Machiavelli, have the status of facts, as do immoral imperatives. Indeed, the distinction between the two kinds of imperatives can hardly be said to exist. He does not counsel evil, for that in itself would be a recognition of the good, and it is the very essence of Machiavelli that in politics there is neither good nor evil, of a moral kind. Politics is the exercise of the Will to Power, which deals not with moral truth but "effectual truth" (*verità effettuale*). Morality can, in certain circumstances, be such an "effectual truth," and Machiavelli is very much aware in his writings that conventional moral sanctions may be quite useful in politics. But he is also very much aware that, in different circumstances, they may not be.

Sir Frederick Pollack claimed that in Machiavelli we meet, for the first time since Aristotle, "the pure passionless curiosity of the man of science." He would have done better to omit the reference to Aristotle, whose idea of "science," and perhaps even of "passionless curiosity," was worlds apart from Machiavelli's.

But he had got the main point nevertheless, which is the close relation be-tween the Machiavellian conception of politics and the modern scientific con-ception of reality.

Why should one not lie or murder in politics? In his *Ethics*, Aristotle gave the answer of classical political thought:

> Not every action nor every passion admits of a mean; for some have names that already imply badness, e.g., shamelessness, envy, and in the case of ac-tions, adultery, theft, murder; for all these and such-like things imply by their names that they are themselves bad, and not the excess or deficiencies of them. It is not possible, then, ever to be right with regard to them; one must always be wrong.

Now, there is a metaphysic behind this, which few take seriously today, and which the very successes of modern science make it almost impossible to take seriously. In its political bearings, this metaphysic assumed that man is a "po-litical animal" in the sense that, possessed of certain natural motions of the soul that urge him to the good, he finds this good is only realizable when the individual is a member of a body politic. This body is like the human beings that comprise it in that it has a "spiritual" reason for existence, and does not aim merely at the longest possible life.

This point of view, in an infinite variety of shadings and with an equal vari-ety of emphases, was basic to all Western political thought before Machiavelli came along to announce: "It is a sound maxim that reprehensible actions may be justified by their effects." Today, we frequently say the same thing, but not in ex-actly the same way; we would certainly avoid the term "reprehensible," as having no place in that sentence. If actions are to be judged by effects, as causes are judged by consequences, it is nonsensical to say that reprehensible actions are to be justified by their effects, for if they are so justified they are not "reprehensible." What often seems like irony in Machiavelli, or a desire to shock the reader, is nothing more than his effort to state the principles of politics as an objective sci-ence in a language that was still permeated by the assumption that politics could not be an objective science, since it was already a branch of ethics; and ethics could not in the very nature of the case be "objective," since its concern was with the good or bad intentions of the subject. And what often seems like ambiguity in Machiavelli is nothing more than a willed indifference to moral judgment. He could praise tyranny or censure it, applaud republicanism or score it; his atti-tude varied with circumstances, for he did not believe it possible to appeal to any other tribunal than brute circumstance.

When Napoleon said, "*J'aime le pouvoir comme artiste*," he was giving expression to an attitude towards politics which Machiavelli was the first to formulate. He preferred a more solemn analogy of himself as a *medico politico*; but it comes to the same thing. Art and medicine and all of natural science have it in common that, in medieval terminology, they do not require "rectitude of the appetite." They are judged only by results. An artist may be a lecher and a murderer, a surgeon may be a sadist; this is irrelevant to the judgment one passes on their work. But is it irrelevant to the work of the statesman? Since Machiavelli we have come to think so; which is why modern politics, all of modern politics, is managerial to the core.

Dante put Brutus in hell, along with Satan and Judas; Machiavelli set the modern tone, extolled him as a defender of republican liberty. In Shakespeare we see the mixed feelings that attend the transition from the first perspective to the second, a transition which might be described, quite literally, as the "profanation" of politics: the removal of political authority, *qua* authority, from the shadows of sanctity that had always enveloped it, and its subjugation to the test of *la verità effettuale*. With this transition, there disappeared all of the crucial problems of the earlier political philosophy. Under what conditions may a subject disobey a legitimate ruler? a tyrant? If disobedience is allowable, what form may it take? What is the relation between the temporal and the spiritual order? For Machiavelli, and for us, these questions do not exist; that is to say, they do exist of course, but we do not grant them *de jure* recognition.

As it happens, Machiavelli's intervention was largely a matter of accident. It was much less a case of his converting later generations than of their sanctifying him. Of science or scientific method, he knew nothing. What he did have was intuition, not of scientific method, but of human reality as it would appear were it simply an object of scientific method. It is an intuitive vision which has never been surpassed for its clarity, not even by our "political science," which does not have the courage of its principles and ceremoniously marks time whenever its method threatens to bring it close to that no-man's-land in which there is no "ought," except what "is."

Since Machiavelli, a dimension has been amputated from man's political existence. The operation was a success; but there are stitches and scars, inevitably. It is in Machiavelli we see them most clearly, for he does not hesitate to wave the stumps at us, in order to make a point. Those riddles one finds in Machiavelli, those ambiguities and ironies—they mark the points where, the soul having been cut away, we are troubled with the illusion that "something" is still there.

1954

" . . . And People
Opening Veins in Baths"

Tacitus

What marks the true greatness of a writer is, first, the peremptory and sovereign way he imposes himself on successive generations of readers; and second, the mystery that attends his ultimate "meaning," his inexhaustibility before the commentator. One is almost tempted to say that his mystery is his meaning; his words impress us as fragments torn from a greater silence, where the whole truth is to be found, though not by us. There are not many such writers. Most of them are poets and dramatists. Some are novelists and philosophers. Very few are historians. Thucydides perhaps belongs among them; Tacitus certainly.

Tacitus is the historian of the extreme situation, without hope and without despair, almost without humanity. Yet, paradoxically, just as the *deus absconditus* [hidden god] of the theologians could be known through his absence, so it is this seeming want of humanity that quickens our own sense of its existence. Thus:

> The general rage against [the fallen favorite] Sejanus was subsiding, calmed by the executions already carried out, yet retribution was now decreed against his remaining children. Therefore, they were taken to prison, the boy understanding what lay ahead, the girl suspecting it so little that many times she asked what wrong she had done, what place she was being taken to, saying that she would not do it again, and that she should be punished as children are. Contemporary writers report that, the execution of a virgin being unheard of, the hangman violated her beside the noose. Then both were strangled and their bodies thrown on the Gemonian steps.

The girl's name we do not know, nor anything else about her. In the blood-spattered pages of the *Annals,* her fate can hardly be called exceptional. Tacitus gives no sign of pity; and whatever it is that the reader feels, pity is not quite the word for it. The effect of this passage may best be compared to an experience most of us probably do not have more than once in our lives—when we dream of our own death, not with any sentimental pathos, but with a cold, clinical detachment, simply seeing it happen, an event among an infinity of events, in an infinity of time and space, and then we awake, feeling in a way we never did before what it means to be a human being in a universe where human beings need not exist.

In his *Agricola,* Tacitus refers to those who were spared by Domitian's terror, and says that they "had outlived both others and themselves." He was one of those who survived himself. Despising Imperial Rome, he served it well, and was in turn well rewarded with high post and privileges. The whole import of his chronicle is that this is a time when nothing can be done, the zero point of the human condition. He condemned those who opposed the regime, for he saw no alternative to it and they only worsened matters; and condemned too those who supported it, for it was base. He censured Seneca for betraying his Stoic-republican principles by toadying to Nero; he censured Thrasea Paetus for being loyal to these same principles and offering resistance to Nero; and he praised both for dying well. Monarchy, aristocracy, and democracy were all unstable forms of government, leading to tyranny. The only good one was a "mixed constitution" as described by Polybius and Cicero; but it was beyond the capacity of men to establish such a state. It was permissible to think about "primeval man, untouched as yet by evil impulse," and his *Germania* is just such a fantasy. But his own age was fatally marked, the people corrupt and beyond redeeming, the barbarians rebellious and menacing. The sole honorable behavior was to avoid contention and die bravely. Nor was there anything to hope for from the gods, "who care nothing for the happiness of men, only for their punishment." All tokens of divine intervention were fraudulent:

> Many prodigies occurred. A woman gave birth to a snake. Another woman was killed in her husband's arms by a thunderbolt. The sun suddenly went dark. . . . But these portents meant nothing. So little were they due to the gods that Nero continued his reign and his crimes for years to come.

The full Tacitean quality does not come through in Professor Michael Grant's new "plain English" translation. On the other hand, its simplicity and readability will presumably attract many readers who might otherwise fight shy of so baroque an historian; and the introduction and appendices are models of erudite popularization. Like Shakespeare, Tacitus will endure almost any loving translation, and Professor Grant's is indisputably that. For, again like Shakespeare, he is complaisant to all human intentions.

And how complaisant! There is a still unwritten chapter in the history of Western political thought that would deal with the varying uses made of Tacitus (and of Machiavelli too, with whom he has such an odd affinity). The classical revival of the Renaissance propelled him into a new and highly ambiguous career—no longer a Roman chronicler, but a political guide to "real" politics as opposed to the "imaginary" politics of the medieval mind. Somehow, by a transvaluation of values we do not even now fully understand, the medieval ideas of a good society, of the moral obligations of ruler and ruled, of a transcendent standard by which political actions were to be measured. All these were suddenly felt to be pretentiously hollow, while the unalloyed hellishness of the *Annals* (especially of Books I–VI, dealing with Tiberius) came to be regarded as a revelation of the "realities" of political life.

It was Guicciardini, one of the founders of *realpolitik* and friend of Machiavelli, who first enunciated this new approach to Tacitus: "Cornelius Tacitus teaches very well those who live under a tyranny how to conduct themselves prudently; as he also teaches tyrants how to found a tyranny." Here was a school for dictators that was also a school for tyrannicides; one chose one's banner and enlisted. Gentle Montaigne saw in Tacitus "a nursery of ethical and political instruction for the aid and ornament of those who have something to do with managing the affairs of the world." And Nicolas Perrot, translating the *Annals* for Richelieu, advised him that "it is in his [Tacitus's] learned writings that one is taught the art of ruling." The new secular monarchies studied the cunning, the hypocrisy, the ruthlessness of Tiberius; courtiers quoted Tacitus and Machiavelli (often confusing the two); this was the essence of royal wisdom. At the same time, however, there were those who found in Tacitus precisely the strength to withstand the new secular tyrannies: Justus Lipsius, the founder of international law, and editor of the first modern edition of Tacitus's works; and Chénier, the French republican dramatist and poet, who declaimed: "*Son nom prononcé fait pâlir les tyrans.*"

The French Revolution even saw the emergence of what one modern historian has called "Red Tacitism," Tacitus as a *sans-culotte*. But by that time the idea of politics as being entirely profane and "realistic" was so taken for granted that interest was declining in Tacitus as a political mentor. Instead of being admired as a political sage, he began to be condemned as a nasty-minded and inaccurate historian. Politics was now safely profane; the need was to make it respectable. Tyrants were to be neither imitated nor opposed. The very idea of tyranny was to be abolished, along with the superstitions of those dark centuries that had never been able to elevate themselves sufficiently to see History and Humanity, but merely men and their deeds. It was Voltaire who sounded the cry, by charging Tacitus with "degrading humanity." And Napoleon, naturally preferring the glory of tyranny to its gore, registered an indignant protest that in the *Annals* one found "nothing save accusations and men accused, persecutions and the persecuted, and people opening veins in baths." The historians of the nineteenth century followed suit and quickly engaged in a coordinated effort to convict Tacitus of historical error, in order to rehabilitate such Tacitean monsters as Tiberius, Nero, and Domitian. It was one of the greatest missionary enterprises in the history of scholarship, and one of the most successful. It is now as difficult to find a historian to speak ill of these men as it once was to find anyone to speak well of them (for even the new absolute monarchs never dared go so far). There is unanimity behind Mommsen's judgment that Tiberius was "the most capable emperor Rome ever had." And his latest biographer, Dr. Gregorio Marañon, a physician-turned-historian, is as eager to "explain" Tiberius as any social worker is to "explain" a juvenile delinquent: he had suffered a childhood trauma when his mother divorced his father to marry Augustus; though sexually feeble he was married to a nymphomaniac, etc., etc. It all makes a plausible and, in a morbid way, fascinating casebook. It has the further advantage that we see the ulcerous and suppurating face of the man, rather than the smooth marble bust of the emperor that the professional historians seem to prefer. But in the end it comes to the same conclusion, that the portrait of Tiberius that Tacitus gives is little less than a slander.

What is striking about this revision of Tacitus is that it is necessarily based on Tacitus himself, since he is our only significant source for the history of the period: and it is Tacitus himself, too, who makes the work so relatively easy. Though he asserted that he wrote *sine ira et studio* [without hate and zealousness], he certainly did not mean by this anything akin to the academic ideal of "objectivity." Evil he might be helpless before, but he could not fail to recognize it, and he assumed that those who did evil were themselves wicked. It is rare that he made a statement of fact about Tiberius without also making a more or less gross insinuation. Thus, we read: "About the same time a serious illness of Julia Augusta made it necessary for the Emperor [Tiberius] to hasten his return to the capital, the harmony between mother and son being still genuine, or their hatred concealed." Usually he was more subtle than this, and there are many occasions when we have to read him very closely indeed to perceive that he has in fact denied what one thought he had said. But it is not at all difficult for a diligent scholar, by snipping off the "facts" from the "value judgments," to compose a new mosaic which is very different from the Tacitean original. To be sure, there remain the corpses, the murdered and mutilated and self-destroyed. These the scholar may dispose of, first, by counting them to demonstrate that their sum was less than astronomical, then by allowing for exaggeration, and finally by turning his attention to the Pax Romana, the efficient imperial administration, and all those other glorious things that make up History.

Now Tacitus had no idea that Tiberius and Nero were making a contribution to History. His problem was: how did they, and all of Rome with them, come to such depravity? His general answer was: under tyrannies men are unmanned. "The ties of our common humanity had been dissolved by the force of terror; and before each advance of cruelty, compassion receded." As for the tyrant, he is simply the most wicked of men, else why should he have become a tyrant in the first place? In this he was but repeating a commonplace of classical political philosophy, which took it for granted that men aspired to tyranny out of an evil impulse. That is why he felt no compunction in ascribing the worst motives to the tyrant's most innocent-looking actions.

We have lost the habit of judging tyrants so harshly, for we are more attentive to their historical rôles, their "objective" tasks, than to their human meanings. It is the supreme virtue of Tacitus that, as we read him, the mists of History fade away, and we see only "persecutions and the persecuted, and people opening veins in baths."

1956

III

DEMOCRACY
IN
AMERICA

"Civil Liberties," 1952

A Study in Confusion

Heard ye not lately of a man
That went beside his witt,
And naked through the citty ran
Wrapt in a frantique fitt?

The above tantalizing bit of seventeenth-century verse was quoted recently in the *London Times Literary Supplement*, in the same issue in which there appeared, elsewhere in its pages, a review of the English edition of Alan Barth's *The Loyalty of Free Men*. This fortuitous juxtaposition was not without its ironic relevance, Mr. Barth's book having been provoked by the "frantique fitt" of McCarthyism, beneath which he saw a cool and calculating assault on the American democracy, and his defense being couched in a cool and calculating eloquence that turns out, upon close examination, to be not nearly the exercise in pure reason it seems.

A close examination, however, Mr. Barth's book and others of its kind have not received. It was hardly to be expected from Senator McCarthy and his friends, who are less famous for their habits of meticulous reading than for their preference for arguing in the large, while the more scholarly sections of American opinion have been so delighted to see the Senator get his, and so soothed by the cadences of a familiar tone, that they have not so much read these books as permitted themselves to be enchanted by them. This enchantment has had its political sequel, for as a result of it there has been drawn a line of battle. On the one side are the men of intellect and sensibility, fair-minded and generous-hearted and confessedly not infallible: the Alan Barths, the Henry Steele Commagers, the Zechariah Chafees, the Howard Mumford Joneses, the

Ralph Barton Perrys, the William O. Douglases, and, rather more tentatively committed, the Francis Biddles. On the other side are the mindless men, the kind who get elected to office when the spirit of the age reverts to primitivism, and who wish, under cover of fighting Communism, to squeeze the nation into a Know-Nothing straitjacket.

The line is drawn, and those liberals who have rallied to their positions on the left of it find themselves ever more pressed against the outer walls of the city. The ready quotations from Jefferson about the trees of liberty and the blood of tyrants, the sonorous repetition of Justice Holmes's dissenting opinions, the schoolmaster's measured accents alternating with prophetic indignation— the whole battery has failed significantly to make an impression on the dominant American mood. Senator McCarthy remains blithely on the offensive, and his critics give ground before him. It is a most exasperating and melancholy situation for liberals to be in; yet in proportion as they fail in strength, they gain in their sense of petulant righteousness.

Is it conceivable that the line was incorrectly drawn in the first place? The liberals are loath to weigh the possibility lest it give comfort to the enemy; Senator McCarthy for his part has no cause for dissatisfaction with things as they are; but those of us who are the displaced persons of this war might reflect on this question to our advantage. Perhaps it is a calamitous error to believe that because a vulgar demagogue lashes out at both Communism and liberalism as identical, it is necessary to protect Communism in order to defend liberalism. This way of putting the matter will surely shock liberals, who are convinced that it is only they who truly understand Communism and who thoughtfully oppose it. They are nonetheless mistaken, and it is a mistake on which McCarthyism waxes fat. For there is one thing that the American people know about Senator McCarthy: he, like them, is unequivocally anti-Communist. About the spokesmen for American liberalism, they feel they know no such thing. And with some justification.

With what justification can be seen from an illustrative incident involving Professor Henry Steele Commager, a distinguished historian who never was a Communist and never will be. In the May 1947 issue of *Harper's*, Professor Commager wrote a spirited article that began as follows:

On May 6 a Russian-born girl, Mrs. Shura Lewis, gave a talk to the students of the Western High School of Washington, D.C. She talked about Russia—its school system, its public health program, the position of women, of the aged, of the workers, the farmers, and the professional classes—and compared, superficially and uncritically, some American and Russian institutions. . . . Mrs. Lewis said nothing that had not been said a thousand times, in speeches, in newspapers, magazines and books. She said nothing that any normal person could find objectionable.

What greatly disturbed Professor Commager was that this inoffensive speech did give rise to a furor in Washington. Congressmen bellowed that our schools were being subverted, the principal of the school came forward with a humble apology, the superintendent of schools for the nation's capital swore it would never happen again, and the speech itself was reprinted (after some discussion of the wisdom of exposing the public to inflammation) in the *Congressional Record* as a horrible example. Professor Commager saw in this a reflection of an anti-Communist hysteria that threatened to engulf all civil liberties, and he pleaded earnestly that reason control the anti-Communist passion, lest we find ourselves saddled with an anti-Communist orthodoxy no less reprehensible than the Communist one. His article was hailed as a kind of liberal manifesto, and was reprinted, alongside John Stuart Mill and John Milton, in Howard Mumford Jones's *Primer of Intellectual Freedom* (1949). Evil won a transient victory in the seats of power, and Good won a permanent niche in the anthologies, a familiar tale.

Familiar, that is, until one goes to the *Congressional Record* and reads through this speech that no "normal person could find objectionable." Mrs. Lewis's English was broken, but her sentiments were whole:

They call it collective farm—the peasants farm and divide up products according to work put in by each individual during the years. As a result of planning, unemployment is completely wiped out. . . .

In Russia right now people absolutely do not worry about today or tomorrow. They never think "All of a sudden I lose a job." That fear doesn't exist among Russian people. . . .

No matter where you live you have to work. What the Russian people have, they are more secure about this. They work. They need not worry much about losing the job. They are free to travel from one place to another, and each person must work 25 years for after that he is able to get a pension. No matter where you work—in this plant or another, 25 years and then you get 50% of your salary and live the rest of your life. . . .

I never appreciated the life in Russia until I live here. Here you have to work hard in order to live, use all your courage not to die. . . .

I read all the papers here and occasionally I go to the Library of Congress and read all papers printed in Moscow. It is very interesting, and when I read these papers always you can see here evidence of press where people talk all the time about having a war, to throw the atomic bomb on Russia, to destroy because they have a system which is very prideful. At the present time Russians are busy to restore all those houses, all those cities, all those towns. Russian people make streets, plants, produce new style of shoes, new fashion of dress, new production, and never do they talk about having a war.

The echoes this awakened in Congress may have been exaggerated, but they were not factitious or beside the point. Obviously, Professor Commager can argue that it will not harm American school children to encounter an occasional Communist apologist in the flesh; one may even go further and say it would do them good. However, in the first place, Mrs. Lewis was not introduced as a Communist apologist but as an informed reporter, and, in the second place, everything she said should have been objectionable to every normal person, and especially to a historian like Professor Commager—for the good and sufficient reason that it was a tissue of lies. For Professor Commager to defend the rights of Communists to free speech is one thing; for him to assert that there is nothing objectionable in mendacious pleading in support of Communism is quite another. The conclusion "any normal person" will draw from such behavior is that, for whatever reason, his critical faculties are less alert when he looks out of the left corner of his eye.

Indeed, the heart of the matter is exactly that he looks at Communism out of the *left* corner of his eye. Professor Commager seems to be seduced by the insidious myth according to which Communism is a political trend continuous with liberalism and democratic socialism, only more impatient and inclined to the fanatical, only more "radical" than its companions who are not quite so "left." It is a myth that Senator McCarthy, for his own ends, is happy to accept, since it allows him to tag a New Dealer as being by nature an embryonic Communist. Neither the Professor nor the Senator is concerned to see that the antithesis of "left" and "right" no longer suits the political realities; that measured by the ideals of the French or even Russian Revolution, Communism today is as counterrevolutionary as Louis XVI or Kolchak ever was; that if one wishes to defend the civil liberties of Communists (as the Senator does not), one must do so on the same grounds that one defends the civil liberties of Nazis and fascists—no more, no less.

Professor Commager might retort that he knows all this full well, and that he is for civil liberties for everyone, fascist, Communist, or what-have-you. But if a Nazi had, in 1938, addressed a high school audience in this country, extolling the accomplishments of Hitler's regime, presenting a thoroughly fictitious account of life in Nazi Germany, never once mentioning the existence of concentration camps, would Professor Commager find in such a speech "nothing that any normal person could find objectionable"? It is doubtless an injustice to him even to conceive of the possibility.

This notion of Communism as "left" and therefore at an opposite pole from fascism, which is "right," appears to have become intrinsic to the liberal outlook. It is embedded in the meretricious historical analogies, in the rolling phrases about "the forces of freedom and those of fear," beneath which there lies the gross metaphysic of the liberal Manichee, apportioning the universe to "forward-looking" and "backward-looking" demiurges. It helps explain how Professor Commager can permit himself to write: "After all, it is no accident that the nations dedicated to freedom won the two great wars of the 20th century and those committed to totalitarianism went under"—when it is not only no accident, it is not even a fact. The same notion is evidenced in Zechariah Chafee's explanation (in his essay in the recent symposium *Civil Liberties Under Attack*) of the origin of Communist fronts: "It is inevitable that the membership of organizations formed to bring about change should include some persons who want a great deal of change"—as if Professor Chafee and the Communists were agreed on the direction of the change, quarreling only over the measure. It is the presupposition from which Ralph Barton Perry (in his new book *The Citizen Decides*) can deduce that Communism is "democratic" by virtue of being a revolt of the "masses" against the "classes," that the Soviet regime is a government "for the people with the consent of the people" though not by the people, and that the Chinese Communist leaders are "hostages" of a popular revolution.

Moreover, after staring out of the left corner of the eye for any length of time, there comes an irrepressible inclination to wink. How else explain, for instance, the attitude Alan Barth takes toward the Hiss-Chambers affair? He can begin a sentence: "Insofar as Chambers may be credited with having told the truth . . ." or: "whatever the guilt of Alger Hiss and whatever the utility of exposing it and punishing it a decade later. . . ." About Whittaker Chambers and the Communist "informer" in general, he is no longer judiciously bland but is knowingly tart: "The ex-Communists, conscious of their betrayal of American values, wanted the comfort of company; they had to show that many others, even many who were highly respected, had been as recreant as they." In other words, Chambers in telling the truth is a man of malice, Hiss in denying it is his defenseless victim. Hiss's guilt is problematic and, in any case, not important; Chambers's wickedness is certain.

On Owen Lattimore, there is liberal unanimity: he got a raw deal. Professor Commager believes (in his contribution to *Civil Liberties Under At-*

tack) that the attack on Lattimore was an attack on "independence and non-conformity." Professor Chafee laments: "Owen Lattimore did his own thinking and look how his services were appreciated." Alan Barth is casually positive: "Dr. Lattimore's ordeal was, of course, only the most spectacular instance of legislative punishment of teachers for expressing their opinions." About the worst that can be said for such arrant nonsense is that it is uttered in all sincerity. For the incontrovertible facts of the case are, "of course," that Owen Lattimore did *not* do his own thinking; that his "ordeal" was the public demonstration of this fact; that he was a faithful and enormously influential fellow-traveler who for more than a decade followed the Communist line as if magnetized by it, including a docile zigzag during the Stalin-Hitler pact. Is it really no legitimate concern of Congress that such a man was appointed adviser to Chiang Kai-shek, that he accompanied Vice President Wallace during his tour of Asia, that he was admired and listened to by important people in the State Department?

In his denunciation of Lattimore's pro-Communist record and in hurling unsubstantiated charges against him (chief of Soviet espionage, etc.), Senator McCarthy may well have been aiming a blow against independence of mind and nonconformity of spirit. For Messrs. Commager, Barth, and Chafee to defend Lattimore's pro-Communist record in order to defend such independence and nonconformity is for them to play the Senator's game, on the losing side.

It is equally futile for liberals to try to match Senator McCarthy's irresponsible declamations with a crafty rhetoric of their own, especially when this rhetoric, while not designedly pro-Communist, is compelled by the logic of disingenuousness and special pleading to become so in effect. The need for disingenuousness arises out of a refusal to see Communism for what it is: a movement guided by conspiracy and aiming at totalitarianism, rather than merely another form of "dissent" or "nonconformity." Hence the liberal argument runs askew of reality and must clothe itself with neat obfuscation. Once again, Professor Commager obliges with a superior specimen:

> The House Un-American Activities Committee has launched an attack on the Lawyers' Guild as a pro-Communist or "subversive" organization. The chief basis for this attack is, as far as we know, that the Guild has proffered its services to the defense of Communists under indictment for violation of the Smith Act. We need not inquire into the accuracy of this charge or into the degree of zeal displayed by the Lawyers' Guild. Let us ask rather what are the logical conclusions to be drawn by the position which the House Committee has adopted? They are two: that certain criminals are so despicable

that they are not entitled to counsel, and that a lawyer who defends a criminal is himself sympathetic to crime.

That phrase in the second sentence, "as far as we know," is curious. It implies strongly that the only conceivable explanation of the Committee's attitude is the action of the Guild in providing lawyers to defend indicted Communists, and that there is no public information which gives plausibility to the Committee's belief that the Guild is a "front" organization, controlled and run by Communists. On the contrary, however, "as far as we know," and we know much further than Professor Commager suggests, the Lawyers' Guild is a Communist creation that, as A. A. Berle stated when he resigned from it in 1940, "is not prepared to take any stand which conflicts with the Communist party line." Moreover, the House Committee on Un-American Activities has collected and published sufficient evidence to demonstrate this beyond cavil, which leads one to think that if Professor Commager spent nearly as much time reading the records of congressional hearings as he does denouncing them, we should all be better off.

The entire third sentence is even more curious: "We need not inquire into the accuracy of this charge or into the degree of zeal displayed by the Lawyers' Guild." If we take "zeal" to mean pro-Communism (in the context, that is all it can mean), then the degree of this zeal and the accuracy of the charge of pro-Communism are precisely what we *do* need to inquire into. How can we know whether to sanction or condemn the Committee's investigation of the Guild as a pro-Communist organization unless we make an effort to find out if the Guild is or is not, in fact, a pro-Communist organization? Even Professor Commager surreptitiously ignores his own disclaimer, as the last two sentences of his paragraph show. Obviously, the two "logical conclusions" flow, not from the Committee's premise, but his own: namely, that the Lawyers' Guild is neither pro-Communist nor subversive. From the Committee's own premise, quite other logical conclusions may be inferred, one of them being that the Committee is engaged in showing up Communist fronts for what they are. Professor Commager's "logic" is a sleight of hand whereby premises that are prejudiced in favor of the Communist interpretation of affairs are made to pass for natural conclusions.

In the same vein, there is a liberal rhetoric of insinuation that works under cover of a high moral posture. Its net effect is to give a backhanded credence to the Communist assertion that it is impossible to oppose Communism vigorously without walking into the arms of Black Reaction. It is the kind of thing represented in the following observation of Alan Barth's:

In the New York trial of eleven Communist Party leaders in 1949, a number of FBI undercover operatives who had joined the party appeared as prosecution witnesses. How widely such agents have been dispersed in labor unions, in lawful voluntary associations, and in political groups is a matter of mere conjecture. But it is certainly a matter of legitimate concern to Americans who care about preservation of the traditional rights of privacy.

A noble sentiment, and the unwary reader assents. Who is against the right to privacy, and who is not prepared to be concerned with its violation? Only the exceptionally attentive will note that the supposed threat to "the traditional rights of privacy" is "a matter of mere conjecture." Whose conjecture? We are not told. Is there any ground for such a conjecture? We are not told that either. Is Mr. Barth against the use of undercover agents in principle? He does not say so. Is he against the use of undercover agents in Communist organizations? He does not say this either. He would seem to be against dispersing FBI agents in bona fide labor unions, lawful voluntary associations, and political groups, and reminds us of the consequences. But who is for it? The answer, which he does not bother to give, is: nobody, and that is why the FBI is doing no such thing and why the whole business is a "matter of mere conjecture." In the course of Mr. Barth's innuendos, however, the onus has been neatly shifted from the Communist conspirators to the FBI agents who identified them.

The same technique of persuasion is at work in such a statement as this one by Professor Commager: "It will be useful to determine, a generation from now, whether those universities that have purged their faculties are actually stronger than they were before the purges occurred—stronger in those essentials that go to make a university." This has about it so trembling an air of bittersweet wisdom that it seems positively boorish to ask: just which universities would Professor Commager describe as "purged"? Surely Columbia is not one of them, for Professor Commager is not the kind of man who would retain his post on a "purged" faculty. Is it Yale? Princeton? Harvard? University of Chicago? The list could be extended indefinitely, and never provoke an affirmative response, for there is not a single university in the United States that can be said to have been, in any meaningful sense of the word, "purged." There have been no more than a handful of cases where Communist college teachers have been dismissed and less than a handful of cases where non-Communists have been unjustly fired as "Reds." To call this a "purge," even regardless of whether or not one thinks Communists have a right to teach in colleges, is to echo Communist propaganda.

Perhaps Professor Commager had in mind the University of California, where several dozen (out of a total of more than a thousand) teachers found the idea of a special loyalty oath—the content of which was irrelevant to their action—so offensive and intolerable that they exercised their constitutional right to refuse to swear it, and consequently had to seek other employment. Granting that the notion of a special oath for teachers is obnoxious, and even conceding that this minority was correct and courageous in its particular re-action to it, is it the part of sobriety to insist, as Professor Commager goes on to do, that the philosophy behind the actions of California's Board of Trustees does not differ "in any essentials" from the philosophy behind the totalitarian control of university teaching? One swallow does not make a spring, or one in-justice an apocalypse.

Despite their fondness for clichés of Communist manufacture, all these liberal spokesmen are sincerely anti-Communist; otherwise, what they have to say would be of little interest to anyone. But their rejection of Commu-nism has all the semblance of a preliminary gesture, a repudiation aiming to linger in the memory as a floating credential. It has little relation to all the en-suing scenes of the political drama, where bad conscience and stubborn pride join to guide the liberal through his role. Did not the major segment of Amer-ican liberalism, as a result of joining hands with the Communists in a Popu-lar Front, go on record as denying the existence of Soviet concentration camps? Did it not give its blessing to the "liquidation" of millions of Soviet "kulaks"? Did it not apologize for the mass purges of 1936–1938, and did it not solemnly approve the grotesque trials of the Old Bolsheviks? Did it not ap-plaud the massacre of the non-Communist left by the GPU [the Soviet secret police] during the Spanish Civil War? All this carries no weight with Alan Barth, who knows that, though a man repeat the Big Lie, so long as he is of a liberal intention he is saved. On the participation of non-Communists in Communist fronts during the thirties, he writes: "In the main, their partici-pation, while it lasted, was not only innocent but altogether praiseworthy."

Even Francis Biddle, who is generally cautious, remarks in his book *The Fear of Freedom*: "What makes an organization subversive? If a vast majority of its members are Communists but its conduct has always been exemplary, advocat-ing desirable social reforms which Communists usually back, it can hardly fit the description." One surmises that Mr. Biddle is not really so politically naïve as this statement, on the face of it, would lead one to believe. He must know what it means to be "subversive," since it was he who, as Attorney General, sent eighteen members of a minuscule Trotskyist sect to jail in 1942 for being just that; he must know how Communists work, how front organizations act as an ancillary to the Communist party apparatus, since this is a matter of common knowledge and Mr. Biddle is uncommonly literate and intelligent. No, it was no elevated unsophistication that urged him on, but rather a sense of shame and a cowardliness to confess that shame. Mr. Biddle, like Mr. Barth, refuses to admit what is now apparent: that a generation of earnest reformers who helped give this country a New Deal should find themselves in retrospect stained with the guilt of having lent aid and comfort to Stalinist tyranny. This is, to be sure, a truth of hindsight, an easy truth. But it is the truth nonetheless, and might as well be owned up to. If American liberalism is not willing to discriminate between its achievements and its sins, it only disarms itself before Senator McCarthy, who is eager to have it appear that its achievements *are* its sins.

There is a false pride, by which liberals persuade themselves that no matter what association a man has had with a Communist enterprise, he is absolutely guiltless of the crimes that Communism has committed so long as he was moved to this association by a generous idealism. There is a political mythology, by which liberals locate Communism over on the "left," in a zone exempt from the unsparing verdict directed against the totalitarian "right." There is also a fear, a fear that the American democracy in an excess of anti-Communism will gather its abundant energy into a wave of "conformism" that will drown all free thought. This pride, this mythology, this fear all unite for a liberal pre-judgment of issues (e.g., the cases of Alger Hiss, Owen Lattimore, William Remington, Harry Dexter White) which is not easy to explain on a purely rational view. It is what stimulates a flood of irrelevant and gaudy prose about loyalty in the abstract ("like love it must be given freely," etc.) while it shuns a careful discussion of Communist disloyalty in the concrete.

Of the three factors, the fear of "conformism" or "orthodoxy" is probably the most influential in its appeal, for it is founded in some degree on objective fact. Alexis de Tocqueville and John Stuart Mill, both friendly critics of the egalitarian trend, pointed out long ago that in every democratic society there is an inherent tendency toward a "despotism of public opinion"; where the majority makes the laws, it may also wish, especially in feverish and unsettled times, to make opinion, lauding the popular and extirpating the unpopular. In America, where the people are more powerful than elsewhere, and where there is, too, a significant tradition of vigilantism, the danger of a despotism of public opinion is proportionately greater. When the State Department is forced to suspend an exhibition abroad of modern American art because some Congressmen denounce it as "Communistic," the danger of such a despotism seems more than academic, and many otherwise sensible people are led to reprehend any attempt to unveil Communist activities or Communist beliefs as a malignant form of "punishment by publicity," which will soon be extended to all opinions that illiterate and narrow-minded Congressmen detest.

What these people do not see is that Communism, because it is a conspiratorial movement, has not the faintest interest in any genuine resistance to the despotism of public opinion. These martyrs whose testament is—"I refuse to answer on the grounds that it might incriminate me"! These "intellectuals" of Hollywood and radio who are outraged at a Congressman's insistence that they say what they actually believe, and who wail that they are in danger of—being excluded from well-paying jobs! Is this the vibrant voice of "nonconformity" and "dissent"? Are these the American rebels of today? Oddly enough, the majority of American liberals seem to think so: they have been moved to indignation by the questions, but never moved to disgust by the answers. Presumably, this is what they think a dissenter looks like, and no sadder commentary is possible on the corruption they have inflicted on themselves. And not only on themselves, for this image of a dissenter happens to coincide with the image held by Joseph McCarthy and Pat McCarran, for whom the dissenter is *per se* a scheming subversive. No greater spur to the despotism of public opinion can be imagined than this identification of free thought with underground conspiracy.

There is only one way the despotism of public opinion can be resisted. That is for a person with unpopular views to express himself, loudly, brazenly, stubbornly, in disregard of the consequences. Such a person may have to suffer for his convictions, as others have suffered before him, and as others will suffer after. But the responsibility for the mind's freedom in a democracy lies with the intransigent thinker, with his courage to shout the truth in the face of the mob, with his faith that truth will win out, and with his maddening commitment to the truth, win or lose. Yet, during all the occasions of the past several years, not a single liberal voice was to say to these strange "victims": "Speak up and damn the consequences! Let them take your job, as they certainly will anyway; tell the truth, you have nothing to lose and honor to gain!" Instead, there were erudite essays on the "right to a job" that would have corroborated William James in his mournful conviction that "the prevalent fear of poverty among our educated classes is the worst moral disease from which our civilization suffers."

Still, unworthy as these "victims" are, may they not, despite themselves, represent the right of the individual to hold whatever opinions he pleases without having to give a public accounting of them? Even if these Communists and Communist sympathizers are despicable, don't they have the right to believe privately anything they please? This is the way the question is frequently put, and it reveals a total misapprehension as to what Communism really is.

Communism is an idea, beyond question. Indeed, it is an Idea, and it is of the essence of this Idea that it is also a conspiracy to subvert every social and political order it does not dominate. It is, furthermore, an Idea that has ceased to have any intellectual status but has become incarnate in the Soviet Union and the official Communist parties, to whose infallible directives unflinching devotion is owed. A person who is captive to this Idea can, at any time, in any place, be called upon to do whatever the Idea, i.e., the Party, thinks necessary. Since this is so, it is of considerably more than private interest if a person is held by the Idea. He is, all appearances to the contrary, a person with different loyalties, and with different canons of scrupulousness, from ours. To grant him an "immunity by silence" is to concede the right to conspiracy, a concession no government ever has made or ever will make.

This sounds exaggerated, as it must, being so foreign to the nature of American political experience. Many of us have known Communists, and most of them conveyed no impression of being conspirators. But then, some of us have known Nazis too, and they conveyed no immediate association with gas chambers. It is quite impossible to judge a political movement by the personality of an individual member. Roosevelt certainly didn't see in Stalin any symptoms of blood lust. Hermann Goering in jail struck one as a clever clown. And there are still plenty of people who can't believe that Alger Hiss ever did any such thing.

No doubt there are some present members of the Communist Party who would, in a showdown, break free of the Idea and rally to the democratic cause. Unfortunately, we have no way of knowing who they are. No doubt there are some present members and fellow-travelers of the Communist Party who would sooner or later get disillusioned with Communism if they were permitted to hold down their present jobs as teachers, civil service workers, etc., whereas they are likely to harden in the face of persecution. Unfortunately, it is quite as impossible to tell the citizens of Oshkosh, some of whom have suffered personal loss as a result of the war in Korea, that there is no harm in having their children taught the three R's by a Communist, as it would have been to persuade the citizens of Flatbush in 1939 that there was no cause for excitement in their children being taught by a Nazi, or to convince a businessman that it is smart practice for him to pay a handsome salary to someone pledged to his "liquidation." No doubt some of these people became Communists after having suffered during the depression, or during a labor conflict, or as a result of race prejudice, and society must bear its share of the blame. Unfortunately, as Fitzjames Stephens remarked many decades ago: "It does not follow that because society caused a fault it is not to punish it. A man who breaks his arm when he is drunk may have to cut it off when he is sober."

The problem of fighting Communism while preserving civil liberties is no simple one, and there is no simple solution. A prerequisite for any solution, however, is, firstly, a proper understanding of Communism for what it is, and secondly, a sense of proportion. So long as liberals agree with Senator McCarthy that the fate of Communism involves the fate of liberalism, and that we must choose between complete civil liberties for everyone and a disregard for civil liberties entirely, we shall make no progress except to chaos. So long as one is either for or against "guilt by association," it is hopeless to try to distinguish between a sober and silly definition of that concept—sober when it is taken to mean, as for instance the Canwell Committee of the State of Washington took it to mean, that anyone who is a member of three or more organizations officially declared subversive is to be considered a Communist; silly when it is taken to mean, as many government loyalty boards take it to mean, that if you have a friend or a relation who is sympathetic to Communism, you are a "bad security risk." So long as Senator McCarthy and the liberals agree that the right of a Communist to teach or be a government employee is a matter of principle, we shall remain distant from that intelligent discrimination between one case and another, and one situation and another, which alone can give us our true bearings. And so long as Senator McCarthy and the liberals are enmeshed in this confusion, the Senator will grow the stronger, for such confusion is the sap of his political life.

Inevitably, liberals will disagree among themselves about the appropriateness of specific actions with regard to Communism and Communists. Inevitably, too, there will always be a basic division and antagonism between liberalism (which is solicitous of freedom) and McCarthyism (which is not). But if a liberal wishes to defend the civil liberties of Communists or of Communist fellow-travelers, he must enter the court of American opinion with clean hands and a clear mind. He must show that he knows the existence of an organized subversive movement such as Communism is a threat to the consensus on which civil society and its liberties are based. He must bluntly acknowledge Communists and fellow-travelers to be what they are, and then, if he so desires, defend the expediency in particular circumstances of allowing them the right to be what they are. He must speak as one of *us*, defending *their* liberties. To the extent he insists that they are on our side, that we can defend our liberties only by uncritically defending theirs, he will be taken as speaking as one of them.

1952

American Ambiguities

The Jacksonian Persuasion

All our efforts to relate ourselves to tradition, to our sources and our origins, are inevitably ambiguous. We look back while marching forward; and march back while looking ahead. On the basis of an appeal to some "original" custom, text, or authority, we make our revolutions and reformations. And if, as has been the case in our own epoch, we may seek a revolution that will mark an end to the tyranny of tradition itself, we find ourselves engaged in a fundamentalist reaction. In America, where the origins are so close at hand, and where a profound piety toward the past combines with a restless urge for innovation, the ambiguities are constant and countless. There is only *one* American political tradition, and every political movement must obtain its sanction, invoking the same memories, the same names, the same archetypal images, even the very same quotations. Jefferson is the patron saint of zealous liberals and vigilant McCarthyites, of northern progressives and southern racists—in his humanitarianism, his agrarianism, his detestation of cities, his suspicion of Big Government, his owning of slaves, and his dim view of slavery as an institution, there is sufficient sustenance for all. America is the country where opposites are always colliding, interpenetrating, changing sides—where the ethereal Emerson and the gentle Thoreau were enthusiastic admirers of that blood-mad assassin, John Brown; where William Jennings Bryan led the "progressive" assault against economic privilege and the teaching of Darwinism in public schools; where a Governor Faubus, in his youth a socialist and always a New Dealer, becomes the spokesman of the "Know-Nothing" rabble. There is, of course, some demagogy in all this, but there is even more sincerity. That is what makes for such a fantastic tangle.

The movement known as Jacksonian democracy has a special place in American history because it was the first to be implicated in this ambiguous relation to tradition, and in the process created party politics in the United States as we have known it ever since. Only a generation or so removed from the founding fathers, it was both near enough to experience the full weight of their authority and remote enough to be self-conscious about its relation to it. The Jacksonians found themselves enmeshed in what Professor Marvin Meyers calls the "Jacksonian paradox," which he defines as follows:

> The fact that the movement which helped to clear the path for laissez-faire capitalism and its culture in America, and the public which in its daily life eagerly entered on that path, held nevertheless in their political conscience an ideal of a chaste republican order, resisting the seductions of risk and novelty, greed and extravagance, rapid motion and complex dealings.

Professor Meyers's book [*The Jacksonian Persuasion*] is part of a reaction among American historians to the view of Jackson, expressed most notably in Arthur Schlesinger Jr.'s *The Age of Jackson*, as in effect a previous incarnation of Franklin D. Roosevelt, a liberal leader of the frontier republic. Ever since Senator McCarthy stirred up the Populist embers, and one was reminded that democratic-patriotic-radicalism in America is a thing of many colors, there has been an increasing reluctance among the intellectual class to bend the knee before bold Old Romans like Jackson who could peremptorily reject the common law ("judge-made law") in the name of the common man. On the other hand, Professor Meyers does not allow his revisionism to be reduced to mere reaction. His mind is beautifully poised, sensitive to every complexity, and, a real novelty in American historiography, his book is written with high literary distinction. It presents to us Jacksonian democracy in its bewildering plenitude, but with a shrewd lucidity that enables us always to take a bearing. And he strikes the finest of balances in his judgment:

> In one form or another, the Jacksonian persuasion has been a perennially powerful strain in American life. It has much to answer for, but also much to claim. In its moment of dominance, it has often obscured political choices for the American people; it has fixed thought on oversimplified dichotomies, moralised where it should have judged, encouraged an ungenerous fundamentalism. And yet the very faults of the persuasion as a guide to prudent statesmanship may have been its strength as a call to justice. For a society inevitably committed to maximizing economic gains, this persuasion in its various forms has been the great effective force provoking men to ask what their nation ought to be.

One of the most fruitful of Professor Meyers's insights is contained in the title. The word "persuasion," which he defines as "a half-formulated moral perspective involving emotional commitment," hits off exactly the strange destiny of ideas in American politics. Parties do not have anything so formal as an ideology, but they do, and must, profess something more explicit than a general ethos. "Persuasion" is a most apt term for what in fact issues from this predicament. It certainly applies to the Jacksonian movement, an upsurge of revolt against the moneyed interests, an upsurge led by real estate speculators, investors, and mercantile adventurers, which spoke as the voice of the People while never getting much more than half the vote, and which gave a sharp momentum to the development of capitalism, urbanism, and industrialism while celebrating the glories of the backwoodsman. Anyone who takes the opportunity to study this episode through Professor Meyers's eyes will gain a priceless initiation into what is most American in American politics.

1958

Republican Virtue versus Servile Institutions

In the end, when all has been said and done, the only authentic criterion for judging any economic or political system, or any set of social institutions, is this: what kind of people emerge from them? In this sense, it is true to say that institutions are made for the people, not vice versa. But today we understand this proposition in a very different way: we worry whether our institutions are sufficiently "responsive" to the people as they are, and assume that any discordance between the two constitutes strong evidence that the institution needs to be changed. Behind this assumption there lies a deeper dogma: that the very idea of helping people to shape themselves in a certain way is both presumptuous and superfluous. Presumptuous, because there is no superior knowledge available as to how people should be shaped. Superfluous, because the people will, if left alone, shape themselves better than anyone or anything can shape them. This might be called the democratic dogma, and it is a very different thing from the republican philosophy which animated this nation during its earlier decades but which gradually has become ever more incomprehensible to us. Indeed, it is by now so incomprehensible we find it difficult even to imagine that, as we remake—"restructure" as we say—our traditional institutions to suit us, we may simply be debasing these institutions so that they will more snugly fit our diminished persons.

It will be said that even to suggest such a hypothesis shows a remarkable lack of faith in the American common people. I would halfheartedly deny that accusation. I do indeed have faith in the common people, only I don't have very much faith in them. Nor is there anything snobbish or, as we now say, "elitist" about such a statement. I include myself among those common people and, knowing myself as I do, I would say that anyone who constructed a political system based on unlimited faith in my good character was someone with a fondness for high-risk enterprises.

To put it another way: the common man is not a fool, and the proof that he is not a fool is that he has such modest faith in himself. On the other hand, the common man is human too, and if politicians go around saying nice things about him, he'll not deny them either. What will happen is that the common man will simply become cynical about politicians and politics and public life in general, and this cynicism will, in the long run, have a deleterious effect on his character. For cynicism about others is always accompanied by a proportionate increase in self-centeredness. And as we become self-centered, we become less open to reason, have a weaker sense of obligation to our fellow citizens.

That it is possible to corrupt a citizenry—or for a citizenry to corrupt itself—is something the Founders understood but which we seem to have forgotten. Today we are sometimes prepared to believe that the people have been deceived into thinking erroneously. But we find it well nigh impossible to admit that they are corrupt, behaving as if they had a bad character as distinct from a bad opinion or two. This is why we tend to take it for granted that all expressions of material grievances by the people must be basically legitimate. After all, people do have intimate, as distinct from abstract, knowledge of their material circumstances. To regard this knowledge as less than authoritative is to cast doubt on their innate capacity for self-government. The Founders permitted themselves to have such doubts, which their political theory then encompassed. We give ourselves no such license. Our instinct is always to assume that, once these material grievances are satisfied, the people's natural goodness of character will reassert itself.

Yet the evidence is much to the contrary: satisfying material grievances, these days, does not seem to calm people or make them more reasonable. It often rather encourages them to be even more unreasonable, and even sometimes to invent grievances as an occasion for being more unreasonable. The relation between satisfying men's material wants, or even material needs, and the quality of their moral nature is evidently an ambiguous and equivocal one.

This ambiguity was something the Founders were much more alert to than we are. They were sufficiently close to their Puritan heritage, and to traditional republican political philosophy, to believe that "luxury," as they called it—by which they meant merely that degree of material well-being which we today call "affluence"—would always represent a grave threat to the spirit of our institutions. None of the Founders, to my knowledge, ever praised their handiwork by suggesting it would lead to a "society of abundance." We may think that the Sears, Roebuck catalog is a splendid testimonial to American civilization. Most of the Founders would have found it a worrisome document. And had they been informed that people were purchasing this incredible variety of merchandise by going into debt, they would have been wildly alarmed.

Perhaps nothing better signifies the difference between the spirit of democratic capitalism in our old Republic and in our contemporary one than their contrasting attitudes toward debt. To be a debtor, in the older view, was to mortgage your future and to surrender a portion of your independence. They regarded indebtedness as a condition to be avoided, if possible. And they had a low opinion of those who were perpetually in debt, or who seemed uncaring as to whether they were in debt or not; such people were then called "feckless." It isn't that the Founders were simply less sophisticated about economics than we are today. They were very sophisticated, in a different way. They judged an economic system, not merely by whether or not it improved one's standard of living, but also by what it did to the character of the people who participated in that system. Our sophistication about economics completely ignores this aspect of the matter, to some degree, one suspects, because we assume that "the character of the people" is inherently unproblematic, but also because we assume that improved material conditions, no matter how achieved, cannot possibly mean an unimproved people.

This last is one expression of that "democratic dogma" which has supplanted the republican philosophy of the early period of this republic. A clear sign of the transformation I am referring to is the way in which the very words "republican" or "republic" have given way before the terms "democratic" or "democracy." This verbal shift mirrors a profound political and psychological change. It is not that the two terms stand for distinctly different conceptions of the proper relations between a citizen and his polity. They need not, and for a long time did not: up until about fifty years ago, they were used without any sense of tension or contrariness existing between them. Indeed, they were frequently and familiarly conjoined together, so that one could speak easily of "our democratic republic" or "our republican democracy" without giving the matter much thought. Yet today the term "republican" has fallen into disfavor, and is rapidly falling into disuse. It is still the title of one of our major parties, but it is not exactly a proud title: Republicans (with a capital "R") do not speak about "republicanism" (with a small "r") but instead, like everyone else, speak about "democracy" and claim to represent the spirit of democracy, properly understood, not the spirit of republicanism, properly understood.

Why does the word "republican" make us so uncomfortable? Why have history textbooks ceased bearing such titles as *The American Republic: From Its Founding to the Present Day* in favor of something like *The Democratic Experiment* or *The Democratic Experience*? Why don't we ever talk about *The Republic Experiment* or *The Republican Experience*? I don't think it is merely fashionable linguistic convention which is at work here, but a much deeper and extremely significant habit of mind. The two terms have assumed, over the decades, very different connotations. "Republican" is something we used to be; "democratic" is what we have become. As a matter of fact, one can put it more strongly than that: being "republican" is what we have been liberated from so that we could become "democratic."

There is no doubt that the term "republican," today, has about it an aura of confinement, constriction, a limitation of possibilities, whereas "democracy" suggests a genial expansiveness. If I were to say to a group of American educators that the purpose of our public schools is to produce republican citizens, they would either assume that I was being hostile or, more likely, that I had meant to say "democratic" and was merely engaging in a literary fancy. They would certainly sense that a school for republican citizens is something different from the kinds of schools they now teach in and administer.

At the root of that term "republican" there lies the idea of self-government. Not merely popular government, and not merely individual liberty, but a popular government and an individual liberty that is defined, and is therefore self-limiting, in a certain way. Self-government is self-definition. It is something strenuous, something which involves our making painful demands upon ourselves, something which directs us to a normative conception of the self to which we should properly aspire. You cannot have "self-government" in the individual case unless you have a clear, if general, idea as to the kind of person you ought to be. And you cannot have self-government collectively unless the members of that collectivity have a clear idea as to the kind of people they want to end up being. The idea of self-government is intrinsically normative and stands in opposition to any social and political system which fails to link popular government or individual liberty to a set of accepted values. That is why it is possible to speak of "republican virtue"; we do not in fact speak of it today but we do not find the phrase meaningless either. On the other hand, one apparently cannot talk about democratic virtue. Not only do we not use that phrase but the very phrase does not exist; it seems not to be a possible political expression. And the reason why this is so must have something to do with the fact that we conceive of democracy as a way of government and a way of life which has liberated us from the confines of such "virtue." We have separated the democratic idea from the idea of self-government.

Montesquieu, whose political philosophy so powerfully shaped the thinking of the Founders, understood that in a large, commercial republic, whose stability was based on an equilibrium of economic interests and a balance of political factions, this stability could very easily dissolve into a war of all against all. To prevent this from happening, he said, one could not rely on any set of institutions but on the "spirit" of its citizens. It is this spirit to which the term "republican virtue" refers.

Because the very word "virtue" so frightens us today, suggesting, as it does, fixed ideas of right and wrong which circumscribe our liberty, it is important to emphasize that "republican virtue," in the American meaning of that phrase, is a very different kind of virtue from, say, Christian virtue or classical virtue as the ancient Greeks understood it. It does not signify an excellence of the soul, a perfection of the person. Our idea of "republican virtue" derives from the Romans, and it is a political conception rather than a religious one. Which is to say, "republican virtue" has fairly modest moral implications, rather than high and ambitious ones. Because these moral implications are so modest, "republican virtue" is compatible with a liberal society in which people can have, within limits, different opinions as to ultimate religious truths and different preferences as to their ways of life. What "republican virtue" asks of people is merely that they be public-spirited.

If this doesn't sound like such a formidable demand, it is because we no longer quite understand what it means to be public-spirited. We think it means to have passionate opinions about the public good and to work furiously to translate these opinions into reality. In truth, public-spiritedness, in its original sense, means almost the opposite of that. It means curbing one's passions and moderating one's opinions in order to achieve a large consensus that will ensure domestic tranquility. We think of public-spiritedness as a form of self-expression, an exercise in self-righteousness. The Founders thought of it as a form of self-control, an exercise in self-government. If we are asked to identify a public-spirited citizen, we are likely to point to someone like Ralph Nader. The Founders pointed to "that noblest Roman of them all," George Washington, as a model for the American citizen. And whatever Ralph Nader's merits may be, they are not George Washington's.

I have said that "republican virtue," in its original American meaning, had only modest moral implications. But it did (and does) have some moral implications, and if we look at George Washington, we see what they are. They include probity, truthfulness, self-reliance, diligence, prudence, and a disinterested concern for the welfare of the republic. In short, they are those virtues which we familiarly associate with "the Protestant ethic" or "the bourgeois ethic," though, as a Jew, I might point out that they could also be properly associated with "the rabbinical ethic," a fact which was well known to the Puritans.

Now, there are two things to be said about such virtues, and about the kind of human character they are supposed to give rise to. First, they are compatible with practically all the religions of Western civilization, including such essentially secular religions as Deism and Stoicism, and are therefore appropriate to a liberal and pluralistic society. And, secondly, they are rather "dull" virtues, precisely because they are so modest in their scope. This "dullness" was always taken to be meritorious, since it meant that you didn't have to be an exceptional person to be a perfectly good citizen. "Republican virtue" is an easy virtue, by the traditional standards of religion and moral philosophy. George Washington is, and was always supposed to be, a model American whom every school boy could assemble from his own parts. So the question naturally arises: if "republican virtue" is so easy, why do we find the very suggestion of it so irksome? More than that: why do we find the very conception of it so repugnant? For the better part of American history, it was thought proper that every American boy should be encouraged to want to grow up to be like George Washington. Today, that would be regarded as a dismal fate, and we have even taken Washington's birthday away from him, for the convenience of a long weekend.

I would say that the basic change in American history took place when it came widely to be believed that it was both natural and right for our republican institutions simply to adapt themselves to the American people, rather than vice versa. It was a gradual change, so gradual that only a few observers took notice of it. For the most part, it was simply accepted as the predestined fulfillment of "the democratic promise" and the full flowering of "the democratic faith"—phrases which are themselves by-products of this transformation. The history of the United States came to be written as the progressive liberation of the American people from all sorts of prior restraints which our rather narrow-minded ancestors insisted on establishing for the people's own good. I think that the history of the United States can indeed be fairly written in these terms. The key question is the degree to which one wishes to regard this history as progressive or otherwise.

We do, of course, regard it as progressive because this history has made the United States into a wealthy and powerful nation. Above all, wealthy: we find sufficient justification in American history by reason of the fact that it has raised our standard of living so spectacularly. But we are not moved to inquire whether this has made us a better people or worse, in terms of the original ideals of this republic. In truth, we cannot imagine how an increase in prosperity could possibly make people worse, rather than better. Both the Old Testament and the New had no difficulty in conceiving such a possibility; neither did John Adams nor Thomas Jefferson. They believed that people, if they lived carelessly and unreflectively, could corrupt themselves. We think the people are naturally good and that only their institutions can be corrupt.

It is not surprising that the first sphere of human action in which this new spirit manifested itself was the economic. It was the American businessman who first liberated himself from the idea of "republican virtue," in order to create as much wealth, as quickly as possible, for himself and for us. Prior to the Civil War, a businessman was a professional man, in the same sense that doctors and clergymen were professional men. That is to say, it was taken for granted that there was a connection between what he did and what he was, between his vocation and his character, a connection that intimated a code of behavior which defined what was "honorable" and what was not. Thus, it was thought to be dishonorable for a businessman to go bankrupt, not because this was a sign of failure but because it meant that he was cheating his creditors who had trusted him. And if a businessman did go bankrupt, it was thought honorable for him to spend the rest of his life paying off his creditors nevertheless, and for his children to assume this burden as well. This may not make any economic sense; our present casual and impersonal attitude toward bankruptcy might be more economically productive. But it did emphatically make *political* sense—if you believe that the effects of economics on our standard of living are less momentous than its effects upon our character.

"Free enterprise," until the Gilded Age, was supposed to be—it wasn't always in fact, but was supposed to be—a form of moral behavior, and the business life was supposed to be a morally satisfying life. I know it will seem incredible but, up until the advent of the morally neutral entrepreneur who is nothing but an economic instrument—up until the Civil War, that is—most Americans seemed to be of the opinion that to be a businessman was to be an honest and trustworthy man. There were greedy and unscrupulous "speculators," of course. But a sharp distinction was made between such "speculators" and businessmen, not least by the businessmen themselves, who did not permit "speculators," no matter how wealthy, to become members of their clubs. The American businessman had "character," as we now say. And he was in good repute among his fellow citizens. Not in the very best repute, it must be said: prior to the Civil War, it was statesmen and soldiers who were the heroes of popular biographies, since they were thought to have an even greater measure of "republican virtue." But businessmen were much respected, and were thought to be an honorable class of men engaged in an honorable activity— i.e., an activity from which they emerged better men than when they first entered it, as a result of the discipline which this activity exercised upon their characters. The institution of business was thought to make for self-improvement and not simply self-enrichment.

This "bourgeois" businessman, about whose life and work there was absolutely nothing value-free, was succeeded by a more "liberated" type, a more "democratic" type, whose attitude toward economic activity was purely instrumental. The businessman ceased being a kind of man and became a kind of function, devoid of any specifically human qualities. Still, it is astonishing how long the bourgeois ethos lingered on. When I was very young, people who bought things on the installment plan were still regarded as feckless and irresponsible. And people who sold things on the installment plan were regarded as engaged in a shady enterprise, because they were, after all, corrupting other people into fecklessness.

All that was in another time, of course, and in another country I sometimes think. Today, businessmen assemble in solemn assembly in order to figure out what they should do to achieve public respect and favor. Their concern is both serious and sincere, and one almost does not have the heart to tell them that their problem is not in the area of *doing* but in the area of *being*. They, like the rest of us, were born into a world they never made, and, again like the rest of us, find it close to impossible to imagine that the trouble they are in is organically related to their having become the kind of successful people our society said they should become.

Another illustration of what I have in mind is the extraordinary increase, in recent years, of strikes which, for quite trivial reasons, inflict enormous damage on the community. I am thinking especially of strikes by policemen, firemen, garbage collectors, and transport workers. These are quite common today, though they were yesterday very rare, and the day before yesterday were close to unthinkable. American trade unions used to be essentially defensive institutions, protecting the human rights and economic position of their members, and their ethos was one of fraternity. They have become purely acquisitive combinations, exercising monopoly power in a spirit of the-public-be-damned. Now, I am not saying that, in some instances, these Americans who go on strike do not have legitimate grievances. On the contrary: I assume they do. But a legitimate grievance can become illegitimate, just as a just war can become unjust, if the means employed are incommensurate with the ends sought. And I must say that I am appalled that a group of American workers should cease performing essential services to their fellow Americans because they seek a 5 percent or 8 percent increase in pay over what they receive or over what was offered them. Something is definitely wrong when that can happen, as it now does with increasing frequency. How can that rather trivial goal possibly justify such aggressive and costly action?

I have used the phrase "that rather trivial goal" in order to put the matter as provocatively as possible. (Sometimes we do have to be provoked to think clearly.) I know I will be told that these workers have a difficult time making ends meet and that a 5 percent or an 8 percent increase is not to be sneered at. That is true enough, but I would also insist it is really beside the point. Very few of our workers live on the margin of subsistence; they are not in the kind of extreme and desperate condition which might justify such extreme and desperate action. The extra money, after taxes have been deducted, will make their situation slightly more comfortable than it was. And for this they are prepared to convulse the community and threaten the livelihood of their fellow citizens, many of whom are surely less well off than they are. This can only be described as selfishness. And that description applies whether one regards their grievances as legitimate or not. Nevertheless, very few of us seem to be able to say this bluntly, without embarrassment. We are more likely to point out that these ordinary people are behaving no differently from many greedy and unscrupulous businessmen. This argument has some truth in it, but what a strange truth it is! It implies, in effect, that the legitimate criteria of behavior in a democracy are to be found somewhere in the vicinity of the lowest common denominator. And, of course, under the pressure of this perverse moral egalitarianism, the lowest common denominator sinks ever lower.

After business and organized labor, just about every other area of American life followed a similar path. Religion may have followed more reluctantly, but follow it did. The sermon which denounced the failings of the congregation slowly gave way to the sermon which denounced the inadequacy of our social, economic, and political institutions. Making demands upon oneself became unpopular; making demands upon others became habitual. It is interesting to recall that, up until about a hundred years ago, it was common for Congress or state legislatures to call, by resolution, for a day of fasting, to take note of some particularly solemn occasion. Moreover, such calls were directed toward all citizens, rich and poor, indiscriminately. It is quite impossible for Congress even to contemplate such a resolution today. And should some brave Congressman introduce such a resolution, it would quickly be studded by amendments exempting all those below a certain level of income or who were engaged in various essential services. We find the very idea of a fast-day barbarous—it violates all the nutritional rules established by the government agencies. And the idea that poor people should fast, just like everyone else, would strike us as utterly preposterous. We know that only people with full stomachs and on a well-balanced diet can be expected to meet such a harsh moral obligation. The fact that our ancestors, who were much poorer than we, thought otherwise is attributed to their lack of enlightenment, as is the fact that, even today, observant Jews and Catholics and Muslims think and act otherwise. Dostoyevsky predicted, in *The Brothers Karamazov*, that when the anti-Christ came, he would have inscribed on his banner: "First feed people, and then ask them to be virtuous." We have improved on that slogan to the extent of adding decent housing, good schools, free medical care, and adequate public transportation as necessary preconditions of virtue. And then we wonder why such benevolence seems not to encourage people to have a good opinion of their political order. It does not occur to us that, in a democracy, if the citizenry lack self-respect they will be incapable of any kind of respect—that to the degree we officially propound a mean and squalid view of humanity, there will emerge mean and squalid human beings. All of us normally become what we are expected to become, and if our society thinks it normal for us to be enslaved to our appetites and our desires rather than to govern them, then we shall come to regard such enslavement as true liberty, and shall simultaneously regard any suggestion of self-government as an infraction of this liberty.

Our politicians have, over these past decades, learned this lesson well, in the sense that they have successfully debased themselves to what they take to be the appropriate common level. The average politician of today sees it as his role to gratify the appetites of the people, to liberate them from deprivation, as we say. The truly creative politician of today is more "far-sighted" in that he discovers new and original deprivations, popularizes them, makes them keenly felt. "What have you done for us lately?" is now assumed to be the absolutely proper question for the citizen to address to his representative, who, in turn, frantically speculates as to what he can do for them tomorrow. What this means, quite simply, is that by the traditional standards of republican political philosophy, American politics today is the politics of demagogy, the politics of bribery. We obscurely recognize this fact by reserving the term "statesman" for those exceptional politicians who hold themselves somewhat aloof from this process of soliciting and pandering, though we are also so suspicious of our own sentiments, which smell ever so slightly of indecent elevation, that we will quickly and cynically wonder whether the "statesman" is merely a politician who is not running for reelection.

If anyone were to suggest that, in a self-governing republic, it should be normal for the people's representatives to wish to be as statesmanlike as possible, continually engaged in a reasonable conversation with their constituents, he would be informed that he is not living in the real world. But this real world is something which we have ourselves constructed. American politics wasn't always like this, and wasn't ever supposed to be like this. Unbelievable though it may seem, there was a time, in living memory, when those who campaigned too energetically for public office were, for that reason alone, viewed with more suspicion. Public office was thought to be a burdensome obligation to which only the more public-spirited would aspire. I don't want to idealize the past or exaggerate its merits; what we are talking about is a matter of degree. The "democratic politician" has always coexisted, in this country, with the "republican statesman." But he certainly never predominated so absolutely as he does today. The one group which seems to understand this situation best of all is the politicians themselves. Most of them will admit, in private conversation, that they would much prefer to be statesmanlike, only they don't see how that is possible. They must, they say, be "responsive" to the people if they are to be able to function at all. The irony is that, as they become ever more "responsive," the people put less and less faith in them and in our political institutions generally.

Very much the same thing has happened in the field of education. When our schools were "republican" institutions, instructing young citizens in the three R's, in elementary civics, and in the rudiments of good manners, they had both self-confidence and universal respect. Today, when they are "democratic" institutions, when they are making few demands on their students but feverishly trying to satisfy all the demands which students make on them, they are in a condition of perpetual crisis. Most of the "progressive" and "liberating" reforms in education, over these past decades, have resulted in most of us being more dissatisfied with American education than was previously the case. You would think that this might give us food for thought, but, no, it only incites us to invent new and better reforms, all in the direction of encouraging students to express more freely their appetites, to more freely indulge their desires. And, inevitably, students end up lacking confidence in these institutions which, lacking all self-confidence, seem to have no other purpose than to pander to them.

And this, I think, is the main point which emerges from the American democratic experience of recent years. People do not have confidence in institutions which do not have confidence in themselves. People do not have respect for institutions which, instead of making demands upon them, are completely subservient to their whims. In short, a people will not respect a polity that has so low an opinion of them that it thinks it absurd to insist that people become better than they are. Not simply more democratic; not simply more free; not simply more affluent; but, in some clear sense, better.

The original republican idea of self-government was what we would today call high-minded. The self which is supposed to govern is necessarily conceived of as being a better self than the self which naturally exists, and the purpose of the republic, in all its aspects, is inherently a self-improving one. The later democratic idea of self-government is based on the premise that one's natural self is the best of all possible selves, and that it is the institutions of society which are inevitably corrupting of natural goodness. These are two very different readings of human nature, and they lead to different kinds of politics. The first results in people making moral demands upon themselves; the second results in people making moral demands upon social reality.

I know of no way in which this philosophical argument about human nature can be settled in the abstract. But our own political experience does, I think, give us some empirical clues as to which reading of human nature is more humanly satisfying. And the evidence seems overwhelmingly favorable to the republican reading. After all, it is a fact that Americans today "have never had it so good," as one says, in the sense that they are wealthier and healthier and enjoy greater personal freedom than did their fathers or grandfathers. But it is also a fact that they don't feel at all good about themselves and their condition, and a great many of our young people seem to feel positively miserable about their human condition. It can hardly be without significance that, among these young especially, the idea of "liberation" from a "repressive" actuality should now be so popular. There are some of us who will delude ourselves into believing that these young people are fretful at the remnants of republican restrictiveness, and they will assert, in the words of Al Smith, that the only sure cure for the ills of democracy is more democracy. If you are committed to the democratic dogma, that is the only possible remark you can make. You are not likely to contemplate the possibility that it is the very society based on this dogma which comes to be felt as "repressive" and from which "liberation" is sought.

Some ten years ago, in the midst of the rebellion on our campuses, an article appeared in the *New York Times Magazine*. It was written by a Yale psychologist, and its title was a quotation from one of the student leaders. That title was "You Don't Know What Hell Is Like Unless You Were Raised in Scarsdale." Now, Scarsdale is one of our most affluent and sophisticated suburbs. It is also, so far as young people are concerned, one of the most tolerant and "permissive" places in America. Nothing is too good or too expensive for the children of Scarsdale. And yet, the children for the most part despise it and leave it as soon as they can.

This is a serious matter. For the American democracy today seems really to have no other purpose than to create more and more Scarsdales, to convert the entire nation into a larger Scarsdale. That is what our political leaders promise us; that is what our economic leaders promise us; and even our religious leaders will issue indictments against the nation because there are still so many people who are "underprivileged" by the Scarsdale standard. But Scarsdale is obviously an experiment that has failed. And the reason, equally obvious I should think, is that the life it proposes to its citizens is so devoid of personal moral substance, and is therefore so meaningless.

We are troubled by this phenomenon, and we wonder why it is that Americans, even as they improve their material conditions, are losing faith in their institutions. We also begin to wonder how these institutions can be made more "responsive" to the people, so as to soothe their discontent. What we do not wish to see is that our institutions are being made ever more "responsive" to the wrong people, to the people as they are, not as they might be. People do not respect institutions which are servile; people only respect a society which makes demands on them, which insists that they become better than they are. Without such a moral conception of the self, without a vivid idea as to the kind of person a citizen is supposed to become, there can be no self-government. And without self-government, the people perish—from boredom, from a lack of self-respect, and from a loss of confidence in their institutions which, they realize, only mirror their alienation from the better selves that lie dormant within their actual selves.

1974

Human Nature and
Social Reform

We are living through a period of much disillusionment with social reform, at least on the part of the majority of the American people. An energetic and articulate minority, to be sure, is still willing to defend the dozens of Great Society programs of the last fifteen years, lamenting only the "niggardliness" with which they were conceived and executed. But even the media, always the last to know, no longer put much stock in any such apologias. "Throwing money at problems" is the way these programs are now described (and dismissed). And even though we continue to do just that, it is all done in a rather mechanical and halfhearted way, simply because we feel we must do something.

What is missing is any kind of serious reflection on our experience with social policy. We seem uninterested in learning from this rich, at least expensive, experience. We are curiously reluctant to analyze why some reforms work, others do not. Not all social reforms fail. Let me point to one which has been an extraordinary success, though it is practically never mentioned in the literature on the subject. I refer to night school at the secondary and postsecondary level. For many decades now, night schools have permitted millions of working-class Americans to acquire an education, and eventually to improve their condition, while supporting themselves and/or their families. Not everyone goes to night school, of course; and many go only quickly to drop out. But these people do not thereby constitute any kind of social problem. In night school, you get only no effects or good effects.

Now, why is this program so successful? The answer is obvious (though not at all trivial): it builds on existing motivations. It doesn't try to reform or rehabilitate the individual. It offers him (or her) an opportunity to achieve an ambition. Let us call this kind of program an "opportunity program," and of such programs we can say flatly: they always work. They may not work as well as we wish or hope. But they are never counterproductive. All of us of a certain age are familiar enough with such opportunity programs, though we don't always recognize them as such. Alcoholics Anonymous, for example, is exactly such a program. In it, people who wish to cease being alcoholics can achieve that goal. As for those who prefer to remain alcoholics—well, there is no program on God's earth which can reform them. Motivation is all.

What is true for alcoholism is also true for drug addiction, juvenile delinquency, and adult criminality. Those who wish to move out of these conditions will be helped by programs that "hook on" to this motivation. The rest will be unaffected by any program. Juvenile delinquency is probably the most interesting of these cases, since most adults would like to think that all young people, in the proper environment, will respond positively to love and care and affection. Well, not all do. We have had for over a century now, in this country and elsewhere, an infinite variety of juvenile delinquency programs. They have all been studied exhaustively by sociologists, criminologists, and social workers, and the findings are dismal. Not a single such program works better than no program at all. This does not mean, fortunately, that all juvenile delinquents are irretrievably doomed to a life of crime. In fact, most juvenile delinquents do not grow up to be professional criminals. The reason is that, as they grow older, their motivations change. Indeed, for these maturing delinquents society does offer an opportunity program that is extraordinarily successful. It is called marriage. Falling in love creates new motivations more powerful (and more benign) than the old. Nothing creates more joy in the heart of a parole officer than the news that one of his charges is getting married.

The case of adult criminals is not so very different. Here, too, we have had hundreds of experiments, in dozens of countries, with prison reform aiming at the rehabilitation of habitual criminals. Not a single such program works better than no program at all, as measured by the rates of recidivism. Once again, if there were such a program you would have heard all about it by now. But, once more again, this does not mean that criminals are a breed apart from the rest of mankind. Their motivations, too, can change. Getting married ("settling down with a good woman") can do it. Religious conversion can do it (which is why it is deplorable that so many prisoners now read law books instead of the Bible). And the weariness of older age—nature's opportunity program, if you will—can do it. Very little else, apparently, can.

What it comes down to is this. There can be no successful social program which does not take seriously, is not realistically attentive to, people's motivations. There is one important exception to this rule. The issue of motivation is irrelevant to people who are dependent by nature (i.e., whose dependency is simply not open to question). I refer, of course, to the old, the halt, the blind, the infirm. Programs that "throw money" at such people are perfectly appropriate. True, one can recklessly if generously throw too much money at them. But that is a question of economic prudence, not of social policy. In principle, all such programs, for such people, work. The reason they work for such people is because their only problem is the lack of money, not the lack of any kind of motivation. But the issue of motivation certainly does arise in connection with our welfare population, whose dependency is social, not natural. The reason our welfare policy has been such a disaster—disastrous, above all, to the people it is supposed to help—is because our reformers thought it would be a slander against human nature even to permit the question of motivation to enter their thinking.

Almost 150 years ago, Alexis de Tocqueville visited England and was quickly struck by the paradox that the wealthiest nation in the world was preeminently perplexed by a massive "pauper problem." Investigating, he soon discovered the explanation for this paradox. Welfare rates had been set so high as to compete successfully with the job rates for unskilled labor. Many people, who preferred nonwork to work, were therefore leaving (or refusing to enter) the labor force. This population, now dependent, was soon corrupted and demoralized by its own unnatural dependency, and manifested all the familiar symptoms of social pathology: abandoned families, drunkenness, sloth, criminality, etc., etc. This is precisely what has happened in the United States in these past fifteen years. (It didn't happen in France, incidentally, which, having no generous welfare program, had no welfare problem.) Why didn't we realize what was happening?

The reason, so far as I can see, has to do with the metaphysics behind modern social thought and the modern impulse to social reform. Our reformers evidently don't much care about opportunity programs; they speak little of them, devise few of them. They care very much, on the other hand, about what we may call "environmental programs"—i.e., programs that enable us (in theory) to change everyone's motivations for the better, through the practical exercise of our unadulterated compassion, our universal benevolence, our gentle paternalistic authority. What it comes down to is that our reformers simply cannot bring themselves to think realistically about human nature. They believe it to be not only originally good, but also incorruptible; hence the liberal tolerance for pornography.

When a slum population wrecks a brand-new housing project, it is the designers of the project who are blamed, never the inhabitants. Those inhabitants are promptly relocated in other housing, which they will also wreck, since there are no rewards or punishments attached to existing motivations. There is thought to be no need for such rewards or punishments, since public officials and our liberal social scientists know that poor people have only good motivations. They know this as a matter of faith, by liberal revelation, as it were. To question this principle of the original goodness of human nature, and its corollary, the ease of improvement of human nature, would also set limits to that most profound of liberal passions, the passion of self-righteous compassion. It is the passion that defines the very essence of modern liberalism, and which, not so incidentally, legitimates the liberal exercise of intrusive authority over our social and economic life. So it is not surprising that, with such a secure anchor in both secular faith and self-interest, the liberal motivation is, of all motivations, the least responsive to messages from the real world.

Still, reality will not be denied. What we call the "neoconservative" impulse today, so evident in both our political parties, is basically a disillusionment with, and disengagement from, the strategy of environmental reform. This does not mean the end of reform itself, as many liberals insist and some conservatives claim. But it does indeed signify a profound shift in the climate of ideas within which reform will henceforth be conceived.

1978

Foundations and the Sin of Pride

The Myth of the Third Sector

Today, I want to talk about the foundation world and the sin of pride—what the Greeks called *hubris*, what the church fathers called *superbia*, namely the desire to do more good than anyone can do, a desire to do good which ends up being a form of the will to power. I think the foundation world today is suffering from the sin of pride.

Let me give you a very clear and specific instance. It is now generally said and widely thought that the foundation world (the nonprofit world, as we say) constitutes a "third sector" in American society. There is, it is said, the private sector, consisting of business enterprise; the public sector, consisting of government; and then we have the third, not-for-profit sector, of which the foundations are the animating core. I would like to suggest to you that there is no third sector. Foundations are part and parcel of the private sector. They are flesh of the flesh, bone of the bone, blood of the blood of the private sector. The notion that foundations in some way constitute a sector of their own, different from, above, and superior to the other two sectors, is an act of pride which will only go before a fall. That fall may consist in the fact that foundations will end up depriving themselves of their sustenance, which comes from the various parts of the private sector. Foundations are creations of the private sector.

In fact, there are only two sectors in our society: the private sector and the governmental sector. The voluntary associations in our nation do not make up a third sector; they are part of the private sector. Churches are part of the private sector. Fraternal organizations are part of the private sector. Even political parties are part of the private sector. There is no high ground which foundations can occupy and from which they can look down upon the other sectors and then try to think up policies, methods of improving the world, which are somehow disinterested in a way that those of the other two sectors are not.

The sin of pride to which I refer shows itself in many other ways. For instance, we hear it said that foundations should be setting the national agenda. But it is politics that sets the national agenda. If foundations want to get into politics, that is their privilege, but they ought to know that what they are then doing is getting into politics. They are not acting in some disinterested way; they are not representing something called "the public interest." In politics everyone represents the public interest, or rather, everyone represents some conception of the public interest, for politics consists of conflicts among different conceptions of the public interest. There is no one conception of the public interest which is right as against all others. I want to emphasize that if foundations are inclined to get involved in politics this way, I think that's perfectly proper, but they ought to know what they are doing. They ought not to think that somehow they are above the political battle. They ought not to think they will not end up bearing the scars of the political battle. They ought not to think that they will be immune to political attack. Shaping the national agenda is part of the political activity of a democracy.

We also hear it said that foundations should stimulate social change, or, to use one of the favorite clichés, be on "the cutting edge" of social change. That, too, is politics. And foundations have no more perception of what is right or wrong in social change, of what is effective or what is desirable, than anyone else who is involved in politics. Foundation people are almost certainly better educated, or at least better schooled, than most people who are involved in politics. But that does not mean that they have a superior understanding of what society needs, in what directions society ought to go, or in what direction society can go.

There is an implicit arrogance in the notion, in the very rhetoric, that a foundation should be on "the cutting edge" of social change. First of all, it assumes you know what the cutting edge is, and you know that it cuts this way, not that way. Secondly, to be on the cutting edge of social change you have to have a complete, comprehensive, theoretical understanding of the social order, of how change is brought about and how you bring about the changes you wish as against the changes you don't wish. There is no such comprehensive theory—never has been, never will be. We do not understand ourselves that well, and we do not understand our neighbors that well. The reason we have politics at all is because the world is full of other people. Other people are never quite like us. That's the way it's always been, and that's the way it's always going to be. The notion, therefore, that any foundation or any group of scholars or any group of thinkers can have a "disinterested" conception of where society should go, one that is not open to political conflict and political argument, is an act of intellectual arrogance which can only end up creating damage to foundations. For not only can't we control social change in a disinterested way, in the end we can't control it at all. We really cannot control social change. We can try. It's very important to try. But the notion that you can come up with a master plan for social change and institute that plan and get the results that you really intended is to overlook the fact that the basic law of politics is that unanticipated consequences are always more important than the anticipated consequences of your actions.

There have been a number of such instances of intellectual arrogance over the past twenty-five or thirty years, some of which I have been involved in, some of which I have just witnessed. I'll mention two of them, both, as it happens, involving the Ford Foundation. Back in the 1950s, the Ford Foundation decided that the behavioral sciences were the key to the future, that the behavioral sciences, like sociology and political science, would really give us a way of controlling human destiny. They would bring about the "politics of the future" and create a better society at the least cost. And so the Ford Foundation devoted tens of millions of dollars to advancing the behavioral sciences in the universities, with great success. Unfortunately, fifteen years later it turned out that the behavioral sciences were in a condition, and to this day are in a condition, of intellectual crisis; the younger scholars, whether conservative or radical, are all in rebellion against the behavioral sciences, which they find very boring, very tedious, and on the whole ineffectual. But the damage that has been done to our universities by the Ford Foundation's presumption in thinking that it knew what should be taught in the universities, that it knew exactly what it should impose on universities within the social sciences, has been enormous. Because professors don't die young. Tens of thousands of professors, with tenure, are now sitting in universities, trained in the behavioral sciences, teaching students who find them all (or most of them) thoroughly unsatisfying.

The other, more famous instance, of course, was the school decentralization fight in New York City. Being a New Yorker, that was something that came very close to the bone. There the act of arrogance was evident, because if there's one law of New York City politics it is: "Thou shalt not polarize racial and ethnic groups." That has been the overriding political law of New York City for 150 years now, but the Ford Foundation blithely went ahead and polarized the city, inflicting enormous damage on the public school system, and on the political system of the city. My impression is that, having caused that damage, it has now lost interest in the subject and has gone on to something else.

Now, I don't want to be misunderstood. It is possible to do good. It really is possible to do good. Doing good isn't even hard. It's just doing a lot of good that is very hard. If your aims are modest, you can accomplish an awful lot. When your aims become elevated beyond a reasonable level, you not only don't accomplish much, but you can cause a great deal of damage. And, in fact, I think that foundations in this country have passed up enormous opportunities to do good, simply because they have found them not sufficiently ambitious.

In my own experience, I spent several years on the Council of the National Endowment for the Humanities (NEH), and it was an organization that I very much favored. In fact, I even helped persuade some of my conservative friends in Congress to vote its appropriation against their inclination. I have avoided speaking to them since. I don't know what I would now say to them. Basically, NEH did a good job; in all fairness, I think it still does half a good job. At the beginning, what NEH did was quite simple and obvious. We supported archaeological expeditions in Turkey. Someone has to support them; they're worth doing. They might discover something interesting; it seems right that NEH should do it. We supported critical editions of major texts. Again, very expensive. Again, someone has to do it, and it seems right that the National Endowment for the Humanities should do it. We went on doing all these very colorless and rather boring, but good things.

But in the end it didn't satisfy a great many people, including people in Congress, including some of the present leaders of foundations. The result is that, when you proposed something along those lines, the reaction became, "Oh goodness, come on, we don't want another edition of classical texts. Let's do something more interesting, let's do something that has an effect on the world." As a consequence, the emphasis at NEH, over these past years, has shifted. A lot of the money is now simply wasted, in my view, on all sorts of dubious "community and cultural activities." I do think that the NEH should support excellent museums. I don't think it ought to support third-rate museums. But, of course, it's now in the business of supporting third-rate ballet troupes, third-rate, fourth-rate museums, spreading the money around state by state, county by county; it has been quite politicized. It still does some good—I'd say half of what it does is still perfectly good. But it just could not be satisfied to do the good things which were not intellectually exciting. They were quite routine but worth doing, and now unfortunately very few foundations are doing them.

I take a more dramatic instance. Everyone is concerned about youth unemployment in the ghetto, as I am, and I have been involved with various foundations and government as well, over the years, in trying to do something about it. It's astonishing how little has been accomplished. The reason so little has been accomplished is that no one was satisfied with doing a little; everyone wanted to do a lot. For instance, it is a scandal in this country that vocational education is in the condition it's in. It is absolutely absurd. Can you imagine a United States of America where there is a shortage of automobile mechanics, and yet there are "unemployable" kids in the ghetto who can strip an automobile in four minutes flat? It just doesn't make sense. But when you try to get a program of vocational education going—and I've tried very hard with various foundations to get a simple program of vocational education going—they say, "No! No! We don't want to train these kids to be automobile mechanics. We want to train them to be doctors, to be surgeons." Let's be reasonable. Not everyone can be a doctor or a surgeon. Some people are going to end up as automobile mechanics. Automobile mechanics have a pretty good career. They make a great deal of money, most of it honestly. But the fact is that it has been impossible to get the resources for so limited a goal.

Foundations talk a great deal about education, and propose grand theories about education. Whenever a foundation comes to me with grand theories about education, I say: "Fine, start a school." Why not? If you have grand and novel theories about education, start a school. But it turns out that those people don't want to start a school. They want to reform the whole public education system, or whatever. But it's very hard to reform the public education system, which is populated by people with interests, ideas, and habits of their own. It's not in their interest to be reformed. So they will take your program and twist it in all sorts of ways. Whereas a foundation can always start a school. Thus it seems reasonable to insist: if you have any good ideas about education, whether it be in the ghetto or elsewhere, *start a school*. But I have never heard of any foundation that started a school, one that would put its theories into effect. A hundred years ago that was assumed to be a very promising way to reform education. These days it is regarded as insufficiently ambitious, too modest in its intent.

Again, turning to the youth of the ghetto, if you say to a foundation: "Look, there are many bright kids in the ghetto who need help, who need scholarships, who need fellowships. Why don't you help them?" the answer to that is: "We want to help those who are really down at the bottom. That's the problem." Indeed that is the problem. Only, helping those at the bottom is not easy, whereas helping those who are at the top, or are moving up, is feasible. It works. If you suggest such a program you are accused of something called "creaming," namely, taking the most able, the most intelligent, the most ambitious, and moving them up while neglecting the rest. But that is the normal way in which all groups move into the mainstream of American life. This is true for all groups, all immigrant groups, all ethnic groups, all racial groups. You begin by moving up those who can be moved up. Their brothers, sisters, cousins, friends, see them moving up and begin to foresee that it's possible. They begin to shape their lives and their habits to follow them. The notion that you go directly to the hard-core unemployable, the high school dropouts, who are "hard-core" for a reason, is utopian. They're not easy to cope with. The notion that you can cope with these people directly, and transform them overnight into willing and eager students, is childish. I'm not saying you can't do it in the case of certain individuals. And if a foundation wanted to focus enormous resources on a few such individuals, it would probably work. But it would be enormously expensive, and in the end you would just be helping a few individuals. The more sensible approach is to do what you can do, help those who wish to be helped, who can be helped, who are already motivated, and hope that others will follow in their path. It is, on the basis of experience, a realistic hope.

I'll never forget my first job, working for a fine mechanic, who was an illiterate and who owned his own factory. After I'd been there a few days, he took me aside and said, "Irving, I want you to remember two things: First, a thing worth doing is worth doing cheaply. And second, if something is too hard to do, find something easier to do." On the whole, I think that's good advice. When things get terribly hard and terribly expensive, it's a sign that, for reasons which you may never understand, it's not going to be doable. Peter Drucker (many years later I read Peter Drucker on management) ends up saying the same thing as my little machine shop owner did, namely, you pour your resources into things that work. You don't spend all your time and energy and money on things that don't work. Do what is doable, and when you do what is doable, it will affect everything else, and you then get the kind of progress in education, or in the economy, or what have you, which brings everyone into the system and from which everyone benefits.

There is a passion for doing good. It is a noble passion, but it is a passion. And all passions have to be controlled. All passions are dangerous unless they are controlled. We have had long experience in the history of Western civi-

lization with people who spend their lives doing good. Nuns, members of religious orders, working in hospitals, in schools. All of them were under a discipline where they were on regular occasions humiliated by their institutions.
That is, if you wanted to do good in the old days, say, in a hospital, at some
point, you emptied bedpans. Now, I'm not saying that all the professionals at
the Robert Wood Johnson Foundation should spend one day a month emptying bedpans. On the other hand, it is useful to have an occasion for humility. It is very easy to sit down and devise a new health delivery service, but
cleaning bedpans gives you an insight into some of the problems inherent in
health delivery service. The passion for doing good, when it was restricted to
religious orders, had a self-correcting mechanism in it. We have no such system
of self-discipline and self-humiliation, so that the tendency toward pride and
arrogance in doing good, the tendency toward an excess of passion and self-
righteousness in doing good, is unchecked.

I want to make one final point, which is really my original point. Foundations came into existence originally to do all the things that needed to be done
that the government did not do in the nineteenth and early twentieth centuries. That was the right thing for foundations to do at that time. However,
the situation has changed today. We have had a reversal. There is almost nothing you can suggest which government is not eager to do. And it seems to me
that foundations, therefore, have a special responsibility to be wary of government and to be a lot more solicitous of their own sector, which, I repeat, is the
private sector. You're not *above* the private sector, by God, you're *in* it. I really
am a little sorry that the Council on Foundations has decided to set up headquarters in Washington. I think that's the wrong signal to the foundation
world. Foundations should not be an adjunct to government. Foundations
should be an adjunct to their own private sector. There is a tendency these
days for everything to become an adjunct to government, just as there is a tendency, when foundations have a good idea, for government to take it and run
away with it. My favorite example of the latter is the Meals on Wheels program. This was a marvelous program, a community program, where people
got together and delivered meals to elderly people who were either house-
bound or confined to their beds. And Congress heard about this and said,
"That's a great idea; we'll do it." So it passed the Meals on Wheels legislation,
but with all sorts of new regulations, so that the community organizations that
had been delivering meals for years were all disqualified because they didn't
have enough professional nutritionists, they didn't have the right number of
this or enough of that, they didn't have the right inspection of their facilities,
etc. So you end up with another government agency doing, in its bureaucratic

and, I am convinced, in the end not very humane way, what neighbors were doing in a very pleasant and humane way. There is clearly a tendency of government, in the name of the welfare state, to expand the conception of the welfare state so far as to be bureaucratically paternalistic. I think foundations should combat this tendency, not encourage it.

In sum, foundations should rethink their situations and their conditions. We live in a pluralistic society. Some foundations are going to be liberal, some are going to be radical, some are going to be conservative, and that's fine. That's the way it should be, as long as they realize that they are being either liberal, conservative, or radical, not somehow representing something called "the common good" which they alone are in a position to define. But I do want to emphasize, in closing, that all of those activities, whether radical, liberal, or conservative, emerge from the private sector, and are a distinctive aspect of our pluralist society. To the degree that our society becomes more centralized, to the degree that government becomes more intrusive in all the affairs of our lives, to that degree, foundations are going to end up in fact being adjuncts of government or being assimilated into government.

Even now it is said—and I have heard foundation executives say it, and I think most people here would probably say it—that the money you people spend is public money, and therefore you have a public responsibility. Now, in what sense is the money you spend public? Under the tax laws, the contributions made to foundations are deductible from income. If you say that that money is public money, you are saying: "Well, the government has the right to all our money, but it doesn't exercise this right at all times or in all respects. It leaves some of that governmental money for us to spend, and therefore we have a public responsibility attached to that money." I think that is socializing money in rhetoric prior to socializing it in fact. The money you people spend is *private* money. It is *not* public money. Money that the government does not take is ours. You can have whatever public responsibilities you wish to assume with that private money. But it is private money. It is the lifeblood of your organizations, and I think it is time foundations gave a little more thought to the source of that lifeblood and to what might be done to making that lifeblood a little more abundant and, shall we say, healthier in composition.

1980

The Spirit of '87

The American Constitution is a highly paradoxical document. Rhetorically, it is dry, legalistic, lacking in eloquence. Substantively, too, while it may not in fact have been "the work of men who believed in original sin," as James Bryce thought, it certainly reveals what one would call a "realistic" view of human nature—i.e., a view that is more alert to the absence of human virtues than to their presence, a view that is skeptical of the ability of human beings to govern themselves without the prior imposition of severe institutional self-restraints. There is no visible "democratic faith" in this Constitution. And yet—and yet it is a founding document that is venerated by a people for whom such a "democratic faith" is about as unquestionable a popular dogma as can be imagined in our secular age.

"Veneration" is not too strong a term, at least so far as popular opinion is concerned. (Scholarly opinion, of course, tends to look askance at such veneration, regarding it as just another popular delusion.) This condition has endured almost from the very beginnings of the nation. Though, as we know, the opposition to ratification of the Constitution was widespread and heated, within a decade such sentiments had evaporated. What that distinguished constitutional scholar E. S. Corwin has called (contemptuously) a "cult of the Constitution" quickly made its appearance. Such terms as "glorious," even "sacred," became the conventional clichés. So strong was this feeling, and so positive a political fact was it deemed to be, that James Madison refused to publish his *Notes on the Constitution* in his lifetime, lest the revelation of disagreements and debates and compromises at the Constitutional Convention have a subversive influence. (Since he enjoyed a long life, those *Notes* were not published until 1840.) Even the Civil War failed to disrupt the popular attitude, since both sides appealed to the Constitution as the vindicator of their positions. When, in 1878, Gladstone made his much-quoted tribute ("the most wonderful work ever struck off at a given time by the brain and purpose of man"), it was immediately accepted as fair and appropriate comment. And it has been accepted as such ever since, despite a flood of muckraking scholarship that began about 1910 and flourished for several decades thereafter. This scholarship, associated with the writings of Charles A. Beard and others, portrayed the Constitution as a repudiation of the principles of the Declaration of Independence by the moneyed interests. But the tide of that scholarship has now subsided; too much of it was pseudo-scholarship, it turned out. In any case, it never really touched the popular nerve.

Obviously, the American Constitution is unlike any other of the world's constitutions, of which by now there are so many. Not only is it the oldest, not only has it "worked" as none other has, it is different in *kind*. This difference was nicely caught by Whittle Johnson in an article in the *Yale Review* almost twenty years ago, when he pointed to the special status of the Constitution as a *covenant*: "What, then, does it mean to be an American? . . . To be an American means to be a member of the 'covenanting community' in which the commitment to freedom under law, having transcended the 'natural' bonds of race, religion, and class, itself takes on transcendent importance."

"A covenanting community"—this, I think, defines with neat precision a crucial dimension of the American body politic. This body politic is not just a "political system," as most of our political science textbooks have it. It is that, of course, but it is also more. This body politic, in the eyes of its citizens, has always had a quasi-sacramental status. It is no exaggeration to say that the Constitution along with the American flag and the Declaration of Independence constitute the symbolic trinity that affirms this status. Even today, young people in public schools recite, in some cases daily, the Pledge of Allegiance to the Flag "and to the Republic for which it stands." Is there anything comparable in any other democratic country? The children are descendants of immigrants who, when they became naturalized citizens, swore their allegiance to the Constitution, perceived as the wonderful fruition of the Declaration of Independence (to which any oath of allegiance is deemed supererogatory.) One learns by heart the Pledge in elementary school; in high school one learns by heart a least the opening sentences of the Declaration along with the preamble to the Constitution ("We, the people . . ."). One doesn't simply memorize them. One learns them by heart, since the recitation is supposed to be heartfelt, an exercise in solemn dedication.

The Flag, the Declaration, the Constitution—these constitute the holy trinity of what Tocqueville called the American "civil religion." As is inevitably the case with holy trinities, the exact relation of each member to the other gives rise to theological (i.e., jurisprudential) disputes, and one such dispute resulted in the bloodiest war in American history. But, on the whole, the American people have felt very comfortable with their trinity, despite all controversies on issues of transubstantiation.

So there is a *spirit* of the Constitution, enveloping the text and transforming it into a covenanting document, a pillar of the American "civil religion." But what is this spirit? Where does it come from? What gives it its sustaining power? It is the failure to address such questions that makes so much—not all, but so much—of the scholarly work on "the intellectual origins of the Constitution" less than satisfactory. This work is very fine indeed in exploring the origins of the American political system, but it too often seems impotent to explain the "spirit" that animates and pervades this system. Thus, there is no doubt that the writings and philosophy of John Locke were a preponderant influence on the authors of the Constitution, but the fact remains that what they wrought was a covenant, not merely a social contract. And the same can be said of all those other very visible intellectual influences: Montesquieu, the British republican pamphleteers of the eighteenth century, the Continental jurists of the era, as well as the Scottish philosophers of the Enlightenment. These influences were real enough, and they must be studied to understand the Constitution as it emerged from the Constitutional Convention. But all of them together do not add up to the Constitution we revere.

The American Constitution has many intellectual fathers, but only one spiritual mother. That mother is the Protestant religion—perhaps one should say the Protestant impulse—in its various American forms. The idea and, more important, the sentiment of the American people as a "covenanting community" comes from Calvinism. The idea of this community being governed by elected representatives comes not from memories of a feudal parliament (as in Europe), but from Puritanism and Presbyterianism. The conviction that all men have equal access to God, that freedom of conscience has divine sanction, that a large measure of individual liberty is consonant with a moral life— all are derived from the impulse toward spiritual individualism of various dissenting and pietist sects, some of whose teachings ended up closer to Deism than to Christianity. What we call the "Protestant ethic" or the "work ethic," a religious or quasi-religious insistence that the exercise of one's mundane responsibilities was a form of piety, comes from Puritanism and then (in a more massive way) from Methodism. Benjamin Franklin's *Poor Richard's Almanack* had very little overt religiosity in it; the author was at most a rather casual Deist. But the book could not have been written, and would not have been widely read, in an environment that had not previously been shaped by the

Protestant experience. That ethic became a moral code for all honest, God-fearing men and women, a code that infused the new "bourgeois" society with a religious aspect. So powerful had this Protestant influence been that Catholicism and Judaism, as they became "Americanized," also became often, after much futile resistance—markedly "Protestantized." Judaism, of course, had always had its own version of this ethic, which is why Puritanism placed such an extraordinary emphasis on the Old Testament.

So the structure and functioning of American government, what might be called its statistics and dynamics, have unquestionably been shaped by secular political philosophers. But what has sanctified their work are popular attitudes derived from religion, not philosophy. After all, "America" existed, as a new nation in embryo, before the Constitutional Convention, before even the Revolution. The various colonial state charters, and the state constitutions during the period 1778–1787, all foreshadowed (if in varying degrees) the basic premises of the Constitution. That "Americans" as a distinctive human type, participating enthusiastically in a distinctive "American way of life," preexisted the Revolution is testified to by the reports of all European visitors. The Revolution delivered the new body politic, the Constitution covenanted it, but it had been conceived out of the wedding of the Protestant ethos with American circumstances.

One legitimate offspring of this marriage circumstance was the early commitment of Americans to the making of money and the acquisition of property—to "bettering their condition," as Adam Smith would later put it. There can be little question but that this predisposition issued from the "Protestant ethic," the belief that a life spent in the legal pursuit of wealth and income could be a righteous life. Not a holy life, certainly, or even the most authentic or admirable of possible human lives, but righteous, even taking its self-imposed limitations into account. This belief has powerful economic effects, as all students of "modernization" know. Moreover, the economic potency of this belief has survived its secularization, which is part of its "Americanization." There is a very great difference between the Presbyterian John Knox and our own Benjamin Franklin. But it is precisely this difference that has allowed generations of immigrants, whatever their religious origins, to join the American covenant, to accept those bourgeois pieties that promised a "better life" without giving any thought to the religious origins of these pieties.

Indeed, so powerful is this Protestant-American impulse to "better one's condition" that it defines the exceptional way Americans subconsciously and automatically think about the politics of their constitutional order. When I teach the Constitution, I like to ask the class this question: "When we elect a representative to Congress, whom does he represent?" Only the occasional European or Latin American student sees the point immediately. The American students, suspecting a trap, are slow to give the obvious answer: he (or she) represents the people in his district, his "constituency." They do come forward with this answer eventually, at which point I inquire: "All of the people in his district—including those who voted against him?" Yes, of course. And suddenly enlightenment dawns: the realization that there is something special about this American assumption. In no other country in the world does the electoral process proceed on any such peculiar assumption. Everywhere else, elected representatives represent mainly their parties and the ideology of their parties, which is identified with the "public interest." Only in America is it taken for granted that they ought to represent, first of all, the economic interests of *all* of their constituents. This can be taken for granted because it has been assumed for two centuries now that all of those voters are more interested in improving their economic condition within the framework of a settled way of life than in any ideology or "cause," or at least expect their political representatives to work toward that economic end rather than expending too much energy promoting any particular ideology or "cause." Surely the main reason that the socialist idea has been so weak in America is the fact that it necessarily violates this political, constitutional assumption.

It follows that the Constitution is inextricably intertwined with the idea of economic progress. It has always been perceived to be so. Up until the Great Depression, it was routine for orators to link American prosperity to the Constitution, as effect to cause. Even today our new immigrants, as they take their oath of citizenship, clearly have this connection very much in mind. But, for many Americans, this linkage has been blurred in recent decades. The increasing secularization and "thinning out" of our "civil religion," while broadening its scope, has both vulgarized it and weakened it. The vulgarization takes the form of conceiving of American society, and bourgeois society in general, as little more than an "acquisitive society" where "free enterprise" flourishes. This provokes an antibourgeois animus among the better educated, who see such a society as a modern version of Plato's "city of pigs," while inciting many of the young to a libertarian hedonism that, by traditional standards, is nothing short of licentious. At the same time, the larger populace becomes uncertain of its "values" (as one now says), and its commitment to our constitutional traditions, though seemingly firm, becomes brittle.

The truth, which we are in danger of forgetting, is that a civil "religion" both engenders and requires a *moral* endorsement of a regime, not simply a utilitarian one. It is such a moral endorsement that always led Americans to believe that their constitutional order is not only efficient or workable, but also just. For such an endorsement to prevail, the "civil religion" must be at least minimally nourished by its religious roots. As the infinitely wise Tocqueville put it: "I do not know whether all Americans have a sincere faith in their religion— for who can search the human heart?—but I am certain that they hold it to be indispensable to the maintenance of republican institutions." The overwhelming majority of Americans still hold to that proposition today, but more anxiously and tentatively. They agree with George Washington when he remarked, in his Farewell Address, that one could only "with caution indulge the supposition that morality can be maintained without religion." But they see this "supposition" unqualifiedly and incautiously insisted upon by the bulk of our educated and professional classes—people who, after all, are really supposed to know about such matters. This makes them confused, unhappy, angry. What kind of polity is it, they wonder, in which we know so much more than our forebears but don't know how to go about explaining to our children right from wrong?

A "covenant" is meaningless unless it is based on moral truths which, if not undisputable in the abstract, are not widely disputed in practice. The source of such moral truth has always been a religious tradition or a composite of religious traditions. Science cannot provide such moral truths, neither can philosophy; both can only offer us reasons for skepticism about them. But a "way of life" involves commitment, and only a religious attachment, however superficial, can provide that. All observers note, and all opinion polls confirm, that Americans as a people are more religious than their West European counterparts. But that this fact may have something to do with the prosperity and political stability of the United States, or with the spirit of patriotism that is still so pervasive in this land, is studiously ignored. The bicentennial of the Constitution would seem to be a suitable occasion not merely for celebrating, not merely for taking thought, but for offering up a prayer on the Constitution's behalf. One assumes it would not object.

1987

The Welfare State's
Spiritual Crisis

By now it is obvious to all who wish to see that we are experiencing a profound crisis of the welfare state. Several crises, in fact. There is the financial crisis now evident in all the Western democracies, where all governments, whether left or right of center, are trying desperately to limit government spending and government commitments.

Though it is this crisis that grabs most of the headlines, it is probably over the long term the least serious. That is because of the two basic laws of economics: what can't happen won't happen, and what must happen will happen. Governments will succeed in edging the welfare state back from the brink of bankruptcy, though at a considerable political cost. That cost will be seen in political convulsions that can be quite scary. Still, after the dust has settled, the welfare state will have been sufficiently trimmed to avoid national bankruptcy, which would be the worst convulsion of all, and one that no government can contemplate as an option.

There is also a social crisis of the welfare state. Fifty years ago, no advocate of the welfare state could imagine that it might be destructive of that most fundamental social institution, the family. But it has been, with a poisonous flowering of those very social pathologies—crime, illegitimacy, drugs, divorce, sexual promiscuity—that it was assumed the welfare state would curb if not eliminate. This has come as such a shock to welfare statists that they have been busy explaining it all away. Their most common hypothesis, by now a dogma of the Left, is that the persistence of economic inequality and the absence of economic opportunity are the root causes of it all. But only those who have succeeded in repressing all historical memories can actually believe that. There are just too many people still alive who can testify that in times past when economic inequality and lack of opportunity were certainly no less evident than today (and for most people were probably much greater), such social pathologies were far less widespread.

One may anticipate that the reining in of the welfare state will ameliorate these problems, at least to some degree. But trimming the welfare state is unlikely to affect the deepest crisis of all, which is spiritual. It may sound odd to talk about the welfare state as if it had a spiritual dimension, as well as an economic and social one. But it does, though less visible to the naked eye and less quantifiable by social scientists. It is a dimension that involves the often subtle ways in which a democratic citizen envisions his government and his political community—envisions rather than simply sees. It is implicated in the way the souls of the citizenry are formed and shaped by the welfare state. What we are witnessing is an alienation from the interest-group politics that incessantly clamors for governmental subventions and that is now an integral part of our democratic politics. It is an alienation that then serves to undermine the legitimacy of the state itself.

Contemplating the decadence of Imperial Rome versus the virility of Republican Rome, the German philosopher Georg Hegel wrote: "The image of the State as a product of his activity disappeared from the soul of the citizen." Today, it is the mission of the welfare state to convince the citizen that he is the product of the state's activity, that he is an importuning subject of the state, no longer a citizen in the classical sense. The fully developed welfare state is a modern version of the feudal castle, guarded by moats and barriers, and offering security and shelter to the loyal population that gathers around it. Ironically, this means that in world affairs the poorer nations that are not welfare states, and are not nearly as risk-averse since they have so little to lose, will be (as they are already becoming) the activist countries, the ones that create the crises and set the international agenda. The most powerful nations in the world—economically, technologically, even militarily—will become citadels of resistance and nothing more.

In this process, the citizen is metamorphosed into the subject. The subject yields up only the right of self-government in return for cradle-to-grave security. He retains many other rights, and even achieves some new ones. He now possesses the right of "individual autonomy" in the sexual sphere, for instance, so that he is "liberated" from all the older social institutions that inhibited promiscuous or near-promiscuous behavior. Unfortunately, it is precisely in the sexual sphere that autonomy is most self-defeating, since the most important joys of sex come from commitments in which others (wives and children most notably) possess claims on us that make of our supposed autonomy a fantasy. Nor does evading those claims give us any help in "the pursuit of happiness." Never has any younger generation found so much loneliness and melancholy as it matures into "sexual liberation."

But then, the welfare state has a constricted notion of the happiness we ought to be pursuing. Since "security" is its keystone and its very reason for being, our welfare state societies are the most risk-averse societies the world has known. Physical health and longevity are the focus of its passions. In this area the welfare state can continually find more and more protective things to do for us. As a result, patriotism—real patriotism, which implies a readiness to die for one's country—is regarded as a form of psychological "extremis," and it is to discourage such mental unbalance that the modern welfare state has practically abolished military parades. The new World War II memorial to be constructed in Washington may show some respect for the endurance of our soldiers, but little for their heroism. The Iwo Jima memorial was the last such to be constructed.

All of this contributes to a spreading spiritual malaise in all our welfare states. As Charles Murray has written: "Responsibility is what keeps our lives from becoming trivial." The transfer of major areas of responsibility to the welfare state, combined with a bland, permissive toleration of moral irresponsibility among the citizenry, is about as fair a description of national decadence as one can imagine. A healthy nation and a respected government have to be capable of idealization—in fiction, poetry, drama, movies, popular songs. Our welfare states are not only incapable of that. They are today actually treated with contempt in these crucial modes of human expression. If you are not willing to die for your country you will soon refuse to take it seriously, and insolent disrespect will replace reverence.

But the welfare state, determinedly secular in its orientation, does not really believe in reverence, an attitude it associates (correctly) with religion. Not that it is openly hostile to religion; it simply treats religion as another consumption good (as an economist would say). The individual is free to shop and choose among all the religions that exist or have ever existed, so long as he takes care to keep his religious beliefs and behavior a private affair, never impinging on the public square. But religion that is merely a private affair has been, until our time, unknown in the annals of mankind, and for good reason. Such religion quickly diminishes into an indoor pleasure, a kind of hobby of one or more individuals, like reading a book or watching television. So it is not astonishing that the search for spirituality has become so fashionable. It is what individuals, liberated from religion, desperately seek as a substitute.

Spirituality is indeed an integral part of all religions, but a minor part, and it cannot be a substitute for the whole. Religion is not some kind of psychic exercise that occasionally offers a transcendental experience. It either shapes one's life, all of one's life, or it vanishes, leaving behind anxious, empty souls that no psychotherapy can reach. And for religion to shape one's life, it needs to be public and communal; it needs to be connected to the dead and the unborn. Religious liberation, like sexual liberation, fails to help us pursue happiness. Together they induce in us an epidemic of "identity crises," which is the peculiar hallmark of our civilization.

It was not supposed to be this way. The secular, social-democratic founders of the modern welfare state really did think that in the kind of welfare state we have today people would be more public-spirited, more high-minded, more humanly "fulfilled." This grave miscalculation, based on a simplistic understanding of human nature and the human condition, may yet turn out to be the saddest of political tragedies in our tragic century. Not the bloodiest, of course, but merely the saddest, as when decent and benevolent political intentions give birth to an increasing and inexorable discontent, individual and national.

1997

The Two Welfare States

The most notable aspect of the current presidential election has been the division that has emerged between the two versions of the welfare state envisaged by the two parties. An older, masculine, paternalistic version of the welfare state is fighting a guerrilla war against a newer and firmly established feminine-maternalistic conception of the welfare state. Nor is this a peculiarly American phenomenon. Something like it is visible in all the Western democracies. Though some intellectuals, especially in Europe, still chatter about conflict between a welfare state and a "free market" state, that polarity ceased to exist almost a century ago.

Fathers want their children to grow up to be self-reliant, self-supporting, and able to cope with a recalcitrant world. Mothers want their children to be as completely protected as possible from such a world and to be gratefully attached to them as long as they live; the avoidance of risk gets very high priority. The original welfare state, from 1900 to 1945, was largely paternalistic in conception, since the trade unions (overwhelmingly male) played such a crucial role in bringing it into being. After World War II, however, as women entered the labor force as well as educational institutions in large number, and as feminist ideas became popular, the welfare state came gradually to be seen less as a helping hand for those in need, a "safety net," and more as a communal exercise in "compassion" toward an ever-expanding proportion of the population. That was the point of the complaint lodged by many feminists against Margaret Thatcher; she had a "manly" rather than "womanly" conception of social policy.

That is the key term in the feminization of social policy, "compassion." Adam Smith talked easily about the importance of "sympathy," but that term lacks the erotic warmth of "compassion." "Sympathy" is most easily directed toward those who want to help themselves and need a helping hand. "Compassion," as we now understand it, is an indiscriminate response to suffering and is always therapeutic. Men can (and do) sympathize with those who are down on their luck, but it needs a woman to feel a deep compassion, shot through with free-floating indignation, for the human suffering of those who have been victimized by the ravages of ill fortune, or even by their own misdeeds. (There is no doubt that George W. Bush's use of the phrase "compassionate conservatism" is an attempt to swim with the maternalistic current.)

Once upon a time, popular journalism knew how to exploit this deep well of "compassion" with the formulaic "sob story," an account of human suffering that would bring tears to a woman's eyes. This was regarded as an inferior form of hack journalism, written by hardened cynics who saw profit where others saw misery. Gradually, however, as more and more women were educated to read and were provided with time to read, it became a quite respectable genre of journalism. And with the advent of mass media, and especially television, it became a dominant form of journalism. The photograph of four American soldiers raising the flag at Iwo Jima was the last "masculine" spectacle enshrined by TV. Since then, it is scenes of war's brutality and human suffering which win the awards.

The feminine, maternal version of the welfare state now has the support not only of public opinion, but of institutions and professions that have been nourished by this state, so that there are large numbers of working women loyal to this state—and men, too, who are loyal to these women. These are now designated collectively as the "helping professions," and include social work, nursing, psychology, public health, librarianship, teaching, and branches of TV journalism. These professions, most of them anyhow, are politically active. It has been noted that the largest single contingent at the Democratic conventions were members of the teachers' unions, and while these included men, one can be certain that none of them ever dared breathe an antifeminist thought. It has hardly been noticed, though it is an interesting fact, that a whole new profession has been recognized in the media. It consists of people who designate themselves, and are then designated by others, as "activists." To be an "activist" has become a recognized occupational specialty with at least quasi-professional status. Needless to say, this activism goes in only one prescribed direction.

Creating this extensive, in some cases massive, maternal welfare state has been an extraordinary achievement in view of the fact that it was created, as it were, ex nihilo. It was not a response to any visible, popular demand but was propelled by the thinking and writing of social scientists and journalists—an instance of what Daniel Patrick Moynihan, back in the late 1960s, foresaw as the "professionalization of reform." This version of the welfare state was officially recognized, and inaugurated and financed, by Lyndon Johnson. There is considerable evidence in the memoirs of his White House staff that LBJ had no clear idea of what he was doing. That did not, of course, matter.

Meanwhile, the masculine version of the welfare state is still a living political idea. In order to survive, it has made concessions, inevitably. "Leave no child behind" is not a traditional, conservative educational slogan. And queuing up to be kissed and blessed by Oprah Winfrey is not a traditional electoral activity. But the original idea still exists and has its victories, most notably in the case of welfare reform. And in the long run it has two things going for it. One is economics, and the other is policy.

The feminine version of the welfare state is inherently expansive—compassion has no limits—and sooner or later it runs into economic counterpressures. This has already happened in the European democracies, where economic growth is impeded by high taxation and overly generous welfare expenditures. It can be predicted with some confidence that those European governments will move, however reluctantly, toward a paternalistic (i.e., limited) version of the welfare state. The Left—a coalition of trade unionists, environmentalists, feminists, and surviving socialists—is already in revolt against "globalization" and "Americanization." It may win the occasional election, but it cannot govern without abandoning its agenda.

The United States is in a much better position, mainly because we now enjoy strong economic growth together with a nice budgetary surplus. But the pressures to spend are there (and quite a few conservative politicians are as easily tempted as liberals are by envisaged electoral rewards). This is especially true for a nation that is a superpower, whose foreign policies require increasing military expenditures. The maternal welfare state positively hates such expenditures, is cutting back on them in Europe, and is doing its best to emasculate the spirit of nationalist patriotism in all the nations of Europe. The United States, however, cannot opt out of world affairs. Nor is there any serious evidence that the majority of Americans wish to disburden themselves of our superpower responsibilities. Even a casual TV viewer can see that our military is still highly popular, which is not at all the case in Europe.

So the maternal-paternal conflict will continue, in a seesaw fashion, until a point arises—and it will, however unimaginable now—when other urgent issues intervene and the welfare state is no longer the focal point of democratic politics.

2000

IV

THE CULTURE AND COUNTERCULTURE

High, Low, and Modern

Some Thoughts on Popular Culture and Popular Government

Rimbaud was unquestionably a great poet. But was he a highbrow? He would generally be so classified today, and yet, the more one considers the matter, the odder it looks. His contemporaries—even his admiring ones, to say nothing of his depreciators—certainly did not see anything "high" about this adventurer bohemian who experimented with vice as energetically as with poetic forms. He himself would have been more than a little astonished at the description. "High" was where the Académie Française was located; Rimbaud was somewhere below, roaming among the cities of the plain.

The term itself, "highbrow," was first publicized in Van Wyck Brooks's historic essay, "America's Coming-of-Age," which appeared in 1915. It is worth remembering that this essay was by way of being a manifesto of "the modern" in literature and art, and that it was, among other things, an attack on the highbrow. By this term, Brooks meant the American equivalent of the French Academy, the "genteel tradition" of letters represented by the New England "Brahmins": Longfellow, Emerson, Lowell, Howells, Aldrich, and company. "Highbrow" culture was "high" culture, that dominating influence on American letters which placed the greatest emphasis, not on creativity itself, but on the continuity of a cultural tradition and the moral role played by art and the artist in the nation's life.

The young moderns, as we know, rejected this notion of cultural statesmanship. They were heirs to a literary tradition only in the sense that it was, in fact, their property, but this property could be used or abused at their pleasure, for they recognized no obligation to it. And they utterly rejected the idea that they were, in any sense, guardians of public morality. This morality wore a Victorian aspect; and so far from preserving it, the young moderns set out to subvert it by every means at their command. It was not, of course, that they— the majority at any rate—were against morality *per se*. What they wanted was to enlarge the moral sense so as to bring into the lives of men (and the arts of men), a freedom, an irreverence, an uninhibitedness, a candor (especially in matters of sex) that had hitherto been lacking.

And no one can say they have not succeeded.

Just as there is a distinction to be made between "highbrow" culture, properly speaking, and the "modern" movement which replaced it, so is there a distinction to be made between the "popular culture" of the last century and the "mass culture" of our own. In the beginning there was only Culture, as defined by tradition and authority. There was never any ambiguity as to who had Culture and who did not—it was entirely a matter of education (though sometimes of self-education). Nor was there any doubt as to who had more or less of it: a man who knew Greek and Hebrew as well as Latin was more Cultured than one who merely knew Latin. Popularizations of this Culture were sometimes provided for the improvement of the uneducated; but not very often.

The uneducated had their entertainments and diversions—singing, dancing, cockfighting, drinking, fornication, and an occasional festivity at the church. Existing as they did without benefit of anthropology, it never occurred to them or anyone else that this kind of thing could be regarded as Culture, or even as a Sub-culture. But with the spread of printing and literacy in the eighteenth and nineteenth centuries, something that could really be called "popular culture" began to emerge and multiply. It was epitomized by the sentimental romance, the Gothic horror tale, the penny-dreadful Western, the inspirational success story, popularizations of scientific and religious matters, the vast literature of self-improvement, self-help, self-education. There was inevitably some confusion as to whether certain commodities were Culture or "popular culture," especially since the novel, as a literary form, itself emerged from "popular culture" and has never disengaged itself from it. But, on the whole, it was pretty clear what was what and who was who. Nor was there much self-consciousness about the difference. One fails to find, in the nineteenth century, any serious concern with "popular culture" as a problem. Educated people could ignore it, when they did not surreptitiously enjoy it. And why not? It was limited in scope, unpretentious in its manner. Most important, it was a highly moral enterprise, in ostensible intent if not always in calculated effect. It accepted the conventional canons—as established by "high" culture— of good and evil, success and failure, in order to weave its narrative around them. Whatever its offense to intelligence and good taste, it did not represent any kind of threat to the moral and political order.

We, in contrast, are very sensitive to "popular culture" as representing just such a threat. To be more exact, we are on the defensive against "mass culture," which is what "popular culture" has become. Whereas "popular culture" was the culture of a class (the uneducated), "mass culture" is a culture shared, to a greater or lesser degree, by everyone. We all watch the same TV shows, read the same advertisements, see the same movies. As a result of the increase in popular wealth, popular taste now has a coercive power such as civilization has never before witnessed. By its sheer massive presence, "mass culture" tends to crowd culture of any other kind to the margins of society.

One does not want to sound like a prig or a snob. Daydreams and diversions are the stuff most people's daily lives are made of; the sentimentality, the inanity, the vulgarity of "mass culture" only become objectionable when they impose themselves upon society with such vigor as to set the tone, suggest the values, establish the context of life both private and public. And this is undeniably what is happening in the modern democracies. And yet one wonders: is it that "mass culture" is so powerful, or that its opposition is so impotent? A clue is provided by the tendency, not in itself so very surprising, of "mass culture" to degenerate into pornography. Now, pornography is, or need be, a problem of no great importance; one certainly would not want to do without it entirely. But what is revealing, as concerns both pornography itself and the larger problem of mass culture, is the complete inability of the "natural" leaders of opinion in the community—the educated class in general, the intellectuals in particular—to deal with this problem.

What is pornography? The fact that we ask this question in genuine puzzlement is itself a cultural phenomenon of the greatest symbolic significance. It testifies to the fact that the educated class has lost its footing. And this, in turn, is connected with the fact that the educated class of today is not "highbrow" at all, but post-highbrow, i.e., "modern." Its difficulties in reaching firm opinions on the "mass culture" which it apprehensively confronts derive from its kinship with it. As Leslie Fiedler has pointed out:

> It has been charged against vulgar art that it is sadistic, fetishistic, brutal, full of terror; that it pictures women with exaggeratedly full breasts and rumps, portrays death on the printed page, is often covertly homosexual, etc., etc. About these charges there are two obvious things to say. First, by and large, they are true. Second, they are also true about much of the most serious art of our time. . . . There is no count of sadism and brutality which

could not be equally proved against Hemingway or Faulkner. . . . Historically, one can make quite a convincing case to prove that our highest and lowest arts come from a common antibourgeois source . . . ; and there is a direct line from Hemingway to O'Hara to Dashiell Hammett to Raymond Chandler to Mickey Spillane.

The educated class of today, formed by the "modern" revolt against the "highbrow," is faced with the difficult task of rejecting pornography without repudiating itself. And the only reason this question of pornography is so provocative is that the startling lack of a ready answer makes it so.

The problem of differentiating between art and pornography has never been easy, if only because some pornographers are awfully talented. In our day, the task is well nigh impossible, and few there are (and these not necessarily the best equipped) who can face it. Thus, most members of the educated class in America will concede that pornography ought to be the object of legal sanctions. But these same people have never defined what pornography is; have never made any effort to discover such a definition; have resisted all urgings that they make such an effort. And, indeed, anyone who displays a genuine concern for the issue is regarded suspiciously as an enemy of art, an enemy of promise, an enemy of the free in spirit.

Instead of facing up to the issue, an elaborate ideology of evasion has been constructed. This ideology employs various arguments, as the occasion allows, but it relies primarily on the arguments from ignorance: we do not know what pornography is because standards of propriety and decency are always changing. We do not know what the effects of pornography are upon the consumer; it is always possible that by the vicarious discharge of sadistic aggressions, an individual's mental health may be, if not improved, then at least maintained in equilibrium. We do not know whether comic books that glorify brutality actually make children more brutal. We do not know—oh, there is so much we do not know! Only the other day a prominent American political scientist at one of our best universities argued before the Federal Communications Commission that it should not interfere with certain "objectionable" TV programs until a massive (and, needless to say, expensive) study had been made to determine what effects, if any, such programs had upon children.

No one can deny that all these arguments from ignorance have an element of truth in them. The only thing wrong with them is that they are impossible to live by. As cautions, they have their merit. But as guides, they lead nowhere. What they add up to is the assertion that we can never be sure of the difference between right and wrong, good and evil. True enough; but that is not the same thing as saying there is *no* difference between right and wrong, good and evil. And if such a distinction is made, it will have a bearing upon how we operate—or allow to operate—our mass entertainment media, our journalism, our book publishing, our educational system.

But who is going to make this authoritative distinction? And how? In the United States, the American Civil Liberties Union is always appearing in court to defend provocatively illustrated magazines, reeking with sadism and sly perversion, against police prosecution; its plea is that such legal action is an interference with literary freedom. And when the prosecuting attorney denies that these sheets can be regarded as literature at all, the ACLU retorts: "It is submitted, however, that any differences are those of taste." And it goes without saying that *de gustibus non* . . . etc. The net result is that the laws against pornography in the United States are enforced in an utterly capricious manner. Edmund Wilson's *Memoirs of Hecate County* is banned in New York State; *Playboy* circulates freely. This is what is bound to happen when the definition of "literature " is something that literary men, as a matter of aesthetic and political principle, refuse to essay.

Here we return to that central fact of the modern cultural situation: the destruction of the older "highbrow" elite whose declared purpose, and recognized function, was to "maintain standards." To some extent this elite was robbed of its authority by the rise of the "scientific expert" as the authoritative figure, in place of the "educated man." And the scientist naturally has a skepticism towards standards in general, emphasizing their "relative" nature. But mainly it was overthrown by the advent of "the modern" in arts and letters—a movement which denied the very legitimacy of this kind of authority, and which insisted that to be genuinely creative the artist had to be free to create his own standards, as well as his own art.

In those cases where fragments of the older elite still survive and exercise some influence (notably in England), they are regarded as figures of fun, rather ludicrous anachronisms. One has only to mention the name of Lord Reith to a London literary audience to evoke a smile—because Lord Reith, as Director General of the British Broadcasting Corporation in its formative years, put great emphasis on "maintaining standards." His BBC was exceedingly proper and unadventurous, respectful towards constituted authority and the taboos of middle-class morals. He was, moreover, solemnly patronizing of his audience. If the BBC provided a Light Program, it was not merely because ordinary people wanted and deserved a spot of fun; the Light Program had to be slanted in such a way that, in theory, it gently led its listeners upwards towards the slightly more serious Home Program; and the Home was similarly inclined towards the Third Program, at which apex one was fortunate enough to listen to either the bland chatter of Oxford dons or learned sermons on original sin.

Lord Reith is gone, and his spirit only intermittently flutters over the airwaves. Instead of the stuffy establishment of yesteryear there is Commercial Television *à l'Américaine* and a BBC television that is scarcely to be distinguished from the commercial variety. Already parents are indignant at the things their children (and, more rarely, themselves) are exposed to. A huge (and expensive) study by the Nuffield Foundation of the effects of TV on children came up with no definite conclusions; but people do not always need a social scientist to tell them what is happening in their homes. Those same sophisticates who were irritated to death by Lord Reith and all he stood for are now outraged by commercial television and all it stands for. But no one knows quite what to do. To be sure, one can always blame America, but not, convincingly, for long.

It is impossible genuinely to mourn the passing of the Mandarins and Brahmins of the older "highbrow" elite. Not all the things said against them were true or fair, by a long shot. But they not only deserved their fate; they positively courted it. Their notion of defending standards came to mean, in practice, a vigilant hostility to creative talent, as against mere mimicry. Above all, they seemed unaware of the fact that young people needed something more in life than the benevolent assurance that they would soon be middle-aged. And so they ended (or are ending) their days as sullen and sneering fulminators against modern "degeneracy" as exemplified by T. S. Eliot, Picasso, Stravinsky, etc.—their only audience, ironically, the popular press.

But now that they are gone, who is to do their job? Someone has to be able to say, with assurance and a measure of authority, what is culture and what is not, what is decent and is not. There must be some group or class that is admittedly competent to decide—not without error, but more wisely than anyone else—questions of moral and cultural value. Otherwise, a necessary and vital element of order in the life of a society will be lacking. Recently, in the United States, religious leaders, educators, and spokesmen for parents' organizations complained to the Federal Communications Commission that there was too much violence on TV. To which they received the official rejoinder that there is a great deal of violence in *Hamlet* too, and how could the United States Government lay down one rule for *Hamlet* and another for *Peter Gunn*? How could the United States government set itself up as an arbiter of taste? This was, presumably, reserved for the advertising agencies who are the only ones to show a passionate interest in the subject.

In England, the London County Council has withdrawn the tax exemption previously granted to the London Library, a private subscription library much used (and much beloved) by scholars, writers, and educated people generally. The Council authorities declared that some people enjoyed going to the movies, others enjoyed going to a library, and why should the pleasure of one be privileged above that of the other? Why indeed? Who is going to come out and say that, as a matter of principle, people who read good books in their leisure time should be privileged as against people who go to the movies? And who, if he does say this, will be listened to?

What it comes down to is this: we seem to have maneuvered ourselves into a situation in which the men of letters, the "intellectual" class, jealous of their own hard-won freedom from previous restrictions and suspicious of the state's meddling with questions of art, have made it extremely difficult for society as a whole to give official recognition to *Hamlet* as against, say, *Headquarters Detective*. Such instances of official recognition do exist, to be sure. But most of them go back some years, and are survivals rather than precedents.

Not only is there no class of people which can be regarded as both representing and forming "public opinion" on matters of culture. The very idea that such a class might exist is fast becoming nebulous. For instance, a prominent American sociologist, until recently a dean in a major university, conducted a study of American reading habits, and arrived at the following conclusions:

> Not only does the frequency of book-reading vary markedly, it is also unevenly distributed among the constituent groups of the community. For a variety of reasons some kinds of people read a great deal more and some not much. The major factor which differentiates readers from non-readers in research to date is education—in the limited sense of number of years of formal schooling. The more years of schooling the individual has, the more likely he is to read books. In one national survey only twelve per cent of the college-educated had not read a book in the preceding year as against seventy-five per cent of those with only grammar school education or less.
>
> Now, this might mean several things. It might mean that additional schooling has improved the individual's basic reading skills, or that it has developed his reading habits, or that it has produced in him the types of interests which are ordinarily satisfied by books, or even that the people who go on to further schooling already have a reading disposition which formal education only reinforces.

The ignorance is feigned, one knows. Our sociologist is not really puzzled as to why educated people read more books than non-educated people. He simply believes that he ought to be puzzled, and that is what is really interesting. For what it means is that the very existence of "culture" in the traditional sense of the term, the very idea of "the cultivated man," is but dimly apprehended. In place of a prescriptive definition of "culture" we have an anthropological-sociological one. "Culture" is whatever people do; some employ "reading skills" directed towards books, others presumably employ "viewing skills" directed towards TV; and the empirical fact that "reading skills" seem to be connected with education is a statistical correlation that needs further research to be explained.

Ludicrous as this is, it is but a *reductio ad absurdum* of a recognizable tendency, within all the Western democracies, for education, even higher education, to divorce itself from the task of forming character, habits, and tastes. Sometimes this is done candidly in the name of vocational training. At other times it proceeds under the guise of allowing "free development" to the students' natural bent. The end result is the same: the disappearance of a class of people which, by virtue of being educated, shares a cultural patrimony and is accepted by the community as providing spokesmen for this patrimony. Even in those places where it is still taken for granted that education has something to do with reading books, what is ignored is that the educated person is one who has learned how to read, enjoy, and profit from certain kinds of books— kinds that are defined by the cultural tradition. Future historians may yet decide that one of the crucial events of our century, perhaps decisive for its cultural and political destiny, was the gradual dissolution and abandonment of the study of the classics as the core of the school curriculum. We all know the many reasons (some of them cogent enough) why this happened. But we fail to appreciate sufficiently the extent to which it destroyed a vital constituency of any well-ordered society; and the manner in which our failure to define a new core for the educational process helped open the way to what can only be called the subversion of public morality in the democratic nations.

Public morality? The phrase sounds almost archaic. Most young people today, if asked what it meant, would probably refer vaguely to prohibitions against necking on the beach during daylight, or perhaps to the disapproval that attaches to a public official who flagrantly appropriates public funds for his private pleasure. Yet until not so very long ago, anyone who had ever given thought to the matter would have asserted, as a matter of course, that the ultimate basis of popular government was what in America was called republican morals, and in England civic virtue. As Edmund Burke put it: "Men are qualified for civil liberty, in exact proportion to their disposition to put moral chains upon their appetites; in proportion as their love of justice is above their rapacity; in proportion as their soundness and sobriety of understanding is above their vanity and presumption." Similar sentiments were expressed by

Madison, Jefferson, and Washington. If Burke was no believer in popular government, it was because he placed a lower estimate on the average man's moral capacities than did the Founders of the United States. There was no disagreement between them, however, on the fact that self-government was a distinctively moral enterprise.

This moral component of political life has, over the past decades, been depreciated. Ours is an age that is hypnotized by Impersonal Forces. We instinctively regard ourselves as their creatures, and we find our freedom in cajoling, mollifying, and humoring them. Much of our political activity can be described, without malice, as efforts to build socialism without socialists, communism without communists, democracy without democrats. Whenever we discuss the prospects for democracy in one of the new nations of Africa or Asia, we analyze the rate of economic growth, the efficiency of the civil service, the loyalty of the armed forces, the number of schools per ten thousand children, etc. We never inquire whether the people display those particular dispositions of mind and character that make popular government workable.

What are these dispositions? This is a large question, and any short answer will be inadequate. But it is not too gross an oversimplification to say that included among them must be: a veneration for the rule of law as against the rule of men; a reliance on common reason as the dominant human motive, as against superstition or passion; a sense of community that transcends class divisions and the recognition of a common good beyond individual benefits; a scrupulous use of liberties towards these ends for which those liberties were granted; a distribution of wealth and inequalities according to principles generally accepted as legitimate; moderation in the temper of public debate and public demeanor; etc. In every historical case one can think of, these attributes have been prior and prerequisite to democratic government. When they did not exist, or where they did not exist sufficiently strongly, democratic government faltered. And if a democratic government fails to sustain and encourage them, it is undermining its own foundations.

For, in the end, democratic government is governed by reasonable public opinion. And reasonable public opinion is not merely one that may be "well-informed" on matters within its comprehension and relevant to its judgment. It is, by definition and above all, an opinion that *wants* to be reasonable and truthful. This is the moral fundament of democracy; and it is this moral fundament that is under constant assault by much of that "mass culture" which is now being distributed through the mass media.

Take advertising, for instance, which plays so dominant a role in modern life that large numbers of people cannot bring themselves to read a magazine or watch a TV show that is not adorned with the familiar ads. They feel it is not really directed at them, that there is something "queer" about it. The bulk of advertising consists of lies, spiced with half-truths. The advertiser knows this; the advertising agencies know it; the consumers know it; the toddling infants know it. The "advertising game" is quite literally that, an effort to sell commodities by producing the most attractive, the most ingenious, the most beguiling hokum. Since everyone understands it is hokum, there is little substance to the nightmarish dread, evoked by some writers, of a society eventually to be ruled by a self-appointed elite of "hidden persuaders." The importation of advertising techniques into political campaigns is a disaster, not because they will produce a political Svengali, not because they play upon credulity, but because they create a universal disbelief and cynicism. Political rhetoric is debauched; the statesman's plea becomes indistinguishable from the huckster's "pitch"; persuasion merges into demagoguery—and is calmly accepted as indispensable to "politics."

Another instance: popular journalism. We are all well aware that a large section of the popular press makes no effort to report the news honestly. Frequently this is a result of political bias; more frequently it flows from a knowledge of what will capture the interest and titillate the prejudices of its readers. This phenomenon is now so common as to seem unremarkable. It is accepted as part of the democratic scheme of things and is shrugged off with an expression of "democratic faith": in a free competition between truth and falsehood for dominion over the minds of men, truth will eventually win out.

Yet no sensible man, contemplating the history of the human race, could seriously claim that truth always prevails over falsehood. And it is interesting to observe that this was not the claim of those who founded and formulated the philosophy of liberal democracy. What they said was that in a free competition between truth and *error*, the victory would finally be on the side of truth. The difference is by no means negligible. It is possible for truth to debate with error, to define itself in the very process of this debate, and for public opinion to be enlightened by the spectacle. But deliberate and cynical falsehood does not merely controvert truth. It challenges the idea which is at the heart of popular government, that the recognition of truth is not only a human but also a civic obligation. There is no such thing as a democratic right to lie, or a democratic freedom to lie. Such a liberty is reserved for a despotic society, whose state has its reasons that the citizen knoweth not. In contrast, democracy has an organic relation to enlightenment and truth.

Yet it is just this relation which is now being cavalierly discarded. Thus, Francis Williams, an experienced and eminent British journalist on the Left, has made a distinction between "serious" and "mass circulation" newspapers, allocating to the former the business of "informing and persuading public opinion" and to the latter the task of "expressing the emotions, and often no doubt the prejudice, ignorance, and silliness, of its readers." This is an entirely novel conception of the function of a free press, and it implies an entirely novel conception of democracy as that system of society which allows people to give the freest expression to their emotions, their ignorance, their silliness. It is doubtful that such a society could exist, but it is certain that no rational argument could be made in its defense, and that no popular government could long survive in it.

It is often said that "mass culture" is the price we pay for democracy. That all depends, of course, on what we mean by democracy. If we mean by democracy nothing more than government which is freely consented to by the people, then this may well be so. In that case, one can either deny that "mass culture" poses any problem at all, and attribute our unease to the influence of "pre-democratic" standards of taste and culture upon our laggard imaginations; or one can seek reassurance in the belief that "mass culture" is only a passing phase of democratic evolution, and that in due course of time the level of popular taste and judgment will rise to nobler heights. Both alternatives involve an act of faith in The People, resting on the premise that what emerges from them is necessarily good and/or necessarily self-correcting.

This may be called the populist religion of democracy, and there is no question but that it is the most common in our day. This can be seen from the frequency with which our publicists and statesmen make appeal to "the democratic faith" and "the democratic creed" as against other faiths and creeds, notably communism. It is also interesting to observe that when the advertising and television industries feel the need to perform acts of "public service" they conceive of their mission as "selling" this democratic faith to all and sundry.

Like all political religions, this one is relatively invulnerable to rational examination and critique. But, again like all political religions, it has to face the test of reality. And the reality seems to be that this idea of popular government, insofar as it is most loyally put into practice, has a tendency to become unpopular. There is certainly more open dissatisfaction with "the democratic faith" in America today than there was fifty years ago, when the barest hint of skepticism was tantamount to treason. Nor is there anything paradoxical about this state of affairs; it simply reflects the fact that what people want (or think they want) is not inevitably identical with, and may even contradict, what they need (i.e., what will truly satisfy them).

But this is not the only conception of democracy. And though it is now sovereign as an ideology, it is not the idea on which democracy in America and Britain was founded and which, to a greater or lesser degree, still rules the actual operations of government. That this is so in the United States is demonstrable by pointing to the existence of the Supreme Court—nine judges, appointed for life, with the power to nullify legislation (no matter how popular) that, in their considered opinion, is "unconstitutional" (a concept more vague than precise). There can be no doubt that, were a constitutional convention to be held today, no such thing as a Supreme Court could be set up; it would be regarded as flagrantly "undemocratic." (In those newer nations of Africa and Asia which have patterned themselves after the American system, either there is no such court or its powers are more formal than real.) Yet the Supreme Court, as originally established, has become an almost sacred institution, with which no politician dares tamper. In part, this is the sanctity that comes naturally with age. But in larger part, it is a tacit recognition that democratic government is something more than government that is popular in its origin: it is government that seeks justice as its aim.

It might be said that this is not a unique characteristic of democratic government, but is rather claimed by governments of all kinds. And it is indeed so. What this emphasizes is merely that democracy is not a self-justifying system of government; that it is not divinely ordained, any more than absolute monarchy is; and that the problem of reconciling popular government with good government is a very real one. And it is when one takes this problem seriously that one must take "mass culture" seriously. We have more evidence than we need or like that popular government can be oppressive, capricious, inadequate to its responsibilities. We have abundant testimony, too, to the truth that institutional safeguards, needed as they are, are not sufficient by themselves to protect a people against its own imprudence, its own passions. For these institutions cannot work unless they are respected, unless their legitimacy is freely acknowledged. And such respect and acknowledgment can only come from a people whose moral sense is sufficiently firm to know, not only that right and wrong exist, but that the distinguishing between them is not something they can achieve instinctively and unaided.

In the measure that people are encouraged to believe that what they want coincides with what they ought to want; in the measure that the mass media conceives it as its function to pander to "the prejudice, ignorance, and silliness" of its audience—in just such a measure is the moral fiber of democracy corrupted. Apologists for the crudities of "mass culture" are fond of pointing out that it is really nothing new, that the favorite sport of the English people, until it was abolished by law in 1835, was bear-baiting. Quite true. But what is overlooked is that, before 1835, there was hardly a thoughtful man who believed the mass of the English people to be ready for self-government by universal suffrage. This is not because (as our textbooks say) the very idea of democracy was novel and unfamiliar. Any educated person of that day knew a great deal about Periclean Athens and the Greek city-state. What he could not see was any resemblance between the Athenians who took part in popular assemblies and the Englishmen who took part in bear-baiting.

According to the Greek philosophers, the virtuous man was the man who exercised "self-government" over himself—over his passions, his impulses, his prejudices, his reasonings. Without such self-government in the individual, there could be no self-government in the state. Modern popular government is, of course, necessarily different from the Greek version. It involves large and representative republics rather than small and direct democracies. Only a utopian could expect virtuous men to be counted in the millions and tens of millions; the very difficulty of educating such a large number precludes it. But it is not utopian—or at least was not thought so by the thinkers of the eighteenth and nineteenth centuries who fathered the democratic idea—to believe that even such large numbers, suitably enlightened by instruction and example, could attain to a general level of decency and responsibility that allowed (though it could not, naturally, guarantee) virtuous and wise leadership to be exercised over them.

Whether such leadership will be forthcoming is the critical question that faces modern democracy. We know perhaps too well that democracy is government of, by, and for the people. What we need to remember is that, according to Thomas Jefferson, democracy was also a system in which "the natural aristocracy" of talent and virtue would find its most perfect fulfillment and satisfaction.

1960

What's Bugging
the Students

No one, except perhaps a few college administrators, mourns the passing of "the silent generation." But it must be said in its favor that at least one knew what the American university students of the 1950s were silent about, and why. They were conformist for plain, indeed, obvious and traditional, conformist reasons. We may have been distressed and vexed by this conformism; we were not mystified by it; whereas we are very much mystified by the nonconformism of the students of the sixties.

Many of the same middle-aged critics who so fervently and eloquently condemned the silent generation are now considerably upset and puzzled at the way students are "misbehaving" these days. One wanted the young to be idealistic, perhaps even somewhat radical, possibly even a bit militant—but not like this! It used to be said that the revolution devours its children. It now appears that these children have devoured this revolution. What is it all about? One thing is fairly clear: the teach-ins, the sit-ins, the lay-downs, the mass picketing, and all the rest are not merely about Vietnam, or civil rights, or the size of classes at Berkeley, or the recognition of Red China. They are about these issues surely, and most sincerely. But there is, transparently, a passion behind the protests that refuses to be satisfied by the various topics which incite it. This passion reaches far beyond politics, as we ordinarily understand that term. Anyone who believes the turbulence will subside once we reach a settlement in Vietnam is in for a rude surprise. Similarly, anyone who thinks of present-day campus radicalism as a kind of overzealous political liberalism, whose extremism derives from nothing more than youthful high spirits, is deceiving himself. What we are witnessing is an event *in* American politics, but not *of* it.

Indeed, one of the most striking features of the new radicalism on the campus is that it is, in one sense, so apolitical. It is a strange experience to see a radical mood in search of a radical program; it is usually very much the other way around. These young American radicals are in the historically unique position of not being able to demand a single piece of legislation from their government—their "platform" is literally without one legislative plank. Their passion for "freedom now" coexists with a remarkable indifference to everything the United States government is doing, or might do, in this direction. If one read every campus leaflet published these past two years and attended every campus or off-campus demonstration, and knew only what one learned from these sources, one would hardly be aware that the Johnson administration had enacted in the area of civil rights the most far-reaching reforms in a century of legislative history. There has been no campus meeting to celebrate the passage of the Civil Rights Act or the Voting Rights Act. There has not even been any meeting criticizing these laws for "not going far enough." It's as if nothing had happened—or, to put it more precisely, as if whatever happens in Washington has nothing to do with the world the students live and act in.

The same sort of thing is to be seen with regard to the war on poverty, a topic upon which students will declaim passionately and with unquestionable sincerity. But it seems that their passion is so pure, their sensibility so fine, that these would be violated by a consideration of anything so vulgar as how to get more money into poor people's pockets. The recent increase in Social Security and the Medicare bill made their way through Congress without the benefit of so much as a benevolent nod from the campuses. Whenever I have mentioned this legislation in conversation, I have received an icy stare of incomprehension and disdain, as if I were some kind of political idiot who actually believed what he read in the *New York Times*.

Even in the single area where one would most expect specific and tangible proposals of reform, the organization of the multiversity, these have not made their appearance. For an entire year the students of the University of California at Berkeley have given dramatic evidence of dissatisfaction with their university experience—and does anyone know specifically what they would like, by way of improvement? The university officials certainly don't know, nor do the regents, nor do the faculty. Some outsiders *think* they know. Berkeley is too large, they say, too anonymous; there is no possibility of a face-to-face community of scholars, young and old. This is true enough. But the Riverside branch of this same university is a small liberal arts college, with great intimacy and comfort, and for the past decade it has had much difficulty in attracting enough students. They all want to go to Berkeley, and the reason, they will explain, is: "That is where the action is."

The denunciations of the multiversity suspiciously resemble the way New Yorkers excoriate "megalopolis"—having come there in the first place, and determinedly remaining there, for no other reason than that New York *is* a megalopolis. All Americans will always insist that they adore small towns and detest great cities, but the movement of population from towns to cities remains strangely unaffected. And Berkeley, even today, has far more student applications than it can handle; one might even say, *especially* today, for I understand that the number of applications has, in fact, slightly increased.

No, the upsurge of left-wing sentiment and left-wing opinion on the American campus today is not the sort of thing progressive parents and educators had in mind ten years ago when they benevolently urged students to become "socially committed" and "more idealistic." They naïvely wished them to have intelligent discussions of Vietnam, not to hurl insults and epithets at Averell Harriman (as happened at Cornell), or tear up their draft cards, or laud the Viet Cong. They wished them to be urbane and tolerant about sex, not to carry placards with dirty words, or demand the sale of contraceptives in the college bookstore. They wished them to be concerned for civic and social equality for the Negro, not to denounce "white America" as a pious fraud, whose "integration" did not differ essentially from South Africa's apartheid, or express sympathy with a mindless (if occasionally eloquent) black nationalism. They wished—they wished, in short, that their children be just like them, only a wee bit bolder and more enlightened. Instead, these children are making it very clear that being just like their parents, progressive or not, is the fate they wish most desperately to avoid.

And this, I think, is the crux of the matter. The new student radicalism is so fundamentally at odds with our conventional political categories because it is, above all, an *existentialist* revolt. The term is unfortunately chic, and ambiguous too. But in this context it has a fairly definite meaning: the students are in rebellion, not so much because things are bad for them, or for others, but because things are what they are for them and for others.

Clues to the meaning of this rebellion may be found in two phrases that now appear ever more commonly in the left-wing campus vocabulary. The first is "organized America." The second is "participatory democracy." "Organized America" is, quite simply, America, and not, as one might think, some transient bureaucratic excrescence on the body of America. As a matter of fact, today's students are immensely skillful in coping with bureaucracies and their paperwork. They fill out forms and applications with a briskness and competence that startle the middle-aged observer. (I would guess that no one over the age of forty could properly fill out a college application form unless he received guidance from some kindly youngster.) What bugs the students is not these trivia but the society they emanate from, the affluent society, welfare state and all. The liberalism (and the radicalism too) of the 1930s and 1940s has borne its fruit, and it tastes bitter to the children, setting their teeth on edge. That is why American students, amidst reasonably general prosperity and under a liberal administration that is expanding the welfare state more aggressively and successfully than anyone had thought possible, feel more "alienated" than ever before. So many college students "go left" for the same reason that so many high school students "go delinquent." They are bored. They see their lives laid out neatly before them; they see themselves moving ahead sedately and more or less inexorably in their professional careers; they know that with a college degree even "failure" in their careers will represent no harsh punishment; they know "it's all laid on"—and they react against this bourgeois utopia their parents so ardently strove for.

One of the unforeseen consequences of the welfare state is that it leaves so little room for personal idealism; another is that it mutes the challenge to self-definition. All this is but another way of saying that it satisfies the anxieties of the middle-aged while stifling the creative energies of the young. Practically every college student these days understands what is meant by an "identity crisis"; it is one of the clichés of the sixties. It is not, perhaps, too much to say that mass picketing on the campus is one of the last, convulsive twitches of a slowly expiring American individualism. American youth, however, has had one grand idealistic experience: the civil rights movement. This has been the formative experience for the activists of the 1960s; it is this movement that gave them a sense of personal power and personal purpose; and it is the civil rights movement which instructed them in the tactics of civil disobedience that are now resorted to at the drop of a hat. Unfortunately, the civil rights movement has had one great drawback: so far from being a proper "dissenting" movement, it has behind it the president, Congress, the courts, the laws of the land, and a majority of public opinion. This fact helps explain why the younger militants have constantly pushed the movement toward "extremes"—for example, demanding utter, complete, and immediate equality of condition for the Negro, as against mere equality of opportunity.

Such equality of condition is what "freedom now" has come to mean. And since this demand cannot be fulfilled without repealing three centuries of history, and since even Lyndon Johnson hasn't figured out a way to do this, there is some satisfaction in such a maneuver. The trouble is that the students do not know how to fulfill this demand either, and are even running out of extremist slogans; which is why so many of them are receptive to the idea of switching their attention to Vietnam, where they can be more splendidly, less ambiguously, in "the opposition."

A second theme of student radicalism today, and a polar twin to the concept of "organized America," is the idea of "participatory democracy." This is a vague notion, but a dynamic one. It expresses a profound hostility toward, and proposes an alternative to, everything that is impersonal, manipulative, "organized" in the American political process. Indeed, many of these students simply dismiss American democracy as a sham, a game played by the "power structure" for its own amusement and in its own interests. True democracy, they insist, can only mean direct democracy, where the people's will is expressed and legislated by the people themselves rather than by elected representatives, most of whom achieve office by deceit and retain office through the substantial support offered them by the vested interests.

One is reminded by this of nothing so much as the Russian Narodniki ("populists," our textbooks call them) of the end of the nineteenth century. They, too, were largely middle-class students who selflessly turned their backs on the careers the Czarist bureaucracy offered them. They, too, "returned to the people," leaving the fleshpots of Petrograd for the villages of the interior, much as our students leave their comfortable homes in New York or Chicago for southern ghettos and slums. And they, too, were hostile to the nascent liberal institutions of their day, seeing political salvation only in a transformed and redeemed people rather than in improvements in any kind of system of representative government. It is also interesting to recall that, though they were as individuals the gentlest and most humane of their time, they nevertheless believed in the justice and efficacy of terrorism against the status quo and assassination against its spokesmen.

The analogy is, of course, very superficial: the United States today is not Czarist Russia of yesterday. But it is nevertheless illuminating, because it helps reveal the inner logic of the idea of "participatory democracy," a logic which proceeds from the most exemplary democratic premises to the most illiberal conclusions. Though few students these days learn it in their social studies course, the Founders of the American republic were exceedingly familiar with the idea of "participatory democracy." As a matter of fact, this was what the word "democracy" usually meant prior to 1789. They rejected "participatory democracy" (they called it "direct democracy") in favor of "representative government" for two reasons. First, they didn't see how it could work in so large and complex a nation, as against a small city-state. Second, and more important, they thought it inconsistent with the idea of free government—that is, a government that respected the liberties of the individual. For participatory democracy requires that all people be fit to govern; and this in turn requires that all people be made fit to govern, by rigid and uniform educational training, constant public indoctrination, close supervision of private morals and beliefs, and so forth. No legislator can be as free as a private citizen, and to make all the people legislators is willy-nilly to abolish the category of private citizen altogether.

This, of course, is exactly what the communists do, after their own fashion. They claim to exemplify a truer, more "direct," more "participatory," more "popular" democracy than is to be found in the representative institutions of the bourgeois West. The claim has a certain plausibility, in that regimes established by mass movements and mass revolutions certainly "involve the people" more than does any merely elected government. The semblance of "involvement" is perpetuated, as we know, through the mass organizations of the communist state, and the fact that it is done under compulsion, and becomes more of a farce with every passing communist year, is one of the inner contradictions both of the communist system and of the myth of direct democracy itself.

These contradictions our left-wing students are not entirely unaware of. Though many of them are, to one degree or another, either pro-communist or belligerently "neutralist," theirs is a very qualified and unconventional version of this attitude; which is why conventional anti-communist propaganda tends to pass them by. They are, for instance, extraordinarily uninterested in the Soviet Union, and they become ever less interested to the degree that the Soviet Union liberalizes its regime—that is to say, to the extent that the Soviet Union becomes merely another "organized" system of rule. What they seek is a pure and self-perpetuating popular revolution, not a "planned economy" or anything like that. And this is why they are so attracted to Castro's Cuba and Mao's China, countries where the popular revolution has not yet become "bourgeoisified." As for mass terror in Cuba and China—well, this actually may be taken as a kind of testimony to the ardor and authenticity of the regime's revolutionary fervor. Our radical students, like other radical students before them, find it possible to be genuinely heartsick at the injustices and brutalities of American society, while blandly approving of injustice and brutality committed elsewhere in the name of "the revolution."

Like other radical student generations before them, they are going to discover one day that their revolution, too, has been betrayed, that "organized society" is what revolutions establish as well as destroy. One hopes they will not be made too miserable by their disillusionment. One also hopes, it must be added, that they won't make *us* too miserable before that day arrives.

1965

Vice and Virtue in
Las Vegas

They smiled indulgently when I said I was going to visit my sister and brother-in-law in Las Vegas. Oddly enough, I was telling the truth—well, half the truth anyway. The other half of the truth, of course, was that I was going to Las Vegas to indulge in the vice of gambling.

I use the word "vice" advisedly. The kind of gambling one does in Las Vegas *is* a vice. We are not, after all, talking about a friendly and convivial game of poker or canasta. That is more in the nature of "gaming" than of gambling. There is nothing friendly or convivial about Las Vegas. It is all impersonal and solitary; one abandons oneself to fantasies of omniscience, of omnipotence, and of getting something for nothing. It most definitely undermines the classical virtues (moderation, self-reliance, self-discipline, thrift, diligence, etc.) while nourishing the classical vices (extravagance, avarice, the lack of social responsibility, etc.). Moralists and psychiatrists agree that this kind of gambling is altogether a bad thing, which is, I suppose, why it is so intensely pleasurable.

I have always been rather fond of Las Vegas because it candidly is an utterly vicious place (i.e., a place for vice). Despite the big-name entertainment and the lavish decor, everyone knows what the business of Las Vegas is, and everyone knows what transactions he has come to participate in. Set in the midst of a barren desert, with no industry of any kind, no pretty scenery or natural charms, Las Vegas exists for sinning and nothing else. Or at least it used to. For Las Vegas is changing. Not only are more and more people coming every year; they are a different kind of people. Las Vegas now boasts a Holiday Inn and a Howard Johnson's. And it is attracting, in ever greater numbers, a Holiday Inn and Howard Johnson's crowd—cluttered station wagons, yelping dogs, whining children, and all. The Chamber of Commerce is very proud of the fact that so many "middle Americans" are now casually stopping off here for a few days of fun and games. I am appalled. It is not only that they will ruin Las Vegas as an authentic city of occasional sin. These are people who are helping to obliterate the distinction between vice and innocent entertainment, a distinction crucial to a self-governing polity, in which (to quote a phrase from "America the Beautiful") we propose to "confirm our soul in self-control."

Las Vegas inverts the normal moral situation: here, vice is public and only virtue is a private affair. Such inversion *is* tolerable so long as one realizes how abnormal it is. But once Las Vegas comes to be regarded as just another vacation resort, to which one takes the family without a qualm, we are in danger of losing our moral bearings. Las Vegas may end up more virtuous, but only by de-moralizing the rest of the country.

The significance of the changes under way in American manners and morals is highlighted by the latest issue of *Forbes* to reach the Las Vegas newsstands. Its lead story, "Gambling: The Hottest Growth Industry?" predicts, with a confidence not to be challenged, the growing legalization of gambling in state after state. The cover is graced with a photograph of the late W. C. Fields peering from behind a "hand" of cards. Only four cards are visible; the fifth is presumably up his sleeve. Now, I yield to no man in my admiration of W. C. Fields. A world without such deviants and eccentrics and rebels against morality would be a curious place. But for a W. C. Fields to emerge in full splendor, he needs a "straight" milieu. One can envisage him easily enough at a typical Holiday Inn, selling snake oil or running a crooked game of bingo. In Las Vegas, he'd be trampled to death by the rush of housewives to the slot machines.

Do we really want to go the way of legalized gambling? There are important issues involved, which no one seems to be seriously discussing. In part, this is because serious discussion of moral issues—e.g., drugs, pornography, sexual promiscuity—goes against the spirit of the age, which would have trouble recognizing a moral issue if it ran over one on Main Street, in broad daylight. But in the case of gambling there is another reason why the moral aspect of the matter is so vigilantly ignored. This is because, when we are talking about legalizing gambling, we are in most cases talking about legalizing it in a very special way, as either socialized industry or a regulated and monopolistic (or at least oligopolistic) "public utility." And we are inclined to think, these days, that such an extension of the public sector represents a natural increment to the "welfare state."

The most common argument in favor of legalizing gambling is that a lot of people gamble anyway, so why make it a criminal activity? Let's "de-criminalize" it and thereby reduce the crime statistics. Despite its superficial plausibility, this argument makes little sense. If it is to be applied to gambling, it can be applied with equal cogency to faith-healing, "pyramid" sales schemes, and all such activities, now illegal, where the victim is a willing participant in the crime. The SEC does not sanction stock market swindles, even where the odds against the investor are scrupulously spelled out somewhere in a prospectus. And gambling, as distinct from what I have called "gaming," is, technically, a swindle; the payoffs on bets must be less than fair, and the overwhelming majority of the "investors" must eventually lose their money, if the gambling enterprise is to survive and prosper.

Besides being unconvincing, this argument in favor of legalized gambling is disingenuous. Just how disingenuous may be discovered by asking the question: if we wish to legalize gambling, why not simply erase the prohibitions from the law books and leave the rest to private enterprise? The rejoinder will be either (a) that gambling under private enterprise will cheat the ordinary gambler more than the state will (which is not always true, as every horse-bettor in New York City knows), or (b) that profits from such a sinful activity as gambling ought not to line private pockets but should rather be directed into the public purse. That last proposition is clearly absurd in its moral logic; as George Will has pointed out, the fact that government cannot prevent people from being self-destructive is no reason for government to enter the self-destruction business on a grand scale. But morally absurd or not, this is the argument that counts. The case for legalized gambling is, at bottom, simply an argument in favor of the government raising revenues by swindling its citizens rather than by taxing them.

The article in *Forbes* makes it quite clear that the impetus for legalized gambling comes from the promise it holds of raising substantial revenues in a "painless" way. When the idea of legalized gambling began to take shape some years back, our state budgets were indeed in bad shape. But today that is no longer the case. For various reasons—revenue sharing, the declining birth rate, general prosperity—most states are now running budgetary surpluses, and tax cuts are becoming more common than tax increases. Nevertheless, there are a great many people in our society whose notion of "progressive" politics is always to be thinking of new ways for the government to spend money for the welfare of its citizens. And since taxation *is* unpopular, these people have persuaded themselves that it is in the public interest for the government to swindle its citizens so that it can then launch programs that would improve their lives, materially and spiritually.

As a result, various forms of legalized gambling are already in existence in several states while other states are contemplating the inauguration of them.

And we have learned something very interesting from our experience so far. This is that legalized gambling, if it is to "work" (i.e., raise revenues), must be run like any other business selling any other commodity. It has to be advertised and promoted: nongamblers have to be *persuaded* to gamble. It has to be attractively packaged: there must be various forms of gambling to suit pocketbooks large and small, and to satisfy diverse tastes for a speculative fling. It must be innovative: new modes of gambling have to be devised and introduced, lest people become bored with losing their money. It must be deceptive: the odds against winning are emphatically not printed on your betting ticket. And both the stakes and the bets have constantly to be increased, so people can ignore their continuing losses while dreaming of an ultimate "killing."

In short, when government gets into the gambling business it necessarily assumes the responsibilities for seeing that this business grows and prospers. In effect, it proclaims that gambling is not a necessary evil but an inherently good thing. And it does this while telling its citizens that, if they are to be good Americans, they should work hard, save their money, shun all get-rich-quick schemes. Is this not ridiculous? Does it really make sense for the government to insist that no one has a legal right to work for a penny less than the minimum wage and for the government then to encourage us all to blow our week's wages at the betting cage? Does it really make sense for the government to enact a mountain of legislation, from SEC registration to the labeling of consumer products, which protects people from unwise expenditures while urging them to make the unwisest expenditure of all, i.e., a gambling bet?

Of course it is ridiculous. And dishonest. And corrupting, of both people and government. But the urge to spend the people's money for the people's welfare is so powerful (and so mindless) that it actually comes to seem proper to cheat the people in order to get this money to spend on their welfare. This is paternalism run amok. I have no doubt that there are some silly anti-*gaming* laws on the books—petty laws, ineffectual laws, which ought simply to be repealed. And if we really are tired and bored with enforcing the laws against *gambling*, then the honest thing to do is to repeal them as well. Gambling will then be the free folly of an individual.

But if we legalize gambling in principle, and then socialize it to boot, we have declared that it is in no way a blameworthy activity. That's going too far. One Las Vegas, far away and only sometimes visited, we can easily tolerate, even benignly tolerate. But one is quite enough.

1973

Reflections of a
Neoconservative

How have my literary, cultural, and political views changed over the past decades? My answer to that question is as clear to me as, I believe, it is to others: I have become more "conservative" in all of those views. The answer, however, gets rather more complicated when one tries to explain the nature of that change and the reasons for it.

Partisan Review had as its self-declared mission the union of "modern sensibility" in literature and the arts with the "radical consciousness" in politics. That mission was accomplished in the 1960s, though in a totally unforeseen way. It is a case, once again, of nothing having failed like success. For it turned out that this "modern sensibility" could be disengaged from the "highbrow" avant-garde tradition that *PR* celebrated and find a powerful, energetic, but, by *PR*'s original standards, debased existence in what was once contemptuously dismissed as the "middlebrow" and "popular" levels of culture.

It is both sad and ironic to observe the ways in which the original elite of *PR*'s *ancien régime* reacted to this new situation. Basically, they, at least most of them, decided that the "modern" they wished to be associated with ended about 1950. Clement Greenberg and Harold Rosenberg, those *enfants terribles* of "modern" art criticism, found themselves writing polemics against the very latest versions of modern sensibility in the arts. The avant-garde was now the old avant-garde, which is to say, the old guard. Meyer Schapiro, the leading academic expositor and defender of impressionism, cubism, expressionism, surrealism, and even abstract expressionism, retreated into his scholarly citadel. Lionel Trilling wrote some typically sensitive and thoughtful essays on the dilemma that he, the first to teach "modern" literature at Columbia University, had created for himself. William Barrett and Lionel Abel turned to the study of contemporary philosophy and ended up more or less "conservative." Along with secession, incrimination, and self-examination, there went co-optation. Mary McCarthy suddenly discovered that the infusion of the "modern sensibility" into the hitherto middlebrow realm of culture permitted her novels and stories to be quite popular and commercially successful. Similarly, a significant number of *PR* writers—McCarthy, Rosenberg, Edmund Wilson, Hannah Arendt—began appearing regularly in the pages of the once-despised *New Yorker*.

Clearly, the new modernism was not anything like the ideal culture *PR* had had in mind. To begin with, it did (does) unquestionably involve a lowering of the entire cultural level. Norman Mailer, whatever his talent, is no James Joyce or William Faulkner, just as Susan Sontag, gifted though she is, is no Lionel Trilling. Moreover, it represented a significant shift from culture as something to be produced to culture as a commodity to be consumed. Whereas "bohemianism" once meant a "lifestyle" organically associated with the presumed endeavor by a chosen few to produce art, it had now become nothing more than a mass "lifestyle" for millions who wished to declare themselves as potential consumers of art. Inevitably, too, "modernism" was thoroughly commercialized in the process. "Serious" writers took it for granted that they ought to be best-sellers, and most in fact now were. The distance between artists and writers, on the one hand, and Madison Avenue and café society, on the other, shrank into nothingness. The comparison of Andy Warhol with Jackson Pollock illustrates the point quite adequately.

Meanwhile, a parallel debasement was occurring in the area of radical thought. As more and more self-declared "socialist" societies emerged in the postwar world, and as they could be clearly perceived to be more or less totalitarian, ranging from the thoroughly disagreeable to the utterly hideous, the viability of the socialist idea itself came into question. Not so, however, with the newer generation of modernists of the 1960s, whose extreme individualism in culture was nicely complemented by an extraordinary tolerance of, even sympathy with, the totalitarian mode in politics. Primarily anticapitalist, antibourgeois, they would take their socialism as they found it, not as an older generation of socialists had once envisioned it. And in the course of the 1960s and 1970s, newer academic versions of Marxism, largely imported from France and Germany, provided a convenient rationalization for this posture. What most of these versions had in common was the belief that "socialism" could be imposed on society by a revolutionary movement of artists, intellectuals, and students—defining all these categories very loosely, of course—and that the evidently hopeless working class had lost the revolutionary charter which Marx had originally granted it. "*L'imagination au pouvoir*," as the Parisian students of

1968 proclaimed—a slogan subsequently put into practice by one student in Paris known to us as Pol Pot.

How did the original *PR* generation react to these developments? In all sorts of ways. Some, like Harold Rosenberg and Meyer Schapiro, kept their distance from the new "radical consciousness" while insisting on their loyalty to an increasingly wispy radical ideal. Others simply ceased to be radical. Some others tried to go with the trend, at least for a while, and to be youthfully radical once more. (Mary McCarthy was the most notable of these.) Philip Rahv made a heroic effort to meld the older radicalism with the new, but he ended up a pathetic, isolated, embittered partisan of a cause without followers. As in culture, so in politics: the new "radical consciousness," like the new "modernist" consciousness, left *Partisan Review* stranded in a time warp.

What went wrong? Or did anything go wrong? When Stalinist totalitarianism emerged out of the Bolshevik revolution, a great many radicals, including those around *Partisan Review*, became intensely interested in the question of whether the seeds of Stalinism were to be found in Bolshevism, or whether Stalinism could be explained (away?) as a creature of special Russian circumstances. The debate around this issue was lively and provocative of thought. And, in the end, the conclusion was inescapable: Stalinism did indeed have roots in Leninism and Bolshevism, so that a revision of the older "radical consciousness" was in order.

It seems to me to be time for another such discussion on the subject of "modernism" and the "radical consciousness." Just where and when did the seeds of eventual decay get planted? Trotsky used to argue that the Soviet Union under Stalin was a "degenerated" workers' state, but still a workers' state worth defending. Similarly, there are those who insist that, though today's "modernism" and today's "radical consciousness" may be "degenerative" specimens of modernism and the radical consciousness, the cultural and political modes themselves are worth defending. Is the second argument destined to go the way of the first?

Even to raise that question, of course, is to define oneself as some kind of conservative, if only an incipient kind of conservative. Just what "conservative" means, politically and culturally, in the last quarter of this turbulent twentieth century, it is not so easy to say. But, then, it is not so easy to say what "radical" or "modernist" means either. We do live, I am convinced, in one of those historic conjunctures when inherited categories of thought, dominant for some two hundred years now, have lost their creative vitality, though not, to be sure, their destructive energies. It is no accident, as one used to say, that there is an ever-growing interest among some of our brightest young people in premodern thinkers. This is a healthy, if still indeterminate, sign.

Meanwhile, for myself, I have reached certain conclusions: that Jane Austen is a greater novelist than Proust or Joyce; that Raphael is a greater painter than Picasso; that T. S. Eliot's later, Christian poetry is much superior to his earlier; that C. S. Lewis is a finer literary and cultural critic than Edmund Wilson; that Aristotle is more worthy of careful study than Marx; that we have more to learn from Tocqueville than from Max Weber; that Adam Smith makes a lot more economic sense than any economist since; that the Founders had a better understanding of democracy than any political scientists since; that . . . well, enough. As I said at the outset, I have become conservative, and whatever ambiguities attach to that term, it should be obvious what it does not mean.

1984

It's Obscene but Is It Art?

Once upon a time, when the idea of a National Endowment for the Arts was under consideration, I had some lively arguments with my conservative friends. I supported the idea, they opposed it. Their opposition was based on the simple and straightforward principle that the state had no business involving itself in this area, which should be left to private philanthropy. I argued that it would be good for our democracy if it showed an official interest in educating the tastes and refining the aesthetic sensibilities of its citizenry.

I won the argument and now wish I hadn't. They were more right than, at the time, they could know. In retrospect, I can see that my error derived from the fact that I really had only a superficial understanding of what was happening in the arts world and no understanding of what this portended for the future evolution of what we now call "the arts community." I was raised in a generation that was taught to appreciate the virtues of modern art, from Renoir to Picasso and even to Jackson Pollock and "abstract expressionism," though I had to admit that this last stage had no appeal to me. "Pop art" and "minimalist art" I tended to dismiss as trendy fads. But what I was utterly unprepared for was the emergence of what is now called "postmodern art," which is a politically charged art that is utterly contemptuous of the notion of educating the tastes and refining the aesthetic sensibilities of the citizenry. Its goal instead is deliberately to outrage those tastes and to trash the very idea of an "aesthetic sensibility."

It is very difficult to convey to people who do not follow the weird goings-on in our culture an appreciation of the animating agenda of the "arts community" today. An ordinary American reads about a woman "performing artist" who prances nude across the stage, with chocolate smeared over her body, and though he may lament the waste of chocolate or nudity, it does not occur to him that she is "making a statement," one that the "arts community"

131

takes seriously indeed. Even museum trustees in Washington, D.C., or Cincinnati—an elite, educated, and affluent group of arts philanthropists—had no idea what Mapplethorpe was up to in his photograph of a man with a bullwhip handle inserted into his rectum. All they knew is that Mapplethorpe was a very talented photographer (which he was), that no such talent could ever create an obscene work (which is false), and that any discriminating judgment on their part was a form of censorship that verged on the sacrilegious. Those trustees are there to raise money and watch the museum's balance sheet. They may or may not know what they like, but they would never presume to assert what is, or is not, "art." To qualify to become a museum trustee these days one must first suffer aesthetic castration.

To reach our current condition, it took a century of "permanent revolution" in the arts, made possible, ironically, by a capitalist economy which created affluent art collectors and entrepreneurial art dealers. "Patrons" of the arts were replaced by "consumers" of the arts, giving the artist an intoxicating freedom. It was the artist, now, who told us what was and was not "art"—not the patron, or the philosopher, or the public. The function of the spectator was to welcome revolutions in taste by permitting himself to be intimidated and indoctrinated by the "arts community," consisting of artists themselves but also and especially (since artists are not usually articulate) art critics, art professors, art dealers, museum directors, etc. The most important spectators who were so intimidated and indoctrinated were the media, which now automatically approach anything declared to be "art" by the "arts community" with the kind of deference, even pseudo-piety, once reserved for the sphere of religion.

As with most revolutions, some impressive creative energies were released, some enduring accomplishments were achieved. But, again as with most revolutions, the longer it lasted the more the destructive impulse began to dominate over the creative. Yesteryear's creative contributions were, after all, what the latest revolutionary phase had to subvert and overthrow. After World War II, it became ever more difficult to distinguish artists from publicity-hungry pseudo-artists, from people "making statements" of one kind or other, such "statements" being the essence of pop art, minimalist art, environmental art, and now postmodern art. That practically all of this activity was infused by an anti-bourgeois ethos was unsurprising, since it was simply mirroring the literary and academic culture in this respect. The bourgeois way of coping with this situation was to purchase and "consume" this art as a commodity, to inventory it, and then at some point to expel it from its system into an underground sump, usually located in the basement of museums. Cooptation, not censorship, was the strategy.

But this strategy does not work with the last and, one suspects, final phase of the revolution we are now witnessing. Today the destructive element has almost completely overwhelmed the creative. What the "arts community" is engaged in is a politics of radical nihilism; it has little interest in, and will openly express contempt for, "art" in any traditional sense of the term. It is no exaggeration to say that the self-destruction of "art" is a key point in its agenda, accompanied by the "deconstruction," not only of bourgeois society, but of Western civilization itself.

"Deconstruction" is an intellectual-ideological movement that is enormously popular in the humanities departments of our universities, which seek to free themselves from the "hegemony" of Dead White Males (DWMs is the common reference) such as Shakespeare or Dante so as to justify offering a university course on, say, the TV program *The Simpsons*. There are no standards of excellence other than those we improvise for ourselves, which is why members of the "arts community" can solemnly believe and assert that whatever they do is "art." The public has the right, nay, the obligation, to support it, but not to question it.

What they do, in fact, is powerfully shaped by certain radical ideological currents; radical feminism, homosexual and lesbian self-celebration, and black racism are among them. This explains why, though it is *de rigeur* to insult public figures, no one in the "arts community" would ever dare insult the Rev. Louis Farrakhan. Any such painting would promptly be vandalized, to the applause of an "arts community" opposed to censorship. It also explains why there is so little pornography, in the traditional sense, in postmodern art. Such pornography evokes lust for heterosexual engagement, which postmodern art disapproves of since it is thought to debase women. Only homosexual and lesbian sex are allowed to be celebrated.

But if pornography is limited to the homosexual sphere, obscenity is unlimited. The purpose of such obscenity is to deride the Judeo-Christian-humanist idea of "human dignity" that Western civilization has fostered. If Western civilization is itself an obscene heritage of racism, sexism, and "elitist" oppression, obscenity is obviously an appropriate response. Where will it all end? One does have the sense that we are witnessing either a final convulsion in the history of modern art (and of modern culture) or, perhaps, a final convulsion in Western civilization itself. Most of us would incline to credit the first alternative. But where does that leave the National Endowment for the Arts, founded in a different time and on quite different assumptions about the role of the arts in American life?

The most obvious response would be to abolish the NEA, perhaps over a period of a few years to mitigate the financial shock. This is not going to happen, however. After all, many major institutions—symphony orchestras, for instance, and large museums—have inevitably become dependent on NEA grants. The trustees of these institutions have considerable influence with members of Congress, who are much happier opening funding spigots than closing them. And the media, it goes without saying, would be horrified at such an effort at "censorship," now redefined to include the absence of government funding. A more limited response would be to move the NEA away from involvement with the most active and turbulent sectors of the "arts community" by requiring that it make only grants of more than $50,000 or $100,000. The institutions receiving this money will be held responsible for any re-grants they make.

Most of the controversial grants one hears of are small to modest. But they do serve an important role in legitimating the activity that is being funded. With $10,000 from the NEA, an "experimental workshop in the arts" can approach foundations and corporations with a plausible claim to respectability. That is precisely why they will fight tooth and nail for the continuation of the small-grants program—grants made by other members of the "arts community," their "peer groups," to their friends and allies. Just how Congress will respond to such a reform, now being bruited, remains to be seen.

But one interesting and important fact has already become clear: our politics today is so spiritually empty, so morally incoherent, that, except for a few brave souls, liberals have been quick to dismiss as "yahoos" anyone who dares to confront this assault on the foundations of liberalism and conservatism alike. A great many conservatives, for their part, having long ago been ideologically disarmed, are more embarrassed than interested at having to cope with this issue at all. Something is definitely rotten in the vital areas of our body politic.

1990

The Way We Were

When I discuss social issues and social problems today, I frequently find myself running up against a blank wall of incomprehension. Most of my interlocutors have no memories of what life was like in America prior to the emergence of the welfare state. They know that things were hard in the 1930s and early 1940s, as indeed they were. The average American in those years had a much lower standard of living than the average black American of today. But, while things were hard, in some important respects they were better. To know this, to appreciate this, it helps to be a senior citizen, especially one born and raised in a working-class neighborhood.

This absence of memory warps the way we think about the present. Take the issue of crime. My younger contemporaries are astonished to learn, are, in truth, disbelieving, when I tell them that, in the midst of the Depression, crime was never an issue that agitated ordinary New Yorkers. Oh yes, there was plenty of crime, and my family was well aware of it, since three cousins of mine spent years in prison. (I hasten to add that my other thirty-one cousins did not.) But most of this crime was either intra-family or organized crime (prostitution, gambling, extortion) that provided sensational headlines but rarely touched the lives of most of us, as today's disorganized crime does. Street crime was practically unheard of; "mugging" was not part of our vocabulary. New York's subways were absolutely safe, even in the dark of night. Rape was rare.

A recent and wonderful book by Professor David Gelernter on New York's World's Fair of 1939 quotes an English visitor: "One may walk the streets without seeing anything more criminal than the solicitation of alms or the manifestation of inebriation." It also quotes a contemporary guidebook: "Don't go to Harlem unless you have an escort. Not because it's dangerous, but because it's dull." In short, though New York was not in other respects a particularly good city to grow up in, considerations of personal safety were not a factor.

Crime is a complicated phenomenon, but I am convinced that the current therapeutic attitude—as distinct from the more traditional, "simple-minded," punitive attitude—toward criminals (and suspected criminals) must bear some of the responsibility for its rise. Prior to the victory of modern liberal dogmas in the early 1950s, the police and the courts could cope with common street crime, as well as burglaries or robberies, without having to defer to a catalog of criminals' constitutional rights, most of which, at the time, were still undiscovered. It may have made for less perfect justice, but it did deter wanton criminality among the young and ensured a more trusting, less fearful society.

Or take education, a subject of such great controversy today. In my youth, there was very little such controversy, as a perusal of the newspapers will reveal. There was then no such thing as a "bad" public school in New York. Oh yes, there were better and less good schools in terms of academic achievement, but this was the result of the kinds of students who attended particular schools— their socioeconomic background, their family situation, their ethnic self-definition with its emphasis, or lack thereof, on the importance of schooling. Everyone understood this, without benefit of sociological inquiry. The schools themselves were held blameless. After all, every school offered the same text-books, the same teaching methods, and the same, or comparable, exams. The only breach in this uniformity was "tracking," which assigned students to classes according to their demonstrated academic abilities. Everyone accepted this as a perfectly sensible educational idea. Class size was large by current standards. Sometimes desks and seats had to be shared. No one saw any educational significance in this, and they were right. Because there were no "troubled" schools, attending the elementary school within walking distance was taken for granted.

The reason there were no "troubled" schools is that "trouble" was not tolerated. Discipline, by our standards, was strict. Students were expected to show respect for their school by being "decently" dressed. Sneakers, for instance, were not allowed in the classrooms. Though so many parents were poor enough to qualify for "relief," they did manage to send their children to school "decently" dressed. And clean, too, for there was a cleanliness code. There were no subsidized lunchrooms, but hungry schoolchildren were not a New York phenomenon. We were told that it was different in the South, where share-croppers were really poor. But what about "troubled" and unruly students? There weren't many, I never heard a student "cussing out" a teacher, and the notion of a student physically attacking a teacher was unimaginable. Most "troubled" students were truants. If their truancy was too gross to be ignored, they were shipped off to a "reformatory." To this day, I don't know exactly what that was, but I do know that those truants seemed much chastened when they returned to class. After elementary school, or when they reached the school leaving age of fifteen, they often "dropped out" (though the phrase itself had not yet been coined). What they did then was their parents' problem, not the school's. Schools existed to educate children who, however reluctantly, were willing to be educated. And educated they were. A reader for the sixth grade in 1940, according to Dr. Gelernter, assumed a knowledge of twenty-five thousand words, as against ten thousand for the 1990 edition. All high school graduates were at least minimally literate and numerate.

Perhaps no other issue excites such hysteria today as does censorship, and the threat it supposedly poses to our liberties. But from the founding of the Republic until 1950, we lived under a system of censorship of pornography and obscenity, and just about the only people who seemed interested in the matter were book publishers mourning lost sales. This censorship was for the most part local, so that books banned in Boston could be bought in, say, New York. Only when the federal government intervened—as in the case of James Joyce's *Ulysses*—were the blunders of censorship highly irritable. In all of American history until 1900, I do not know of a single case where the prohibition against pornography/obscenity was directed against political speech, political writings, or scholarly books. So much for its hypothetical "chilling effect." As for its harming artistic creativity, it is worth noting that the same cultural historians who froth at the mouth at the very mention of censorship casually refer to the decades from 1920 to 1950 as the "golden age" of Hollywood (despite censorship by the Hayes Office), of the American novel, and of the American theater. When Fiorello La Guardia was mayor of New York, he decided unilaterally that it was subversive of the quality of life in that city for people to be free to attend burlesque shows (the forerunners of our own topless dancing). The courts upheld his right to make them illegal. Those shows then moved to Jersey City, but very few New Yorkers bothered to follow them. If "free expression" in New York City suffered from La Guardia's action, it has occurred to no one to try to demonstrate it.

Today, if an artist is denied a grant from the National Endowment for the Arts, he or she screams "censorship." Today, if a school board decides that certain books are inappropriate for its school library, the librarian cries "censorship." The American Library Association has convinced itself that only the school librarian has the constitutional right of book selection. Hollywood, for its part, has decided that it is a "creative community," populated by "artists," so that any interference with its pursuit of prosperity by producing entertainment with soft porn, hard porn, or obscene violence is a censorship that threatens all freedom of expression, and our civil and human rights as well. The confusion between liberty and license, or entitlement and privilege, is one of the least endearing traits of the American character today.

I am not suggesting either the desirability or possibility of a return to the status quo. Those things don't happen. But I do think it would be of great benefit to this nation if the sanctity of contemporary liberal dogmas, which generate so much mindless liberal hysteria, were kept in skeptical, historical perspective.

1995

V

CAPITALISM, CONSERVATISM, AND NEOCONSERVATISM

Old Truths and the
New Conservatism

Macaulay in 1832 referred to "conservative" as "the new cant word." The way things are going in America today, one is tempted to echo this sentiment. Not only are we all socialists now; we are all conservatives as well. It used to be one of the fixed characteristics of an American conservative that he should deny he was one; now it appears to be expected of every liberal that he should insist that he is the real conservative. As if the air were not already oppressive with the ghosts of dead ideas and extinct passions. The prevalence of liberalism is bad enough; the mere addition of conservatism would be intolerable.

Just what do these words mean? If one can rid oneself of habitual predisposition long enough to gaze at "liberal" and "conservative" in all their literal nakedness, one experiences a kind of vertigo. A conservative, presumably, is one who is hostile to substantial changes in the status quo—this makes Mr. Khrushchev a Russian conservative. A liberal is less easy to specify, the word having many vague associations; but it will surely apply to, among others, those who insist that the laws and their administration conform more perfectly to the demands of popular opinion (like the late Senator McCarthy, for instance?). Or who believe in the greatest possible freedom for the individual as against the state (like the late Senator Taft?). I suppose there are people who, under the sign of consistency, will allow themselves to be led to such conclusions. After all, in 1830 a section of the victorious French liberals announced that they would henceforth call themselves conservatives, since they were for the conservation of the liberal regime. Most of us, however, would be inclined to estimate this sort of thing as bordering on the frivolous, and would venture to explain that what defines a conservative or liberal is not so much his attitude toward permanence and change *per se*, but

140

the principles on which the attitude itself rests. That is to say: a liberal is one who believes in liberalism, a conservative one who believes in conservatism, and anyone without an "ism" to his name is by definition a more or less astute opportunist.

Now, it may please us to think that everyone is born either a little liberal or a little conservative. It may please us so much, indeed, that we conveniently forget there was a time when no one was. The dissociation of the political sensibility is as much an historical event as the dissociation of the poetical sensibility about which literary critics of our day are so concerned. Up to the French Revolution, which can be taken as the opening of the modern political era, the history of political philosophy knows nothing of liberals and conservatives. There was a clash of principles, yes; of moral, political, and theological principles. And there was a continual clash of interests. But there was no controversy over one's relation to the historical process itself, while it is precisely this relation which is the essential quality of both liberalism and conservatism, just as it is the interpretation of this relation that sets them at odds.

The only people who, prior to modern times, ever believed that politics could or should be oriented round a vision of the historical process were those chiliasts and millenarists—the Beghards, the Anabaptists, the Fifth Monarchy men, all the subterranean streams fed by the Christian apocalyptic—who felt that the Second Coming was imminent and that it was therefore an appropriate moment for the reign of prophets to supersede that of temporal powers. These movements, though they caused no end of political excitement, gave rise to nothing that could properly be called a political philosophy. If the End of Time is at hand, one does not want to be caught philosophizing about politics. For the rest, though there were a great number of men who were either for or against changes in the political order in which they lived, they did not possess, and apparently did not even feel the lack of, an inclusive title upon "change" or "order" as such. In this moonstruck world of flux, in which everything that is born must perish, what earthly sense could it make to be against change? And since man is a political being, part of a larger chain of being, who could not be for order? Providence existed, of course, but it was inscrutable; to claim foreknowledge of history was an invitation to burning.

When and how all this was transformed into the modern temper, historians are still trying to figure out. It was a long process, and a devious one. Doubtless it had something to do with the rise of modern science and technology, which gave man a power over things he never before possessed. It also had something to do with the "revival of antiquity" in the Renaissance, which struck a secular note especially in the field of politics (what we loosely call "Machiavellianism"). And then there were the changes of religious sensibility that accompanied the Reformation. These and other happenings culminated in the Enlightenment, which was literally that: a revealing to all mankind of hitherto forbidden secrets, in particular the mystery of Providence—or as it was soon to be called, of History. Mankind could now have positive knowledge of time's arrow, could even chart and direct its course. The idea of Providence had always implied that God worked in dark ways, using evil itself for His good ends; these ways were now open to human inspection, imitation, and even improvement in the interests of efficiency. Utopias, which had once been "no-where," were now in the range of human vision.

All of classical (i.e., pre-Enlightenment) political thought agreed that there was such a thing as a "best regime," but this was taken to exist in speech rather than in deed, to be imaginable but not realizable in the ordinary course of events. (This was certainly Thomas More's attitude toward his own "Utopia.") It was a standard for measuring the actual; but it was not, and could not be seriously proposed as, the working goal of the actual. The Enlightenment changed all this. After 1789, politics ceased to be considered as the prudent management of men and circumstances, in order to become the "realization of ideas." It became possible for Dostoyevsky, on the extreme right, to assert that "the problems of God and immortality are the same as those of socialism, but seen from a different angle"—a sentiment heartily endorsed on the extreme left by Marx and his followers. Political thinking became irredeemably ideological, an imposition of ideas on political life rather than an emergence of policy from living experience. The "isms" began to breed.

Conservatism was born only a year after the Revolution, with the publication of Edmund Burke's *Reflections on the Revolution in France*. As Professor Leo Strauss has demonstrated, Burke himself was no conservative; the very word, in its political meaning, did not come into being until some four decades later. His critique of the French Revolution was based on the classical premise that theory cannot be the sole or sufficient guide to practice; and his attack on "speculatism" in politics, as well as his high praise of History, must be understood in this light. It is because he was not a "conservative" that Burke could, without contradiction, defend the American Revolution and criticize the French. His principles in both cases were the same: whatever the "rights of man" or the "rights of sovereignty," politics consists in the prudent exercise of these rights rather than the mere flat assertion of them. Nevertheless, there was in Burke's rhetoric and style a reverential attachment to things old and established and ailing with age that fixes him as the source and origin of modern conservatism. This modern conservatism is an ideological retort to the revolutionary ideology. Against the "ideas" and "values" of the Revolution it poses other "ideas" and "values"; and it, too, demands that society "realize" these values. It is no accident that the most eloquent spokesmen for conservatism in the nineteenth and twentieth centuries could not accurately be called men of politics at all, but were essentially men of letters. Just as the French Revolution grew out of the dreams of the *Encyclopédistes*, all the revolutionary trends and tendencies grew out of the dreams of what might be called the anti-*Encyclopédistes*: Scott, Coleridge, Carlyle, de Maistre, Bonald, Novalis, et al. This fact helps explain two of the most extraordinary aspects of modern conservatism: first, its amateur helplessness before the specific problems of a dynamic industrial society; and second, the relative ease with which it merges into revolutionary right-wing movements that aim to "realize" conservative values in a radical and ruthless way.

One of the more amusing results of this dominance of political thinking by ideology is the great difficulty of "placing" those modern political philosophers who manage to carry on the genuinely classical tradition. Burke himself is one such example: admired equally by the liberal Macaulay and the socialist Laski, his bust is in all the pantheons. A more striking instance, perhaps, is Tocqueville, against whom no one can find anything to say. And then there are Madison and Lincoln, revered by all parties and partisans.

But another, and far more interesting, result is the way in which political platitudes have taken on a polemical coloration, so that the simple truths, the wisdom, inherent in them have become anything but self-evident, as they ought to be and once were. Take the following:

> Want of appreciation of distant objects and remote consequences; where an object is desired, want both of an adequate sense of practical difficulties, and of the sagacity necessary for eluding them; disregard of simple traditions, and of maxims sanctioned by experience; an undervaluing of the importance of fixed rules, when immediate purposes require a departure from them—these are among the acknowledged dangers of popular government; and there is the still greater, though less recognized, danger of being ruled by a spirit of suspicious and intolerant mediocrity.

In a quiet moment, a liberal would accept the truth of this observation, particularly if he were aware of its source, which is John Stuart Mill. But it is not the kind of observation he would himself commonly make, because its tenor runs against the mythology of liberalism, which does not like to contemplate the possibility that popular government, like all forms of government, has its own peculiar evils and weaknesses, not to be overcome by Human Evolution, or the March of Time. The sentence, therefore, takes on a "conservative" edge, becoming (and often enough intended as) a challenge to the liberal myth rather than a statement of political fact. And its simple truth is elbowed aside to make room for the conflict of ideologies.

Similarly, there is Burke's statement that "a disposition to preserve and an ability to improve, taken together, would be my standard of a statesman." Peter Viereck, in his excellent little book *Conservatism: From John Adams to Churchill*, takes this as "the perfect definition of the evolutionary kind of conservative." But Burke is not here a "conservative" any more than he is a "conservative" when (repeating Aristotle) he says that prudence is the first of the moral and political virtues. He is uttering a proverbial cliché that no man of worldly experience is likely to dispute, and is pointing to a criterion that we do in fact apply to those who claim recognition as "statesmen"—though not to prophets, saviors, or redeemers of any complexion. The same holds true for Professor Viereck's summation of the conservative temperament as containing a distrust of human nature and of untested innovations, with a trust in historical continuity and a traditional framework of action. These are well-known characteristics of the temperament of all governments, indeed, of all authorities, whether political or no. There is as little point in prescribing them as in deploring them. This is what authority means.

The difficulty, then, with the "conservative revival" is that truths it rediscovers and proclaims, though true enough, must remain incomplete and distorted so long as they are not taken matter-of-factly but as the rejoinder of conservat*ism* to liberal*ism*. For, in fact, they are not the truths of conservat*ism* but those truths about man as a political creature that the very existence of the "isms" themselves, as ideologies and world outlooks, inevitably obscures. Their status as truths presupposes a view of politics that sees it as a field to be claimed, not by the aesthetic imagination, nor by pure reason, but by practical morality; a view of political action as arising out of the concrete dilemma, never from the abstract problem. They cannot, by their very nature, be belligerent truths or party truths without thereby descending to a level on which they cannot live. Once they become controversial, they lose their potency, which is to define and delimit the area of reasonable controversy.

But in face of the utopian *Weltanschauung* offered by modern liberalism and radicalism, there is apparently an irresistible need (even a political necessity) to offer a counter-*Weltanschauung* of one's own. In opposition to doctrinaire rationalism in politics there is called forth a doctrinaire irrationalism. Our politics is so sodden with all of those inarticulate feelings which used to find sanctuary in religion that people seem unmoved by political programs that are not also mythologies. This is, in fact, one of the classic weaknesses of popular democracy. Conservat*ism* is a sign of that weakness rather than a corrective to it.

This is all the truer in that our modern democracies are societies undergoing a permanent technological revolution. The unceasing tumultuous change that we live through every day of our lives makes nonsense of all the "isms." The direction of this change and its corollaries and consequences are utterly unforeseeable. Both liberalism and conservatism limp frantically after the event; both are more frightened than they allow; and both are far more helpless than they pretend. That, no doubt, is why so much of the liberal-conservative quarrel in the United States has hardly anything to do with politics, strictly speaking. The locus of this debate is primarily in the just sphere of education. It involves above all the image of man into which we should like to see the child mature. It is a clash of visions, of philosophies of life, loyalty, and death—just the sort of thing that one would expect from a collision of ideologies. And in such a collision, the old truths of political philosophy, and political philosophy itself as a disinterested contemplation of *la condition politique de l'homme,* are crushed.

So far as concerns foreign policy, economic affairs, and what used to be called "social reform," the difference between the "liberal" and "conservative" viewpoints is becoming ever more difficult to perceive. There are agitated remnants to be sure. If one reads *The Nation,* one gathers that it would be downright sinful for anyone to speculate on the suitability of a restricted franchise, rather than universal suffrage, to countries like India or Burma where the majority of the people are illiterate and impoverished. And if one reads the *National Review,* one would think it a gross impiety for a nation's economic system to be suited to the habits, the character, and the capacities of the people who inhabit it, rather than to the divine commandments handed down by (or is it only to?) Professor von Mises. But these are anachronisms, if noisy ones. The major ideological trends are intermingling and intermarrying. When Professor Frank Tannenbaum writes: "Trade unionism is the conservative movement of our time. . . . In practice, though not in words, it denies the heritage that stems from the French Revolution and from English liberalism" [i.e., "the atomization of society and the isolation of man"]—one sees what he means, but his way of putting it can only confuse. Trade unions, though liberals are accustomed to praise them, are not "liberal" institutions. They are not "conservative" institutions either. They are postliberal institutions, and therefore postconservative as well.

Nor is this a uniquely American phenomenon; it characterizes almost all the nations of the West. The passions that set in motion the Age of Ideology—for so we might denominate the last century and a half—are slowly receding. Both the liberal and the conservative flight from reality are, in retrospect, becoming every day more incomprehensible. Anyone who has had occasion to teach the young knows that even such recent controversial issues as the New Deal and isolationism simply pass them by; they can no more comprehend them than they can the division in the early Christian Church between those who said Jesus was *homoousios* and those who insisted he was *homoiousios* [the "same" or "similar" substance]. What economists call "the revolution of rising expectations" is still with us, and will remain with us so long as science and technology can promise to make a cornucopia out of every wasteland. But these expectations are more and more becoming nonpolitical. Salvation is no longer sought through political action; and, most important, political parties are less likely to regard themselves as "movements." (This is not the case, unhappily, in Asia and Africa, which are "backward" in more than the economic sense; they seem determined to "catch up" with the West mainly by recapitulating its errors.)

The idea of "good government" is becoming once again meaningful, an idea that naturally flows from classical philosophy, in which the political principle of the state is justice rather than either "freedom" (liberal) or "order" (conservative). At the same time, new authorities in social life are emerging to replace those shattered or discredited during the last 150 years. Whether one calls this the "managerial revolution" or the "twentieth-century capitalist revolution" is of little consequence, as are the labels "socialism," "state capitalism," or "the managed economy" when applied to the same, or very similar, facts. The modern epoch has created a whole new set of "rights"—economic, social, political, and cultural—never conceived as being possessed by the ordinary citizen. Now there is emerging a new set of obligations to match these rights, a process that makes both liberals and conservatives uneasy: the one, because it somehow seems an infringement of the abstract idea of freedom; the other, because new obligations take for granted the permanence of these new rights, which conservatism (in its dream of a restoration) is reluctant to concede. But the trend continues, and must grow stronger, for it flows from the old truths of political existence which cannot be forever suppressed.

In short, liberalism and conservatism, which once between them expressed the pathos of revolution, now between them express the irritability of men faced with a new reality that is as contemptuously irrelevant to their hopes as to their fears, and which every day makes utter nonsense of their dogmas. It is, I think, an intuitive recognition of this situation that makes so many, even of our most articulate people, unclear in their own minds as to whether they are proper "liberals" or "conservatives." This confusion is a sign of health, not of decadence; of vigor, not lassitude. It is a tribute paid by the all-exhausted rhetoric of the Age of Ideology to the fact that we are now living in the second half of the twentieth century: a strange time, so unlike all the futures that were ever projected for us that it offers us the invaluable opportunity to, in the words of Karl Jaspers, *"ganz gegenwätig zu sein"* [be utterly committed to the present].

1958

What Is a
"Neoconservative"?

There can no longer be any question about it. I am, for better or worse, a "neo-conservative" intellectual. *Newsweek*, *Time*, and the *New York Times* have all identified me as such, and that settles the matter. As with the original Adam, theirs is the power to give names to all the political creatures in the land, who in turn can only be grateful for having been rescued from anonymity.

So I have no complaint. On the other hand, I must report that some of my friends who have been identified as fellow neoconservatives are less complaisant about this business. Daniel Patrick Moynihan, for instance, suggests that he is a modern version of a Wilsonian progressive. Professor Daniel Bell of Harvard asserts that he is, as he always has been, a right-wing social-democrat. I keep telling them (and others) that such resistance to Higher Authority is not only useless, it positively verges on sedition. But they retort that this is a free country, which the Garden of Eden was not.

Before this situation gets out of control and spreads great turmoil among the citizenry, I should like to offer my services as a mediator. There can be no doubt that the political tendency deemed neoconservative does exist, that it is represented in such journals as *The Public Interest* and *Commentary*, that it has become quite influential of late in shaping political attitudes in intellectual and academic circles, and that its views have even infiltrated the world of media and government. But it is also true that it is only a tendency, not a clearly defined "movement," that there is much heterogeneity in it, and that to those who do not closely follow intellectual controversy in America the term "conservative" can be misleading.

Let me see, therefore, if I can briefly outline the substance beneath the label, the vague consensus that seems to affiliate men and women who are frequently not even aware that they are part of a tendency, much less a neocon-servative one. It's a real enough thing we are talking about; I am not disputing that. But, at the moment, it needs describing more than it needs naming.

1. Neoconservatism is not at all hostile to the idea of a welfare state, but it is critical of the Great Society version of this welfare state. In general, it approves of those social reforms that, while providing needed security and comfort to the individual in our dynamic, urbanized society, do so with a minimum of bureaucratic intrusion in the individual's affairs. Such reforms would include, of course, social security, unemployment insur-ance, some form of national health insurance, some kind of family assis-tance plan, etc. In contrast, it is skeptical of those social programs that create vast and energetic bureaucracies to "solve social problems." In short, while being for the welfare state, it is opposed to the paternalistic state. It also believes that this welfare state will best promote the com-mon good if it is conceived in such a way as not to go bankrupt.

2. Neoconservatism has great respect—it is fair to say it has learned to have great respect—for the power of the market to respond efficiently to eco-nomic realities while preserving the maximum degree of individual free-dom. Though willing to interfere with the market for overriding social purposes, it prefers to do so by "rigging" the market, or even creating new markets, rather than by direct bureaucratic controls. Thus it is more likely to favor housing vouchers for the poor than government-built low-income projects.

3. Neoconservatism tends to be respectful of traditional values and insti-tutions: religion, the family, the "high culture" of Western civilization. If there is any one thing that neoconservatives are unanimous about, it is their dislike of the "counterculture" that has played so remarkable a role in American life over these past fifteen years. Neoconservatives are well aware that traditional values and institutions do change in time, but they prefer that such change be gradual and organic. They believe that the individual who is abruptly "liberated" from the sovereignty of tradi-tional values will soon find himself experiencing the vertigo and despair of nihilism. Nor do they put much credence in the notion that individ-uals can "create" their own values and then incorporate them into a sat-isfying "lifestyle." Values emerge out of the experience of generations and represent the accumulated wisdom of these generations; they simply can-not be got out of rap sessions about "identity" or "authenticity."

4. Neoconservatism affirms the traditional American idea of equality, but rejects egalitarianism—the equality of condition for all citizens—as a proper goal for government to pursue. The equality proclaimed by the Declaration of Independence is an equality of natural rights, including the right to become unequal (within limits) in wealth, or public esteem, or influence. Without that right, equality becomes the enemy of liberty. To put it in more homely terms: the encouragement of equality of opportunity is always a proper concern of democratic government. But it is a dangerous sophistry to insist that there is no true equality of opportunity unless and until everyone ends up with equal shares of everything.

5. In foreign policy, neoconservatism believes that American democracy is not likely to survive for long in a world that is overwhelmingly hostile to American values, if only because our transactions (economic and diplomatic) with other nations are bound eventually to have a profound impact on our own domestic economic and political system. So neoconservatives are critical of the post-Vietnam isolationism now so popular in Congress, and many are suspicious of "détente" as well. On specific issues of foreign policy, however, the neoconservative consensus is a weak one. In the case of Vietnam, neoconservatives went every which way.

So there it is—oversimplified but not, I think, distorted. Not all neoconservatives will accept all of those tenets; but most will accept most of them. Is neoconservatism the right label for this constellation of attitudes? I don't mind it. But then, if the political spectrum moved rightward and we should become "neoliberal" tomorrow, I could accept that too. As a matter of fact, I wouldn't be too surprised if just that happened.

1976

Toward a "New" Economics?

We do not dance even yet to a new tune. But change is in the air. We hear but indistinctly what were once the clearest and most distinguishable voices which have ever instructed political mankind.

So wrote John Maynard Keynes in 1926, in a book called *The End of Laissez-Faire.* He was pointing to the intellectual impotence of the prevailing economic orthodoxy, which seemed less and less capable of explaining what was happening to the economic universe, and quite incapable of providing a coherent set of economic policies which statesmen could look to with confidence. And, of course, he was predicting, with a prescience matched only by his self-assurance, the emergence of a new economics, what we today call Keynesian or neo-Keynesian economics, to replace the old.

It all came to pass as he foretold. During the next fifty years, Keynesianism established itself as the new economic orthodoxy. Even conservative politicians eventually were to be heard saying cheerfully, "We are all Keynesians now." But the number of politicians saying it has, in the past five years, dwindled remarkably. For the Keynesian orthodoxy itself is showing clear signs of sclerosis, even senility, and is well on the way to suffering the fate of its predecessor. It cannot explain the key economic phenomenon of our time, "stagflation," i.e., the coexistence of inflation and unemployment. And the "stimuli" it recommends mysteriously fail to stimulate, but only enfeeble. In desperation, Keynesian economists are now beginning to recommend that we consider seriously the virtues of wage and price controls. Well, for such advice we don't need economists. Politicians have always been able to think up such "cures" for themselves.

The "classical" economics which Keynes challenged really had no theory of economic policy. Its major contributions were in the area of microeconomics—specifically, the rational allocation of scarce resources—and its work in this area is of enduring validity. As for the economy as a whole, the "classical" tradition assumed that equilibrium at a high level of employment was a "natural" and potentially steady state. It could not convincingly explain recessions or depressions, and its advice to governments consisted of little more than keeping the budget in balance and letting things follow their natural course. Good advice, on the whole, but not for all seasons. Keynes perceived this deficiency even before the Great Depression made it obvious to everyone, and he spent a decade developing a new theory to correct it. This involved the creation of "macroeconomics" as an independent field of economic theory, in which efforts were made to explain the general level of economic activity by establishing the "proper" relations of aggregate demand to other aggregates (e.g., GNP, national income, etc.).

At the heart of his own "general theory" was the proposition that a modern economy was naturally unstable because it had an inherent tendency toward a deficiency in aggregate demand, or to put it another way, once full employment is reached, people's propensity to save tended to outweigh their tendency to invest. The maintenance of high demand, therefore, became the central object of economic policy, regardless of its unbalancing effect on the budget. And economic policy consisted of government's manipulation of fiscal and monetary affairs—"fine-tuning," we have come to call it—to achieve a level of demand that would ensure full employment and prosperity.

That Keynes was a giant in the history of economic theory is beyond question. "Macroeconomics" is here to stay and will remain his permanent testament, as will governmental responsibility for the level of employment. But, with every passing year, his limitations have also become more apparent. For instance, his extraordinarily cavalier attitude toward budget deficits—"deficits don't matter," as his leading disciple put it—may have soothed the consciences (and quickened the appetites) of politicians, but it never did make any obvious economic sense. Why should a nation's debt be a different economic species from a family's debt? The only visible difference is that a nation can pass on its indebtedness to future generations, while parents have no such right vis-à-vis their children. But does that make it any less real or burdensome? A "psychohistorian" might wonder whether the fact that Keynes himself was childless might have had something to do with shaping this attitude.

Similarly, a cultural historian might properly wonder to what degree the fact that Keynes was a charter member of the "Bloomsbury circle"—a group of talented upper-class aesthetes—had a bearing on his faith in government's ability to "manage" the economy. His masterwork, *The General Theory of Employment, Interest, and Money*, reveals a frank disdain for the traditional bourgeois virtues (thrift, industry, diligence) and for the bourgeoisie as a class. There is also a strong implication that ordinary people are just too shortsighted to make capitalism work, and that they need the likes of John Maynard Keynes to manage the system for them.

None of this would matter much if his policy prescriptions worked. But they don't. Financing those "unimportant" budgetary deficits turns out to cause inflation. And to the degree that the deficits give rise to heavier taxation, the economy stagnates. It also turns out that the effectiveness of governmental stimulus to the demand side of the economy, accompanied by governmental stifling of the supply side (through taxation), only works if everyone is under the spell of a "money illusion"—i.e., if they notice only the increased number of dollars in hand, and fail to observe that each dollar has lost some of its purchasing power. But the people are cleverer than Keynes thought. They do make the requisite observation; they demand that their purchasing power be maintained; and inflation swells from a ripple to a wave to an oceanic storm.

In response to this crisis in the theory of economic policy, a "new" economics is beginning to emerge. Based on the critique of Keynesianism by the "monetarist" school, as further developed (in a rather heterodox way) in the work of such economists as Robert Mundell and Arthur Laffer, and as vigorously publicized by Jude Wanniski of the *Wall Street Journal* and Congressman Jack Kemp (R-N.Y.), it is still in an embryonic condition and the world has not yet taken much notice of it. To requote Keynes: "We do not dance even yet to a new tune. But change is in the air." One uses the inverted commas around that term "new" because, in truth, much of the "new" economics is very old—as old as Adam Smith, say. Its focus is on economic growth, rather than on economic equilibrium or disequilibrium, and it sees such growth arising from a free response (e.g., investment, hard work, etc.) to the economic incentives of a free market. It does retain the Keynesian macroeconomic apparatus for diagnostic purposes, but its inclination is "conservative" rather than "liberal"—i.e., it believes that only the private sector can bring us sustained economic growth, and that whatever tasks one might wish to assign to the public sector, economic growth cannot be one of them.

This "new" economics is sometimes described, rather cumbersomely, as "supply-side fiscal policy." (There is also an international monetary aspect which a critic has called, not inaccurately, "global monetarism," but that is another story.) It arises in opposition to the Keynesian notion that an increase in demand, by itself, will increase supply and therefore accelerate economic growth. The "new" economics asserts that an increase in demand, where the

natural incentives to economic growth are stifled, will result simply in inflation. It is only an increase in *productivity*, which converts latent into actual
demand by bringing commodities (old and new) to market at prices people
can afford, that generates economic growth.

At the moment, and under existing circumstances, the major emphasis by
far of the "new" economics is on the need for a substantial, across-the-board
cut in tax rates, because it is the high level of tax rates that is stifling incentives
to growth. This has caused some concern and confusion among Republican
Congressmen, and business executives too, who sense a continuation of the
Keynesian unconcern with budget deficits. But the "new" economics is all in
favor of balanced budgets, only it believes that, to achieve such a goal, temporary imbalances may be required. Its emphasis on tax-cutting flows from its
conviction that this will, through economic growth, eventually lead to a balanced budget. Simply to reduce government expenditures, in a depressed economy, creates too many problems. (And a ruthless dismantling of the welfare
state is, in any case, unthinkable.) It is only a substantial tax cut that will, in
time, permit us to reduce the *relative* size of the public sector by an expansion
of the private sector.

This is a highly simplified and much foreshortened version of a set of economic ideas that is beginning to reshape our thinking on economic policy. Its
political appeal to conservatives is obvious (just as the political appeal of Keynesianism to liberals was obvious) and helps explain the recent willingness of
Congressional Republicans to vote in favor of a permanent tax cut despite the
state of the budget. They were not "playing politics," as some critics claimed.
They were acting on an economic theory which, if only dimly understood,
was nevertheless persuasive. After all, as Congressman Kemp has pointed out,
all that Republicans were urging is a tax cut similar to the Kennedy tax program of 1963, which was also made in the face of a deficit. And it worked. The
deficit soon declined and employment went up.

It is hard to overestimate the importance of the fact that, for the first time in
half a century, it is the economic philosophy of conservatives that is showing
signs of intellectual vigor, while the economic philosophy of liberalism keeps
tying itself into ever more elaborate knots. As some sage once observed: you can't
beat a horse with no horse. Conservatives, who believe in limited government
and a strong private sector, may be in the process of acquiring a horse.

1977

No Cheers for
the Profit Motive

Every now and then, I find myself having a conversation with a business leader who slaps me on the back, tells me how much he agrees with what I have written or said, and urges me to go back to the academic community where I am to impress upon my fellow professors and students what a splendid thing "the profit motive" really is. Since such occasions do not lend themselves to philosophical discussion, I smile weakly, mumble something unintelligible, and change the subject as quickly as possible.

The question I leave unasked is: Why should anyone want to sing the praises of "the profit motive"? And who ever has? The Old Testament does no such thing; and the New Testament definitely does no such thing. Nor did the ancient philosophers, or the medieval theologians, or such founders of modern political thought as Thomas Hobbes, John Locke, or James Madison. Nor, for that matter, did Adam Smith—though this may come as a surprise to many who have never really read that fine thinker, and whose understanding of him has come thirdhand via some current exponents of "free enterprise."

It is, in my opinion, as absurd to praise the profit motive—i.e., economic action based on self-interest—as it is to condemn it. The human impulse to such action is, like the sexual impulse, a natural fact. So far from being a virtue, self-interested action (again, like sexual action) is an intrinsic aspect of human nature that falls under the shadow of "original sin" (or whatever the theological counterpart is in non-Christian religions, and they all do have such a counterpart). Perfect human beings—i.e., saints—do not engage in such self-interested, acquisitive actions; and it is quite impossible to believe that, after our Redeemer cometh, business will go on as usual. Or sex, for that matter. Or politics, which is still another natural activity of unredeemed humanity.

Fortunately for all of us, the world is not so constructed that only virtuous intentions and virtuous actions contribute to our happiness and prosperity. There is a Jewish teaching to the effect that God created the "evil urge" because the world, as created, could not exist without it; and the Christian teaching of "*o felix culpa*" ("Oh happy Fall") works to the same effect. It is the sexual urge that is a precondition of the family, in which men and women find some degree of temporal contentment, even sometimes happiness. It is from the sin of pride and the will to power that governments emerge, which permit human beings to lead lives of sociability, rather than existences that are, as Hobbes reminds us, "solitary, poor, nasty, brutish, and short." And it is on the acquisitive impulse that economic orders are built, which permit men to enjoy the fruits of creation.

The socialist ideal, as elaborated in the nineteenth and twentieth centuries, can be summarily dismissed as utopian precisely because it envisages an economic order in which everyone is motivated by a virtuous commitment to the well-being of all his fellow men, rather than being guided by self-interest. It is an attractive ideal, of course, especially to young people with little experience of the real world. But there never has been such an economic order; there never will be such an economic order; there cannot in principle be such an economic order. For it to exist would require a kind of radical transfiguration of human nature that only a messianic deliverance can bring us. And though socialism is messianic enough in its pretensions, it turns out to be all-too-human in actuality.

Ironically, one of the ways in which capitalism responded to this socialist challenge was by debasing, distorting, and vulgarizing its own self-definition. Looking back, one is hard put to say who has done more damage to capitalism, its apologists or its critics. It begins with the Reverend Malthus, who refuted socialist utopianism by "proving" that, as you improved the condition of the poor, you encouraged them to multiply their numbers so rapidly that they soon relapsed into their previous poverty. At a time when democratic sentiments were spreading like wildfire, it is hard to imagine a less beguiling message, or one less likely to persuade people that a capitalist economic order should engage their loyalty. Fortunately, Malthus was utterly wrong in his analysis. Nevertheless, even as ordinary men and women were gradually (if unevenly) beginning to enjoy the fruits of economic growth, capitalist apologetics for many decades persisted in its adherence to Malthusian doctrine. Somehow it seemed not to occur to the apologists that their refutation of socialism was also an indictment of capitalism.

A more "positive" apologetic for capitalism was later elaborated as a consequence of the popularity of various forms of "social Darwinism." It was in this context that (as best I can determine) the term "free enterprise" gained currency, as did the notion that the "profit motive" was the motor force which ensured the "survival of the fittest" through competition, and therewith the progressive improvement of the human race. Like Malthusianism, this doctrine was self-defeating in a democratic age, since it did not offer much solace or hope to those (perhaps the majority) who, not being among the fittest, had the worst chances of survival. But unlike Malthusianism, which was suffused with Christian resignation, this doctrine represented the first clear break between capitalist apologetics and the Judeo-Christian tradition, especially the moral components of this tradition. Whereas naked political ambition still did not dare speak its name and seek moral status, naked economic ambition now could.

The twentieth century widened this break between capitalist apologetics and the Judeo-Christian tradition as the defense of capitalism came to be expressed more boldly in terms of a hedonistic, "libertarian" ethic. There are today some writers and scholars who, instead of worshiping the Golden Calf, worship the Sears, Roebuck catalog and all the "alternative lifestyles" that capitalist affluence permits the individual to choose from. There is a secular faith here in the capacity of the "autonomous" individual to create his own moral order, to perfect his humanity by a process of original "creativity." In the eyes of the Judeo-Christian tradition, of course, this vision is as utopian as socialism itself, and, in many respects, far less admirable. On the whole, the business community has remained too "bourgeois" to embrace such libertarian apologetics, preferring to stick with a vague and eclectic defense of "free enterprise" and "the profit motive" as being a Good Thing, both in and of itself and because it is connected with other good things. There is truth in this claim, but to understand what kind of truth it is, one should turn back to Adam Smith, the first and still the best apologist for capitalism.

Adam Smith had nothing flattering to say about the "profit motive" *per se*, or even about businessmen as a class. The virtues he celebrated were those familiar to the Judeo-Christian tradition: sympathy, compassion, generosity, public-spiritedness. His great and original contribution, however, was to point out how the sum of self-interested economic actions, in themselves nonmoral, resulted in an institution, the market economy, that was moral because it permitted everyone to better his condition even though each participant sought only his own particular good. A market economy, by promoting economic growth and the most effective allocation of resources, helped render the human estate more habitable. Moreover, it did so in such a way as to encourage the self-reliance and spirit of responsibility of the individual, therewith shaping characters capable of self-governance and, ultimately, of constituting a self-governing polity of free men. Such a polity had always been admired, as an ideal, by political philosophers throughout the ages. They just didn't think it realizable. Adam Smith indicated a way in which it could become a reality.

In short, Adam Smith did for the realm of economics what the medieval theologians had done for the realm of politics. These latter, though never singing the praises of political ambition, saw it as respectable, as a natural and irrepressible impulse which, as if by a "Hidden Hand," resulted in the creation of an institution necessary for the good of all—i.e., government. Most of them did not, however, extend the same tolerance to self-interested economic activity, which they openly despised. It was Adam Smith who first established the respectability—not the morality, just the respectability—of economic self-interest by demonstrating the benign consequences that such activity, taken as a whole, gave rise to. In so doing, he made possible the unprecedented economic growth and economic prosperity of the past two centuries, as well as the concurrent spread of liberal and limited government.

Adam Smith gave moral status to an acquisitive economy, but he was far too close to the Judeo-Christian tradition to have kind words for an acquisitive *society*, one in which "the profit motive" was perceived as good-in-itself instead of being merely respectable. The evolution of capitalist apologetics from Smith's day to our own has witnessed a gradual "liberation" of the capitalist idea from its Judeo-Christian moorings—most such apologetics being the work of economists, who do not know how to think in moral terms. The upshot is that the business class today, when faced, for instance, with issues of "social responsibility" or "business ethics," flounders helplessly, even though there is a veritable library of traditional, Judeo-Christian commentaries and exegesis on exactly such moral issues. Just as our current apologists for "liberated sex" end up with a tangle of moral conundrums (such as the moral status of homosexuality), so our defenders of "the profit motive" and "free enterprise," pure and simple, end up with seemingly insoluble moral dilemmas involving the relation of private to public interests.

But that is a subject for another day.

1979

Ideology and
Supply-Side Economics

The terms being applied—by the media, by politicians, by economists—to President Reagan's economic program, and most particularly to the tax-cutting aspect of this program, are "bold," "revolutionary," "a risky experiment," and so on. Clearly, a great many people are nervous about "supply-side" economics, and seem to have difficulty understanding its rationale. This is quite odd. For there is nothing really bold, or revolutionary, or experimental about this program. Nor is it at all difficult to understand.

Indeed, the trouble with the thing we call supply-side economics is that it is just too simple, too easy to understand. Accustomed as we are to the increasing complexity of the natural sciences, and the occult jargon of the social sciences, we are inclined to be suspicious of transparent simplicity, which we are likely to equate with naïveté or wishful thinking. The average person, listening to an exposition of supply-side economics, will nod his head at every point, but, after it is done, will remain incredulous. If it is that obvious, what is the fuss and controversy all about? The average economist, on the other hand, is only too likely to be indignant, outraged, and contemptuously dismissive: what is the point of his hard-won expertise in sophisticated economic theory if economic policy can be reduced to such plain terms?

It must be said that the term itself, "supply-side economics," may be a source of initial confusion. It originates in deliberate contrast to the prevailing Keynesian approach, which emphasizes the need for government to manage and manipulate, through fiscal and monetary policies, aggregate demand so as to maintain full employment. Supply-side economists say government cannot really do this, no matter how many clever economists it hires, but that if business enterprise is permitted to function with a minimum of interference, it will invest and innovate, so as to *create* the requisite demand for the goods it produces.

There is certainly a difference in perspective here. Supply-side economists look at the economy from ground level, as it were—i.e., from the point of view of the entrepreneurs and investors who are identified as the prime movers. Keynesian economists look at the economy from above, from the standpoint of a government that is a *deus ex machina*, and which, in its omniscience, intervenes discreetly to preserve a harmonious economic universe. But it is wrong to infer that we live in a Manichean world in which Supply and Demand are continually at odds, so that we always are having to declare allegiance to one as against the other. They are, rather, opposite sides of the same coin, coexisting of necessity, and there can be no question of choosing between them. More precisely, it is absurd economically to think in terms of such a choice. Beyond a certain point, a tax on production becomes a tax on consumption; the goods become too expensive and demand falls. Similarly, beyond a certain point a tax on consumption becomes a tax on production; the decrease in demand inhibits supply. Shifting taxes from the one to the other may provide marginal benefits on occasion. But a tax on commercial transactions and economic activity is always a tax on *both* production and consumption.

When, however, one moves from a purely analytical-economic mode of thought to a political-ideological one—when, in short, one moves from economic analysis to economic policy—then the difference in perspective has significant implications. Supply-side economics naturally gives rise to an emphasis on growth, not redistribution. It aims at improving everyone's economic circumstances over time, but not necessarily in the same degree or in the same period of time. The aggregate demand created by economic activity, as seen from the supply side, is indifferent to the issue of equality. Its bias is consequently in favor of a free market for economic activity because this provides the most powerful economic incentives for investment, innovation, and growth. Those, on the other hand, for whom economic equality is at least as important as economic growth will always want to see government "restructure" this aggregate demand and will be indifferent to the issue of economic incentives.

However, there is another, incidental but important, source of controversy which has already been referred to, and that is the threat that supply-side economics represents to the economics profession as at present constituted. There can be little doubt that the nature of the controversy would be a lot clearer, and we would all be less befuddled, if it were not for the fact that so many distinguished economists are publicly accusing supply-side economics of being inconsistent with the principles of economic science as these are taught in graduate school and incarnated in, say, articles in the *American Economic Review*. To make matters worse, the accusation has a lot of truth in it, which is why so much of the writing in favor of supply-side economics originates outside the academic universe. Thus one cannot understand the controversy over supply-side economics without paying some attention to the condition of the economics profession and to its vested interests, both intellectual and material. This condition is, at the moment, painfully ambiguous.

For more than three decades, we have all been looking to our best economists for guidance on economic policy. To that end we even established, after World War II, an extraordinary institution called the Council of Economic Advisers: three economists, with staff, who are supposed to provide the president and Congress with authoritative guidance on our economic problems, prospects, and policies. One must emphasize that word "authoritative." Those economists are not brought to Washington to offer their personal opinions, but rather to provide us with expert, scientific advice.

From what do their authority and expertise derive? They derive from the ambitious reconstruction of economic science after World War II in which the scheme of Keynesian macroeconomics was wedded to new, rigorous, analytical, largely mathematical techniques so as to provide, not a general, abstract model of the economic "system"—the nineteenth century gave us that—but a specific model of *our* economy at *this* particular time. Such a model consists of hundreds of complex correlations, spawned by econometric research, which relate one aspect of our national economic activity to another (or to many others), all fed into a computer which, having been properly programmed, can inform us as to where our economy has been coming from (to adopt a useful term from another part of the culture), where it is now, and whither it is drifting. It is this enterprise, which has come to be called "the neoclassical synthesis," or "neo-Keynesian" economics, that has defined the nature of economic expertise, the acquisition of which is the dominant goal of graduate studies. And because a mastery of advanced mathematics has been so crucial to the enterprise, economists have secured the mantle of a true scientific elite, often incomprehensible, always indispensable.

It all went reasonably well for a couple of decades, though just *what* went reasonably well is itself one source of controversy. The neo-Keynesians will say that their sound analysis and good advice were at least partly responsible for our healthy economy from 1945 to 1970. Critics will argue that it was the existence of a healthy economy, created by businessmen and statesmen blissfully ignorant of sophisticated economic theories, that permitted economists to bask in a kind of reflected glory. (These critics point to the remarkable economic recoveries of Germany and Japan in a period when those nations had yet to learn of the neoclassical synthesis.) But there can be no dispute over the fact that, beginning around 1970, it ceased going well and began to go badly. Not only were those annual forecasts too often very wide of the mark (especially with regard to inflation), but our economics establishment—for that is what it is by now—could not explain the phenomenon of "stagflation," a combination of inflation and lagging economic growth that neo-Keynesian theory regards as an impossibility. A note of desperation began to creep into the writings of the economists themselves. Professors of economics who had for years patiently explained to their students the folly (in peacetime) of wage and price and rent controls suddenly began to look upon them with a more sympathetic eye.

But for such a prescription one does not need economists. Ever since the beginnings of time, governments have been quite capable of thinking up such peremptory "solutions" to their economic problems all by themselves. The equivalent in politics is rule under martial law, no doubt necessary in extreme emergencies, but not a subject on which political theory or political philosophy has anything to say. Simultaneously, and inevitably, a great many people began to take a hard and critical look at the presuppositions of neo-Keynesian economics, and, above all, at the model of the economy upon which it relies. That there are some anomalies in this model had always been conceded. Thus, since the wages of cleaning women are counted in the Gross National Product while the labor of housewives is not, one could easily achieve a huge increase in GNP (and presumably we would all be wealthier) if every housewife were to rent herself out to do her neighbor's cleaning instead of doing her own cleaning herself. Similarly, there has always been a problem about "investment" by governments. The typical macroeconomics model is incapable of distinguishing among the building of roads, the building of warships, and the building of pyramids, all of which are counted simply as "expenditures," though their economic status is obviously very disparate. And there are other difficulties with the model that many economists have been aware of, but which they also have thought could be regarded merely as a limitation of models *per se*, rather than a serious flaw in this particular model.

The new critique of the neo-Keynesian model, however, went far beyond such relatively familiar anomalies. Essentially it asserted that this kind of model, for all its complexity and sophistication—or one can even say because of its complexity and sophistication—reveals profound misconceptions about the nature of economic behavior, and especially about the kind of economic behavior that leads to economic growth. It is important to realize that the conventional models are utterly blind to entrepreneurship and innovation (technological or otherwise). They can deal with quantifiable aggregates (like "investment"), but what cannot be quantified they ignore. Basically, theirs is a kind of Newtonian model of an economic system, with all the "forces" balancing each other out, except sometimes when (for reasons still unclear) there is a mismatch between overall supply and overall demand, on which occasions the government, like some benign deity, pumps in the missing quantity of demand and restores the system to equilibrium. All specifically human motivations, intentions, aspirations are ignored. It is the results of past human behavior that the model blandly reflects, and always after the fact. In a sense, the revolt against neo-Keynesian economics is part of a larger revulsion, visible in other social sciences as well, against behaviorism as an adequate guide to human reality.

Economists attuned to the theories incarnated in such models cannot explain the "whys" of economic phenomena. They cannot, for instance, explain why economies grow, and why some economies grow faster than others. They try to come up with such an explanation, of course. By now the literature on "growth theory"—much of it mathematical and arcane—fills a good-sized library. But as our current textbooks on economic growth will admit, after hundreds of pages in which the various theories of diverse economists are adumbrated, there is nothing near a consensus about this issue. Is that surprising? Only if we forget that economics is still a "social" science—the most methodologically rigorous of them all, to be sure, but still a social science—and not a "natural" science like physics or chemistry. We are hardly astonished, after all, if our political scientists fail to come up with a rigorous theory of political change, or if our sociologists fail to come up with a rigorous theory of social change, one which informs us precisely and authoritatively as to where our polity and society have been, where they are, where they are going. That is because we understand intuitively that any such theory, dealing with human beings, would require a degree of self-knowledge, of our present characters and personalities, from which we could make strong inferences as to our future motivations and actions, which is, by the nature of things, unavailable. (If we had any such complete self-knowledge we would be God, the Being in Whom thought and existence are one.) But economics, in striving to become an objective and positive science like physics, has promised us exactly this kind of self-knowledge, at least insofar as we are economic men and women. It has not been able to deliver on such a grandiose promise, has, in truth, reached a dead end in its efforts to do so.

In all fairness, one must say that not all economists have been co-opted into this ambitious intellectual enterprise. The "neo-Austrians," headed by

Friedrich Hayek, have always been very skeptical of the utility of such mathematical models, and of the ability of economic analysis to provide the kind of exact, quantitative answers—how much? how long? when?—that politicians naturally yearn for (and the media always assume to be available). The neo-Marxists, too, more interested in the dynamics of economic change than in the static calibrations of economic phenomena at any one point in time, have made trenchant criticisms of the prevailing mode of economic theorizing. But the economics profession as a whole remains committed to the neoclassical or neo-Keynesian synthesis, and practically every course in macroeconomics introduces the student to it.

Supply-side economics may be viewed as a kind of "humanistic" rebellion against the mathematical-mechanical type of economic analysis in which economic aggregates, themselves dubious in nature, are related to one another so as to achieve a supposedly accurate series of snapshots of the economic universe we inhabit, something comparable to the universe we perceive when we go to a planetarium. Supply-side economics is uninterested in such a beautifully architected equilibrium because it believes this is the wrong paradigm for understanding an economy that consists of the purposive yet inconstant behavior of millions of individuals. Purposive, because economic behavior generally has as its goal the improvement of one's economic conditions. Inconstant, because only the individual himself can define "improvement" for us, and his behavior will be profoundly influenced by all sorts of contingent factors—religious heritage, family relations, and, not least, the actions of government.

So far from being new or revolutionary, supply-side economics is frankly reactionary. "Back to Adam Smith" can be fairly designated as its motto. Not, however, in the sense of returning to some purist version of laissez-faire; all supply-siders agree (as would have Adam Smith, author of *The Theory of Moral Sentiments*) that, when a society is sufficiently affluent to provide a safety net for those unable to participate fully in the economy, we all have a moral obligation to see that such provision is made. "Back to Adam Smith" has to be understood, rather, as "Back to *The Wealth of Nations*" as the paradigm for economic reasoning, a book that makes sense to any literate person with some worldly experience (as distinct from book-learning, which often inclines the reader toward otherworldliness). It may sound incredible, but supply-side economics really does believe that, if you want an economic education, *The Wealth of Nations* is still the best book to read. Indeed, the publicists of supply-side economics—Jude Wanniski in *The Way the World Works* and George Gilder in *Wealth and Poverty*—will readily allow that their books are but elaborations on themes by Adam Smith.

Nothing conveys more clearly the radically different perspectives on economic activity of supply-side and neo-Keynesian theory than the issue of incentives. It is an issue about which much confusion exists, and the confusion arises because contemporary economists are uneducated in the world of business, i.e., in the world of *real* economic activity. They are trained instead in the world of economic analysis, which stands in relation to business as academic political science stands in relation to politics. It is a distant relation, which easily warps one's perspective. Political scientists know that it is ambition which energizes the political system, but in their models—and yes, they have them—ambition is simply taken for granted, as a constant in magnitude and quality. Similarly, all economists know that incentives energize the economic system, but in their models they take incentives for granted, as a constant in magnitude and quality. In both cases, the reason is the same: since political ambition and economic incentives are essentially subjective and nonmeasurable essences, there is no place for them in an objective, quantified model.

Supply-side economics takes incentives—the innate human impulse to better one's condition, as Adam Smith would put it—as the *fons et origo* of economic activity and, most important, of economic growth. We do indeed know of primitive cultures where that impulse is either weak or missing and where economic growth is, as a consequence, also weak or missing. We know, too, of historical societies where the impulse has been frustrated by religious or political authorities, and where economic growth has been sporadic and cyclical. It is only with the emergence of a modern, commercial civilization, in which self-interested transactions in the marketplace are morally vindicated and politically tolerated, that the impulse to better one's condition becomes translated into steady, progressive economic growth over decades and centuries.

Now, one way of frustrating that impulse, and economic growth as well, is to tax it. This accords with both common sense and common observation. As a matter of fact, it is a proposition that any economist, even the most devoted neo-Keynesian, will casually agree to. But when you suggest that one way of encouraging economic growth is to decrease the taxes on economic activity, many of these same economists will suddenly and inexplicably balk. This balkiness is unquestionably ideological. These are people who are persuaded that the "collective goods" our taxes pay for—not only public works but also a more equal distribution of income—give us fair value, if not in purely economic terms. This is a perfectly sensible argument in defense of a tax system, but it is rarely made in the United States in 1981, presumably because it is not so evident that our taxes are actually getting us our "money's worth" in those collective goods. Instead, these economists engage in the most curious kind of research to refute the notion that anyone's incentive will be affected by a cut in taxes. This research involves polling people, asking them whether they will work harder if their taxes are cut by 10 percent or 20 percent, or will they, perhaps, just consume more, by way of goods or leisure? Such studies often find that it makes little or no difference. And such studies are not worth the paper they are printed on. They are parodies of what economic analysis should be.

Who on earth ever said that, in a commercial society such as ours, we achieve economic growth by having to work harder? On the contrary, the whole point of economic growth is that people should work less hard, but more productively. The human impulse to work less hard is just as strong as the human impulse to better one's condition, always has been, one suspects always will be. It is the genius of market capitalism to satisfy both of these impulses at once by encouraging entrepreneurship, the incentive to innovate, among that minority of human beings who are, unlike most of us, peculiarly "economic activists." The existence of such human beings—of entrepreneurs who, by innovating, make us all more productive without necessarily being less lazy—is simply ignored in the atomistic poll data or the aggregate statistics that economists so solemnly analyze.

It does not matter in the least whether you or I will respond to a tax cut by sharpening our economic incentives. Some of us will, some of us will not. What does matter is that there is, out there, in the real business world as distinct from the academic world of the economists, a minority who will respond in this way—not necessarily the nicest people, not necessarily the smartest people, but the ones who, for whatever reason, relish economic success. For such people, the incentives to save and invest (and invest again) are extraordinarily powerful, and it is the incentives of these "economic activists" that are blunted and thwarted by a heavy tax burden. True, if we knew who they were in advance, we could cut only *their* taxes. But we only know who they are after the fact.

Still, taxes do have to be paid to acquire the necessary and desirable level of public services, and the question is immediately posed: how do we know, in fact, that taxes are too high? To put it another way: how do we know, since people do value many of those public services (if in varying measure), that our tax level is so high as to have a deleterious effect on economic incentives? This brings us to the so-called Laffer curve, a simple but powerful concept that is not in the least new; one can find an excellent summary of it by Ibn Khaldun in the fourteenth century. All that the Laffer curve says is that, after a certain point, a tax, or the tax level as a whole, can become counterproductive. It is the point at which people experience taxes as an excessive and unfair burden—they are not getting their "money's worth" for the tax they pay—with the result that their incentives to economic activity are adversely affected. The tax, in effect, represses economic activity to such an extent that, if it were substantially reduced, the government would end up collecting more in tax revenues, since there would be a lot more economic activity contributing to these tax revenues.

None of this is controversial; every economist would concede the general validity of the point; every citizen, from his own experience, can provide anecdotal confirmation. (Under Prohibition, when the tax on liquor was 100 percent, the government's tax revenues were zero; when the tax was lowered, revenues sharply increased.) The question that academic critics of the Laffer curve raise is whether the American tax system has gone beyond the point of diminishing returns. "How do we know this?" they ask querulously. "Prove it," they demand. To judge by last November's election results, a clear majority of Americans are already convinced. But academic economists want academic proof, not, one suspects, because of their devotion to pure science, but because they would really prefer that government collect money and redistribute it more equally than see everyone improve his condition unequally through untrammeled economic growth.

The academic question as to whether we are beyond the point of diminishing returns in our tax system is unanswerable in strictly academic terms. It is a matter for political judgment, since it all depends on how people feel about the level of taxation. In wartime they feel one way; in peacetime, another. Yes, people always do grumble about taxes, at just about any level, but they don't always do something about it. They don't always make strenuous efforts to avoid or evade; they don't always regard overtime (at time-and-a-half pay) with indifference or hostility. On the other hand, a housewife thinking of entering the job market will certainly think twice if her take-home pay barely covers the cost of the babysitter.

Though one cannot provide the kind of elegant, mathematical proof economists wish, there are in fact some persuasive signs that the American economy has gone too far up on the Laffer curve. One is our flourishing (because untaxed) underground economy; just how large it is, no one knows, but that it is very much larger today than yesterday, no one can deny. This underground economy is a new phenomenon in American society, and a most unhealthy one. Another such sign is the tens of billions of dollars that seek and find legal tax shelters, investments that would not exist except for their relative tax advantage and which are therefore, by definition as it were, uneconomic. The volume of such commercial transactions, based on tax evasion and tax avoidance, is so enormous that even a slight shift, resulting from a lowering of tax rates, would bring substantial tax revenues to the Treasury. More precise than this, one cannot be, but in any case the demand for precise estimates of revenues gained and lost as a result of a decrease in tax rates is largely a smokescreen. The real opposition to the Laffer curve has less to do with economics than with liberal egalitarianism.

If the Laffer curve indicated that a cut only in tax rates for those in the lower-income bracket would pay for itself in recouped tax revenues, the demand for precision would vanish overnight. It cannot, however, show any such thing, since the major portion of our income tax is paid by people in upper-income brackets. (That is where the income is.) Does anyone really think that, even if we could prove beyond the shadow of a doubt that reducing the tax rates on more affluent Americans would result in their actually paying more in taxes than they now do, the reductions would become less controversial? There are many people, including quite a few economists, for whom it is more important to have a symbolic tax rate of 70 percent on very high incomes even if very few of the rich actually pay it, than to have an effective tax rate of, say, 40 percent which many of the rich would pay instead of fooling around with (often problematic) tax shelters.

But there are some thoughtful people who, having little quarrel with the general tenor of supply-side economics, nevertheless wonder whether it is appropriate in today's inflationary economy. It is these people, genuinely concerned about inflation as our overriding problem, who feel that cuts in tax rates, for rich and poor alike, should wait upon our prior success in bringing down the rate of inflation. Since many of these critics of Kemp-Roth are themselves conservatives who supported Ronald Reagan—one thinks of Arthur Burns, Herbert Stein, and presumably Paul Volcker—and since their criticism is clearly not ideological, they are all the more influential, especially within the financial and business communities. For such as these, it is not the tax cuts themselves that are "bold" and "radical," but the fact that they are being contemplated in a particular economic environment, one of an unprecedentedly high and sustained peacetime rate of inflation. And it is their disinterested concern over this issue which has served to fuel the criticisms of others who, while warning solemnly against "radical experimentation" in economic policy, have a different species of fish to fry.

The conservative case against reliance on supply-side economics in present circumstances cannot be lightly dismissed. It has a long and solid tradition of classical economic thought behind it. The only question is whether it is relevant to today's environment, both economic and political. That classical tradition has its own policy for coping with inflation. And, in truth, it is a policy that has always worked. It involves slowing down the rate of growth of the money supply to bring it in line with the growth in productivity. It also involves reducing governmental expenditures and bringing the budget into balance, this, to preclude the necessity of the Federal Reserve Board "monetizing" a deficit. Both of these measures, taken jointly, induce a recession, during which all of the distortions caused by inflation are "purged" from (or "wrung out of") the economic system. After the recession has achieved this effect, a normal economic recovery may be expected to set in, and non-inflationary growth is once again possible.

That is the prescription, and it is a prescription for recession as a cure for inflation. This must be emphasized because, understandably enough, its advocates tend not to stress it. Only Hayek has been candid enough to say openly that we need a recession. Unfortunately, many of the politicians and businessmen who are swayed by these arguments do not, on their own, fully comprehend the implications of those arguments. I have noted that these policies have in fact worked in the past. But would they work under the present, truly novel, circumstances? Can they even be tried under these circumstances? The answer to the first question is: probably not. The answer to the second is: certainly not.

One of the novel things about our present economic condition is not merely the endemic high inflation but the existence of a welfare state. This means that as the economy slows down, government expenditures actually increase, as the number of people who are now "in need" increases, and all sorts of welfare programs are triggered. The deficit, instead of going down, tends to go up, especially since tax revenues are also decreasing. As a result, whereas a relatively shallow and short-lived recession could do the trick in a pre–welfare state economy, what is now required is a deep and prolonged recession. (This is what Margaret Thatcher has discovered, to her dismay.) The economic costs of such a recession are so enormous as to make it a most questionable instrument of policy. And the political costs are, to put it bluntly, intolerable. In this decade of the 1980s, no administration, no political party, certainly not this Republican administration or the Republican Party, can survive association with policies that bring on a long and severe recession. Once upon a time, in a different world, it was possible; it no longer is. All those politicians who are now, in innocence and good faith, advocating such policies would be the first to panic when the recession arrived, and would predictably opt for any scheme at hand to deal with it.

That is why the Reagan administration has added a cut in tax rates, for business firms and individuals, to the traditional dual strategy of fighting inflation by slowing down the growth of the money supply and of government spending. It is the only possible answer to our predicament, encouraging economic growth so as to annul or at least ameliorate the recessionary effects of other anti-inflationary policies. Some hostile economists have triumphantly pointed out that what we have here is a case of policies moving in opposite directions. Yes, and so does the policy of providing poor people with both welfare and job opportunities at the same time. Mixed solutions of this kind are as appropriate to economic policy as to social policy, and for the same reason: they are the only solutions that, under the circumstances, make practical sense.

Will it work? There are plenty of good reasons for thinking it will. True, it might temporarily increase the deficit and the national debt, but if the predicted growth eventually occurs, both deficit and debt will be imposed on a larger and stronger economy which can easily support them. Moreover, we do have some solid historical evidence that the "feedback" effects of cuts in tax rates, in terms of increased tax revenues, are always larger than our economists and Treasury officials, whose econometric models cannot cope with such "feedback" effects, expect to be the case. This is what happened with the Kennedy-Johnson tax cuts, which were as large, in terms of the 1964 economy, as the Reagan tax cuts are in the 1981 economy. There is no reason why it should not happen again.

One final point, often overlooked. Because of the increase in social security taxes that has taken effect this year, and because of automatic "bracket creep" in the income tax resulting from inflation, we shall in effect be experiencing something like a $40 billion tax increase in 1981. No economist of any persuasion, no politician of any persuasion, no commentator (liberal or conservative) has been heard to say that such a tax increase would be good for the economy in its present condition. Yet many of these same people are volubly disturbed by a tax cut that will, in 1981, at best keep our tax burden in a steady state, and in 1982 only alleviate it modestly.

Somehow, the current condition of economic theory, combined with existing ideological trends, has given us a level of public discourse on economic policy that is disgracefully inadequate to our economic and political realities. No one, critical though he may be, seems even to feel the need to offer a practicable alternative to Reagan's economic policy. One even suspects that many critics of supply-side economics want above all to see it fail, since its success would threaten their ideological investments.

1981

American Conservatism

1945–1995

The Public Interest was born well before the term "neoconservative" was invented, and will, I trust, be alive and active when the term is of only historical interest. That time may even be now, as the distinction between conservative and neoconservative has been blurred almost beyond recognition. Still, the distinction has not yet been entirely extinguished—it still turns up when Jeane Kirkpatrick's views on foreign policy are mentioned—so this may be a suitable moment to look back and define the role that neoconservatism, and *The Public Interest* specifically, has played in the history of American conservatism since the end of World War II. (A quite different, but equally useful, essay could be written on its role in the history of postwar liberalism.)

In that half-century, as I see it, American conservatism has gone through three stages. First there was the renewal of what might be called traditional conservatism, centered around William F. Buckley's *National Review* and having the goal of reprogramming the Republican Party into a solidly conservative political instrument. This led to the nomination of Barry Goldwater in 1964 and the ensuing electoral debacle. That debacle, however, had the result of consolidating and expanding conservative influence within the Republican Party. This is not as paradoxical as it appears. After all, the comparable debacle of McGovern's defeat in 1972 resulted in the left wing of American liberalism, whose candidate he was, gaining effective control of the Democratic Party. Inner-party dynamics can be far more important than election results, on which the media and public attention naturally focus.

Second, there was the influence of the neoconservative impulse. Originally, this impulse looked to the Democratic Party for political expression, but by the mid-1970s that was obviously an expectation difficult to sustain, and a gradual, often reluctant, shift toward the Republican Party got under way. (There are still quite a few Democratic neoconservatives, most of whom by now quietly vote Republican.) *The Public Interest* was the focal point of this neoconservative impulse, though much of its impact was the result of its influence on the younger men and women who were ensconced in the editorial and "op-ed" departments of the *Wall Street Journal*. Neoconservatism differed in many important respects from traditional conservatism, but had no program of its own. Basically, it wanted the Republican Party to cease playing defensive politics, to be forward-looking rather than backward-looking. Some of us actually dared to suggest that the party should be more "ideological," although "ideology" is not a term pleasing to American ears. In the end, the notion of an activist "agenda" has become ever more integral to Republican political thinking, doing the work of "ideology" though in a peculiarly pragmatic American way. The substance of any specific agenda may not have much to do with neoconservatism, but the moving spirit does.

Third, there has been the emergence, over the past decades, of religion-based, morally concerned, political conservatism. In the long run, this may be the most important of all. Though the media persist in portraying the religious conservatives as aggressive fanatics, in fact their motivation has been primarily defensive, a reaction against the popular counterculture, against the doctrinaire secularism of the Supreme Court, and against a government that taxes them heavily while removing all traces of morality and religion from public education, for example, even as it subsidizes all sorts of activities and programs that are outrages against traditional morality. The religious faith behind this reaction has been steadily gaining in both intensity and popularity, especially among Protestant evangelicals, and may well now have a dynamism of its own. It is not at all unimaginable that the United States is headed for a bitter and sustained *Kulturkampf* that could overwhelm conventional notions of what is and what is not political.

Let me look at the evolution of postwar conservatism from the perspective of a neoconservative. When *National Review* was founded in 1955, I regarded it as an eccentricity on the ideological landscape; it seemed so completely out of phase. Essentially it continued the polemic against the New Deal that characterized American conservatism, as represented by the Republican Party, throughout the 1930s and 1940s. As a child of the Depression who was outraged at the spectacle of idle factories, unused resources, and vast unemployment all coexisting, I could not take seriously the seemingly blind faith in "free enterprise" that was the primal certainty of *National Review*. I simply found this point of view irrelevant. So did practically everyone else at the time, at least the "everyone else" I knew or read.

To some aspects of the conservative message I was certainly vulnerable, even then. Though a liberal, I had never been enamored with those beliefs that constituted an orthodox liberal outlook. Thus, I had always been in favor of capital punishment. I never believed that criminality could be "cured" by therapeutic treatment. I never doubted that school prayer was a perfectly sensible idea. I was convinced that the "basics"—rote learning and memorization—offered the young the best opportunity for learning. I thought that "sexual permissiveness," in all its guises, was an absurd idea. I regarded the ideal of a "world without war" as utopian, and "making the world safe for democracy" a futile enterprise. So I could honestly say that I would welcome the appearance of a conservative magazine, a magazine that was reflective (in the Burke-Tocqueville tradition), one that would help refine and elevate public discourse. What I meant, I now suspect, was that I would welcome a conservative magazine that was not overly offensive to liberal sensibilities, a magazine that did not aim to destroy liberalism but to complement it.

National Review was certainly not that. It was brash, even vulgar in its antiliberal polemics. There was something collegiate—sophomoric, to be blunt—about its high-spiritedness, and its general tone was anti-intellectual. Above all, it seemed to me simple-minded in its "anti-statism" in general and its contempt for all social reforms in particular. There is little doubt that its "anti-statism" revivified, for a lot of people, even younger people, the dormant nerves of anti–New Deal fervor. Ten years earlier, the popularity of Friedrich Hayek's *The Road to Serfdom* had already signified the possibility of such a revival. But I had not read that book, and though I have come to admire his later writings in political philosophy and intellectual history, I still haven't read it. The reason is that I did not believe for a moment that the American people would allow themselves to be seduced or coerced along any such path. I deemed that kind of "anti-statism" to be a species of political hysteria, and I felt its reaction to the New Deal excessive. So I did not take *National Review* seriously as a political journal.

Which, it turns out, was a mistake, the kind of mistake that intellectuals are especially prone to make in politics. We say, repeatedly, that ideas have consequences, which is true, but what we have in mind are complex, thoughtful, and well-articulated ideas. What we so easily overlook is the fact that simple ideas, allied to passion and organization, also have consequences. *National Review*, it turns out, was part of a larger movement that created institutions which shaped and trained several thousand young conservatives, not so much to go forth and proclaim the gospel as to go into the Republican Party and gain control of it. This they did, most effectively, over the next decade. The result was that it was Goldwater, and not Nelson Rockefeller, who was the Republican Party's nominee in 1964. Nor did Goldwater's defeat change the reality that liberal Republicanism had suffered a mortal wound and the eastern, "establishment" wing of the party had yielded dominance to the conservative wing. The Nixon years were a troubled time of transition, and for the younger conservatives in that administration it was a disaster. But the course had been set. It was the *National Review* idol Ronald Reagan who won the nomination in 1980, and today—despite the George Bush interregnum—the Republican Party is unquestionably a conservative party. But what kind of conservative party? Much has happened since those early years in the 1950s, and the conservatism of *National Review* has largely been reshaped by the emergence of new currents of conservative thought.

One such current was what came to be called "neoconservatism," and its origins can be traced to the founding of *The Public Interest* thirty years ago. Not that the founders of this journal had any such political goal. We were all liberals, of a kind, in 1965. But it turned out that most of us were the kind of liberals who were destined to play a role in the conservative revival. The dozen or so scholars and intellectuals who were the nucleus of the new venture were in a state of dissatisfaction with the liberal temper of the age. But at that time, the conservatism of *National Review* interested us not at all. There were many points of repulsion, but it was *NR*'s primordial (as we saw it) hostility to the New Deal that created a gulf between us and them. We were all children of the Depression, most of us from lower-middle-class or working-class families, a significant number of us urban Jews for whom the 1930s had been years of desperation, and we felt a measure of loyalty to the spirit of the New Deal if not to all its programs and policies. Nor did we see it as representing any kind of "statist" or socialist threat to the American democracy. As James Q. Wilson, one of the "founding fathers," recently wrote in *The New Republic* (May 22, 1995):

> American liberalism, like America in general, is different. Created by the New Deal but drawing on features of the earlier progressive movement, liberalism here, unlike the liberalism found in many European nations, never took seriously the idea of nationalizing major industries, only occasionally and then without much conviction proposed any major distribution of income, and merely flirted with centralized economic planning. A welfare state was created, but compared to the welfare state in many other industrialized nations, the American version offered less generous benefits to the unemployed, provided no children's allowances and restricted tax-supported medical care to veterans, the elderly and the very poor.

All of us had ideas on how to improve, even reconstruct, this welfare state; we were meliorists, not opponents, and only measured critics. It was when the Great Society programs were launched that we began to distance ourselves, slowly and reluctantly, from the newest version of official liberalism. But it was not only the Great Society that affected us. The *Zeitgeist* of the 1960s was, in retrospect, really quite bizarre. "Automation," for instance, was a prime bogeyman, as was the corollary prospect of a "push-button society" in which workers would experience a surfeit of leisure they were not equipped to handle. The Ford Foundation and other trendy institutions had many conferences and sponsored many books on "the problem of leisure," while Lyndon Johnson appointed a Commission on Automation. Fortunately, Daniel Bell was on that commission, and, together with Robert Solow of MIT, he composed a sensible report. This experience with the automation-leisure scare moved Dan Bell and myself to contemplate the founding of this magazine. Someone, we felt, had to continue talking modest sense, even if grandiose nonsense was temporarily so very popular.

The tone of *The Public Interest*, from the outset, was skeptical, pragmatic, meliorist. We were especially provoked by the widespread acceptance of left-wing sociological ideas that were incorporated in the War on Poverty. The most egregious such idea was the Community Action Program, which would mobilize the urban poor, especially the black poor, to "fight city hall," literally. The prescribed cure for poverty was defined as militant political action, even revolutionary political action, that would result in the redistribution of income and wealth. This idea, spawned by the Jacobins in the French Revolution, has probably been the most popular and pernicious belief of the past two centuries, distorting expectations and destroying the economies of many a Third World country. We at *The Public Interest*, having known poverty firsthand—the authors of the War on Poverty were mainly upper-middle-class types—and witnessed the ways poverty was overcome in reality, by gradual economic growth with the concomitant growth of economic opportunity, were utterly contemptuous of this idea. And our attitude had surprising echoes in unexpected places.

The reason was that most of us were social scientists, and as Pat Moynihan put it, the best use of social science is to refute false social science. Since we live in an age when "experts" are overvalued, the social science in *The Public Interest* had its effect. Actually, one could have reached the same, sound conclusions from the study of history, or even just looking, not at people mired in poverty, but at those poor people who had managed to move out of poverty—people who were all around us. But that's not the kind of testimony that Congressional committees and the media were looking for.

As *The Public Interest* continued on its modest way, at first with a circulation of two thousand to three thousand, all sorts of portentous things were happening around us, which made us feel, and made us appear to be, more conservative than we had anticipated. One was the student rebellion of the late 1960s, a rebellion aimed primarily at the liberal professoriate; the small minority of conservative professors were largely ignored. This assault reminded many liberal professors that their liberalism had implicit limits, beyond which lay some quite conservative assumptions about the nature of authority in general and in a university in particular. There is nothing like the utopian idiocies of the extreme left—the "infantile" left, as Lenin called it—to stir thoughts of moderation among the centrist majority. And from such thoughts of moderation, some second thoughts about the implications of moderation are bound to develop, and these second thoughts will always, in that context or that situation, turn out to involve a conservative modification of the original liberalism.

The student rebellion had, of course, close ties with the emerging counterculture, which set out to scandalize and delegitimize the regnant liberalism in its own bold and brash way. Liberal professors and liberal intellectuals liked, at that time, to think of themselves as "broad-minded," but they were nevertheless shocked. It's one thing to give scholarly approval to historical, sociological, and psychological studies that demonstrated our conventional family structure to be less universal, more "culture-bound," than one had realized. It is quite another thing to see one's children enticed into sexual promiscuity, drugs, and suicide. The liberal professoriate, and many members of the intellectual community, had always kept its distance from "bourgeois society," and always tried to be "objective" about bourgeois mores. Now, a great many discovered, albeit reluctantly, that they had been bourgeois all along.

Soon, *The Public Interest* no longer stood alone. *Commentary*, which had for some years flirted with the left, veered sharply in a neoconservative direction. Even more important was the arrival of Robert Bartley as editor of the editorial page of the *Wall Street Journal*. He quickly melded the familiar anti-statist views of the *Journal* with the neoconservative critique of contemporary liberalism. This trio of publications suddenly became something like a national force, and politicians and editorial writers began to pay attention.

What kind of force was it? It is not easy, even in retrospect, to answer that question in a crisp and clear way. I would say that there were three distinctive aspects to the neoconservative "movement" (a rather grandiose term, given its modest dimensions). First, the political tonality was different. This was surely the result of our liberal heritage, which predisposed us to be forward-looking, not in any sense dour and reactionary. I once remarked, semi-facetiously, that to be a neoconservative one had to be of a cheerful disposition, no matter how depressing the current outlook. In America all successful politics is the politics of hope, a mood not noticeable in traditional American conservatism. The way to win, in politics as in sport, is to think of yourself as a winner. The pathos of being proved right, while losing, is always a great temptation to a conservative minority in opposition.

Secondly, it follows that our natural impulse was melioristic. From the out-set, I was mindful of the injunction of my first editor at *Commentary*, Elliot Cohen, that you can't beat a horse with no horse. Even while being critical of the Great Society, *The Public Interest* was always interested in proposing alter-nate reforms, alternate legislation, that would achieve the desired aims more securely, and without the downside effects. This was something that did not much interest traditional conservatism, with its emphatic "anti-statist" focus. The difference also had something to do with the fact that traditional conser-vatives had many distinguished economists in their ranks, and economics is above all the science of limits, a great nay-saying enterprise. Among the core so-cial scientists around *The Public Interest* there were no economists. (They came later, as we "matured.") This explains my own rather cavalier attitude toward the budget deficit and other monetary or fiscal problems. The task, as I saw it, was to create a new majority, which evidently would mean a conservative majority, which came to mean, in turn, a Republican majority, so political effectiveness was the priority, not the accounting deficiencies of government.

Thirdly, neoconservatives, at least the New Yorkers among them, came out of an intellectual milieu in which some large ideas, ideas with a philosophic or ideological dimension, were taken very seriously. This was of little significance in the early years of neoconservatism, but it did become very important as the nation found itself in a third stage of postwar conservative history, a stage in which religious conservatism became an active force in American politics.

Active religion-based conservatism did not become a political force in the United States because of either religion or conservatism. Its activism was pro-voked by militant liberalism and the militant secularism associated with it. This liberalism and this secularism, in the postwar years, came to dominate the Democratic Party, the educational establishment, the media, the law schools, the judiciary, the major schools of divinity, the bishops of the Catholic Church, and the bureaucracies of the "mainline" Protestant denominations. One day, so to speak, millions of American Christians—most of them, as it happens, registered Democrats—came to the realization that they were insti-tutionally isolated and impotent. They quite naturally wanted their children to be raised as well-behaved Christians but discovered that their authority over their own children had been subverted and usurped by an aggressive, secular liberalism that now dominated our public education system and our popular culture. They looked at our high schools and saw that gay and lesbian organizations were free to distribute their literature to the students but that religious organizations were not. They saw condoms being distributed to adolescent teenagers while the Supreme Court forbade the posting of the Ten Commandments on the classroom wall. And so they rebelled and did the only thing left for them to do; they began to organize politically. In so doing they may very well have initiated a sea-change in American politics and American life.

Inevitably, the conservative Christians began to seek links with traditional conservatives, since they shared common enemies: liberal government, a left-liberal educational establishment, a judiciary besotted with liberal dogmas. But this alliance worked smoothly only up to a point. The trouble with traditional conservatism, especially those segments dominated by a purely economic conservatism, was that it tended to be libertarian and even secular-minded when it came to the kinds of moral and social issues that agitated Christian conservatives. There is an important difference between the kind of "liberty" dear to the hearts of economic conservatives and leaders of the business community, and the "ordered liberty" that any serious religion would have in mind. This contradiction became obvious in Ronald Reagan's appointees to the Federal Communications Commission, men who were enthusiastic about deregulation but indifferent about opening the doors to pornography. That same contradiction is today glaringly obvious within the Republican Party, which economic conservatives have dominated ever since the post–Civil War period.

Oddly enough, the Christian conservatives found it easier to get along with the neoconservatives, many of whom come from an intellectual background and an intellectual milieu that is more concerned with criticizing liberalism than with criticizing "statism." It was primarily the neoconservative criticism of welfare for corrupting the souls of its recipients, as against the traditional conservative emphasis on the waste of taxpayers' money, that helped make welfare reform a major issue for religious conservatives. Similarly, the troubled condition of the modern family was a concern of both secular neoconservatives and Christian conservatives before it became a popular conservative topic. Not that this now matters all that much, since the merger of neoconservatism and traditional conservatism, under way since the election of Ronald Reagan, is largely complete. Even the term "neoconservative" is not much used, "conservative" now having stretched its meaning to be more inclusive. But today's traditional, libertarian, economically focused conservatives are still strong enough to win local or statewide elections and to dominate the United States Senate. This is a source of constant irritation to Christian conservatives.

So the assimilation of Christian conservatives into American conservatism is still in its relatively early stages, and it is creating serious tensions. To some degree, this is because Christian conservatism is a "movement," not simply a political party, and like all movements of this kind it has its various factions, some of whom are more committed to demonstrating the steadfastness of their Christian faith than to exercising political influence. To some degree, too, the secular temper of the business community—not densely populated by Bible-reading types—has a powerful grip on the Republican political imagination, as well as on its finances. It is even possible that Christian conservatism will fragment into new political parties. The conventional political wisdom, wedded to our two-party system, would assume that this would mark the political demise of Christian conservatism. That is possible. But it is also possible that the two-party system, however deeply rooted in our history, is not going to be with us forever.

In any case, I think it is probably an error to focus so narrowly on the role of Christian conservatism in American politics. The born-again Christian impulse is, above all, a religious impulse that looks well beyond any political horizon. It is my sense that this impulse will grow in the years ahead, whatever the political fortunes or misfortunes of Christian political conservatism. We have lived through a century of ever more extreme hedonism, antinomianism, personal and sexual individualism, licentiousness (as it used to be called), and no one who has bothered to read a bit of history ought to be surprised if it culminates in some kind of aggressive religious awakening. So the rise of Christian political conservatism may turn out to be a prelude to something far more important, involving the place of religion in American life, including American public life. Just what form this renewed religious impulse will take no one can foresee. We—all of us—could be in for some shocking surprises.

1995

The Right Stuff

I remember the day very well, back in 1956, when I arrived at my office at *Encounter*, of which I was then co-editor, and found on my desk an unsolicited manuscript by Michael Oakeshott. This, I thought, is the way every editor's day should begin, with an over-the-transom arrival of an essay by one of the finest living political thinkers and certainly the finest stylist. The manuscript was called "On Being Conservative," and I read it with pleasure and appreciation. It was beautifully written, subtle in its argument, delicate in its perceptions, and full of sentences and paragraphs that merit the attention of anthologists for decades, perhaps even centuries, to come. Fortunately, this essay is to be found in his book, *Rationalism in Politics*. I say "fortunately" because, after loving every line of this essay, I sat down and wrote to Michael, rejecting it.

I forget what disingenuous circumlocutions I invented for that letter, probably something about its being both too abstract and too specifically British in its frame of reference for our journal. But the truth is that, while I admired the essay immensely, I did not really like it. Which is another way of saying that I disagreed with it. At that time, I was not sure why I disagreed with it. Today, looking back over the past forty years, I can see why. I was American, Michael was English. I was then in the earliest stages of intellectual pregnancy with those dispositions that later merged as neoconservatism. And American neoconservatism is very different from the kind of ideal English conservatism that Oakeshott was celebrating so brilliantly. It is also different from the much less ideal conservatism that still dominates the Conservative Party.

Conservatism in the United States today is on a different track from that of Britain and Western Europe—I insist on the distinction—and it is reasonable to think that one of us may be on the better track. Oakeshott's essay focuses on what he calls "the conservative disposition." Let him describe that disposition in his own lovely language:

The general characteristics of this disposition . . . centre upon a propensity to use and enjoy what is available rather than what was or may be. . . . What is esteemed is the present, and it is esteemed not on account of connections with a remote antiquity, nor because it is recognised to be more admirable than any possible alternative, but on account of its familiarity. . . . To be conservative, then, is to prefer the familiar to the unknown, to prefer the tried to the untried, fact to mystery, the actual to the possible, the limited to the unbounded, the near to the distant . . . the convenient to the perfect, present laughter to utopian bliss.

These words are bound to strike a chord in the souls of any reader, since all of us, in varying degrees, participate in such a disposition. What we call civilization is itself based on the power of this disposition. But even as I respond to Oakeshott's ideal conservatism, I know, as I knew back in 1956, that it is not for me. And this for two reasons. First, it is irredeemably secular, as I, being a Jewish conservative, am not. Were I a Christian conservative, my reaction would be the same. For it is impossible for any religious person to have the kinds of attitudes toward the past and the future that Oakeshott's conservative disposition celebrates. Our scriptures and our daily prayer book link us to the past and to the future with an intensity lacking in Oakeshott's vision. Not that this religious dimension of our humanity in any way denigrates the present, in all its fullness. Judaism especially, being a more this-worldly religion than Christianity, moves us to sanctify the present in our daily lives, while always reminding us that we are capable of doing so only through God's grace to our distant forefathers. And of course, the whole purpose of sanctifying the present is to prepare humanity for a redemptive future.

In short, Oakeshott's ideal conservative society is a society without religion, since all religions bind us as securely to past and future as to the present. The conservative disposition is real enough, but without the religious dimension, it is thin gruel. In the concluding sentence of his inaugural lecture at the London School of Economics, Oakeshott made that magnificent biblical declaration to the effect that this is the best of all possible worlds and everything in it is a necessary evil. But his conservative disposition offers us no guidance in coping with all those necessary evils, which can tear our lives apart and destroy whatever equanimity we have achieved as a result of reading the writers of philosophy.

Second, Oakeshott's conservative disposition runs squarely against the American grain. Oh, Americans possess such a disposition all right. Despite all one reads about the frustrations of American life, it is the rare American who dreams of moving to another land. We are, in some respects, a very conservative people, but not quite in the Oakeshottian sense. To begin with, we have a most emphatic relation to our past—an ideological relation, some would say. In the United States today, all school children, in all fifty states, begin their day with a recitation of the Pledge of Allegiance to the Flag and to the Constitution. There is no national legislation to this effect; it is entirely up to the states. Despite some efforts by radical educators, no state has removed this prescription. In addition, there is the extraordinary fact that at the opening of every high school, college, and professional sporting event players and spectators rise to their feet and sing the national anthem. And it is not a good idea to fail to do so. The United States today is the most vibrantly patriotic of all the Western democracies. Some might say—a sophisticated European would surely be tempted to say—that this merely demonstrates that the United States is, in some crucial respects, a premodern country. Perhaps so. Or perhaps we are a postmodern country; one should not exclude that possibility.

Behind this ideological patriotism is the fact that the United States is a creedal nation. Being American has nothing to do with ethnicity, or blood ties of any kind, or lineage, or length of residence even. What we scornfully call nativism in the United States is what passes for authentic patriotism among many Germans and Frenchmen. None of this is surprising if you recall that the United States is literally a nation of immigrants and in the course of time has developed astonishing powers of assimilation. What is surprising is the intensity of patriotism generated by this fact, an intensity owing to the great fact that assimilation in the United States is like a conversion experience, in which a new creed replaces an old.

This creed and this ideological fervor are suffused with a kind of religious sensibility. Indeed, American patriotism was born out of the sensibility of Protestant dissent. In the last two centuries, our increasingly secular outlook has tempered this sensibility, so that sociologists now blandly refer to an American civic religion that unites the community with secular ties. The concept of a civic religion has its validity, up to a point. We are no longer the "nation under God" as we once casually defined ourselves. But that reservoir of religiosity is still there, and these still waters run deep. Most Americans thought Soviet Communism to be an awful idea, and a terrible reality, simply because it was "atheistic and godless," and so doomed. They did not have to read Hayek to come to this conclusion.

There are tensions between American religiosity and the more secular civic religion, but they coexist because they also have much in common. They subscribe equally to a version of the Judeo-Christian moral tradition. Both are individualistic when it comes to economic matters, wedding the Protestant ethic to the philosophy of Adam Smith. Both approve of economic growth, as a character-building exercise and as a way of improving the human condition. And both are, in general, future-oriented and progressive in their political vision. When Americans deplore the present they always assume that it can be improved upon; American politics is about the controversial choices this entails. Today there is so much to deplore in this present that Oakeshott's paean to present-mindedness is singularly inapt.

All of this is by way of a background explanation to what I see as a major divergence today between American conservatism and British conservatism. It is a divergence with significant implications for the future of the Western democracies. The difference can be summed up this way. Conservatism in the United States today is a movement, a popular movement, not a faction within any political party. Although most conservatives vote Republican, they are not party loyalists, and the party has to woo them to win their votes. The movement is issue-oriented. It will happily combine with the Republicans if the party is "right" on the issues. If not, it will walk away. This troubled relationship between the conservative movement and the Republicans is a key to the understanding of American politics today. The conservative movement is a powerful force within the party, but it does not dominate. And there is no possibility of the party ever dominating the movement.

American conservatism after the Second World War begins to take shape with the American publication of Hayek's *The Road to Serfdom* in 1943 and the founding in 1955 of William F. Buckley's *National Review*. Previously, there had been a small circle who were admirers of the Jeffersonian, quasi-anarchist teaching of the likes of Albert Jay Nock, but no one paid much attention to them. Hayek's polemic against socialism did strike a chord, however, especially among members of the business community. There may have been people converted from statism to anti-statism by that book, but my impression is that most admirers of the book were already pro–free market. What Hayek did was to mobilize them intellectually, and to make their views more respectable. I have to confess that I still have not read *The Road to Serfdom*, although I am a great admirer of Hayek's later writings in intellectual history and political philosophy. The reason was, and is, that not for a moment did I believe that the United States was on any kind of road to serfdom. Socialism has never had much of a presence in America, and besides, having gone through a brief Trotskyist phase in my college days, I needed no instruction on socialist illusions or the evils of Soviet Communism.

Still, it is fair to say that an anti-socialist, anti-statist perspective dominated the thinking and politically active part of American conservatism from 1945 to the Goldwater campaign of 1964. William F. Buckley's *National Review* represented this point of view, and it gradually helped recruit enough younger political activists to become a force within the Republican Party. The Nixon elections of 1968 and 1972, however, revealed that, even when winning elections, largely through Democratic default, the basic principles of postwar conservatism had little purchase on American realities. And yet, from the ashes of the Goldwater-Nixon debacles there arose Ronald Reagan, to become a popular two-term president. What happened?

Two things, I would say. First, although certainly not in order of political significance, was the emergence of an intellectual trend that later came to be called neoconservatism. This trend, in which I was deeply involved, differed in one crucial respect from its conservative predecessors: its chosen enemy was contemporary liberalism, not socialism or statism in the abstract. (About communism, as distinct, say, from Soviet foreign policy, we had almost nothing to say, we were so utterly hostile to it.) The dozen or so academics and intellectuals who formed the original core of neoconservatism, located at *The Public Interest*, a journal Daniel Bell and I founded in 1965, were all disillusioned liberals: disillusioned with the newest twists and turns of that liberalism, but also (in varying degrees) with their past liberalism whose inherent philosophical flaws now became visible.

The symbol of the influence of neoconservative thinking on the Republican Party was the fact that Ronald Reagan could praise Franklin D. Roosevelt as a great American president—praise echoed by Newt Gingrich a dozen years later. The message was clear: the Republican Party was no longer interested in destroying the welfare state, but intended rather to reconstruct it along more economical and humane lines. The emphasis on more "humane" is another sign of neoconservative influence. Whereas traditional conservatism had tried to focus attention on welfare cheating, the writings of various neoconservatives emphasized the terrible, demoralizing effects of our welfare system on the recipients of welfare themselves. It was no longer a matter of simply saving the budget from welfare expenditures but of redeeming the welfare population from the kind of exploitation involved in a system that created and encouraged dependency. The new message gave a moral dimension to welfare reform that it had lacked.

To the surprise of most observers, the critique of liberalism by neoconservative intellectuals, such as Leo Strauss, was in some ways more effective than the older attack on statism. Paradoxically, precisely because there was no socialist movement, no ideological statist movement in the United States, the neoconservative critique went deeper, and was more radical, than conservative critiques in Britain or Europe. Who would have thought it possible, fifty years ago, that in 1996, one-third of the American public would designate itself as conservative while only 17 percent designated itself as liberal, with the rest claiming the label of "moderate." To bring contemporary liberalism into disrepute—its simplistic views of human nature, its utopian social philosophy, its secularist animus against religion—is no small achievement.

The second, and most spectacular, thing that happened was the emergence of religious conservatives as a force to be reckoned with. This has no parallel in any of the other Western democracies. It has been estimated that something like one-third of the U.S. electorate are (or claim to be) regular churchgoers. Not all of them are conservative, but the majority are. Insofar as they are anti-statist, as most are, it is not only on economic grounds. These religious conservatives see, quite clearly and correctly, that statism in the United States is organically linked with secular liberalism, that many of the programs of the welfare state have a powerful anti-religious animus. School prayer is a very live issue among the religious conservatives not because public schools are especially suitable places for young people to pray in, but because our educational system, dominated by the teachers' unions, the schools of education, and the liberal politicians who count on their active electoral support, is biased in an anti-religious way.

Conservative politicians woo the religious conservatives, but only neoconservatives can really speak to them. Many neoconservative intellectuals are not themselves religiously observant in their private lives, although more and more are coming to be. This leads to accusations by liberals of hypocrisy or cold-blooded political instrumentalism. But such accusations miss the point. All political philosophers prior to the twentieth century, regardless of their personal piety, understood the importance of religion in the life of the political community. Neoconservatives, because of their interest in and attachment to classical political philosophy, share this understanding. Just as there is a difference between being pious and being observant, so there is a difference between being observant and being religious. As it happens, a disproportionate number of neoconservatives are Jewish, and within the Jewish community such distinctions have always been blurred. In any case, more and more Christians and Jews these days, who themselves have a secular lifestyle, are seeing to it that their children are raised within a religious tradition. Modern secularism has such affinities to moral nihilism that even those who wish simply to affirm or reaffirm moral values have little choice but to seek a grounding for such values in a religious tradition.

Most foreign journalists, like their American counterparts, tend to be secularist in outlook and therefore have difficulty in understanding what is happening within American politics. One has only to read the American reporting in such a distinguished journal as *The Economist* to experience this difficulty, to read reporting that is sophisticated, blandly superficial, and misleading. It is not only religion that creates this difficulty, there is also the equally significant issue of populism. American democracy regularly witnesses populist upsurges. European and British observers, along with most American scholars, tend to describe them as spasms or even paroxysms. But they are nothing of the sort. They are built into the very structure of American politics in a way that is alien to British or European politics, where "politics" is what the government says or does. In a sense, it is fair to say that contemporary political journalism, as well as most political scholarship, is statist in its preconceptions and vision. Whenever a populist upsurge occurs, as is the case today, national politics in the United States trails way behind local politics.

In the United States, most school boards are locally elected, and school board politics is the way most adult Americans begin their political education. If you are looking for some of the reasons for the strength of American conservatism today, watching local school board politics is a good, although difficult, place to begin—difficult because there are so many such school boards, and the issues that cause contention vary from place to place. Still, had we been paying attention, we would be better prepared to appreciate the frustrations of so many American parents with the educational establishment. It is not simply that their children do not often get a decent education in the basics, but that the counterculture born after the Second World War has captured the school system itself, and has been codified in the leading schools of education. Parents are loath to argue with educators, who are presumed to be the experts, and when they do argue they are sufficiently confused and intimidated to argue badly. But anxiety, a diffuse terror even, about what kinds of mature young people their children will grow up to be is widespread. Sooner or later, politicians emerge to tap this kind of anxiety. That is why the so-called social issues, or more accurately moral issues, are so powerful today. The Clinton administration, convinced (as most liberals are) that economic issues are at the center of politics, finds itself bewildered and impotent when confronted by such issues. Economic frustration liberals are sensitive to, but moral frustration is incomprehensible to them.

In Washington, D.C., the most liberal and statist city in the nation, school board politics is unworthy of the attention of the national media. Our liberal media do not mind presidential primaries or primaries for governorships, which fit into their framework of politics-as-a-horse-race. But they hate primaries for lower offices: that is local news and unworthy of their attention. Referendums—a legacy of the progressive movement that is institutionalized in many of our states—are now equally despised because they introduce a wild card into the established political game and are more successfully used by conservative activists. Our secular liberal media are horrified by politicians who mix religion with politics because they are convinced that religion is, at best, a private affair. A politician who so much as mentions Jesus Christ alarms them.

Ironically, Washington and the liberal media have been unprepared for conservative changes within the media itself. Our national news magazines, our half-dozen or so newspapers that claim national attention, and our national television networks are all liberal, more or less, and feel that they share the journalistic mission of enlightening (as well as entertaining) the American public. They have tried, somewhat less than halfheartedly, to give representation to the conservative viewpoint whenever they sense that this viewpoint has become popular. But they were utterly unprepared for the sudden emergence and swift rise of radio talk shows, which now rival television's daytime soap operas in popularity. These talk shows are overwhelmingly conservative in their politics and populist in their rhetoric.

All of this happened without anyone planning it or anticipating it. It was made possible by the federal structure of our polity and by the fact that there are well over a thousand local radio stations. Once a local program host, Rush Limbaugh, for instance, becomes popular, other stations, always eager for listeners, will rush to broadcast him. And if, for competitive reasons, they cannot do so, they will try hard to invent their own popular conservative talk shows. The owners of these stations are interested primarily in making money, not in spreading any kind of liberal enlightenment. And given the near absence of government regulation, the market works.

In the United States, there is always a latent populist potential simply because the structure of our polity and of our economy make it possible for *vox populi* to find expression. This populist potential disturbs political theorists, even conservative ones who fear that populist dissatisfaction can have an anti-capitalist thrust. In fact, this has rarely been the case in the United States. Even the original populist movement at the beginning of this century, generally identified as belonging to the left, was not really so. It was hostile to big business, not to the free market. It is interesting to note that today populist opinion, as every poll shows, is more concerned about cutting the federal deficit than about lowering taxes, which has come as a great surprise to many con-servatives, who learned in their political science courses that "the people" al-ways want to be pandered to. It is also worth noting that the current Republican Congress is turning a cold shoulder to the lobbyists of the big cor-porations while exuding friendliness to those organizations that represent smaller businesses. This upsets many conservative economists who point to statistics that show the economic importance of multinational corporations. Which only shows that the statistics of economists, along with those of the public opinion poll, are best ignored by a conservative government that is in-terested not merely in being reelected but in creating an enduring national conservative majority.

In foreign policy, too, the new conservative populism is playing a crucial, although as yet ambiguous, role. The liberal Democrats, ever since 1930, have been interventionist and multilateralist in foreign policy. The conservative Re-publicans have tended to be nationalist and isolationist. This situation is changing. Liberal Democrats are much less interested in seeing the United States play a major role in world affairs. In contrast, Republicans now favor in-ternational free trade; while still nationalist, they are no longer isolationist. Just how those trends will develop in the future is unknowable. The Republi-cans have a special problem in defining a nationalist foreign policy in a post–Cold War world. But multilateralism is dead, so far as both parties are concerned. This is something our European allies (and our own State Depart-ment) seem not to understand. It is not that U.S. opinion has turned hostile to the United Nations and NATO. Rather, there is not enough interest in such organizations to breed hostility.

This populist conservatism, now the trend in American conservatism, has its own internal problems. There are still traditional conservatives who are sus-picious of populism. Many of them are still in the Senate, but even in the House of Representatives there is internal dissent. The "right to life" move-ment, like the abolitionists of a century and a half ago, are fanatically deter-mined to make the best the enemy of the good. Then there are all those newly elected Republican governors, critical of the welfare state but reluctant to give up federal funds that help them cope with their own budgetary shortfalls. Talk of an abrupt conservative revolution is hyperbole, even if it does inspire the troops. There will surely be defeats ahead, some of them self-inflicted.

The United States today shares all of the evils, all of the problems, to be found among the Western democracies, sometimes in an exaggerated form. But it is also the only Western democracy that is witnessing a serious conser-vative revival that is an active response to these evils and problems. The fact that it is a populist conservatism dismays the conservative elites of Britain and Western Europe, who prefer a more orderly and dignified kind of conservatism. It is true that populism can be a danger to our democratic orders. But it is also true that populism can be a corrective to the defects of democratic order, defects often arising from the intellectual influence and the entrepreneurial politics of our democratic elites. Classical political thought was wary of democracy because it saw the people as fickle, envious, and inherently turbulent. They had no knowledge of democracies where the people were conservative and the educated elites that governed them were ideological, always busy provoking disorder and discontent in the name of some utopian goal. Populist conservatism is a distinctly modern phenomenon, and conservative thinking has not yet caught up with it. That is why the "exceptional" kind of conservative politics we are now witnessing in the United States is so important. It could turn out to represent the "last, best hope" of contemporary conservatism.

1996

The Neoconservative
Persuasion

What exactly is neoconservatism? Journalists, and now even presidential candidates, speak with an enviable confidence on who or what is "neoconservative," and seem to assume the meaning is fully revealed in the name. Those of us who are designated as "neocons" are amused, flattered, or dismissive, depending on the context. It is reasonable to wonder: is there any "there" there? Even I, frequently referred to as the "godfather" of all those neocons, have had my moments of wonderment. A few years ago I said (and, alas, wrote) that neoconservatism had had its own distinctive qualities in its early years, but by now had been absorbed into the mainstream of American conservatism. I was wrong, and the reason I was wrong is that, ever since its origin among disillusioned liberal intellectuals in the 1970s, what we call neoconservatism has been one of those intellectual undercurrents that surface only intermittently. It is not a "movement," as the conspiratorial critics would have it. Neoconservatism is what the late historian of Jacksonian America, Marvin Meyers, called a "persuasion," one that manifests itself over time, but erratically, and one whose meaning we clearly glimpse only in retrospect.

Viewed in this way, one can say that the historical task and political purpose of neoconservatism would seem to be this: to convert the Republican Party, and American conservatism in general, against their respective wills, into a new kind of conservative politics suitable to governing a modern democracy. That this new conservative politics is distinctly American is beyond doubt. There is nothing like neoconservatism in Europe, and most European conservatives are highly skeptical of its legitimacy. The fact that conservatism in the United States is so much healthier than in Europe, so much more politically effective, surely has something to do with the existence of neoconservatism. But

Europeans, who think it absurd to look to the United States for lessons in political innovation, resolutely refuse to consider this possibility.

Neoconservatism is the first variant of American conservatism in the past century that is in the "American grain." It is hopeful, not lugubrious; forward-looking, not nostalgic; and its general tone is cheerful, not grim or dyspeptic. Its twentieth-century heroes tend to be TR, FDR, and Ronald Reagan. Such Republican and conservative worthies as Calvin Coolidge, Herbert Hoover, Dwight Eisenhower, and Barry Goldwater are politely overlooked. Of course, those worthies are in no way overlooked by a large, probably the largest, segment of the Republican Party, with the result that most Republican politicians know nothing and could not care less about neoconservatism. Nevertheless, they cannot be blind to the fact that neoconservative policies, reaching out beyond the traditional political and financial base, have helped make the very idea of political conservatism more acceptable to a majority of American voters. Nor has it passed official notice that it is the neoconservative public policies, not the traditional Republican ones, which result in popular Republican presidencies.

One of these policies, most visible and controversial, is cutting tax rates in order to stimulate steady economic growth. This policy was not invented by neocons, and it was not the particularities of tax cuts that interested them, but rather the steady focus on economic growth. Neocons are familiar with intellectual history and aware that it is only in the last two centuries that democracy has become a respectable option among political thinkers. In earlier times, democracy meant an inherently turbulent political regime, with the "have-nots" and the "haves" engaged in a perpetual and utterly destructive class struggle. It was only the prospect of economic growth in which everyone prospered, if not equally or simultaneously, that gave modern democracies their legitimacy and durability.

The cost of this emphasis on economic growth has been an attitude toward public finance that is far less risk-averse than is the case among more traditional conservatives. Neocons would prefer not to have large budget deficits, but it is in the nature of democracy, because it seems to be in the nature of human nature, that political demagogy will frequently result in economic recklessness, so that one sometimes must shoulder budgetary deficits as the cost (temporarily, one hopes) of pursuing economic growth. It is a basic assumption of neoconservatism that, as a consequence of the spread of affluence among all classes, a property-owning and tax-paying population will, in time, become less vulnerable to egalitarian illusions and demagogic appeals and more sensible about the fundamentals of economic reckoning.

This leads to the issue of the role of the state. Neocons do not like the concentration of services in the welfare state and are happy to study alternative ways of delivering these services. But they are impatient with the Hayekian notion that we are on "the road to serfdom." Neocons do not feel that kind of alarm or anxiety about the growth of the state in the past century, seeing it as natural, indeed inevitable. Because they tend to be more interested in history than economics or sociology, they know that the nineteenth-century idea, so neatly propounded by Herbert Spencer in his *The Man versus the State*, was a historical eccentricity. People have always preferred strong government to weak government, although they certainly have no liking for anything that smacks of overly intrusive government. Neocons feel at home in today's America to a degree that more traditional conservatives do not. Though they find much to be critical about, they tend to seek intellectual guidance in the democratic wisdom of Tocqueville rather than in the Tory nostalgia of, say, Russell Kirk.

But it is only to a degree that neocons are comfortable in modern America. The steady decline in our democratic culture, sinking to new levels of vulgarity, does unite neocons with traditional conservatives, though not with those libertarian conservatives who are conservative in economics but unmindful of the culture. The upshot is a quite unexpected alliance between neocons, who include a fair proportion of secular intellectuals, and religious traditionalists. They are united on issues concerning the quality of education, the relations of church and state, the regulation of pornography, and the like, all of which they regard as proper candidates for the government's attention. And since the Republican Party now has a substantial base among the religious, this gives neocons a certain influence and even power. Because religious conservatism is so feeble in Europe, the neoconservative potential there is correspondingly weak.

And then, of course, there is foreign policy, the area of American politics where neoconservatism has recently been the focus of media attention. This is surprising since there is no set of neoconservative beliefs concerning foreign policy, only a set of attitudes derived from historical experience. (The favorite neoconservative text on foreign affairs, thanks to Professors Leo Strauss of Chicago and Donald Kagan of Yale, is Thucydides on the Peloponnesian War.) These attitudes can be summarized in the following "theses" (as a Marxist would say). First, patriotism is a natural and healthy sentiment and should be encouraged by both private and public institutions. Precisely because we are a nation of immigrants, this is a powerful American sentiment. Second, world government is a terrible idea since it can lead to world tyranny. International institutions that point to an ultimate world government should be regarded with the deepest suspicion. Third, statesmen should, above all, have the ability to distinguish friends from enemies. This is not as easy as it sounds, as the history of the Cold War revealed. The number of intelligent men who could not count the Soviet Union as an enemy, even though this was its own self-definition, was absolutely astonishing.

Finally, for a great power, the "national interest" is not a geographical term, except for fairly prosaic matters like trade and environmental regulation. A smaller nation might appropriately feel that its national interest begins and ends at its borders, so that its foreign policy is almost always in a defensive mode. A larger nation has more extensive interests. And large nations whose identity is ideological, like the Soviet Union of yesteryear and the United States of today, inevitably have ideological interests in addition to more material concerns. Barring extraordinary events, the United States will always feel obliged to defend, if possible, a democratic nation under attack from nondemocratic forces, external or internal. That is why it was in our national interest to come to the defense of France and Britain in World War II. That is why we feel it necessary to defend Israel today, when its survival is threatened. No complicated geopolitical calculations of national interest are necessary.

Behind all this is a fact: the incredible military superiority of the United States vis-à-vis the nations of the rest of the world, in any imaginable combination. This superiority was planned by no one, and even today there are many Americans who are in denial. To a large extent, it all happened as a result of our bad luck. During the fifty years after World War II, while Europe was at peace and the Soviet Union largely relied on surrogates to do its fighting, the United States was involved in a whole series of wars: the Korean War, the Vietnam War, the Gulf War, the Kosovo conflict, the Afghan War, and the Iraq War. The result was that our military spending expanded more or less in line with our economic growth, while Europe's democracies cut back their military spending in favor of social welfare programs. The Soviet Union spent profusely but wastefully, so that its military collapsed along with its economy.

Suddenly, after two decades during which "imperial decline" and "imperial overstretch" were the academic and journalistic watchwords, the United States emerged as uniquely powerful. The "magic" of compound interest over half a century had its effect on our military budget, as did the cumulative scientific and technological research of our armed forces. With power come responsibilities, whether sought or not, whether welcome or not. And it is a fact that if you have the kind of power we now have, either you will find opportunities to use it, or the world will discover them for you. The older, traditional elements in the Republican Party have difficulty coming to terms with this new reality in foreign affairs, just as they cannot reconcile economic conservatism with social and cultural conservatism. But by one of those accidents historians ponder, our current president and his administration turn out to be quite at home in this new political environment, although it is clear they did not anticipate this role any more than their party as a whole did. As a result, neoconservatism began enjoying a second life, at a time when its obituaries were still being published.

2003

VI

FOREIGN POLICY
AND IDEOLOGY

The Ironies of
Neo-Isolationism

"The cunning of Reason"—this was Hegel's classic phrase which summed up his sense of history: of men marching backwards into their futures, pursuing an impossible dream while creating a necessary world. One is reminded of this Hegelian metaphor by the spectacle of the present debate over the future of American foreign policy. It is a debate charged with intense emotions attached to past experience, specifically, to one experience of the recent past: the Vietnam War. It was, indeed, an illuminating (and, for many, an emotionally shattering) event. But one need not be a German philosopher to wonder if it makes sense to understand American foreign policy in terms of our Vietnam experience, rather than trying to understand Vietnam in the light of the enduring imperatives which shape American foreign policy.

The irony implicit in any attempt to construct a foreign policy that would solve yesterday's problems is well illustrated by current efforts of Congress to limit executive discretion in sending American troops overseas. The legislation that is proposed would require Congressional sanction after thirty days, otherwise, the troops would have to be withdrawn and all military operations would cease. As I write, it is not clear that Congress will ever pass such a law over the inevitable presidential veto. But there is certainly widespread support for it, both inside Congress and out, as a reaction to the long and bloody Vietnam War. So let us assume it does become law, either now or sometime in the future. What would be its effects?

One possible answer is that it would have no effect whatsoever. After all, though the law assumes that American presidents decide to send troops overseas in an arbitrary and capricious way, whereas Congress is more prudent and deliberative, there is really no evidence for any such assumption. Presidents always do take Congressional and public opinion into account when making a decision of this kind. There is little doubt that, had such a law existed in the early 1960s, Congress would have given the necessary sanction to President Kennedy. It did in fact subsequently give such sanction to President Johnson on many different occasions. True, it now wishes it hadn't, and the proposed law embodies this retrospective wish. But, as the memories of Vietnam fade, and as new crises arise which will have no obvious parallel to Vietnam, there is far more likely to be concord than dissent between Congress and the executive on any issue of military intervention. Indeed, it is hard to think of a single instance in American history when the president insisted on sending American troops abroad against the wishes of a majority in Congress. So the new legislation would cope with a hitherto nonexistent contingency.

Another possible answer is that the law, if passed, would have exactly the opposite effect of that intended. A president who thought it important to intervene quickly in some part of the world, and who was uncertain of the support he might receive in Congress, would look at that thirty-day deadline and decide that he would have to intervene massively so as to ensure a quick success. In other words, such a law might mean that military intervention abroad, when it occurred, would be on a large scale rather than a limited one. And what if the president misjudged the situation and his massive intervention, after thirty days, had not reached a military conclusion? Would Congress really decide that an army of, say, fifty thousand U.S. soldiers should promptly surrender? Or should withdraw helter-skelter, suffering severe losses and great humiliation? Or that the American government should promptly sue for peace on the enemy's terms? None of these alternatives is at all likely. So the law, by tempting the president to intervene on a larger scale rather than a smaller one, would end by making disengagement and withdrawal less easy to accomplish.

In addition, there is the further important fact that the soldiers we are talking about will be, not conscripts, but professionals. In this respect, all future military interventions overseas (short of a major war) will differ radically from our Vietnam experience. One can even go further and suggest that the major, lasting consequence of the Vietnam War will be the creation of a large, professional, standing American army. Yet in debates over foreign policy this matter is either ignored or regarded as tangential. One of the reasons for the odd inattention to such a striking, new phenomenon is that many observers seem convinced that it cannot really endure, that the effort to create a professional army will founder for lack of volunteers. And it is true that, at the moment, the military forces are having some difficulty in filling their recruiting quotas. But that, surely, is the result of the high eligibility standards that still prevail. The army has been "spoiled" by conscription, which permitted it to select, from a large available pool, fairly well-educated recruits with unblemished civilian records; high school dropouts, for instance, have not been welcome, nor have those with records of juvenile delinquency. It is doubtless convenient for the military leadership to have such "quality" manpower, but it is absurd for the military to claim, as it still does, that it "needs" such recruits. All professional armies rely on "dropouts," from school and/or society, to fill their ranks, and the armies then organize themselves so as to make the military jobs fit available manpower, rather than vice versa. The U.S. military will doubtless follow suit, once it realizes what it is still reluctant to concede, that peacetime conscription is no longer a real possibility.

It was in a spasm of revulsion against the Vietnam War that peacetime conscription came to a legislative end. The war had become so unpopular, among young people especially, that Congress didn't have to think very hard about letting the draft expire. But it also didn't bother to think very hard about the implications of what it was doing for American foreign policy. Had it given such thought to the matter, it might have realized that one clear consequence of relying on a professional army was to increase the president's discretion with regard to military intervention, wherever and whenever he thinks necessary. But where neo-isolationist passions are so strong, interventionist consequences are not as evident as in a calmer moment they would be. Only a handful of observers have taken notice of this important event, most notably Joseph Califano Jr., a former assistant to Lyndon B. Johnson, who wrote: "By removing the middle class from even the threat of conscription, we remove perhaps the greatest inhibition on a President's decision to wage war." Mr. Califano went on to argue that opponents of the Vietnam War (among whom he is to be numbered) were making a terrible mistake in permitting a professional army to emerge from the shambles of that war. But his arguments have fallen on deaf ears. People are too busy repealing the Vietnam War to pay attention to the actual, as distinct from the intended, results of their actions.

To be sure, if the United States were to revert to a strictly isolationist position in foreign affairs, then it wouldn't much matter whether we had a conscript or volunteer army. But the chances of any such reversion are remote, despite Vietnam. Our economy is an integral part of the world economy; our heterogeneous people have strong feelings about different areas of the world (Israel, South Africa, Ireland, Eastern Europe); our "cosmopolitan" civilization, international in its essence, could not reconvert itself into the provincial America of yesterday ("Our Town" is now a suburban city boasting a state university campus). We have too much power to disclaim responsibility for what happens to our friends and neighbors, and as a democratic republic have too much conscience to steel ourselves to utter indifference to the fate of others. The neo-isolationist impulse is, literally, a "reactionary" one, a reaction against Vietnam, a nostalgic yearning for past simplicities.

It will soon spend itself, perhaps in two years, perhaps in five, perhaps in ten. The exact timing doesn't matter. What does matter is that, when next we are militarily engaged overseas, it will be with professional soldiery, not with a "citizens' army." There will be "no more Vietnams," but not exactly in the sense that the phrase is commonly thought to have. There will be no more gradual, limited interventions with military conscripts. Those who infer from this fact that there will be no interventions at all, short of a declaration of war by Congress, are trying to control the future by rewriting the past in their mind's eye. That kind of political magic is as effective as political magic usually is.

1973

Notes on the Yom Kippur War

Since the outbreak of war in the Middle East, I have been getting up at dawn to listen anxiously to the radio reports. I sit there, in a silent city, glued to the transistor radio, cursing the inane ads as they jangle my raw nerves, then listening glumly to the news bulletins when they do come. Things have not been going so well for Israel, as in my bones I had always feared might be the case. No prescience on my part, just a Jewish instinct for impending disaster, an instinct that has been grotesquely overdeveloped in the course of generations by a kind of "natural selection," you might say. I am one of those Jews who has never been able to take Jewish good fortune seriously, but rather suspect it as a deception. Only misfortune is real.

I find that I am irritated, too, with almost everyone. Irritated at those of my friends who ring me up for one reason or another, and somehow never get around to mentioning what is happening in the Middle East. It's like having major surgery in the family and discovering that the world would prefer to take no notice of it. I am annoyed, too, at Israel for having been so smug, and for having failed to confront the realities of her situation. I am most annoyed at those urbane Jewish liberals who claim to see "both sides" of this conflict and apportion blame and responsibility with academic detachment. Oddly enough, I cannot work up any real feelings against the Arabs, who are behaving—well, like Arabs. I'll explain that remark in a moment.

Why am I so deeply affected? I am not an Orthodox Jew, and only a barely observant one. I am not a Zionist, and I did not find my two visits to Israel to be particularly exhilarating experiences. Truth to tell, I found Israeli society, on the whole, quite exasperating, and none of the Israeli ways of life—there are several to choose from—had any great appeal for me. Still, I care desperately.

I think it is because I sense, deep down, that what happens to Israel will be decisive for Jewish history, and for the kinds of lives my grandchildren and great-grandchildren will be leading.

Should Israel be extinguished in a bloodbath, it could be the end of three thousand years of Jewish history. In the course of World War II, two out of every five Jews on this earth were slaughtered for no other reason than that they were Jews. But that holocaust was in part redeemed, was given some meaning, by the astonishing emergence of the State of Israel, a sudden and unanticipated answer to two thousand years of daily prayer. If that fantastic dream, now realized, should turn into just another Jewish nightmare, a great many Jews are going to conclude, reluctantly but inevitably, that the burden of Jewish history is just too grievous to bequeath to one's descendants, and they will opt out. It is not likely they'll be converted to Christianity; there is, alas, so little of it left to be converted to. It is more probable that they will simply drift into that spiritual void which so many educated and "sophisticated" people inhabit these days, and which is destroying the very soul of Western civilization. There are enough Jews there already, so far as I am concerned, and I'd rather not see the rest of us propelled into that ghastly, identity-less existence, where all you can pass on to your children is a life insurance policy.

I suppose what it comes down to is that, though you don't have to be religious to be Jewish, being Jewish may eventually tend to make you, in some mysterious way, religious, at least minimally. When I find myself reciting a Jewish prayer, in which I avow that we are worthy of God's grace because of the virtue of "our fathers"—Abraham, Isaac, Jacob—and despite our own sinfulness, I find myself taking the prayer literally. They are my "fathers," after all; I am the distant seed of their loins. And this being true, perhaps the rest is true too. So any war in which the existence of Israel may be at stake becomes for me a special kind of war, not a conventional crisis in "international relations." In such a war, not only is the whole of the Jewish past at stake, but also the whole of the Jewish future. If that past and that future, and the meaning which unites them, is to be killed in dubious battle—this is to think the truly unthinkable, in Jewish terms.

I have said that I find it hard to be angry at the Arabs, and that is the truth. Unfortunately, when I try to explain what I mean, people think I am being frivolous. That is because we in the West, most of us anyway, have so little sense of history, cannot take religious beliefs seriously, and are so resolutely inattentive to the ways in which history and religion shape national character. Indeed, the use of that term, "national character," is distinctly frowned upon these days. There isn't supposed to be any such thing, every one of us presumably being born into "one world." What nonsense. The Arabs are an extraordinarily proud people, in some ways a quite noble people, whose religion assures them that they have been chosen for a superior destiny. The Jews, too, of course, have a notion of themselves as "a chosen people," but the Jewish idea is moral, not political in nature. The Arabs, in contrast, believe that it is unnatural for them to be politically or militarily inferior to any other people. Centuries of subordination, even of foreign occupation, have made only a small impression on this profound conviction. For Arabs, the glories of medieval empire are like yesterday; the intervening centuries are a lamentable hiatus, of no intrinsic significance or even of much interest, and "soon" to be annulled by foredestined triumph.

But, surely, it will be argued, this Arab vision of history and of the world is bound to be dissipated by industrialization, and oil royalties, and urbanization, and television, and what we call "modernization." The only reason we can even entertain such a thesis is that we, the moderns of the Western world, are so smugly certain that our "progressive" view of history is the absolutely true one, and that to become modern must mean a gradual conversion to our own liberal-secular materialism. The Nazi experience should have suggested to us that there are other possibilities, but we won that war and therefore concluded that we had refuted and foreclosed these other possibilities. We are now, once again, learning otherwise. The Arabs, simply because they are becoming more "modernized," are not going to become "just like us." (Nor are the Chinese, or the Africans, I am confident.) True, their "national character" might indeed change in the course of future generations—everything changes, sooner or later—but a centuries-old way of life, and a way of looking at life, is not going to be transformed overnight, just to suit our convenience.

What this means, in actual political terms, is that it is wishful thinking to expect, in our lifetime, that the Arabs are going to be "reasonable" vis-à-vis Israel, or foreign oil companies, or anything else which they regard as an infringement of their historic rights over the areas settled by the Arab people (or assimilated, by conquest or conversion, into the Arab world). Their idea of "reasonableness" is utterly different from ours. They are less interested in making money or in the world's good opinion than in reviving a lost grandeur. In short, they are behaving exactly as they have always behaved, and as they said they would behave. True, they speak a different tongue at the United Nations Assembly, and therefore appear hypocritical. But they are not really hypocritical at all; they are merely talking the kind of diplomatic jargon which they know we regard as proper and suitable for intercourse among nations. They don't talk that way at home, in their newspapers, in their magazines, on their radio and television. One might almost say their rhetoric at the United Nations is a form of politeness; they understand how painful we would find candor.

One of the things that most exasperated me in Israel was the unwillingness to face up to Arab realities. Many of my Israeli friends could not confront the fact that the Arab nations do not accept, and will not in the foreseeable future accept, the existence of a non-Arab nation in "their" Middle East. The most they will concede is the survival of a limited Jewish community in a binational Palestine which would be part of the Arab world. They may agree to cease-fires, or truces, or armistices, and they may even temporarily recognize demilitarized zones if it is to their advantage to do so. But they will not sign any treaty giving *de jure* recognition to a Jewish state. No Arab leader has ever hinted at such a possibility, and it is utopian to think otherwise.

Utopianism, however, is a kind of political orthodoxy in Israel. The dominant political tradition of Israel is democratic-socialist, and the original Jewish settlers in Palestine, in the first decades of this century, envisioned the creation of a "cooperative commonwealth": egalitarian, fraternal, pacific. Just where the Arabs would fit into this lovely picture they never clearly said, but they seemed to think that the sheer perfection of Israeli society would so enchant the Arab masses as to transform them, too, into secular, humanitarian socialists. They also took it for granted that, as the Arabs of the Middle East became more prosperous and better-schooled, they would be only too happy to join Israel in the task of "making the desert bloom."

Incredibly enough, this is still the basic Israeli outlook, despite the evident fact that it is the better-educated, middle-class Arabs, and most especially the college students, who are most rabidly anti-Israel. The Israelis actually feel (or at least think) that time, in the form of the economic development of the Arab nations, is inevitably on their side. It might be, but there is no obvious inevitability about it. When I was in Jerusalem fifteen months ago, at a conference of intellectuals, I timidly questioned this thesis. I was promptly accused of lacking all appreciation of the idealism which was the essence of the Zionist movement and which was the moving spirit behind this Jewish state.

1973

What's Wrong with NATO?

According to a recent report by the International Institute for Strategic Studies, the London-based research center, NATO is in trouble. Western Europe and the United States, the study points out, appear to have different attitudes and policies toward the Middle East, Central America, and Poland, different perceptions of the Soviet threat, different conceptions of the proper economic relations between the West and the Russians; and there seems to be a belief in Europe that the Reagan administration is somewhat too casual about the possibilities of nuclear war.

Such commentary is true as far as it goes, but it does not go far enough. The cracks keep appearing in this antiquated, bureaucratic alliance that has been in existence now for more than three decades. We keep papering over the cracks, but they resurface faster than we can repair them. It is becoming ever clearer that the Atlantic alliance, as we have understood it and been comfortable with it for so many years, is gradually emptying itself of all meaning. In fact, the public disillusionment on both sides of the Atlantic with Europe's security arrangements, especially the excessive reliance on nuclear weapons, is such that a radical reconstruction may be the only way to keep NATO from disintegrating entirely.

I think we can look back and see that three faults have appeared in the Atlantic alliance, and they are truly basic. The first has to do with the so-called nuclear umbrella—the American nuclear umbrella—over Europe. About four years ago, at a NATO conference in Brussels, I read a paper called "Does NATO Exist?" to a small seminar. My answer was in the negative, based on my belief that the nuclear umbrella no longer offered real shelter. The talk was not well received, and the NATO aides did not take it too seriously. The following day, however, Henry Kissinger gave a speech to the conference, a public speech with all the media of Europe present, and strongly implied that the

American nuclear umbrella no longer existed. At which point all hell broke loose. Every European chancellery immediately got on to the State Department and demanded to know, "Does this signify a change in American policy?" And the State Department got on to Kissinger and said, "My God, what have you done?" And Kissinger then issued a "clarification," saying he had been completely misunderstood, that of course the American nuclear umbrella was still there, in place, and the Europeans could have absolute confidence in the American determination to use intercontinental nuclear weapons in the defense of Europe.

Kissinger had evidently forgotten that he really did not have freedom of speech. When you are Henry Kissinger you cannot say what you mean because everyone assumes that you speak either for the State Department or for some sovereign power or, in his case, for yourself as a sovereign power. But there is no question as to what he meant, just as there is no question as to where the truth lies. It should be obvious to everyone that, once the Soviet Union achieved nuclear parity with the United States, the whole notion of the nuclear umbrella became much less credible. It is one thing for the United States to say, and for Europeans to believe, that we shall send ICBMs to destroy the Soviet Union if it presumes to attack Western Europe, all this at a time when the Russians cannot respond in kind. It is quite another thing for the president of the United States to declare that, because the Russians have dared to attack Western Europe, I will press the red button even if it means that my country will be destroyed in a nuclear exchange with Moscow.

Will any president actually do that? I have discussed this matter with friends (and former friends) in the Pentagon and the State Department. Their reaction is: "You must not write those things, you must not say those things; the Russians will hear you. So long as they believe the president will press the red button, that is all that counts." When I persist in asking: "But will the president press that red button?" they say, "Well, it is not certain that he won't." That is the official view: it is not certain that he won't. In my view, it is as certain as anything can be in the political universe that he won't. It strikes me as absurd to think that a president is going to risk the destruction of the United States by inaugurating a nuclear holocaust because Russian tanks have moved into West Germany and our conventional forces on the Continent have failed to stop them.

Today the nuclear umbrella is 99 percent bluff. Mutual assured destruction, the threat upon which the umbrella over Europe relies, really no longer exists as a believable strategy. One can imagine the United States responding to a Soviet attack on the American homeland with, in effect, a suicidal gesture, saying, "All right, you are going to obliterate us, we will obliterate you, just for the satisfaction of it." But it is unimaginable, really, that the United States is going to engage in a mutual holocaust with the Soviet Union in order to protect Western Europe. How is it possible, then, that so many European leaders are willing to join the Pentagon and the State Department in pretending that the umbrella exists? Part of this pretense is wishful thinking. There is a fantasy that has been popular in Europe for many years now that the next European war will consist of Soviet missiles and American missiles flying over Europe and obliterating the two superpowers while leaving Europe untouched. A seductive fantasy, from the European point of view.

But the main reason why the idea of the nuclear umbrella has any credibility among Europeans is the presence over there of something like 200,000 troops and their dependents. Europe doesn't need 200,000 American soldiers to fight a conventional war; it has plenty of soldiers of its own and the military significance of the American soldiers is marginal. In the European mind, they are there as hostages to make certain that if the Soviet Union does overrun Western Europe in a conventional war, the president will be under severe pressure, seeing an American army decimated, to press that red button. Which is one reason why those American troops are not going to remain in Europe for very long. This situation can be accurately perceived in the United States as well as in Europe, and American Congressmen can now be heard wondering aloud whether it truly makes sense to have those hostages over there. I have little doubt that, in the years ahead, this concern will become more acute. There is no active public opinion in favor of keeping those troops in Europe, only public passivity before a long-standing commitment. Nor is there any active Congressional opinion in favor of it if the only function of those troops is to act as sacrificial hostages. Sooner or later such passive acceptance of an inherited military strategy will drain away into nothingness.

The second fault in the Atlantic alliance as now constituted is a reliance on the doctrine of graduated deterrence. Under this doctrine, we provide conventional forces in Western Europe to help the Europeans cope with a conventional Soviet attack; our combined forces are not large enough to defeat a Soviet attack, but they are strong enough to give the Russians some pause. If they don't pause, then we will shoot tactical atomic weapons at them, and that should give them pause. If they then fire back tactical atomic weapons at us, we will let loose the intermediate-range nuclear missiles now scheduled to be placed in Europe, wreaking havoc on crucial Russian military installations all the way to Moscow. And if the Russians reply by destroying Western Europe with their SS-20s, already in place, well, then the elected leaders of the United States, Britain, and France press their red buttons and give us mutual assured destruction.

This whole idea of graduated deterrence was inaugurated in the late 1950s and early 1960s as a way of saving Europe the trouble of permanent, large-scale military mobilizations and of providing a much cheaper defense than would large standing armies with conventional weaponry. Somehow, the possibility that the Russians would quickly achieve parity or better in tactical nuclear weapons and intermediate-range weapons was never seriously explored. They have done so, of course. The upshot is that the strategy of graduated deterrence now scares Western Europe more than it does the Russians. That, I think, helps explain the strength of the antinuclear movement in Western Europe, a movement that is absurd in its dreams of a non-nuclear world but perfectly understandable in its human origins. For it is truly insane for Western Europe to begin any nuclear exchange that could well end in its annihilation. Moreover, a great many Europeans suspect that once Europe is destroyed in a limited nuclear exchange and the United States faces mutual assured destruction, American leaders will sit down with Soviet leaders and negotiate. And who can say with confidence that such a scenario is unlikely?

When one raises this issue with NATO officials, they say: "Well, we really don't expect to have a nuclear exchange in Germany at the level of tactical nuclear weapons or even intermediate-range nuclear weapons; that is not the point of the strategy. The point is to deter the Russians." Yes, of course, but there is no such thing as a surefire deterrent. What if, after all, the Russians are not deterred? Is NATO bluffing about its tactical nuclear weapons? The answer one gets is: "But they don't know whether or not we are bluffing, and the truth is that we don't know whether or not we are bluffing." Is this a sensible military policy, to engage in bluffing the enemy and bluffing yourself at the same time? It creates a significant uncertainty for the Russians, to be sure, but also for the democratic polities of Western Europe. And it is becoming clear that the totalitarian Soviet Union can endure such uncertainties with greater fortitude.

Moreover, we can rely on the Russians, who are very astute in their strategic thinking, to probe the bluff. It is most unlikely that Soviet tanks are going to start rolling en masse through West Germany. There is no reason to think the Russians want, literally, to occupy Western Europe as distinct from "Finlandizing" it. They have enough problems with their Eastern European satellites. Besides, they have more interesting alternatives. They might, for instance, consider a new Berlin blockade, using SAM missiles to prevent an airlift. What would NATO do in the face of such an action? Would it really send its tanks rolling through East Germany or would it choose to negotiate West Berlin away? To ask this question is to answer it.

Or let us assume that one day the Russians say they have been provoked (they are very easily provoked) in northern Norway—someone has done something nasty to some Russian submarine—and they then proceed to occupy the northern littoral of Norway. Not many Norwegians live there, but it is an area of considerable strategic importance. Now, as it happens, Norway is a member of NATO. So what do we do if the Russians occupy the northern strip, an area that is indefensible against Russian conventional forces? Do we start sending troops to fight a war, perhaps, eventually, a nuclear war, on Norwegian soil? How will the Norwegians react to that idea? Or do we use NATO forces against a Soviet target closer at hand, say, East Germany? The fact is we have no credible plan to cope with any such Russian probe, not in Berlin, not in Norway, not in Turkey. Yet if such probes prove successful, the demoralization of Western Europe would proceed apace.

In truth, there really is only one viable military strategy for Western Europe. That is to build up NATO's conventional forces so as to be able to fight, and win, a conventional war against the Soviet Union, while at the same time possessing a second-strike tactical and strategic nuclear capability strong enough to inhibit the Russians from initiating nuclear warfare. We must stop frightening the citizenry of Western Europe to death, which is what we are doing with our overemphasis on nuclear warfare and nuclear weapons. We need conventional forces of sufficient size and strength to inflict military defeat upon an aggressor. And, obviously, since even a conventional conflict on NATO territory could be devastating to the area, NATO planning should be such that any conventional war should be fought, not in Western Europe, but in Eastern Europe. Nations that are serious about defending themselves do not hunker down behind a Maginot Line, which is what NATO is doing. The kind of buildup of conventional forces required for such a viable strategy would be very expensive and would require a significant mobilization of Western Europe's resources. The question is: does the will to make these sacrifices for European security exist among the peoples and governments of Western Europe?

When one discusses this issue with informed European observers, one is quickly assured that it does not exist, that it is unrealistic to think that the British government or the West German government or the Danish government will spend more money on military hardware and troops and inevitably slow down their spending on the various programs lumped together under the rubric of social welfare. No government can do it, these observers insist, and no government has the will even to try to do it. But the people who say this do not fully realize the import of what they are saying. What they are saying is, in effect: "Look, we can't have larger armies. We can't cut our social expenditures. The political will for that just does not exist. But when it comes to using nuclear weapons and risking nuclear annihilation, you can count on us." That is hardly a plausible assurance. A nation unwilling to curb its social expenditures in order to build up its conventional military forces will not take upon itself the burden of igniting a nuclear war on its own territory. It will figure out ways and reasons for not doing so. If the will for conventional warfare is lacking, the will for nuclear warfare is lacking, *a fortiori*, and the whole NATO doctrine of graduated deterrence makes no sense whatsoever.

What the Europeans really hope is that any confrontation with the Russians will escalate quickly into a Soviet-American nuclear confrontation, so that those "graduated" stages, during which they may be annihilated, will be passed over. In effect, the governments of Western Europe are asking the United States to run the risk of a nuclear holocaust so that they don't have to cut their social welfare budgets. This is not a very attractive proposition from the point of view of the American national interest. The American national interest, and in the longer term, I think, the European national interest as well, is to try to see to it that any conflict that might emerge in Europe will remain at the conventional level rather than move quickly to the nuclear level. Of course, if the Russians initiate a nuclear attack, we would presumably respond in kind. But short of that prospect, it seems clear that the willingness to use strong conventional forces in conventional ways and on enemy territory must be revived in Europe. Otherwise NATO is void of meaning.

As NATO is now constituted, European suspicion of American intentions is so active as to subvert the will to resist Soviet pressure. The question constantly being posed is: "Who is using whom?" More and more Europeans are convinced that the United States would prefer to see a nuclear war confined to Western Europe, and that the American commitment to "go the last mile" in nuclear warfare is suspect. This is a reasonable suspicion, based on a sensible reading of the American national interest. And it is an ineradicable suspicion, given the present structure and strategy of NATO.

The third fault in the Atlantic alliance involves differences in attitudes and policies toward the Soviet Union. It is often said that these differences flow from varying perceptions and theories as to what the Soviet system is like, whence it has come, whither it is going. I think this is a half-truth. The other half is that the differences flow from the different conceptions the United

States and Western Europe have of their own roles in the world. The United States is, and the American people wish it to be, a world power. In fact, the American people wish it to be *the* world power, which may not be entirely possible. But no president of the United States is going around saying that the United States must be number two. Presidents still say the United States must be number one—even though they understand that being number one is not so easy anymore, and that it isn't even clear exactly what being number one means. In any case, the American people do have the sense of themselves as a world power, which means they have some sense of themselves as shaping a world order and world civilization that will be congruent, however imperfectly, with American interests and American ideals.

Western Europe, in contrast, has entered what can fairly be described as a regional-isolationist phase, with a policy toward the Soviet Union based on the assumption of permanent military inferiority, a policy that one might call, at the risk of giving offense, "therapeutic appeasement." The rationale for this policy is that "time is on our side," that the Soviet Union is a young country, that the Communist socioeconomic system has its troubles, and that as the Russians "mature" they are bound to become more civil in their foreign policy. Therefore, many Europeans say, we should help them mature, help them build a more productive economic infrastructure through trade and investment, negotiate with them ceaselessly even if it is—temporarily—unproductive.

The American rationale for American policy is much less sophisticated, though not necessarily less valid. This is that the Soviet Union is an immoral, brutal, expansionist power and has been so under successive leaderships, and that so long as it is a Soviet union, that is, a Communist regime, it will continue to be so. Nothing better exemplifies the clash between the two perspectives than the sham arms control negotiations that we are now involved in with the Soviet Union. I use that word "sham" advisedly. The Reagan administration never wanted to enter these negotiations, because in the past the Russians always used such occasions to gain a military advantage. The United States was dragged into the current negotiations by the leaders of the Western European governments, who said they had to demonstrate to their people that their intentions were honorably peaceful before any intermediate-range nuclear missiles could be installed to balance the Russian's SS-20s. Is it not a little odd that these democratically elected governments of Western Europe should have to prove to their people that they are not "warmongers," and that the best way to accomplish this is to engage in arms control negotiations that will be at best pointless and at worst the prelude to a treaty that further increases Soviet military superiority in Europe?

In short, the governments of the Western alliance have been for some time now engaged in miseducating and misleading their own public opinion on the possibilities of arms control, encouraging all sorts of wishful thinking about Soviet intentions. So wishful is this thinking, and so successful have our own governments been in deluding us, that in all of the controversy over the SS-20s, Pershings, and cruise missiles, no one seems to have asked the question: "Why did the Russians in the mid-1970s begin to put those SS-20s in place?" They didn't have to, if it was merely military security they were concerned about. The Russians already had a preponderance of power in Europe, a preponderance of nuclear as well as conventional power. So why did the Soviet leaders decide to do what they must have known would be exceedingly provocative—namely, install these new, very powerful, very accurate missiles? The only possible explanation is that the Russians are not satisfied with having a clear edge in the balance of power in Europe; they want an overwhelming preponderance of power over Western Europe. They want Western Europe to be radically inferior militarily, radically vulnerable, to the Soviet Union. One can further assume that if they wish to achieve such overwhelming superiority they intend to do something with it, like intimidating the nations of Western Europe to pursue policies, economic and political, which are skewed toward the interests of the Soviet Union.

The question of Soviet intentions has not been addressed by the Europeans because it raises the troublesome question of Soviet ideology. Unlike the Europeans, most Americans do see themselves as engaged in an ideological war with the Soviet Union, one that will determine the nature of the future world order. Will it be an order that, in some sense, continues the liberal, democratic, capitalist traditions of the West, or will it be some version of Soviet Communism, Chinese Communism, or some other kind of Communism yet to be invented? That this is the fundamental issue, the Soviet government and the American people (if not always the American government) understand clearly enough.

It is fascinating to listen to Western Europeans who complain that the trouble with Americans is that they think they are in an ideological war with the Soviet Union, even though the Russians say plainly, over and over again, that they are in an ideological war with us. Finding it inconvenient to face up to the reality of that ideological war, Europeans refuse to take Soviet ideological statements seriously. But that they are seriously meant is evidenced by the way those within the Soviet orbit are treated when they fail to take them seriously. President Reagan is accused of igniting the Cold War all over again. But, in reality, the Cold War has never ended, not since the conclusion of World War II.

Our State Department, our presidents, all the leaders of Western Europe have talked about détente, but there is no détente, and there never has been. And most Americans, despite their miseducation at the hands of the media, the State Department, and successive administrations, have never succumbed to this mirage. Indeed, to the extent that President Reagan speaks as if the Cold War were a reality, he is merely bringing American rhetoric into line with American opinion, as well as with world realities.

In fact, I think we are in the process of witnessing a basic sea-change in American foreign policy, although it may take some years before it emerges in a recognizable form. The era of liberal internationalism, extending from World War II until 1980, has pretty much petered out. The old liberal establishment that ran American foreign policy and that basically agreed with the European view of the world has lost, to a large degree, its credibility, its authority, and its political influence. We don't hear people talking about "winning the hearts and minds" of Europeans or Africans or Asians anymore; that phrase has vanished from the American vocabulary. The United States is becoming a much more nationalistic country, a country much more concerned about its national interest and more willing to act unilaterally if necessary to pursue its national interest.

This is the real predicament that NATO now faces. The new national mood in the United States could wreck the Atlantic alliance unless certain basic changes are made, though it is the reconstruction of the Western alliance that most Americans would certainly prefer. After all, the nations of Western Europe are democracies; they share our political values, we want them as allies, and we want them to want us as an ally. In order to achieve a firm alliance, however, papering over the cracks will not work. What we need to do is to reconstruct NATO before it falls apart. If we have learned anything from the NATO experience of the last thirty years, it is the rediscovery of an old truth: dependency corrupts and absolute dependency corrupts absolutely. To the degree that Europe has been dependent upon the United States, the European will has been corrupted and European political vitality has diminished. A reconstructed NATO could reverse that process. But it would have to be an all-European NATO, with the United States an ally but not a member.

An all-European NATO, with its own nuclear weapons and its own military strategy, would not have to worry about whether it was serving American interests, not its own, in pursuing this or that policy. If it wanted intermediate-range nuclear missiles, we would provide them, but only on request. If it wanted them at sea, instead of on land, it could put them at sea. The only way the nations of Western Europe are going to regain the self-confidence that they should have, and the will to engage in international affairs in a resolute way, is if there were a European NATO with a large degree of military independence from the United States. An independent NATO, with its own nuclear deterrent, responsible for the defense of Western Europe, willing to make the sacrifices to fight (with American help, if necessary) and win a conventional war with the Soviet Union should such a war break out—that is the NATO of the future, if NATO is to survive at all.

Such a European alliance might regain its self-respect, a feeling of control over its own national destinies, and, above all, it might recapture the spirit of nationalism that is indispensable to any successful foreign policy. You cannot in this century have a successful foreign policy that does not encompass the nationalist impulse. One of the problems with the involvement of the United States in NATO is that it dilutes that nationalist impulse. Nationalism in Western Europe is up for grabs, and unless it is seized by political parties that believe in our values and traditions, it could be seized by people with less palatable aspirations.

A new Atlantic alliance between the United States and an all-European NATO would be possible and desirable, with Europeans as willing partners of the United States under terms to be freely negotiated. But if this is to come about, we must subject the NATO that now exists, a very sick NATO, to shock treatment. Nothing less will suffice.

1983

International Law and
International Lies

One of the most distressing aspects of American foreign policy today is the felt need of our government to lie to the American people when it takes an action, or adopts a policy, that it believes to be necessary for the integrity of our national interests. The invasion of Grenada was a most illuminating case in point.

Why did we invade Grenada? According to the White House and State Department, the main reason was the danger to American medical students in Grenada because of the political turbulence there. This was not, of course, the real reason. After all, we simply could have airlifted those students out instead of sending the Marines in. The real reasons, obvious enough to all, were the fear of the other Caribbean governments before a new and potentially troublesome Soviet puppet-state in their area, and our own fear of still another Soviet military base in our "backyard." Both fears were legitimate and reasonable, yet they were conveyed to the American people only in an undertone, with the emphasis going to those presumably endangered students. This led one wag, at the time, to suggest that the United States scatter a few thousand medical students among those countries we thought we might at some future date have reason to invade. The contempt for our official hypocrisy implicit in this remark was perfectly justifiable.

In foreign policy, doing the right thing for the wrong reasons can, in the longer term, be as counterproductive as doing the wrong thing for the right reason (e.g., our feeble and costly intervention in Lebanon). This is especially true in a democracy, where a very important function of government is educative. Such a government must rely on popular approval for its actions, and this approval will never be wholehearted if the people have grounds to think their government makes a habit of deception and double-talk. To be sure, everyone understands that, in some instances, a government may have to resort to diplomatic duplicity to conceal a secret but necessary action (e.g., the use of the CIA in helping friends and damaging enemies). But such duplicity is utterly unacceptable when American troops are involved in an overt military action. Then, a decent minimum of candor is required. There may be little harm in "dressing up" this candor with some exaggerated rhetoric; all governments do that, as do all nongovernmental organizations when they describe their motivation for embarking on a course of action. But outright lying and downright hypocrisy are not acceptable, if only because they will soon be exposed for what they are and the government's credibility, abroad and at home, will then be severely impaired.

So why did we lie about Grenada? Some State Department officials have said privately that there may not have been a lie, that, in fact, we might never have been able to intervene in Grenada had those medical students not been there. If this was the case, American foreign policy is in a worse condition than even its severest critics had imagined. For it is obvious to most Americans, relying simply on common sense and moral intuition, that the intervention was utterly justified, with or without medical students. And, indeed, one is fairly certain it was this same common sense and moral intuition that moved President Reagan to send in the troops. But, apparently, a straightforward appeal to this common sense and moral intuition was thought to be an inadequate justification. Hence, the focus on those students.

It must be emphasized that according to very reliable information, both the State Department and the White House took no pleasure in this exercise in obfuscation. They did it reluctantly, and because they thought they had to. They found themselves in a position where they could not explain their action without seeming to violate principles the U.S. government had been expounding for decades, and that were articulated in a whole array of treaties to which we had solemnly subscribed. These principles are the principles of "international law," as this body of doctrine has developed since World War I. And it is this body of doctrine that still dominates official American thinking about foreign policy, a mode of thought that can be summed up in the phrase "liberal internationalism."

The relevant principles are few and can be succinctly stated. (1) There exists a worldwide "community of nations" dedicated to the preservation of peace among its members. (2) To achieve peace, this community has explicitly, in such documents as the charter of the United Nations, made illegal and therefore impermissible certain actions by member governments. (3) The most important such action defined as illegal and impermissible is "aggression," i.e., the violation of any and all existing borders by a unilateral military action. It is these principles that administration after administration has assured the American people we most sincerely believe in. And it was these very principles we violated—rightly, in the opinion of almost all Americans—when we moved into Grenada. One can now appreciate the quandary our State Department found itself in. It desperately needed a legalistic fiction to render legitimate an action that, under that very conception of international law we insist we adhere to, was quite improper. It found that legal fiction in the convenient presence of those medical students.

This is not, alas, the last time our government is going to find itself in such a quandary. It will be stranded there again and again as it tries to reconcile the realities of great-power politics with the "liberal internationalist" way of thinking about foreign policy. They are, in truth, not reconcilable, since this entire doctrine of "international law," as developed since World War I, and especially since World War II, is itself one vast fiction. It is a fiction abused callously, or ignored ruthlessly, by those nations that, unlike the Western democracies, never took it seriously in the first place. For us, however, it is a fiction that induces irresoluteness, guilt, and queasy hypocrisy whenever we are forced to confront the realities of the world we live in. It is a world without a "world community" committed to a universal definition of law and order and civilized behavior. It is a world in which national interests and national values (whether religious or secular) easily override all paper commitments to a vision of universal peace. It is a world that, as someone once said, is a "dangerous place," in which terrorism, subversion, and naked aggression are no less common than ever before. For the United States to try to conduct its foreign policy according to principles that are visionary rather than sensibly realistic is the kind of suicidal folly future historians will find it well nigh impossible to comprehend.

It is not that international law is a completely meaningless idea. There is an entire body of international law, going back several centuries, that represents a considerable step forward in civilized behavior among nations. And behind this basically secular tradition lies the specifically Christian tradition of the "just war" and the preconditions thereto. These traditions of international law are today embodied in various treaties that affect the treatment of prisoners of war, the treatment of enemy civilians in case of war, the rights of neutrals, etc. They have also been embodied in treaties of non-aggression, non-belligerency, and non-intervention, but always with the understanding, usually explicit, that misbehavior by one party to the treaty annuls the treaty itself. These older traditions of international law still exist and play a most useful role. But beginning with our own Woodrow Wilson, a new conception of international law began to emerge, achieving its full flower with the founding of the United Nations after World War II. Its ambitions were and are positively messianic: to "abolish war" among nations, to subordinate all national interests and national values to the serene judgment of "the international community," and, in effect, to render it unnecessary for any nation to have a vigorous foreign policy of its own. This is, of course, an ancient vision, but it is fair to say that only in our century did statesmen and political philosophers think it a realistic agenda for an unredeemed humanity.

This new version of international law, and the liberal internationalist foreign policy associated with it, has played out its string. The senselessness of its assumptions becomes more apparent with every passing day. The American people see this; witness the popularity of any American ambassador to the UN who vigorously asserts American interests and values against that organization. Many higher officials in the State Department understand it well enough, but they are prisoners of what is by now a powerful conventional rhetoric, a set of intellectual habits that pervade the media, academia, and public discourse on foreign affairs.

The sad fact of the matter is that we do not have available, in the American political tradition, a mode of thinking about foreign policy that is appropriate to our condition today. The older nationalist-isolationism is clearly irrelevant to our condition as a great power that aims to shape a world congruent with our ideals, while confronting another world power, a militant world power, with the same aim but contradictory ideals. Theodore Roosevelt's combination of nationalism and internationalism seemed to offer promise of an interesting alternative, until it foundered on a foolish mimicry of European imperialism. Liberal internationalism, because it is incarnate in a host of international treaties and organizations, still predominates, but it is a theory both empty of substance and at war with reality.

A new way of looking at and thinking about American foreign policy will eventually emerge. What one may call "reality therapy" will see to it. Meanwhile, however, we shall have to rely on our common sense and moral intuition to cope with the challenges of the near future.

1985

"Human Rights"

The Hidden Agenda

To the best of my knowledge, the first time the issue of "human rights" became a focus for a major foreign policy debate in a Western democracy occurred a little more than a century ago in Britain, when Gladstone divided the country because of the massacre of some twelve thousand Bulgarians by their Turkish rulers.

Gladstone was a believing Christian, with an intensity of religious commitment that, in the United States today, would surely be regarded as a disqualification for high office. He was appalled that the British government, under Disraeli, seemed unmoved by the massacre of Bulgarian Christians by Turkish Muslims. And Disraeli was indeed unmoved. Though nominally a Christian, he could hardly be called a believer, much less a true believer. What he did care very much about was preventing Russia, the self-appointed Slavic "protector" of Bulgarians and other Balkan peoples under Turkish rule, from liquidating the Turkish empire and acquiring Constantinople and the Dardanelles in the process. He saw this as a serious threat to the new British empire he was in the process of creating, an empire that would include India and Cyprus, with the area in between (Afghanistan, Egypt, etc.) a British sphere of influence. For Disraeli, Russia's imperial ambitions were the main enemy, and it was to frustrate these ambitions that he tried to preserve the integrity of the Turkish empire, even if it meant a war with Russia, which he was prepared to contemplate. In the event, the Turkish empire was beyond salvaging, but at the Congress of Berlin, Disraeli was still able to come away with "peace with honor"—i.e., with Cyprus in hand and the Dardanelles out of Soviet reach. As a concession to the Tsar, the Bulgarians did get some dilution of Turkish sovereignty, but for Disraeli this was distinctly a minor matter.

In the brief period that intervened between the original Bulgarian massacre and the Congress of Berlin, Gladstone did more than denounce Disraeli for lack of Christian compassion. He elaborated an alternative view of Britain's role in the world and of an appropriate British foreign policy. It was, quite simply, an anti-imperialist view, a candidly "little England" view. He thought it ridiculous for Queen Victoria to become Empress of India, and saw no point in having Cyprus as a colony or in establishing military outposts in Afghanistan. He believed in self-determination for the Christian peoples of the Balkans and did not give a damn for the Turkish empire, which he regarded as a barbaric relic, but he was not about to do anything to "liberate" those Christian peoples. And while he did not like the idea of Russia acquiring the Dardanelles, he did not think it was worth a war to prevent it. This was not just a point of view, it was a program. When Gladstone returned to office in 1880, however, the "facts" that Disraeli had created, the public opinion that had been solidified behind them, as well as the coercive necessities of international power politics, prevented Gladstone from carrying out his program. He never left any doubt as to what he would have preferred to do, had he been free to do it. But he was not free, and the issue of "human rights" slid once again to the distant margins of British foreign policy.

When one looks back at this episode, one is struck by what one can only call the "innocence" with which the issue was raised and debated. Ever since the end of World War II, in contrast, when "human rights" again became of international concern, the entire discussion has been tainted with disingenuousness. For the past four decades, a concern for "human rights" has not simply and mainly been opposed to a hard-headed and hard-hearted *realpolitik*. On the contrary, despite the sea of sentimentality on which the issue of "human rights" has floated, that issue has, as often as not, been an accessory to a certain kind of ideological politics.

Today, most discussions of "human rights" are misleading because beneath the surface there is almost always a hidden agenda. An issue of "human rights" today is all too likely to be an issue exploited in bad faith. Am I questioning the sincerity of the thousands of "human rights" activists in the United States and elsewhere? Well, sincerity in politics is a tricky affair. It is more common in politics than cynics think, but even political activists can have difficulty knowing what it is they are being sincere about. It is not always easy to distinguish between sincerity and a passionate self-righteousness that cares only for the purity of conscience which inhabits a posturing self. Many of the most ardent northern abolitionists, prior to the Civil War, were so offended by slavery that they urged that the South be encouraged to secede. Were they being sincere about slavery, or about their own moral fastidiousness? God only knows.

There is no doubt that most Americans who exhibit a passionate interest in "human rights" are moved primarily by humanitarian motives, usually by an understandable, even commendable, outrage at one particular abuse directed against a particular person or group of persons. It is then very easy for them to slide into a feverish humanitarianism which disorients their senses when they confront issues of foreign policy. In such a condition, they are easily manipulable by those who have a professional, as distinct from a simple, humanitarian interest in "human rights."

Yes, one must certainly respect the courage of those human rights activists who live and operate in countries and under circumstances where self-sacrifice is a possible consequence of their commitment. Yet it also has to be said that even some of those who make this exemplary commitment do not necessarily care about "human rights" in any general sense. Thus, I do not share the widespread admiration for Archbishop Tutu of South Africa, because I am reasonably certain that if and when the African National Congress comes to power, he will be a vocal apologist for its tyranny and brutality. My certainty on this score derives from his placid acquiescence in the brutality and tyranny of existing black African regimes.

On the whole, then, I think the question of "sincerity" is best left aside when discussing "human rights" agitation. Much human rights agitation today appears to exemplify what Hegel called "negative activity"—a fanaticism of the abstract that assaults the actual without having in mind any practical plans for improving the actual. In politics such "negative activity," whatever its motivation, always ends up serving a positive political purpose. It seems to me that the key question today is whether such activity is linked to a "hidden agenda." Much of the time, I would argue, this is the case. Moreover, it is this linkage that explains why the issue of "human rights" has achieved such extraordinary prominence in our time.

The era of bad faith in "human rights" began soon after the conclusion of World War II, with the United Nations' Universal Declaration of Human Rights in 1948. This document has been widely criticized for the bland way it equates "social and economic rights" (the right to a job, the right to medical care, vacations with pay) with the kinds of traditional political rights (government by consent of the governed, due process of law, etc.) that have prevailed in the liberal democracies. But there was more than intellectual error or enthusiastic idealism at work here. The document was an important first step in establishing something like a moral equivalence between liberal capitalist democracies and communist or self-styled socialist regimes. This was the hidden agenda that gave birth to this text.

It is probable that most of those in the West who endorsed the Declaration did not realize what was happening. They shortsightedly perceived only immediate advantages to their own political agendas. The trade unions were delighted to see their long-standing demands elevated to the level of "human rights." Liberals eager to construct a welfare state were pleased to think that they were now enlarging the sphere of "human rights." So, naturally, were social-democrats, for whom the welfare state is a necessary transitional regime toward some kind of socialist society. To the degree that these groups shared a common ideological purpose it was the denigration of "old-fashioned" property rights in order to create a more egalitarian society—and to this same degree, they were complicitous with the "hidden agenda," even if they didn't fully realize its implications. On the other hand, some of those involved in the composition and promulgation of this text knew exactly what they were doing, and were fully aware of its implications.

Those implications, spelled out over the succeeding decades, have been momentous. To begin with, the Declaration legitimized the notion that totalitarian or authoritarian societies that emphasize "social and economic rights" as part of an official egalitarian ideology have their own distinctive virtues as well as their obvious vices, to be balanced against the virtues and vices of liberal-capitalist societies. While this did not usually result in a literal "moral equivalence," it did frustrate any effort at a strong comparative moral judgment. It is not too much to say that what was involved was nothing less than a firm step toward the moral disarmament of the West.

Perhaps an even more important intellectual consequence of this new conception of "human rights" was the near-magical transvaluation of a venerable political idea: the idea of tyranny. Clearly, any authoritarian or totalitarian regime officially dedicated to an egalitarian ideology and officially committed to the entire spectrum of "social and economic rights" could not simply be described as a tyranny, even though the kinds of political rights distinctive of liberal societies were nonexistent. This helps to explain what to many thoughtful people is otherwise a mystery, or a sheer perversity: why the majority of liberals in the West extend such an extraordinary tolerance toward "left-wing" tyrants.

Traditional liberalism spoke not of "human rights" but of individual rights, these being almost exclusively rights vis-à-vis government. It explicitly recognized only one "social or economic right": the right to property, including the "property" of one's labor power. This right was thought to be the cornerstone of all those political rights that collectively defined a liberal order. In and of it-self, of course, it was not a sufficient basis for those rights, but it was deemed a necessary basis for those rights. Nothing in the experience of the past three centuries has invalidated this thesis. Political liberties exist only in societies that respect individual rights, including property rights. True, the degree of respect (or nonrespect) will vary from country to country, and from time to time. Moreover, in all liberal societies today, property rights have been lim-ited by various entitlements that some would call "social and economic rights," although they are never constitutionally defined as such. But wherever these entitlements are given a massive priority as part of an egalitarian ethos, a lib-eral society either will not exist or will not endure for long.

To put it bluntly: the effect of the "hidden agenda" was to help delegitimate the market economy ("capitalism") that is an indispensable precondition of a traditional liberal ("bourgeois") society. It had the further implication of cast-ing into doubt the moral status of American foreign policy, which has never thought it appropriate to concern itself with "social and economic rights" in other countries. The importance of this latter implication has been gradually revealed over the course of the past two decades. It is today the primary "hid-den agenda" of most activist organizations concerned with "human rights."

I have to emphasize (lest I seem paranoid) that many of the people involved in these organizations are naïve innocents. But among the organizers and lead-ers there are always some full-time professionals who are sophisticated enough to know exactly what they are doing. "Human rights" indeed is only one aspect of their endeavors. It has been documented, though little notice has been taken of this, that many of the same people who are among the leaders of "human rights" agitation are also active in antinuclear agitation, arms control agita-tion, extremist environmentalist agitation, unilateral disarmament agitation, anti-aid-to-the-*contras* agitation, radical feminist agitation, as well as all sorts of organizations that sponsor "friendship" programs with left-wing regimes. Since these are not only energetic people but very intelligent as well, they have been very successful in giving the issue of "human rights" a special "spin" in a certain direction.

Take, for instance, the question of "torture" which has become so promi-nent in "human rights" agitation. Note that I put the word in quotation marks, because one of the successes of the "human rights" movement has been to broaden the definition of "torture" to include what would otherwise be clas-sified as "police brutality." Americans would be disapproving of but not out-raged at police brutality or the use of third-degree methods against prisoners in distant lands. We are, after all, familiar enough with this phenomenon at home, and would not be surprised to learn that it is far more common in "less civilized" (i.e., most other) countries. But torture, real torture, is an abomination to the bourgeois-liberal sensibility, a violation of that sense of human dignity which is at the very root of our liberal individualism. So a focus on torture is a brilliant bit of public relations.

The question that should be asked, but isn't, is: why is torture such an issue now, when in years past it never even entered any discussion of international relations? Is torture more common today than it was, say, thirty years ago? There is no reason to think so. In a country like Turkey there has always been a thin line between sheer brutality and outright torture in its prisons. But Turkey, a member of NATO, is an important military ally of the United States. Are we really willing to help destabilize its government in the interest of prison reform? And are those who are so willing really more interested in prison reform than in such destabilization?

In fact, torture (and police brutality too) may well be less common in the world today because of the power of the media to expose such abuses. In general, actual torture is used today mainly in countries where it has been a traditional practice for centuries. It is also likely to be used in circumstances of a guerrilla insurrection (urban or rural) where the police and military, themselves targets (and often victims) of assassination, are determined to acquire information that might help them suppress the rebellion. That there is provocation to torture is not, of course, a justification, since civilized opinion properly decided long ago that there is no justification, whatever the circumstances. But by focusing on instances of torture (or of police brutality now counted as torture), the "human rights" activists score an important point: they help legitimate the insurrection that today generally comes from the left, while doing their bit to discredit those governments that are trying to suppress the insurrection.

Critics of the "human rights" organizations assert that these organizations operate on a double standard—they seek out authoritarian governments that are on good terms with the United States and emphasize the violations (real or supposed) of "human rights" that occur there, but tend to be relatively unexcited, or at least much less excited, about violations of "human rights" by authoritarian or totalitarian anti-American governments. Indeed, the government that gains this privileged status need not even be left-wing, so long as it is clearly anti-American. Note the disproportionate lack of interest in the state of "human rights" in Syria or Iran, as contrasted with the intense interest in Israel.

To this the "human rights" activists reply, with plausibility, that it makes sense for them to direct their energies to situations where it is reasonable to assume that the United States government is capable of exercising some benign influence, and where, therefore, it bears a degree of moral responsibility for failing to exercise this influence. To which the critics retort that the "human rights" activists are themselves guilty of moral turpitude because of their failure to distinguish between what Joshua Muravchik calls "individual abuses" and "systemic deformities," the latter characterizing totalitarian communist regimes as distinct from merely authoritarian regimes. To which the "human rights" spokesmen then reply that this distinction between "totalitarian" and "authoritarian" regimes is a species of "Cold War" sophistry, since the suffering of the victim of torture or police brutality under either regime is unvarnished, indistinguishable suffering.

I must confess that, though my sympathies are all with the critics of the "human rights" movement, I find this debate to be essentially sterile. To begin with, the perspective of the victim, whether in war or peace, is the stuff of which poetry (or perhaps theology) is made, not politics, and certainly not foreign policy. To invert Tolstoy's aphorism, all victims are alike in their suffering and humiliation. But not all political regimes in which suffering and humiliation exist are alike. The difference between totalitarian *societies* and authoritarian *governments* is obvious enough, though one of the purposes of focusing on the individual indignities suffered under both regimes is precisely to blur this obvious distinction. True, not all totalitarian societies are identical—there are important national differences that create shades and hues of totalitarianism—nor are they immune to change. But though there may arise an occasional instance where the distinction between an authoritarian and totalitarian policy is less easy to make, the distinction is of crucial significance for an understanding of twentieth-century history and politics.

Authoritarian governments have existed throughout history and may fairly be regarded as preliberal realities. Whether they are "destined" to become liberal or totalitarian societies, or to evolve into some social form still unimaginable, is an interesting question of political philosophy. But no one can seriously claim that the numerous authoritarian regimes now scattered all over the world constitute any kind of threat to liberal America or the liberal West. Totalitarian societies, on the other hand, are postliberal realities. They emerge out of an explicit rejection of the Western liberal tradition, are the declared enemies of this tradition, and aim to supersede it. It is impossible to write a history of international relations in the twentieth century without making the rise of postliberal totalitarianism (whether of the right or left) the central event of the era, or without making the "Cold War" between the liberal democracies and the new totalitarian states the central focus around which everything else revolves. It is, in contrast, perfectly possible to write a history of international relations in the twentieth century without ever bothering to mention something called "authoritarianism." In fact, the histories that have been written all do exemplify both this impossibility and this possibility.

It is not an accident that most "human rights" activists, and all "human rights" publicists or theorists, insist on denying either the existence or the importance of the totalitarian-authoritarian distinction. In the abstract, there would seem to be no need for them to do so. There are actually some "human rights" activists who do ignore this whole issue. Like the clergy of yesteryear, they are impelled by the simple desire to alleviate human suffering, without paying attention to politics. But these are a minority, even among the clergy of today. The "human rights" movement is decidedly political. Its need to obfuscate the totalitarian-authoritarian distinction flows from its political intentions, its desire to deny that the "Cold War" is anything but a paranoid fantasy of a bourgeois-capitalist establishment, to minimize the totalitarian threat to liberal-democratic nations, to unnerve American foreign policy by constantly exposing the "immorality" of its relations with authoritarian allies, etc. In short, to repeat: its purpose, the hidden agenda of its "negative activity," is the moral disarmament of the bourgeois-capitalist West.

It is interesting, by the way, to note that the "human rights" movement is far less influential in Western Europe, and is taken far less seriously by governments there, than is the case in the United States. No European foreign office has to engage in the idiotic political arithmetic which Congress has imposed on our State Department, whereby every year it solemnly tots up the "human rights" situation in dozens of countries. It is an inherently absurd enterprise. If women in Switzerland don't have the vote, while they do in Romania, does that make Romania in any way more respectful of "human rights" than Switzerland? And how does one even apply the concept of "human rights" to Saudi Arabia, a medieval nation rather than a modern state? Why are we so silly as to get involved in this sort of thing, while European governments do not? Are the peoples across the Atlantic less concerned with human rights than we are?

I don't think so. I believe, rather, that the difference is that Western Europe has real, live, important socialist parties, while the United States does not. The result is that those Americans who, in Europe, would belong to socialist or social-democratic parties are forced to channel their political energies into "causes" which, in sum, approximate as closely as possible to those parties' programs. The upshot is that the European left is far more candid than its American counterpart, and has less need for any hidden agendas. When one reads books by European socialists on foreign affairs—the recent writings of Regis Debray can serve as an example—"human rights" is, at most, a very subordinate theme, and the theme is sometimes not struck at all. These writings suffer from all kinds of illusions, but they are illusions that flow from avowed ideological convictions. In the United States, where it is imprudent to avow a socialist ideology, those convictions go underground and then emerge in "causes" such as "human rights" or "arms control" or "unilateral nuclear disarmament," which present themselves as apolitical or transpolitical.

Precisely because they seem so nonpolitical or transpolitical, they can actually be more radical in substance. No European country has an Arms Control and Disarmament Agency, whose function is presumably to thwart the militarist proclivities of our Defense Department. Similarly, no European country has an Assistant Secretary of State for Human Rights, whose function is presumably to thwart the immoral proclivities of our State Department. True, the notion of negotiating an "arms control" agreement with the Soviet Union is at least as popular in Western Europe as in the United States. But in Western Europe this notion is often based on a real (or not-unrealistic) anxiety that a conflict between the two superpowers could easily and quickly result in Western Europe becoming a devastated nuclear battlefield, even if the source of this conflict lies outside Western Europe itself or is marginal to Western European interests. It is this fear that motivates many of the more serious "antinuclear" activists over there. In the United States, however, "antinuclear" and "arms control" publicists are more akin to the anti-American, pro-Soviet left in Europe. They are persuaded that it is a "Cold War" American foreign policy which threatens the world with nuclear devastation, and that a more "conciliatory" (i.e., appeasing) posture toward the Soviet Union and its allies will avert such a catastrophe. They display little fear of Soviet intentions, much fearful anxiety about our own White House, Pentagon, and State Department. It is this distrust of the United States and of its status as a world power—what in Europe would be called "anti-Americanism"—that motivates our more passionate "antinuclear" advocates and impels them to support *any* formula acceptable to the Soviets, and to adopt an appeasing mode in foreign policy. Such appeasement is their hidden—not deeply hidden, it must be said—agenda.

There is no other explanation, so far as I can see, for the pertinacity of various leading "arms control" advocates, when by now one would have expected them to be thoroughly disillusioned with the whole affair. This includes many who were involved in the negotiation of the SALT I agreement, an agreement that never would have been signed, never could have been signed, if it had been understood beforehand that the Soviets would promptly install over five hundred intermediate-range warheads aimed at Western Europe, something that, it turned out, was permitted (though certainly never envisaged) under the SALT I agreement. The lack of subsequent disillusionment among such knowledgeable people, the fact that their passion for the "arms control process" remains undiminished, is something that requires interpretation.

What makes American foreign policy so vulnerable to "human rights" agitation? The explanation is not far to seek: this foreign policy has, must have, an ineradicable moral-ideological component. We are indeed engaged in a profound ideological conflict with the Soviet Union, a conflict that dominates world politics. But it is both a simplification and a distortion to describe it as a conflict about "human rights." It is, rather, a conflict over the very definition of "human rights," and the point of this conflict is to determine who will have the power to define "human rights" for future generations. In that sense, the United States cannot evade the urgencies and the ambiguities of "power politics."

The relation of such "power politics" to the American "public philosophy" makes for tension and complications in our foreign policy. *Realpolitik* à la Disraeli is unthinkable in America, since it runs against the very grain of our political ethos. Ours is a nation based on a universal creed, and there is an unquenchable missionary element in our foreign policy. We do aim to "make the world safe for democracy"—eventually, and in those places and at those times where conditions permit democracy to flourish. Every American administration in our history has felt compelled, though some have been more enthusiastic than others, to use our influence, wherever possible, to see that other governments respect our conception of individual rights as the foundation of a just regime and a good society.

On the other hand, only two presidents in our history have tried to emulate Gladstone in making the missionary element the very centerpiece of American foreign policy. The first was Woodrow Wilson, who believed that his enterprise would achieve its success by creating a world organization that in turn would form a "community of nations" pledged to respect the principles we hold dear—with disrespect being curbed by a broadened (Wilson would have said "heightened") definition of international law, to be enforced by this new "world community." It was a utopian vision to which many eminent Americans still pay lip service, but which no serious person can any longer take at face value. Today, all that is left of the Wilsonian dream is a host of international organizations that are at best debating societies, at worst sinks of corruption. There is also an array of treaty obligations that the United

States thoughtlessly entered into and from which we are now gingerly trying to free ourselves.

The second president, of course, was Jimmy Carter, who fully accepted the expanded version of "human rights" (including social and economic rights) and who then tried to give the American missionary impulse a unilateralist thrust. But he soon was forced to recognize that the world is a complex and recalcitrant place, full of other peoples with other ideas, and that while proclaiming high-minded principles was one thing, unilateral American efforts to reshape world realities according to our national vision were an enterprise necessarily limited in scope, often very limited. The rights of individuals in other lands are a matter of concern for Americans. One may even say it is an integral part of our national interest. But it is usually a concern that claims no centrality in our foreign policy, since it has to be weighed against all those other interests which make up our national interest.

Secretary of State Cyrus Vance, one of the original "human rights" enthusiasts, was not in office more than a month before he felt constrained to issue the following statement:

> We will speak frankly about injustice both at home and abroad. We do not intend, however, to be strident or polemical, but we do believe that an abiding respect for human rights is a human value of fundamental importance and that it must be nourished. We will not comment on each and every issue, but we will from time to time comment when we see a threat to human rights, when we believe it constructive to do so.

Well—yes. If one is willing to stipulate that by "human rights" one means pretty much what used to be called "individual rights," then any American president could have endorsed that statement. Ronald Reagan, I am certain, would be happy to endorse it. The United States (in this respect like the Soviet Union) does stand for something in the world, and its foreign policy must, to the degree that the world permits, respect the principles of its establishment. But it is the nature of foreign policy to operate, most of the time, in the realm of necessity rather than the realm of freedom. So while it is fair to assert that the ideological basis of American foreign policy gives it a permanent moral dimension which itself delimits the scope of any purely "realistic" policy, these limits have to be broad enough to permit foreign policy to be effective.

Just how broad or narrow these limits are will depend on circumstances. Probably the "purest," most moral, least self-interested foreign policy action ever taken on behalf of "human rights" was the British navy's suppression of the slave trade in the nineteenth century. This action was made possible by many factors: Britain's massive superiority in sea power, the unimportance of the "Third World" countries involved, the nonexistence (as compared with today) of a complex structure of international law and international organizations. So while Britain's action was wholly admirable, one also has to point out that it was costless, or as close to costless as makes no matter.

It is conceivable that the United States might, one of these days, find itself in a more or less comparable situation, and it is certainly to be hoped that it would then take a comparable action. But such situations are likely to be rare. Like all great nations, the United States does conceive itself as having some kind of "civilizing mission." But, lacking an "imperialist" impulse, we are not usually inclined to accomplish this mission through forceful intervention. Presumably if a Pol Pot regime came to power in Central America and began a genocidal campaign against its own people, we might very well intervene. On the other hand, we did not intervene in Cambodia, nor have we even dreamed of intervening in Africa, where tribal genocide is not uncommon. Unilateral military intervention by the United States on behalf of "human rights" would have to overcome resistance from both our enemies and our allies. And steps short of military intervention will almost always be more symbolic than real. True, symbolic action may sometimes be better than no action at all. But over time the impact, both at home and abroad, of a series of mainly symbolic actions will be negligible. Worse, they will be interpreted as a sign of weakness, not strength, of moralistic impotence rather than moral energy. If this is our situation today, and the experience of the Carter administration has confirmed that it is, why has the message failed to get through to the "human rights" constituency? The reason, I suggest, is that this constituency has its own agenda, and that "human rights" is a useful rhetoric in which to promote it.

A final point: there are some conservative (or non-left) "human rights" activists who feel that this theme can be exploited for purposes of anti-communist and anti-totalitarian propaganda. It is impossible not to admire the diligence with which they expose the sufferings of people under communism, and this kind of candid ideological warfare does serve to remind us of the nature of the enemy, a reminder that is always timely. But there is reason to wonder whether this strategy, on its own, can be effective over the longer term. There cannot be many people who do not already know about conditions in the Soviet Union. The question is: Why don't they care? Why are most of the major Christian churches in the United States so utterly indifferent to the persecution of Christianity in the Soviet Union and in Soviet-occupied Eastern Europe? If this be ignorance, it is a special kind of willful ignorance.

Such willful ignorance, I would suggest, has two sources. First, since the Soviet Union has its own (Marxist) conception of "human rights," about which it is brutally assertive and in no way apologetic, it does seem quixotically futile to criticize it for not sharing our traditional-liberal political philosophy. Second, and more important, there are many who believe the Soviet model is flawed but who nevertheless regard it as a respectable alternative to our own, which they perceive as at least equally flawed, or even flawed to a greater degree. The sad and simple truth is that, once one has lost faith in the traditional-liberal model, one feels deprived of the moral authority to challenge the Soviet model and one then loses all interest in doing so. It is this loss of faith that feeds the organized "human rights" movement, and gives it an "anti-American" bias. To this loss of faith, mere anti-communism is no answer.

There is also a significant cost involved in such an anti-communist "human rights" campaign. To avoid accusations of unprincipled conservative bias, it is inevitably pushed toward making "human rights" a central issue in determining American policy toward South Korea, Chile, Indonesia, the Philippines, etc.—which is, after all, exactly what our anti-American "human rights" activists wish. In effect, the conservative campaign has the unintended consequence of legitimating the "human rights" efforts of the left. The so-called human rights activists inside the Soviet Union, or at least the more sophisticated among them, understand this problem well enough. They certainly do appreciate efforts in the West to alleviate the suffering of those who oppose particular policies of the Soviet system. This is justification enough for such efforts, whatever their limited success. But those activists inside the Soviet Union also have a hidden agenda, one of which I thoroughly approve. To the extent that the "human rights" issue offers them some protection as well as some leverage, they are morally entitled to use it. It is also politically prudent for them to emphasize it. Unfortunately, such hidden agendas are easily read by the Soviet authorities, who have had so much experience in writing them.

1986–1987

Conflicts That Can't Be Resolved

Three more bombs went off in Jerusalem yesterday, killing at least 6 people and injuring more than 165. The Islamic terrorist group Hamas claimed responsibility. Back in Washington, the Clinton administration uttered the usual platitudes and talked of postponing Secretary of State Madeleine Albright's planned peace mission to the Middle East next week. But already the administration is pondering ways to save the "peace process."

Peace processes are proliferating all over the world, along with the violence that gave birth to them. There is the Middle East peace process, of course, but peace processes are also at work in the Cyprus conflict between Greeks and Turks, the Northern Ireland conflict between Catholics and Protestants, the Korean conflict between communists and non-communists, the Bosnian conflict between just about everyone, and in many other conflicts around the globe. Nor are they limited to international conflicts. In the California Legislature a bill has been proposed authorizing a Peace Process Task Force to oversee truces in gang warfare. So many "peace processes" and so little peace! What's going on?

Well, what's going on is the familiar story of a social science theory being promoted to politicians who find it an attractive and easy option. The theory in question is "conflict resolution," by now a venerable department of social psychology with some thousands of "experts" who are happy to sell their services to foundations, government agencies, or troubled nations. Our State Department is thoroughly under the sway of this theory—aren't diplomats by training experts at conflict resolution?—and so is the United States Institute of Peace, whose latest bulletin features a summary of a speech by Joseph Duffy, director of the U.S. Information Agency. It reads: "The new information technologies are transforming international relations, opening up new possibilities for conflict prevention, management and resolution." Just how these technologies are to perform this task we are not told, nor is there any hint of why they do not seem to be working effectively in all those peace processes under way. But the basic idea of a "peace process" as a most desirable alternative to violent conflict is very attractive to these enchanted by the therapeutic approach to all of life's problems. It is equally attractive to political leaders who perceive it as a way of "doing something nice" without really doing anything.

Still, it is hard to find a peace process that has accomplished anything, anywhere. That is because "conflict resolution" is itself a rather pompous, high-sounding theory with a very skimpy, simple-minded psychological basis. The axiom of this theory is that harmony among human beings is more natural than conflict—no original sin here!—and that if only we can get the parties in conflict to talk to one another, the level of "mistrust" will decline and mutual understanding increase, until at some point the conflict itself will subside. It is thinkable that such an approach to marriage counseling might in some cases be productive, but its extension to the level of statecraft, or to any conflict between collective entities, is an extreme case of academic hubris.

When collective entities clash, it is usually because their interests are at odds. Mediation may in some instances be helpful. But mediation and conflict resolution are two different things. Conflict resolution focuses on the psychological attitudes prevalent within the two entities, and tries to reform them. Mediation focuses on the interests at issue, tries to envisage a settlement minimally satisfactory to both parties, and then aims to persuade them to move to such a settlement. A crucial difference between mediation and conflict resolution is that the former has a compromise as its limited goal, where the latter has "better trust and understanding" as its goal, on the assumption that this will inevitably mark the end of conflict and the advent of pacific harmony.

Mediation played an important role in bringing the recent United Parcel Service strike to an end. One doubts very much that it resulted in "better trust and understanding" on either side. But the sphere of conflict was limited at the outset; UPS did not wish to break the Teamsters union, and the union had no desire to destroy UPS. A mediator in such a situation operates within a fairly well-defined realm of possibilities, and hopes to nudge the contestants toward a realization of one of these possibilities. The reason the "peace process" gets nowhere in places like Northern Ireland and Cyprus is that no mediator can envisage an end situation satisfactory to both parties. An expert in conflict resolution can easily and always envisage a radical reformation of feelings, attitudes, and sentiments in the populations involved, so that the problem, as it were, resolves itself. Unfortunately, he is not in possession of a therapy to create such a miracle.

The best-publicized "peace process," of course, is directed at Israeli Jews and Palestinian Arabs in the Middle East. In this process, our State Department plays a crucial but muddled role. It is in part a cool mediator, in part a fuzzy therapist in conflict resolution. Its step-by-step approach is justified in terms of "building mutual trust," but the nature and direction of these steps strongly suggests that the department does indeed have an end in view. Unfortunately, it is not an end ever likely to be acceptable to either Jews or Arabs, which is why it is best obscured by conflict resolution rhetoric.

It seems clear to any attentive observer that the "final solution" the State Department has in mind is that Israel should return to its 1968 borders (perhaps with minor revisions) and the Palestinians should have their own state on the West Bank. The tip-off came when the Netanyahu government "leaked" a proposed map of the West Bank, based on something like a fifty-fifty partition. It was the first time an Israeli government ever publicly contemplated such a partition, and a mediator, playing his traditional role, would have explored whatever possibilities were inherent in this move. There is little doubt that the terms of any such partition were negotiable. But the State Department never discussed this idea with the Arabs or the Israelis. It simply ignored it as a distraction from the "peace process."

But it is extremely doubtful that Israeli public opinion, whatever Israeli party is in office, will ever accept the State Department's ideal solution. It would pose too many obvious problems for Israel's military security. The only reason the Arabs launched their war in 1968 was because Israel's geography, with the middle of the country only thirteen miles wide, made it seem so vulnerable. Israelis have no desire to return to that status quo. The Arabs would surely be happy to accept the State Department's goal, but for how long? The Palestinian media, and Palestinian leaders speaking to their own people in their own media, have given clear signals that their goals have a further reach: sharp limits on Israeli immigration, return of an unspecified number of Arab refugees, even the dismantling of a specifically Jewish state. The State Department is dismissive of such rhetoric, since it would render hopeless the dream of an eventual "conflict resolution." But there is plenty of evidence that the Palestinians are not so dismissive, which is why the State Department has never asked the Palestinian leaders explicitly to disavow such an agenda. And neither are the Israelis, listening to this rhetoric on Arab radio and reading it in Arab newspapers, so dismissive. How can they be?

The only reason the Mideast "peace process" gathers so much attention is because of American leverage over Israel, which has produced results. In fact, these results only reveal the "peace process" to be another name for an appeasement process, whereby Israel makes concessions and Arabs simply demand more. But that cannot go on much longer, as Israeli patience has pretty much reached the end of its tether. The Mideast "peace process" is fated to end in a stalemate, just like the Northern Ireland, Cyprus, and all the other "peace processes." Perhaps this will persuade the State Department there really is a difference between the art of diplomatic mediation and the social science of "conflict resolution." On the other hand, perhaps not.

1997

VII

JUDAISM
AND
CHRISTIANITY

The Myth of
the Supra-Human Jew

The Theological Stigma

THE STIGMA

"Anyone who is not instinctively disgusted by the Synagogue is unworthy of a dog's respect." So wrote Léon Bloy in 1905 in his book, *Le Salut par les Juifs*— "Salvation Through the Jews"—a title taken from Christ's words in the Gospel of Saint John: *Salus ex Judaeis est*. A strange sentiment for a book so titled, and one suspects the presence of the spirit of irony. Yet close reading fails to disclose any irony, and serves only to convince the reader that Bloy intended to express both these sentiments with the utmost seriousness. How could he?

In her volume of autobiography, *We Have Been Friends Together*, Raïssa Maritain has a long and interesting discussion of Bloy, this disgusted, lonely, poverty-stricken, exalted prophet of Catholicism. "Pilgrim of the Absolute" he called himself, while a contemporary described him as a "cathedral gargoyle who pours down the waters of heaven on the good and on the evil." He is a striking figure, a man of deep feeling, a brilliant rhetorician, a near-saint. Certainly, much can be forgiven him, including ill-tempered statements like the one above; they might be regarded as unclean froth on the surface of a vigorous and profound ocean of religious feeling.

Such a case for forgiveness is presented by Mme. Maritain. Since she herself was born a Jewess, and holds what are known as "liberal" views on the subject of human rights, her pleading is genuine and not open to suspicion. She points out that this simple soul (and he was simple for all that he was profound) had a "medieval horror" of the Jews as a deicide people, and that "he expressed this detestation in terms that were sometimes inadmissible." On the other hand, he attacked in unequivocal words the cheap *racist* anti-Semitism that was then becoming voluble, and even, in later years, modified his invective so as not to be linked in any way with these latter. To clinch her defense, there are all the wonderfully flattering things that Léon Bloy did say about the Jews. Salvation through the Jews—he meant it, passionately.

Still, after having done justice to Bloy, there remains the problem—the problem of the place of the Jew in the Christian religion that could provoke such a bewildering duality of emotion; for Bloy's opinions are, in startling clarity, Christian opinions. The Greco-Roman world disliked the Jews: they were stiff-necked, proud, barbaric, stubborn, almost, a sovereign might say, rebellious. It was an imperial dislike, and certainly no Roman ever had the idea of salvation arising from these people. It was left for the Christians to do that.

What is the Christian conception of the Jew? Jacques Maritain, in his book on anti-Semitism, defines the position of the Jew as follows:

> Between Israel and the world, as between the Church and the world, there is a supra-human relation. . . . The bond which unifies Israel is not simply the bond of flesh and blood, or that of an ethico-historical community; it is a sacred and supra-historical bond, of promise and yearning. . . . But since the day when it stumbled, because its leaders chose the world, it is bound, prisoner and victim of the world which it loves, but *of which* it is not, shall not be, and can never be [Maritain's italics].

There is then a mystery about the Jew as there is a mystery about the Apostolic Church. Just as the Church can never be exhaustively defined by a secular vocabulary, so the Jew cannot be explained as, say, the Muslim, the Hindu, or even the Christian can be explained. His being cannot be circumscribed within the area of natural man. He bears a stigma, a theological stigma, that perforce makes him more than human. Or is it less? Or both?

Bloy, in denouncing the scribbling of some contemporary Jew-baiters, wrote: "Formerly the Jews were detested, they were gladly massacred, but they were not scorned *as a race*. On the contrary, they were respected and feared, and the Church prayed for them." "Gladly massacred"—"respected"—"feared." We begin to see the outlines of the stigma.

One more witness, Ernest Renan: "Several times we have called attention to the curious circumstance that the Jews . . . harbour in their bosom two extremes, the struggle between good and evil. . . . The best of all men have been Jews and the most wicked of all men also have been Jews." He is high up to the heavens, and he is low to the very depths of hell, but never does the Jew stand with two feet upon earth.

CURSED AND DIVINE

Many writers have presented the case of the "demonic" Jew as a product of the Western (i.e., Christian) unconscious. Those who read Joshua Trachtenberg's *The Devil and the Jews* will find ample source material. Medieval Europe saw the Jew as an ally of the Devil, a sly, subhuman, evil creature who incited Christian man, tempted him, damned him. He, the Jew, was at the root of evil, temporal and spiritual, and was attacked as such. He was more than the bystanding scapegoat, the victim of all thwarted desires. He was assumed to be at the source of the frustration itself.

It does not need an expert in psychoanalysis to see that the Devil himself was an ambivalent symbol. He was the imaginative projection of unlawful lust and unsanctioned desire at the same time that the guilt of experiencing these desires was transferred to him, so that it could be fought and chastised at a distance. The Jew, as an ally of the Devil (when he was not that gentleman himself), was a convenient target for the guilty unconscious of the mass of men. Like the Devil, he was unremittingly pursued. The popular belief in the excessive sensuality of the Jews, and those crude medieval drawings of the Devil with his enormous testicles, drawings that aroused gasps of thrilled horror—surely there can be no misunderstanding this. The medieval Christian in pillaging the Jews was purifying himself conveniently and at no expense. On the contrary, his wages were glory and righteousness.

So far, so good. We have here one insight into the perennial sources of anti-Semitism. For, though the Devil may have disappeared from the scene, the psychic mechanism has not changed significantly since the Middle Ages. But it is only half the story. Trachtenberg refers to the moral and dogmatic scruples expressed by the Church against anti-Semitic excesses, and deplores the lack of control of these scruples over the lower clergy and the masses. But might it not be that the beliefs behind these very scruples were themselves at the root of Jew-hatred? The belief that the Jew was in league with the Devil has been investigated ably, but what has not been emphasized enough is the hatred of the Jew that arises from the belief that he is in league with God.

In what sense is the Jew in league with God, that is, the Christian God? That sense is expressly defined in the apologetic literature of the Church. The Jews are witnesses of the Incarnation and Crucifixion, and that is their function until the end of time. They bear living testimony to the truths of Church doctrine. As witnesses, they are doomed to inhabit the earth for eternity, until the day of the Resurrection, when they will be converted to the true faith. Their historical dispersion is the price they pay for this guarantee of deathlessness. The Wandering Jew is the complete symbol: the homeless, ever-living witness to the advent of Christ on earth.

Let us quote Bloy again: "The thought of the Church in every age has been that holiness is inherent in this exceptional, unique and indispensable people who are protected by God, preserved as the apple of his eye in the midst of destruction of so many peoples, for the accomplishment of his ulterior designs."

The Jews, then, do not appear on the historical stage in the same way as ordinary men. They are not born to it, have no natural right to it. They are allowed—nay, enjoined—to settle on the fringe because they are related to the producer, though they are not at all on good terms with him. They exist on divine sufferance, and in their own suffering. The rest of the cast have their suspicions, and their resentment. No one likes to be spied upon, even by agents of the supernatural, of God himself. Especially of God himself. They mutter to themselves and one bright voice calls out:

Kill them all; God knows his own.

DEATH OF A GOD

The Jew is holy and divine. He is also sacrificial in season. The excuse for persecuting the Jew is the charge of deicide, a charge leveled against him once every year in the Catholic ceremony on Good Friday. But, obviously, this cannot be taken seriously, except in the most trifling technical way. The Jews who participated in the Crucifixion must have acted under divine guidance (God is omniscient and omnipotent) as a proxy for Man, all men. Christendom must bear the guilt of this act along with the Jews. But Christendom also bears its own special guilt: that of continually desiring the crucifixion and death of its God.

The Middle Ages reveled in inordinately long and detailed descriptions of the sufferings of Christ on the cross. Trachtenberg remarks: "One cannot escape the impression that an abysmal guilt feeling drove Christendom to re-murder Jesus, the personification of its uneasy conscience . . . and to seek release by projecting its guilt upon the Jews." Thus the hatred of the deicide Jews is a sublimation of an instinct toward deicide, a castigation of it.

It is also more. It is an ill-disguised attack upon Christ and Christianity, not merely a sublimation, but also a genuine satisfaction of the desire to kill God. When the Jews are persecuted for having killed Christ, they are also being persecuted for sustaining his memory. For, and we tend to forget this, the blood of Christ was Jewish blood, and conversely, Jewish blood is the blood of Christ. In killing the Jew, the Christian is committing the long-desired, the abhorred, deicide.

Léon Bloy: "The Blood shed upon the Cross for the redemption of humankind, as well as that which each day is shed invisibly in the Chalice of the Sacrament of the Altar, is naturally and supernaturally Jewish blood—the immense river of Hebrew blood whose source is in Abraham and whose mouth is the Five Wounds of Christ."

"Kill them all; God knows his own." Can any Christian hear this without shuddering at the naked blasphemy?

The Bible says that the Jews will exist until the end of time. What a burden, and what a temptation, what a provocation, to give the lie to the Holy Book by exterminating them beforehand! With that, who knows what other sacred, irksome sanctions might be annulled? Even original sin perhaps, and man's dolorous existence on earth. What vistas of freedom! Will they never die off?

Pope Innocent III saw the danger, and warned: "The Jews are the living witnesses of the truth of Christianity. The Christian must not exterminate the Jews, for by so doing he would himself lose the knowledge of the law."

Words like these, however, only added fuel to the fire by assuring the Jew-killers that their wildest hopes were well founded. To abrogate the law, to see God dead once and for all, and to have men's secret lusts dance unrestrainedly under the open sky. . . . Will the Jews never die off?

The Jews, too, believe that they are holy and elect, the chosen people. Not as Christian dogma would have them believe it, but after their own fashion, holding fast to some sense of a special election and destiny, and in one way or another to the promise of the Messiah, or a messianic age, when peace and justice will at last come to them and to the world. The Jews, too, believe by their own religion that they are eternal. The influence of these two dogmas, Christian and Jewish, has its effect upon the rebellious Christian. His revolt is doomed to failure before it has begun, and he comes to recognize this. But this knowledge only goads him on to more desperate measures. To humiliate, to mock, to slaughter, only to find your victim impassive upon a pedestal of persecution, unshakeable—it is enough to drive the best family man into a frenzy of despair.

THE BURDEN OF GUILT

With the years, and the centuries, the burden of guilt grows heavier and heavier. For the guilt is cumulative, from generation to generation. The sins of anti-

Semitism are like a snowball, rolling downhill, gathering weight and speed. Its path is irreversible, the damage unatoneable.

To use another metaphor: the original murder leaves behind black and dirty traces that point an accusing finger. They must be erased, which means a further series of murders, and these, in turn, leave new traces. The accusation becomes ever more oppressive. All that can be hoped for is a convulsive miracle of elimination, the destruction of all clues and witnesses without exception.

The anti-Semite is doubly guilty: he is guilty of the Passion of Christ and he is guilty of the Passion of Israel.

A German anti-Semite, Hans Blueher, writing under the Weimar Republic, complained naïvely: "One of the greatest political assets of the Kingdom of Judah, which accompanies the curse on its blood, is its general capacity to draw a host-nation under the shadow of the curse. This it does by provoking a pogrom and thus bringing guilt upon the hosts." That, presumably, is what some people mean when they complain of the Machiavellian ethic of a Jew.

Sit in the darkness of the movie house with a Christian audience when pictures of concentration camps are shown upon the screen. There is a silence, a silence that whispers. "Ugh! How horrible!" And then the bent, scrawny, smiling survivors are shown, and the silence whispers: "Are they then truly eternal? It cannot be, for the world's burden of guilt would be too intolerable. Will they never die off?"

Even as they ask, they know the answer. No, they will never die off. In one of his letters, Rainer Maria Rilke wrote: "These people are fruitful even in their eradication." The popular mind amends this to: fruitful *because* of their eradication. It combines the belief in Jewish unnaturalness with the belief in Jewish sensuality. It is a lascivious thought, as must be any that links, contrary to all law and tradition, the sensual with the non-natural.

This grudging, salacious admission of the futility of their revolt does not quiet the Christian rebel. He must gird up his loins to try again. For as long as the Jew is before him, with his theological stigma, his unnatural accusing presence, the blasphemer cannot have peace.

THE UNSPOKEN VIRTUE

There are decent people; probably, under favorable circumstances, they form a majority. These people are civilized; that is, they have a more secure control over their desires, are more sensitive to the consequences of their actions. They partake of the nihilistic, sinful urge of their fellow men, but they never permit it to flower dangerously. Unless, of course, they are unduly provoked. There is always this "unless." "There is a limit to patience—that's going too far—" and so on their apologies run when civilization and decency go by the board and they leap into sacrilege. This is not to say that the leap necessarily takes place. But neither does it say that it necessarily does not.

This decency may be described as the Christian virtue of not being anti-Semitic. As a virtue, it is a good thing. But, also as a virtue, it has a lamentable tendency to offer itself for defilement.

We see this virtue in all its strength and weakness in England today. The British are a tolerant, human, and generous people. Their historical record with regard to the question of anti-Semitism is comparatively good. But, at present, they are undergoing a trial of temptation. Their soldiers in Palestine (never mind why they are there!) are being attacked by Jewish terrorists. Naturally, there is resentment and anger at this; that is perfectly human. What is not so pleasant is the form that this resentment takes.

In all organs of opinion and among all classes of people, there is pride in the "forbearance" shown by British troops in Palestine. What this means, and it comes out bluntly in ordinary conversation, is the restraint the British have displayed in not behaving as the Nazis did, or the Cossacks in pre-Revolutionary Russia. There is never any question of treating dissident Arabs, or Burmese, or Malayans in such a fashion. It is recognized tacitly that where the Jews are concerned, a special latitude of humanity (or inhumanity, rather) exists. Those who do not take advantage of this full latitude demonstrate "forbearance" and may pat themselves upon the back. The average Briton, proud of his tolerance and democratic institutions, when he reads of the Palestine terrorists, clenches his teeth and murmurs to himself: "They had better watch out." He is not thinking here of an ordinary opponent upon whom he will turn. He means, watch out for anti-Semitism. His self-control is admirable and all that sort of thing, but there are limits—understand?—and beyond those limits lie the ghetto, the pogrom, the concentration camp. Those punishments are linked peculiarly to the Jews. It is the way a Christian, when out of patience, reproves them.

In other words, the British are very much worried that they may be pushed into the horror of anti-Semitism. Let us pray that this special virtue, too, will be possessed of that famous British bulldog tenacity, and will not snap under the strain.

THE SECRET BEHIND THE MAN

Contemporaneously with Léon Bloy lived another great French Catholic, Charles Péguy. The similarities between the two men are striking. Both were poor, proud, sensitive, brilliant; both were outside the mainstream of twentieth-century thought, and both were scorned because of it. Bloy, possibly, was the "saintlier" of the two, for Péguy had the faculty of getting involved in political and personal squabbles. On the other hand, Péguy was a truly great poet whose full stature is only beginning to be recognized.

Péguy, too, wrote about the Jews. There are some critics who say that his discussion of Israel in *Notre Jeunesse* ("Our Youth") is the finest ever written. He was what is called pro-Semitic, and in Péguy's case this is something of an understatement. Personal events had gone into the formation of this attitude: his activity in the Dreyfus affair, his intense friendship with Bernard Lazare, his poignant, frustrated romance with a Jewish girl. Along with this went a heart whose capacity for love was only equaled by its capacity for contempt. Once Péguy had discovered what he thought to be the truth, he refused to equivocate or compromise. The very scent of anti-Semitism would send him into a rage. In 1912, he broke off his friendship with Georges Sorel because the latter would not support Péguy's efforts to obtain the Prix Goncourt for Julien Benda, a Jew.

For Péguy, the Jews were the carnal voice and temporal body of the Godhead. He wrote of Bernard Lazare: "There was not a trace of feeling, not a thought, not a shade of emotion that was not drawn and ordered by an order fifty centuries old . . . ; a whole race and a whole world on his bowed shoulders; . . . and a heart consumed by fire, the fire of his race, consumed by the fire of his people; the fiery heart, the ardent mind, and the burning coal on the prophetic lips."

Noble sentiments nobly expressed. It would seem almost perverse to cavil at them. Yet, if only he had described a man instead of a myth incarnate. It is so easy for these noble words to be handled by a charlatan, like a glittering coin, until the reverse side turns up. Blueher does just this: "Every Jew, irrespective of his intentions or what he thinks are his intentions, is subject to the missionary commands of the messianic kingdom represented by the reigning Prince of the Diaspora." And he further remarks the Jewish "organic plastic talent for mimicry. It has something to hide."

There is no question of relating the two views. One is not responsible for the other. They are absolutely opposed. But opposed as are the two sides of a coin. Both sides are necessary in order to make the coin legal tender. To speak plainly: so long as the Jew is anything but entirely human, so long as he bears the theological stigma, so long as he is in essence mysterious and extra-human, he can be described as the devil (sub-human) as easily as he can be described as something divine (super-human). When the stigma is enforced, the "truths" of anti-Semitism, far more influential than their contraries, are predetermined, and no antidefamation campaign can hope to really touch them. Witness Blue-her: "Henry Ford's highly important book on *The International Jew* is largely valid, though there is not a true word in it." If the Jew is outside the realm of the human, the human criteria of evidence, logic, and proof are not relevant to judgments concerning him.

THE SECULARIZATION OF THE STIGMA

Since the French Revolution and Napoleon, the stigma has, among the more "advanced" nations, changed its color. With the decline of religion as a force in men's lives, the Jew is condemned less and less in sacred terms and more and more in profane. The new charge against him is that of "race," that is, of anti-nationalism. The Jew is, to borrow an epithet beloved of Maurras and Chesterton, a "Bedouin" among nations. His self-imposed task is that of national dissolution. He can belong to religion, family, property, but never to any nation. For Jehovah has promised him the empire of the world, and he cannot be placated with anything less. Today, excessive nationalism seeks and finds an ally in anti-Semitism.

This change, while significant, leaves the original form of the stigma unchanged. The Jew is so easily designated as the stranger within the gates because he is, to begin with, the Stranger par excellence, the Stranger on earth itself. All variant and temporary types of anti-Semitism are fed by the deep subterranean wish that discovers the Jew to be—the Devil, a God, a holy witness, a finger of guilt—anything but a man.

This altered coloration of the stigma coincides with a change in the worldly status and ambitions of Israel itself. The literal advent of the Messiah was pushed into the background by the stirring call to liberty, fraternity, equality. The Jew began to explore the possibility of a tolerable existence in this world; he became excited and agitated at the prospect of the rule of reason and good-will among men, a rule which would relieve his depressed condition. With the echoes of the French Revolution ringing in his ears, the Jew began his dedication to the task of social amelioration. Not all Jews, of course. Many would have nothing less than the Messiah and stayed by their holy books. Others found special reasons for washing their hands of this secular idealism. But the participation of the Jews, with a vigor disproportionate to their numerical influence, in these new movements of the nineteenth and twentieth centuries has been widely commented upon. So impressed have some observers been that they would have it an essential ingredient of Judaism itself. Jacques Maritain declares that "Israel passionately hopes, waits, yearns for the coming of

God on earth, the kingdom of *God here below*. With an eternal will, a super-natural will, it desires justice in time, in nature, and in the cities of man." And: "Israel teaches the world to be discontented and restless as long as the world has not God; it stimulates the movement of history."

Here, Maritain has seized upon a historical truth and polished it until it shines forth as a theological insight, true for eternity. He might assert that many modern Jewish thinkers have insisted upon this secular mission of Israel; he could even point to certain passages in the Talmud that could conceivably support such an interpretation, though many authorities, I believe, will contend that prior to the Enlightenment and Emancipation, the idea of salvation among the Jews was a distinctively otherworldly idea. However, quarrels of historical interpretation, though relevant, are not the issue. Many religions have diverse and far-reaching claims made in their name without these claims being accepted at face value in the popular ideological market. What is noteworthy and exceptional in this particular case is that the Christian world, Protestant as well as Catholic, should be so willing at the present time to accept such claims, made in behalf of an alien religion, in all their literalness. It was not always so. A medieval or Renaissance theologian would have found Maritain's dialectics incomprehensible if not heretical.

But why argue? Is not this vision of Israel as the "communion of mundane hope" a rather flattering one? Perhaps. But, running so close to the ancient stigma, the non-natural historical task of the Jews as a mystic unity, it is a dangerous sort of flattery. If the Jew is of the "communion of mundane hope," he becomes at the same time the object of all wrathful hopelessness. Again we are presented only with the nicer side of the coin. Flip it over, and there is to be read the raucous accusation of "Jew-Bolshevism."

Divine mission or secular mission—the missionary runs his risks. If the Jew is the "stimulating" and "exasperating" agent of progress, he must bear the brunt of the failures of progress, and failures there are sure to be. With each collapse of government and economic order, men will run in anger and disillusion from their attempts at betterment. Where is an easier object for this anger than the mythical Jew who started the whole affair? "This Jew, this instigating devil who with his persuasiveness tempts men to improve themselves—away with him and back to the good old days [smartly gilded in imagination]. After all, what was good enough for our fathers, etc., etc." The fault does not lie in the lack of foresight, the lack of intelligence, the individual's greed. No, it is transferred to the Jew with his absurd, intolerable, misleading optimism. It is the Jew who is blamed for having led mankind out of the Garden of Eden of the past. He is the Great Deceiver.

This does not mean that the Jew should "play it safe" and abstain from all social movements. Not at all. He has the right and the duty to participate, just as does every citizen, every human being. But when well-meaning lyricists, Christian or Jewish, hold out to him the treasure of his "divine, suffering mission," he should return the gift with as much haste as is consistent with good manners. Unfortunately, there is never an element of choice. The stigma is gratuitously pinned onto the Jew without any previous inquiries as to his wishes.

THE TRIPLE ANXIETY

The Jew, because of his theological stigma, bears the anxieties generated by the Christian religion. Because of the stigma in its secularized form, he bears most acutely the anxieties, the contingencies, of his epoch. Thus the anxieties of both Christian man and secular man descend upon him. It is not surprising, then, that the anxieties of man himself, as a conditioned, limited, imperfect being, should also seek him out. By a supreme analogy, the Jew's fate is man's fate, and is seen as such in the world's eye. The Jew is the eternal embodiment and symbol of man as victim, man suffering, man beaten down by nature and the world. And it is inevitable for a man to hate his own suffering and his fate when he sees it mirrored in the suffering and the fate of another.

Rilke saw this point: "The mobility and nomadism of man's inner center, its independence . . . *this spiritual vagrancy* came into the world through the fortunes of the Jews." This vagrancy promotes the despair of man who sees his life as a journey toward death and who sees in his death a lifetime's work. His self-hatred becomes Jew-hatred. The Jew is made over into the looking-glass of humanity. Men warp the glass in every possible way so that their image shall come out over-large and handsome. But it is a perverse glass, perverse as fate itself, and occasionally men see themselves diminish furiously, threaten to disappear. Then they smash the glass.

THE FINAL SHAME?

There is a tendency among some Jewish thinkers to accept the stigma and glorify it. That is understandable; one does the best with what one has. It is not a solution that will commend itself to those who are not possessed of a martyr complex, and besides, it means grafting an essentially foreign ideology onto the body of Jewish religious thought.

It is time, I think, that a distinction is drawn between that concept of the "chosen people" which plays a unique role in Jewish theology, as an affirmation of the loving contract between God and man, and the more modern interpretations that are based, in one form or another, directly or by reaction, upon the stigma of the supra-natural Jew. Judaism is neither a divinely intoxicated form of liberalism nor an intellectual's masochistic apologia for the historical sufferings and present alienation of the Jews. It is a religion—and a religion of quite ordinary men.

Now, after the efficient massacre of European Jewry, the stigma becomes more and more intolerable. One reason why so many Jews feel a secret pride in the terroristic acts in Palestine (the practical merits and demerits of these acts are something else again) is because they constitute a debasement, a debasement to the human. Is not that, in a way, the final shame?

D. H. Lawrence, a strong anti-Semite in his own right, wrote: "And it will be left for the Jews to utter the final and great death-cry of this epoch: the Christians are not reduced sufficiently." So they will, if the stigma, in all its variants, is not obliterated. Or is it already too late, and did the cry pass unheard in the general commotion?

1947

How Basic Is "Basic Judaism"?

A Comfortable Religion for
an Uncomfortable World

Rabbi Milton Steinberg's little book, *Basic Judaism*, is in good part addressed to me, as one of those who "are groping to establish rapport with the Jewish tradition, standing at the synagogue's door 'heart in, head out.'" It is a provocative book, as would be expected from a man who is so able an exponent of the Re-constructionist version of Conservative Judaism, and who writes with such learning and grace. But it provoked in me, along with an appreciation of its virtues, a considerable unease at its often hollow ring. Rabbi Steinberg will hardly regard my positive and negative reactions as presumptuous. After all, the purpose of his book was to set unsynagogued Jews like myself to thinking about the Jewish religion and their relationship to it.

In writing this book, Rabbi Steinberg has tried to be fair and objective in reporting the various differences, creedal and ritual, within the body of Israel. This is what the Orthodox think, this is what the Reformed think, and here is the golden mean of the Conservatives; so runs the argument in many of the chapters. But beneath all these differences, Rabbi Steinberg insists, there is an unbreakable thread of unity, of agreement, that he calls "basic Judaism."

One must confess to some misgivings about the whole concept of a basic Judaism, or of a basic religion of any kind, for that matter. To be sure, Judaism has always been concerned to protect its unity against the conflict of contradictory interpretations; in this, the sense of the precarious position of the community in the Diaspora played its role. The Talmud itself endeavored to ward off the possibility of schism. Is it not written: "Whatsoever any earnest scholar will innovate in the future, lo this was already spoken at Sinai"? The unity in Judaism that Rabbi Steinberg proclaims is a unity of historical fact.

A unity of historical accident, one is tempted to say. For it is not a unity that has anything to do with philosophy, world outlook, or immediate inner experience. There is, of course, a common original text, the Torah, and to a certain extent a common fund of images and memories. But these, while necessary conditions, do not in themselves make up a religion; a core of intellectual conviction is equally necessary.

Actually, all the events that shattered Christendom into the conflicting denominations we know today have had their parallel in Jewish history. The difference is that the oppressive weight of world hostility has restrained the centrifugal impulse created by these events. We may consider this a blessing if we wish. But we must be wary that the search for "basic Judaism" is not merely an escape from intellectual responsibility, from responsibility to one's beliefs. It is a fact, however depressing, that there is today no defining *Weltanschauung* in being a Jew, just as there is none in being a Christian, just as there is none in being a man. And if we tolerate such concepts as basic Judaism, basic Christianity, basic Buddhism, and so on, why should we not settle for basic religion, in which everything is so watered down and vague that no one's religious sentiments are excluded from participation? No such settlement is possible because it would simply reflect the atrophy of the religious sentiment itself.

If we are to have a *Weltanschauung*, it has to be constructed—by each man, by each group of thinkers, by each generation. It is a question of picking and choosing from what tradition and the present have to offer, of acceptance, rejection (no matter how discreet), and reconstruction. The Orthodox might retort that it is indecent to weigh religions in the open, so to speak. There is something unpleasant in this public pinching, scrutinizing, and fingering of beliefs for which one's ancestors, and even one's family, perhaps, have suffered and died. (This sense of propriety must explain, at least in part, the traditional reluctance of Judaism to engage in overt theological controversy.) The only defense for doing so, true if inadequate, is that the ruling self-consciousness of our times spares nothing its dry uncomfortable glare, not even a Judaism bereft of the protective shell of the ghetto.

Contemporary Jewish theology is, in its various branches (including the Orthodox), a more or less self-conscious construction of Judaism, a careful mixture of past and present in the hope that the mixture will turn out to be a true solution. This is especially the case with Rabbi Steinberg's Conservative Judaism; its careful middle-of-the-road tone should not be allowed to obscure its essentially creative purpose. His point of view is an important one by virtue of its great influence on the American Jewish community; it is also important because it is shared to a surprisingly large extent by thinkers whom we would not ordinarily assign to the same category as Rabbi Steinberg. There is a world of difference between the great mystic-philosopher Martin Buber and the urbane rationalist Milton Steinberg; yet it is surprising how much they do have in common when one gets down to points of doctrine.

My primary concern, genuine if possibly selfish, is: what does this kind of contemporary Jewish theology have to offer to people like me? I believe that it does have valuable positive insights to offer, and that they do establish a claim of Judaism upon me; I also feel that what it has to offer is not quite enough. First, I would like to indicate, in a necessarily sketchy manner, what I consider these positive insights to be.

The creedal basis of Judaism is not overt, but implicit. Since Jews have always belonged to Judaism by belonging to a historical people and culture, there was never a pressing need to set forth the faith in logically pure propositions. There are dogmas, but they are not integrated into a hierarchic, syllogistic structure. Judaism is less a religious system than a system of living religiously. As Martin Buber has written: "In the religious life of Judaism primary importance is not given to dogma, but to the remembrance and expectation of a concrete situation: the meeting of God with men. Dogma can only arise where detachment is the prevailing attitude to the concrete, lived moment." In other words, to use a currently popular term, Judaism is an existential religion. What this means is that Judaism thinks in the categories of life; it does not try to adapt life to the categories of thought. The law and the Prophets taught the truths of life and not the truths of philosophy; the "religious life" includes all of life, in its full particularity. If we think of religion as an eternally continuing dialogue between man and God (and this is already a Jewish conception), then the language of this dialogue is life—not prayer, meditation, contemplation, ecstasy, good deeds, or anything else, but all of life.

All well and good—but how about God? How does Judaism justify its belief in God's existence? There are innumerable procedures of justification, and Jews at one time or another have tried them all: reason and revelation, first cause and final purpose, and so on. But what is striking about these endeavors is the ironic ease with which one can supplant the other as soon as strategy indicates the need for such a move. Judaism believes in God because—well, to begin with, because Judaism has a covenant with God. Does one sign a contract with a non-entity? And if stupid lawyers, mainly *apikorsim* [heretics, unbelievers], cannot read the handwriting, what does that prove? Judaism has always respected the intellect, up to a point. There is a saying: where there are two Jews there are three opinions. The "proofs" of God by metaphysics, natural reason, science, sophistry, etc., all in the long run cancel each other out, and we are left with a deity whose existence is essentially noncontroversial. It all comes down to the fact that Judaism has faith in God, and it accepts a belief in God for the good and sufficient reason that it believes He exists. Is this arguing in a circle? Well, then, it is arguing in a circle. But it is a circle of words, and outside this circle lies life, and man—and God.

There is hardly any such thing as Jewish "apologetics"; the medieval texts of the "golden age" which can claim that title are outside the subsequent channels of study and concern. Apologetics is the science of defending a belief from attack. For the quarrel to be meaningful, both attacker and attacked must have the same criteria of evidence and proof. Christianity, exposed to the influence of Aristotelian philosophy and modern science, was forced to some degree to accept the criteria of practical and theoretical reason. Postmedieval Judaism, in its insularity of the ghetto, was oblivious to both the criteria and the quarrel, and by the time the ghetto was disrupted, theology was already out of season. This may be more historical fortune than essential virtue, but in any case, there it is. Judaism has always insisted upon the salvation of the world rather than the knowledge of things. All modern science and philosophy, having separated man from the world for purposes of pure knowing, is now desperately trying to put them back together again. (All, that is, except the logical positivists with their mincing distaste for "unanswerable questions," who incline to see the life of man as a kind of grammatical misadventure.) Judaism has never left the whole of man's existence to pursue other hares. Man finds religion in his life, he "proves" it with his life; life is a dialogue with God. That is what Pascal must have meant when he wrote on a slip of paper that he always carried near his heart: "The God of Abraham, the God of Isaac, the God of Jacob—not the God of the philosophers."

The modern world has suffered much damage by permitting the scientists to appropriate the vocabulary of meaningful and authoritative discourse as their own and only their own. To "analyze," in the scientific sense of the word, is to express a thing as a function of something else. And if a thing cannot be expressed as a function of something else, it simply doesn't "exist" so far as the scientist is concerned. "Love," as we use the word, has no place in the scientific vocabulary (not even, I would insist, in the vocabulary of psychoanalysis). Nor does "God." Why that should give everyone—except the scientists!—an inferiority complex with regard to their beliefs in Love and God is one of the wonders of our times. Similarly, science has preempted the word "truth" to refer to a valid proposition issuing from a previous series of propositions, some of which may refer to experimental procedures. Perhaps we had better choose another word, like "authentic," for those statements of religion, poetry, and sheer human wisdom that were formerly thought to be "true." But then some hardheaded gentleman will quickly rise to point out that these statements are not true.

George Foote Moore, the distinguished historian of Judaism, has written: "Jewish monotheism was reached neither by postulating the unity of nature nor by speculation on the unity of Being—the physical or the metaphysical approach of science and philosophy—but by way of the unity of the moral order in the history of the world." The world is no play of phenomena and noumena, matter and spirit; it is the daily life ready to be made sacrament, prepared for an act of redemption. According to certain rabbinic teachings, the act of Creation was inspired by the souls of the unborn pious, and the world owes its continued existence to these pious men (*zaddikim*). Abraham was assured by God that at any one time there could be found thirty men his equal in saintliness; without them the world could not endure.

That evil exists is undeniable; that it is often triumphant is equally evident. Yet, as is seen in the Book of Job, the tragic solution is unacceptable in Judaism. Though evil be inexplicable and ineradicable, the end of human activity is positive and constructive. Judaism forbids man to doubt this; in his deepest extremity, the most that a man is permitted to do is to repeat after Job: "I will lay mine hand upon my mouth." In the *Kaddish* prayer, offered up for the souls of the dead, God is praised and death is not so much as mentioned. "And God saw everything that He had made, and behold, it was very good" (Genesis). This goodness was never vitiated by man's ejection from paradise. Adam fell and men learned to know good and evil, but the world did not fall with him.

Whereas for Kierkegaard the love of God was incommensurable with all of reality, for Judaism there is an unbreakable bond between the love of God and the love of all reality. There are few echoes of Christian-Oriental asceticism to be found in Judaism. For a Jew, virtue is a pleasure; even when it is a sacrifice, a great sacrifice, it is a pleasure. There is no place for wanton sensuality, but neither is the human body considered corrupt or degraded. In the old ghettos on a Friday night the pious Jew would perfume himself and comb his hair before he went to prayer, would fervently chant the Song of Songs at the table, and after the Sabbath supper, the best meal of the week, he generally went to bed with his wife. It was right to do this on the Sabbath, because the union of husband and wife gives us the image of the union of God with the *shekhina* [manifestation of God]. It was also allowed to break the holiness of the Sabbath for the purpose of making marriage arrangements. Thus did Judaism attempt to achieve the old prayer that runs: "O Lord, let me worship thee not only with my good inclination, but also with my evil inclination." By hallowing the earthly, potential evil was transmuted into actual good.

How far is this from the Catholic mind! "The law of divine love knows no mercy. Love truly sacrifices: it desires the death of everything not itself" (Mélanie de la Salette). This contrast between Jewish and Christian attitudes toward the material world comes out strikingly in their different estimations of poverty. Léon Bloy was a Catholic who always stretched Catholic doctrine to its furthermost limit. When a coin is given to a beggar with bad grace, he wrote, the coin "pierces the poor man's hand, falls, pierces the earth, makes holes in the sun, flies over the firmament and compromises the universe." All this happens because poverty is a form of holiness, and must be honored as such. It is a highly poetic view, a transvaluation of values, if only on a verbal level as far as most of Bloy's fellow Catholics are concerned.

Among the Jews it is otherwise. Poverty is a gift of God, a product of His boundless mercy along with all other human states. But it has no preferential value; the good things of life are too well appreciated. On the contrary, poverty is thoroughly undesirable, like an early death, whether issuing from God's mercy or not. Tevye, the pauper in Sholem Aleichem's stories, puts this succinctly: "With God's help I starved to death—I and my wife and children—three times a day, not counting supper." God's blessings must be accepted, but there is no law against an ironic comment on His dispensation. To be poor among the Jews . . . is to be poor. That and nothing else. If you don't know what that means, Sholem Aleichem will explain it to you: "Among us Jews, poverty has many faces and many aspects. A poor man is an unlucky man, he is a pauper, a beggar, a *schnorrer*, a starveling, a tramp, or a plain failure." He goes on to say that one can surpass poverty by laughing at it, by refusing to be degraded, but that is a matter of human dignity, not supernatural grace.

Since Judaism posits "the moral order in the history of the world," it is impossible to separate doctrine from ethic or either from the people that created them. For Judaism, the relationship between the real and the ideal is active, not cognitive. When Hillel was asked to summarize the Torah in one commandment, he replied: "That which is hurtful to thee do not to thy neighbor. This is the whole doctrine. The rest is commentary. Now go forth and learn." Whereas the Greeks subsumed ethics under the intellect (philosophy), Jewish ethics are subsumed under the working of the will (law). The

Fall was the primal failure of will, but man's spiritual and moral nature was unaffected, and his moral responsibility in no way relieved. The freedom of man's will has never been seriously challenged within Jewish thought. On the contrary: not only is man's responsibility for himself assumed, but also his responsibility for his fellow men, and for God himself.

There is no vicarious salvation in Judaism; each man must save his own soul. At the same time, Judaism is directed toward the salvation of the community, for which individual salvation paves the way; on the Day of Atonement, Jews pray for the remission of communal sins as well as private ones. "Separate not thyself from the community," Hillel said, and indeed Jewish eulogies of the joys and virtues of communal life so resemble those of John Dewey that it will sometimes happen to me in reading one or the other that the images of the New England small village and the East European ghetto will merge into an incongruous coincidence.

Nor is Judaism ethnocentric. "The righteous of all people have their share in the world to come" is quite another matter than "outside the church there is no salvation." A non-Jew has only the seven commandments of the sons of Noah to perform in order to be eligible for the best the next world has to offer. The Jews, on the other hand, as the "chosen people," have a greater burden of duties and obligations. The Rabbi of Kosnitz, it is reported, used to pray: "And if you will not yet redeem Israel, then redeem at any rate the *goyim*." There is in this plea a commingled despair and appreciation of the advantages likely to accrue to the Jews if the *goyim* were redeemed. But there is also a pure breath of genuine universalism.

Man is responsible for his own fate, for his community's fate—and for God's fate. The world was created for the sake of those who can exercise the power to choose God; if God is not chosen, His purpose is wrecked. Each instant is filled with all time insofar as the moral act, the act of redemption, is concerned. This is the significance of the messianic task. Not a blinding angel on a fiery steed come to supersede the world; the world is not to be superseded at all, but to be redeemed, that is, consummated. It is the *zaddik*, living his moral life in seclusion, unidentifiable, who carries on and defends the messianic purpose. "Not thine to finish the task, but neither art thou free to exempt thyself from it." It is from this conception of man's divine responsibility that springs the stubborn hope, the blind optimism, that has been so frequently observed (and misinterpreted) in Judaism. In the daily prayer, it states: "Happy are we; how goodly is our portion and how fair is our lot." But to my mind, the classic example of Jewish transcendent hope lies in the Hasidic tale that begins: "It is told: dangerous plots against the Jews were brewing in the emperor's palace. Then Rabbi Shmelke and his disciple Moshe Leib of Sasov set out for Vienna to put an end to such plans. . . ."

These are, in brief and in part, the insights, indigenous to Judaism, that I find so valuable. Valuable, yet insufficient. There is something lacking in this kind of Judaism, a note that is absent, a key that is never struck, that subverts one's appreciation of the total effect. It is not an easy thing to designate, this element that is wanting. Perhaps the best way to approach it is to make the statement: as far as most non-Jewish intellectuals are concerned, and for many Jewish intellectuals too, the greatest and most influential Jewish thinker of the twentieth century is Franz Kafka. And Kafka was a great and influential thinker and writer insofar as he was a Jewish heretic; a heretic to whom Judaism offered itself in its full magnificence, but who could not choose to accept it. "What have I in common with Jews?" he asked. "I have almost nothing in common with myself." To the extent that Judaism refuses to explore the basis of this rejection, it delivers itself up to irrelevancy—or worse.

In effect, Rabbi Steinberg's "basic Judaism," and not his alone, seems to be directed toward a happier era than our own, to a better humanity than we know. His is a religion of the good deed and the good community, in a time when the quality of the good deed is anything but self-evident, and the good community is only a dream of something that might have existed. It strikes me—and I say this with no disingenuousness—as considerably too good for us. And in the absence of a corresponding genuine goodness without, it fixes itself upon the imitation directly at hand, so that the noble intention is used to the advantage of the ignoble fact. Consequently, it is not astonishing that there runs through Rabbi Steinberg's book a colored thread of superficiality, even vulgarity, that entwines itself into the very warp and woof of his theology.

What happens is that Rabbi Steinberg accommodates his religious views with facility to the outlook of an American "Main Street" in its New Deal variant. What is worse, this accommodation represents not merely Rabbi Steinberg's state of mind, but also the state of mind of a large section of the American rabbinate, and much of the American Jewish community in general. It results in the perversion of the Jewish religion into a doctrine of social (and sociable) principles, the transformation of messianism into a shallow, if sincere, humanitarianism, plus a thoroughgoing insensitivity to present-day spiritual problems. Rabbi Steinberg's Judaism is reduced to an earnestly moral sociopolitical liberalism, with divine sanction to boot. What are we to make of a rabbi who claims for the Mishnah and the Talmud that they guarantee the right to strike—thereby providing Holy Writ with the satisfaction of having paved the way for the National Labor Relations Act! Obviously, Rabbi Steinberg is entitled to his political opinions. He is even privileged, if he so desires, to seek divine sanction for them, though this strikes me as a daring and somewhat purposeless venture. But, in fact, what he is doing is to justify and ennoble his religious beliefs by parading what he deems to be their enlightened sociopolitical implications.

It is social philosophy that is his talking point, and not religion. Judaism, Rabbi Steinberg finds, has an immanent political doctrine that adds up to "political democracy, to a modification of capitalism in the direction of democracy, and a world state." How convenient. . . . But what is this but an oblique way of saying that one of the merits of Judaism is that it permits its believers to read *The New Republic* with untroubled soul? And what kind of belief in messianism is it that finds itself represented in such diverse figures as Saint Augustine, Tennyson, and Hegel? And what a grotesque selection! Rabbi Steinberg's Judaism is obviously native American. That is to say, in its heart it has no faith in the effectuality of religion on the American scene, and hastens to adopt a vocabulary with a higher popularity rating at the first opportunity. Genial and well-wishing, appropriate company for a businessman's luncheon. When he says, "All good men are Messiahs," it rings with all the fervor and conviction of "Any boy can grow up to be president."

The spiritual distress of the modern world does not arise merely because man perversely chooses to do evil rather than good. If it were as uncomplicated as all that, present-day Judaism, even Rabbi Steinberg's Judaism, would have the answer right at hand. The horror that breathes into our faces is the realization that evil may come by doing good—not merely *intending* to do good, but *doing* it. That is the trap of social action that the movements of progress and enlightenment of the nineteenth and twentieth centuries fell into; and we, whether "best minds" or ordinary citizens, haven't the faintest inkling how to get out. Universal literacy has led to popular demagogy and mass mania; modern medicine finds unparalleled opportunities unleashed by the atomic bomb; the shortening of the working day goes hand in hand with the breakup of the family and the derangement of the sexual sentiment.

A century of incessant effort to the building of a humane life-on-earth has led with fantastic ease to a victorious life-in-death. To say, with someone like Sidney Hook, that the disaster is a result of our having failed to carry out the full implications of these high ideals, or our having misconstrued them, is in itself an unfounded assertion, not subject to test by experience. Moreover, it is the kind of assertion that our situation does not encourage; indeed, the situation makes it appear superbly beside the point.

There is a difference between the doctrine of original sin, which is open to many objections and which can have no place in Judaism, and the *fact* of sin. Judaism, today, and especially liberal Judaism, despite the horrors of modern totalitarianism, seems unable to recognize sin when it sees it. It does see the evil of individual wickedly minded men (or nations), but it refuses to assign to evil its full and menacing stature. It has preferred to dress itself up in the clothes of nineteenth-century liberalism in order to attend a twentieth-century execution. The transcendental hope of Judaism has settled into uncomprehending, complacent euphoria.

Consequently, Judaism looks blankly at the current trends toward a "theology of crisis." Sometimes it allies itself with the "naturalists" and "progressives" and talks of a "failure of nerve," thereby missing the point. For the trend in religious thinking (except in Judaism) is away from certitude, harmony, and peace. These are left to the self-styled "humanists." Or else it nods approvingly at the fact that God is a word once again in currency, without looking into the "how" and "wherefore." The "theology of crisis" represents a genuine discovery, though by no means a novel one. The gulf between man and righteousness has widened with frightening rapidity. And against the soothing inanities, generally either social or psychoanalytical, that gush forth from rabbinical pulpits, there is the chord struck by Kafka's sardonic judgment: "Plenty of hope—for God—no end of hope—only not for us."

That Judaism has escaped relatively scot-free from the ideological conflict between science and religion of the last few centuries is, as I have pointed out, a valuable asset. Yet it has had its drawbacks too. The poignant sorrow over "the death of God," the striving for faith in a faithless world, has been relatively unknown to it. At a time when Judaism is in need of a worldview, its perspective is still catastrophically narrow. Intellectual timidity, cultural immaturity, a reluctance to venture to extremes even when the extreme has become banal and quotidian—these are the outstanding features of contemporary Jewish thought.

We are beginning to wonder, and discuss, the question "why Jews are in the world," even if, to date, we have ended with hoary platitudes. We have scarcely dared to ask "why *goyim* in the world?"—an important question, it must be conceded. Perhaps we are afraid that we will not be able to stop there, but will go on to the semi-blasphemous question "why men in the world?" Yet, if theology today is to ask any question, the last one is the most pertinent, whether it be asked by Jew, Protestant, Catholic, or atheist. A Jewish analysis of "the human condition" usually (with too rare exception) turns up as an analysis of the "condition of the Jews." Judaism, at the present moment, seems shy of asking the important questions for fear its answers might be inadequate.

Judaism is trying to approximate to a genuine theology through a heightening of the social conscience because its intellectual base is constantly narrowing. The prophetic vein has been abandoned (to be grabbed up by Protestant neo-Orthodoxy). The Law has buried itself in a dugout at the threat of the modern secular, and insane, world. What we have left are political lectures, fund-raising, Zionism, interfaith activities, public relations, social work, and so on. It may be that I have no right to ask Judaism to take all this into account. The fault might as easily be mine for feeling these problems, as it is Judaism's for not managing them competently. Or perhaps, whether one speaks blandly or tragically when walking off the cliff edge that is the twentieth century, it is a matter only of personal vanity. But that is in itself a theological speculation.

1948

The Political Dilemma
of American Jews

Jews have a long history, and with that long history goes a long memory. So it is entirely to be expected that the political loyalties and habits of mind of a Jewish community should change very slowly, so slowly, sometimes, that an odd divergence can occur between Jewish thinking and the developing social, political, and economic realities. It is not so much that Jews do not see what is going on; they just do not believe it when they do see it. In politics, seeing is not always believing. Memories, and the cast of mind into which those memories become encrusted—one can fairly call it an ideological cast of mind—often enough will not only obscure the reality but will actually prevail over it for a surprisingly long time.

Something of this sort, it seems to me, is happening in the American Jewish community today. Over the past two decades, the political landscape with which American Jews are familiar, and in which they are accustomed to take their bearings, has been shifting in all sorts of unexpected ways. A sense of disorientation has slowly been pervading the political consciousness of American Jews, causing uneasiness and discomfort. Inevitably and understandably, the initial reaction, and still the dominant reaction, is that such changes are superficial and transient, and that the old, familiar markers will enable one to make one's way. But beneath this reaction is the growing apprehension that perhaps this is not so, that perhaps the political geography of the United States has undergone a more basic realignment of its features, and that it is time for a reorientation.

Erik Erikson, in his biography of Luther, defines three critical stages in the life cycle of an individual. The first is a crisis in identity, the second a crisis of conscience (involving one's responsibility to others), and the third a crisis of integrity (a coming to terms with historical actuality). The American Jewish community is in the process of experiencing all these life-cycle crises simultaneously. No wonder there is so much bewilderment and anxiety.

Let us look at three changes in the American political landscape that were not anticipated, and that are now contributing to these crises. The most striking change has been the emergence of Jesse Jackson as *the* political leader of American blacks. Jackson stands for black nationalism—what the media mindlessly persist in calling "black pride"—with a dash of anti-Semitism added for good measure. He is not a "civil rights" leader of the familiar kind only somewhat more militant. He has radically redefined the role of black political leadership in this country. Even if he should pass from the scene, for one reason or another, there will be no reversion to the *status quo ante*. He has, with extraordinary entrepreneurial skill, shown the way, and there will be plenty of others eager to follow.

This was not supposed to happen. American Jews had anticipated a quite different scenario to emerge from the civil rights movement, in which they were so deeply involved. That involvement was natural because Jews, as a religious and ethnic minority, have for centuries experienced a deprivation of civil rights and are therefore keenly aware of how important it is that equality in civil rights be enjoyed by all minorities—religious, ethnic, or racial. This explains why, for most of the history of the NAACP and the Urban League, Jewish money played such a large role in keeping those institutions afloat. It also explains why so many individual Jews participated so energetically, over these past twenty years, in the civil rights movement itself. That movement was victorious. What are now called civil rights issues are marginal legal quarrels, and more often than not involve women rather than blacks. So far as civil rights, traditionally understood, are concerned, there now exists a comprehensive body of law, emerging from either Congress or the courts, which defines and protects the rights of blacks. The very fact that such cities as Chicago, Philadelphia, Los Angeles, Atlanta, and Birmingham—Birmingham!—now have black mayors pretty much tells the story.

Nor is it surprising that these black mayors were elected with Jewish support, which in some cases was decisive. For until yesterday, relations between the Jewish community and the official black leadership continued to be most amiable. In Congress, black Congressmen usually voted "correctly," from the Jewish point of view, on Israel, while Jewish Congressmen usually voted "correctly" on domestic legislation that the black leadership endorsed. The black-Jewish political coalition outlasted the civil rights movement itself, and there seemed no reason why it should not endure. The strength of the attachment of

Jews—or perhaps one should say of the major Jewish organizations and their leaders—to this coalition is best revealed by the debate over affirmative action. Affirmative action has come to be judicially and bureaucratically defined in terms of racial and ethnic quotas in hiring and firing, what has been called "positive discrimination." This is utterly repugnant, in principle, to Jews. Indeed, Jews had always felt so keenly about this sort of thing that they had fought long and hard, and in the end successfully, to prevent the introduction of religious identification in the census. To this day, all major Jewish organizations are on record as supporting "affirmative action" in the original sense of encouraging the advancement of minorities, but remain opposed to quotas. Nevertheless, once the definition of affirmative action as implying quotas became an issue of considerable importance to the black leadership, the major Jewish organizations split on whether to oppose it outright in the courts, so powerful was the desire of Jewish leaders to continue cooperating with their black counterparts.

So what went wrong? Where did Jesse Jackson come from, and why? Well, coincident with the civil rights movement, another social-political phenomenon occurred that was of great significance to the black community. This was the construction, by Congress, of an extensive (and expensive) range of social programs, under the rubric of the "Great Society." These programs were intended to repair the social and economic condition of American blacks, even while their political condition was being elevated to the plane of equality by the civil rights movement. And even as the civil rights movement succeeded, the Great Society programs failed, at least as far as most blacks were concerned. Out of this failure, Jesse Jackson emerged.

It is not to be thought that the Great Society programs were simply a waste of money. Some were, some were not. But where benefits did occur, it was largely the middle class that enjoyed them. Much of the population of the black ghettos was in no condition to exploit those benefits. It is nice to provide free lunches for poor schoolchildren, and it is unquestionably nice for the nutritionists, the food service industry, and the farmers. But what availeth that free lunch to a black mother if her son, at the same time, gets hooked on drugs or is involved in criminal activities, while her teenage daughter becomes pregnant? The sad truth is that the social disorganization and individual demoralization within the black ghettos have overwhelmed whatever positive effects those social programs were expected to have, or even might have had.

And there is good reason to think that the Great Society programs themselves had something to do with this social disorganization and individual demoralization. It may not be literally true that dependency (like power) tends to corrupt and that absolute dependency (like absolute power) tends to corrupt absolutely. But there is truth enough in that proposition to give pause. After all, how else explain the fact that the increasing breakdown of the black ghetto family and the proliferation of all sorts of social and individual pathologies parallel so neatly, in time and place, the institution of all those social programs? The people who devised, legislated, and applied these programs surely expected no such consequences and are now at a loss for an explanation. It is reasonable, however, to take seriously the possibility that the two phenomena have a causal connection.

In any case, it is out of the frustration of the black ghetto—frustration arising from the fact that neither the winning of political civil rights nor the enactment of those Great Society programs transformed or even ameliorated the condition of the black ghettos—that Jesse Jackson has built his mass appeal. It is worth recalling that, before becoming a candidate, he spoke with refreshing candor of the need for blacks to help themselves rather than relying on white handouts that left them mired in poverty and misery. This was not a theme that the established black leadership had the courage to enunciate. But apparently there was greater political potential in black nationalism than in black self-help, and Jackson himself has by now substituted the former for the latter. The frustration of ghetto blacks, moreover, is as sharply felt by that portion of the black population, about half, whose condition has dramatically improved over the past decades. Racial solidarity is as natural a feeling as religious or ethnic, so it is not surprising that many middle-class blacks, especially the young and upwardly mobile, are sympathetic to Jesse Jackson. Nor is it surprising that the older, established black leadership has been so utterly disarmed before his campaign. They, after all, had bet all their chips on the civil rights struggle and the Great Society programs. Confronted with the enduring, brutal realities of ghetto life today, they are mute and impotent. The upshot is that the long alliance between Jewish and black organizations is coming apart. Jesse Jackson has substituted Arab money for Jewish money. In foreign policy he is pro–Third World and anti-American, pro-PLO and anti-Israel; and he is on the way to making this the quasi-official foreign policy of the black community. In domestic policy he is vaguely, but unambiguously, well to the left of anything that one could call "liberal." And his role in future elections, which is bound to be significant, will only make things worse. He has already indicated that he will be coming to New York in 1985 to back and stump for a properly militant black candidate against Mayor Koch in the Democratic primaries. The black-Jewish polarization that would ensue is almost too scary to contemplate.

The rise of the Moral Majority is another new feature of the American landscape that baffles Jews. They did not expect it, do not understand it, and do not know what to do about it. One of the reasons—perhaps the main reason—they do not know what to do about it is the fact that the Moral Majority is strongly pro-Israel. To say this was unexpected is a wild understatement. If one had informed American Jews fifteen years ago that there was to be a powerful revival of Protestant fundamentalism, and as a political as well as religious force, they would surely have been alarmed, since they would have assumed that any such revival might tend to be anti-Semitic and anti-Israel. But the Moral Majority is neither.

To be sure, occasionally a fundamentalist preacher will say something to the effect that God cannot be expected to heed the prayers of non-Protestant fundamentalists. At which point many Jewish organizations react in a predictable way: they sound the alarm against an incipient anti-Semitism. But the alarm rings hollow. After all, why should Jews care about the theology of a fundamentalist preacher when they do not for a moment believe that he speaks with any authority on the question of God's attentiveness to human prayer? And what do such theological abstractions matter as against the mundane fact that this same preacher is vigorously pro-Israel?

Some Jews, enmeshed in the liberal time warp, refuse to take this mundane fact seriously. They are wrong. Just how wrong they are can be seen by asking the question: how significant would it be for American Jews if the Moral Majority were *anti*-Israel? The answer is easy and inescapable: it would be of major significance. Indeed, it would generally be regarded by Jews as a very alarming matter. So it is ironic, and puzzling, that American Jews appear to be not all that interested in, and certainly not enthusiastic about, the fact that the Moral Majority is unequivocally pro-Israel.

One reason for the peculiar Jewish reaction here is that this phenomenon does not fall into the spectrum of the familiar and expected. But there are other reasons too, of considerable significance in their own way. For the Moral Majority is simultaneously committed to a set of "social issues"—school prayer, anti-abortion, the relation of church and state in general—that tend to evoke a hostile reaction among most (though not all) American Jews. How does one go about balancing the pros and cons of this matter? And to what degree is this hostile reaction itself worthy of some second thoughts? That balancing should not, in truth, require much intellectual effort. From a purely expediential point of view, it is obvious that the campaign of the Moral Majority around these "social issues" is meeting with practically no success, and so there is little reason for Jewish alarm. Neither Congress nor (more important) the judiciary is at all forthcoming, and the Reagan administration has got absolutely nowhere in its espousal of these issues. In contrast, anti-Israel sentiment has been distinctly on the rise, and the support of the Moral Majority could, in the near future, turn out to be decisive for the very existence of the Jewish state. This is the way the Israeli government has struck its own balance vis-à-vis the Moral Majority, and it is hard to see why American Jews should come up with a different bottom line. But the expediential point of view is not enough if the Moral Majority's support of Israel is not to wither and die on the vine. That will happen if it continues to evoke so muffled and embarrassed a response from the American Jewish community. American Jews really do need to revise their thinking about some, at least, of these controversial social issues, even from the point of view of expediency. Moreover, it is becoming ever more clear that it is time they did so in any case, Moral Majority or no Moral Majority.

Ever since the Holocaust and the emergence of the state of Israel, American Jews have been reaching toward a more explicit and meaningful Jewish identity and have been moving away from the universalist secular humanism that was so prominent a feature of their prewar thinking. But while American Jews want to become more Jewish, they do not want American Christians to become more Christian. This is an untenable point of view. First, because of the hypocrisy involved. Why should there be a Hanukkah candelabrum at Central Park, as there is, but no Christmas crèche? Second, because the quest for a religious identity is not confined to Jews. It is, in the postwar world, a general phenomenon experienced by Jews, Christians, and Muslims alike. It does not seem, moreover, to be a passing phenomenon but rather derives from an authentic crisis, a moral and spiritual crisis as well as a crisis in Western liberal-secular thought. Is there any point in Jews hanging on, dogmatically and hypocritically, to their opinions of yesteryear when it is a new era we are confronting? Is it not time for Jews to sit back, curb their habitual reflexes about the "proper" relations of state and religion in the United States, and think seriously about how they can most comfortably exist (and survive) in a world in which religious identity will become increasingly important? In short, is it not time for an agonizing reappraisal?

The relation of American Jews to American foreign policy is, every day, becoming more and more bizarre, more and more tormented by self-contradiction. It is a situation that cannot last. Sooner or later, American Jews are going to have to make very hard choices—hard, because they will go against a deeply imprinted grain.

To select one issue that is profoundly symptomatic because it touches on such a sensitive ideological nerve: the United Nations and the attitude of our major Jewish organizations to it. We all know—one would have to be deaf and dumb not to know—that the UN is, above all, an organization bent on delegitimizing, even eventually destroying, the state of Israel. More than half the time, the UN and its associated organizations are busy pursuing this mission. The rest of the time they are preoccupied with serving as a forum for a Third World critique of the United States, and of the West in general, of which Israel is perceived (correctly) to be an integral part. "Zionism is racism" is a doctrine officially proclaimed by the UN, while at no time has the UN shown the slightest interest in protecting the rights of Jews (and other minorities) in the Soviet Union or in Muslim nations. It would seem to follow logically that the American Jewish community should be hostile to the UN, should like to see the United States dissociate itself from it to the greatest possible degree, should even wish to see it vanish from our political horizon. Why not, after all? But logic, apparently, plays very little role in defining Jewish attitudes toward the United Nations. Nostalgia for what it was once hoped the UN would be is stronger than the clear perception of what the UN indubitably is. If ever there was a case of a group of people desperately evading the most obvious of political realities, this is it.

To be sure, Jews (like most other Americans) are full of admiration for Daniel Patrick Moynihan or Jeane Kirkpatrick when they boldly stand up for Israel, and America, at the UN. They are honored with plaques, scrolls, honorary degrees, banquets, etc. But that is as far as it goes. Just let anyone suggest that the Jewish reaction to the UN, as it now exists, should go somewhat further and suddenly all the Jewish organizations have lost their tongue. When efforts are made in Congress to cut the American financial contribution to the UN—we now provide 25 percent of the budget—the American Jewish community remains on the sidelines. When the Reagan administration decided to withdraw from that scandalous entity called UNESCO, the American Jewish community could think of nothing supportive to say, at least openly. Even Ambassador Charles Lichenstein's semi-jocular remark to the effect that, if the UN wished to relocate its headquarters elsewhere, he would be on the dock waving an enthusiastic farewell, was greeted by the Jewish community with a frigid silence. Meanwhile, the United Nations Association, along with other organizations that "educate" people toward a "positive" view of the UN, are financed most generously by Jewish contributors. Here the discrepancy between the reality and Jewish ideological obstinacy is positively stunning. The UN has become a very different organization from what Jews and Jewish organizations, in the immediate postwar years, anticipated and hoped it would be. They certainly never expected that the covenant against "genocide," for which

American Jewry lobbied in the UN so persistently and, finally, successfully, would serve as a basis for attacks against Israel, as it is, repeatedly. The actuality has diverged wildly from the dream. But the dream still exercises its dominion over the Jewish imagination.

The vision of a "community of nations" living peaceably under international law, so eloquently articulated by Immanuel Kant in the eighteenth century, has been an organic part of the ideology of Western liberalism ever since. It has had a special appeal to Jews, both because of its biblical roots and because Jews, as Jews, would obviously be much more secure and comfortable in such a world. No single ethnic or religious group in the United States has produced such a disproportionate number of scholars in the field of international law as have Jews, and no other group has been so reluctant to recognize that this messianic vision, when applied to political actualities, has proved to be political utopianism, wishful thinking.

It is not that international law itself is in essence utopian. The emergence, in the two centuries preceding Kant, of principles of decent international behavior was a genuine contribution toward making international relations less anarchic, less "Machiavellian," less casually brutal than they had been or otherwise would have been. But this pre-Kantian conception of international law was much more modest in its ambitions and more realistic in its assumptions than the notion of international law we are familiar with. It recognized, for instance, that the intervention of nations in the affairs of other nations was both proper and inevitable under certain conditions, and that the violation of national frontiers could not always be classified as immoral "aggression." To the degree that international law has any substantial meaning in the world today, it rests on this pre-Kantian basis rather than on the kind of grandiose principles associated with the League of Nations and the United Nations.

An extraordinary number of Jews, however, remain loyal to those grandiose principles. As a result, their thinking about foreign affairs is incoherent to an equally extraordinary degree. When Israel bombed and destroyed the Iraqi nuclear reactor, most American Jews realized that this was a sensible thing to do and that there was nothing "illegal" or "immoral" about the act, but they could not figure out a way to say this. Approval at the personal level was matched by embarrassed double-talk at the official level as Jewish leaders tried to talk their way out of a rhetorical trap of their own construction. In addition to incoherence, there is positive schizophrenia. All Jews would be pleased if Ronald Reagan were publicly to reproach the Soviet Union on the issue of Jewish emigration, but would be less happy if his reproach were aimed at the suppression of all religious freedoms under that "godless" regime. This, it is felt, might be construed as undue intervention in Soviet Russia's internal affairs, and might "worsen international tensions," "aggravate the Cold War," etc., etc.

One can muddle through with such incoherence and schizophrenia for a while, but sooner or later the world demands that one talk sense. Such a demand is being imposed on American Jews today. The older liberal internationalism, which was the basis of American foreign policy after the end of World War II and the basis of our membership in the United Nations, is rapidly disintegrating. The Third World uses the UN when it can, ignores it when convenient. So do the Soviet Union and the other communist countries. There is no "community of nations," and the grand principles of the UN Charter are cynically abused for the purposes of *realpolitik*. The United States is being forced to choose between being an active, great power in the world as it exists, or gradually retiring into a quasi-isolationism that leaves our moral purity undefiled and the world to its own devices.

The Democratic Party today, and especially its most liberal wing, is clearly moving toward this second alternative. It is a movement made all the easier by the unspoken (because uneasy) liberal assumption that left-wing totalitarian movements, paying lip service to principles that have a superficial affinity with liberal ideas, will evolve into less totalitarian and more liberal regimes. This assumption flies in the face of the fact that the most evident political reality of the twentieth century is the revolt against the liberal economic and political order and the liberal ideal of self-government. That this revolt is sometimes explicitly "reactionary" or sometimes "progressive" in its political metaphysics is of interest to historians of ideas, but has little bearing on the construction of foreign policy. Indeed, what is most striking in recent decades is the convergence between yesteryear's totalitarian governments of the Right and today's totalitarian regimes of the Left. The similarities between Castro's Cuba and Mussolini's Italy are far more striking than their differences.

Isolationism has a strong traditional appeal to the American people, and one can understand why it should reemerge today, or why the prospect of fighting "dirty little wars" in remote places should be so repugnant. What is difficult to understand is why American Jews seem to be among those who are not shocked and appalled by this new trend. Can anyone believe that an American government which, in righteous moralistic *hauteur*, refuses to intervene to prevent a communist takeover of Central America will intervene to counterbalance Soviet participation in an assault on Israel? Can anyone believe that the American people could make sense of such contradictory behavior? Yet a large number of American Jews, perhaps even a majority, appear to believe it.

Have these Jews taken leave of their reason? Of course not. It is simply that their thinking is beclouded by anachronistic presuppositions about the kind of world we live in and about the appropriate responses by the United States to the kind of world we live in. This real world is rife with conflict and savagery. It is a world in which liberalism is very much on the defensive, in which public opinion runs in the grooves established by power, in which people back winners not losers, and in which winners not losers provide the models of the future. In such a world, we are constrained to take our allies where and how we find them, even if they are authoritarian (e.g., Turkey), even if they are totalitarian (e.g., China).

If American Jews truly wish to be non-interventionist, they have to cease being so concerned with Israel, with Jews in the Soviet Union, or indeed with Jews anywhere else. To demand that an American government be interventionist exclusively on behalf of Jewish interests and none other—well, to state that demand is to reveal its absurdity. Yet most of our major Jewish organizations have ended up maneuvering themselves into exactly this position. They cannot even bring themselves openly to support the indispensable precondition for the exercise of American influence on behalf of Jewish interests in the world: a large and powerful military establishment that can, if necessary, fight and win dirty little (or not so little) wars in faraway places. It is the winning or losing of such wars that will determine the kind of world our children inherit, not striking pious postures or exuding moralistic rhetoric.

To quote Erik Erikson once again: "In some period of his history, and in some phases of his life cycle, man needs a new ideological orientation as surely and as sorely as he must have light and air." Today is such a period for the American Jewish community. For two centuries, Western Jewry has been wedded to the intellectual traditions and political movements that had their roots in the Enlightenment. This was understandable and inevitable, since it was this current of thought and these movements, liberal or left-of-liberal, which achieved religious toleration and civic equality for Jews. Conservative thinkers and conservative political parties tended to be hostile to Jewish aspirations, or at best coolly indifferent. In the United States, founded as it was in the flush of Enlightenment enthusiasm, the division between liberalism and conservatism was never that pregnant with meaning for Jews. Nevertheless, as relatively new immigrants, Jews found liberal opinion and liberal politicians more congenial in their attitudes, more sensitive to Jewish concerns. For the most part they still do. The kind of social discrimination—in country clubs, business luncheon clubs, within the corporate community generally—that Jews experience even today is generally at the hands of people who express conservative opinions and are likely to vote Republican. This form of discrimination affects only a fraction of the Jewish population, but that fraction includes those upper-middle-class, affluent Jews who are active in community affairs and provide the leadership of Jewish organizations.

Still, the world changes and will continue to change no matter how stubbornly Jews stick their heads in the sand and hope that yesteryear's realities will return. The American Jewish community needs the light of reason and the refreshing air of candid discourse if the world is not to pass it by. It must begin to see things as they are, not as it would like them to be. One of the things it must see, on the domestic level, is that the liberal consensus and the liberal coalition that have dominated American politics since the inauguration of Franklin D. Roosevelt are disintegrating, at least so far as Jews are concerned. The blacks may or may not remain members of this coalition—one presumes they probably will—but if they do, it will be on a new set of terms. Though a great many Jews will gallantly try to swallow these terms, in the end the American Jewish community will gag on them. Can anyone doubt that, henceforth, the black caucus in Congress will be inclined to think that military or economic aid for Israel can be better spent for social programs in the ghettos? This is what Jesse Jackson thinks, this is what he says, and what Jesse Jackson thinks and says today is what the black caucus will think and say tomorrow. And can anyone doubt that, under a Mondale or Hart presidency, our next ambassador to the UN will be more like Andrew Young than Jeane Kirkpatrick? All of these terms have been set by Jesse Jackson, and he means them most seriously. He must mean them seriously if he is to maintain his political leadership of the black community. His mission has been to incorporate a Third World view of politics into the American political spectrum, especially into the portion of that spectrum dealing with foreign affairs, and if he cannot do this within the Democratic Party he will either desert that party or his enthusiastic followers will desert him. His die is cast.

But the increasing and tragic polarization between blacks and Jews is only one feature of the disengagement of the liberal coalition from Jewish interests. Another is the changes that are occurring in one of the traditional bastions of that coalition, namely, the trade unions. This reality is masked by the fact that the current head of the AFL-CIO, Lane Kirkland, is an old-fashioned liberal, a Henry Jackson type of liberal—in short, the kind of liberal Jews have cooperated with so amiably in the past. But Kirkland, alas, is not forever, and one can already see the ground shifting beneath his feet. It is, so far as American Jews are concerned, an ominous shift. To begin with, there is the little-noticed fact that the so-called Jewish unions are on the verge of disappearing. The

Amalgamated Clothing Workers, the International Ladies' Garment Workers, the American Federation of Teachers, still have Jewish leaders with close ties to the Jewish community. But their membership is already overwhelmingly black, Hispanic, and Oriental, and future leaders will have no reason to be especially concerned with Jewish issues.

Meanwhile, organized labor itself is moving away from the nonpolitical tradition of Samuel Gompers and is developing closer official ties with the Democratic Party. As this happens, the unions themselves naturally take on the ideological coloration of their political allies. If one wants to get a sense of what this can mean, one has simply to look at the "educational materials" prepared by the National Education Association—once a professional association, now more a union—and observe how "fair" it is to the PLO, how coolly skeptical it is of Israel's virtues. The AFL-CIO's executive council, too, is moving to distance itself from Lane Kirkland's "old-fashioned" views on foreign policy. All in all, organized labor in the United States is reshaping itself in the mold of European trade-unionism, with an organic connection to a social-democratic party and with an ideology to suit. That ideology, as expressed, for instance, in the conferences and publications of the Socialist International, is pro–Third World, anti-Israel. It is now far more left than it is traditionally liberal. But then, liberalism itself, in the United States as elsewhere, has moved distinctly to the left in the past two decades.

This shift is very evident in a third pillar of the older liberal coalition, that class of people we call "the intellectuals," those in academia, the media, and the foundation world. These men and women used to be predominantly liberal. Today, it is fair to describe most of them as being to the left of the older liberalism. In the case of the media, the transition has been obvious enough, as reportage on Middle Eastern events has made clear. Here, too, we are witnessing a process that is not peculiarly American. In Britain, France, Germany, Italy, the media are even more highly critical of Israel, compassionate toward the PLO. We are witnessing the coming of age, the accession to positions of power and influence in all the institutions of the media, of the youthful rebels of the 1960s. Their attitudes may have softened somewhat, but they have not been significantly reshaped. In the case of academia, these attitudes have actually sharpened rather than softened. The academic community today, populated by the graduate students of the 1960s, and insulated from worldly experience, is more openly and vigorously left-wing than ever before in American history. The most influential intellectual tendency among academicians today is Marxism, in a dozen or more different versions, some of them so far from the original as to perplex older Marxists, but all of them pointing in the same political direction. Just what that direction is may be inferred from the fact, and it is a fact, that an invitation to Ambassador Jeane Kirkpatrick to speak on campus will cause intense controversy in faculty councils, with quite a few professors going so far as to encourage student harassment should she appear. Meanwhile, such invitations go out routinely to Third World spokesmen, whose anti-Israel and anti-American remarks are listened to respectfully.

In short, while American Jews have for the most part persisted in their loyalty to the politics of American liberalism, that politics has blandly and remorselessly distanced itself from them. For the first time in living memory, Jews are finding themselves in the old condition of being politically homeless. It is possible, though far from certain, that Jews in the West will find a new home, however uncomfortable, in the conservative and neoconservative politics that, in reaction to liberalism's leftward drift, seems to be gaining momentum. But whether this conservatism will be keenly enough interested in Jews to offer tolerable lodging to them is itself an open question. What is no longer an open question is the dissociation that has occurred, and is daily occurring, between the American Jewish community and its traditional allies. That is an established fact—and one that American Jews must candidly confront.

1984

Liberalism and
American Jews

American Jews, in their overwhelming majority, are politically rooted in a liberal tradition. That is presumably why, as Milton Himmelfarb has noted, Jews in this country have the economic status of white Anglo-Saxon Episcopalians but vote more like low-income Hispanics. How to explain this anomaly, unique in the American experience? The Irish and the Italians, as they move up the economic ladder, are far more likely to shed the urban-immigrant liberalism of their parents and grandparents, shifting rather predictably to one version or another of suburban conservatism (of which interest-group liberalism is a subspecies). They perceive their interests in a new way, and vote these interests. Such a shift is what a student of sociology would expect. Why has it not happened among America's Jews? Why are they so different? Is there a single answer that can serve as an explanation?

I think there is, though it is a single answer that is not a simple answer. It has to do with the meaning of that "liberalism" to which American Jews seem so stubbornly attached, a meaning that is itself a special compound of Jewish political history and Jewish religious history over the past two centuries. So powerful is this meaning that it has become, for many Jews, an integral aspect of their self-definition as Jews. There are now some signs that this self-definition is finally eroding in the face of a circumstantial reality that repels its solicitation. But it is interesting to note that Jews who move away from their familiar (and familial) liberalism still tend to describe themselves as "disillusioned," whereas their Irish and Italian counterparts find such a movement to be natural, not at all traumatic, and not calling for any self-conscious reflection.

To be disillusioned one must have had illusions. The liberalism of the modern Jew is one that has been especially rich in illusions. Obviously, those illusions have been not merely illusions; to retain the loyalty of Jews for so long a time, they had to be nourished by the real, outside world. "Jewish liberalism"—and the term is neither invidious nor inappropriate—is organically connected to a larger non-Jewish liberalism that has tended to dominate the intellectual (even spiritual) life of Western Europe ever since the French Revolution. It is the intensity and obstinacy of the Jewish commitment to this liberalism that is so special.

To this liberalism, and not to another. We are talking about Continental "radical" liberalism, the liberalism that gave rise to the French Revolution and which, stubbornly (if not altogether successfully) resisting opportunities for disillusionment, has remained loyal to the ideals of that revolution ever since. What was liberal about this liberalism was its opposition to monarchy and aristocracy, the *ancien régime*, which was seen as oppressive, corrupt, and decadent. What was radical about this liberalism was the belief that a new order could be constructed, to be governed by a new, "enlightened" state which would be representative of man's finer instincts, his most elevated thoughts. By the early decades of the nineteenth century, this belief began to incorporate a fundamental distrust and detestation of the market economy, which was perceived as incarnating self-interest as the guiding principle of the new social order. Such a focus on self-interest was thought to be inimical to "enlightened" government, which should be the master, not the servant, of social and economic realities. It is this polarity between "enlightened," powerful, intrusive government and the principle of self-interest as the bedrock of our economic system which is the driving force behind all modern socialism, whether in its social-democratic or Leninist versions.

There is, of course, another liberal tradition with a quite different conception of "liberalism." This is the Anglo-Scottish-American tradition, represented by such thinkers as John Locke, David Hume, Adam Smith, and the authors of *The Federalist Papers*. Though this tradition had a certain popularity in Continental Europe prior to the French Revolution, it has always been viewed by Continental liberalism as a mere prolegomenon to the more "authentic" and more radical liberal ideals emerging from the French Revolution. In Anglo-Scottish-American liberalism, it is an enlightened, civil *society* that is prized, while *government* is regarded as a continuing threat to individual liberty— including the liberty to pursue, within a large sphere of action, one's self-interest. Such individual liberty is the root principle of this new order. In the end, it is whether one regards a "bourgeois" civil society more favorably than an "enlightened" state, or vice versa, that determines whether one leans to

Anglo-Scottish-American liberalism or to the radical liberalism of the Continental political tradition.

The difference between the two liberalisms can be fairly described, in quasi-Marxist terms, as the difference between a "bourgeois" and a "post-bourgeois" ideology, exemplified in the American and French Revolutions, respectively. The ideals of the American Revolution were (and are) individual liberty, social and political equality, and representative government. The ideals of the French Revolution stressed economic equality, political community, and a government, freely elected or not, that claimed to represent a sovereign popular will. It is understandable, therefore, that socialist thinkers and socialist movements of the nineteenth and twentieth centuries all looked back to the French Revolution as the appropriate paradigm of what a "real" revolution should look like, while the American Revolution was regarded, if at all, as a marginal event. Leon Trotsky's magisterial *History of the Russian Revolution*, for instance, takes the French precedent (or the Jacobin version thereof) as authoritative in explaining the "natural" history of revolutions in general, and specifically of the Russian Revolution in which he played so notable a part. This explains why the drama Trotsky reconstructs is so coherent, so plausible, though also more fictional than real.

That European Jews should have been legatees of the political ideology of the French Revolution was inevitable under the circumstances that prevailed. They had, properly speaking, no political philosophy or political traditions of their own, after all; even today, and even in the state of Israel, there is no identifiable "Jewish" political thought. They knew nothing of Anglo-American political theory and not much more about the far-off American Revolution. The individualism of Anglo-American political theory, in any case, evoked few echoes, still evokes few echoes, in a communally oriented Judaism. In addition, and most important, the ideology of the French Revolution, throughout the nineteenth century, did offer European Jewry tangible benefits of the utmost significance, while the opponents of this ideology were likely to be adherents of an established Christian church and of an established social-political order which, at the very least, discriminated against Jews, or at most totally excluded them from membership in the civil society.

It was the ideology of the French Revolution, incarnated in Napoleon, that liberated European Jewry from confinement in the ghetto. Just how much this may have meant at the time may be grasped from a reading of Martin Buber's fascinating imaginative reconstructions in his novel, *For the Sake of Heaven*, in which Orthodox Jews in a Central European ghetto conclude ecstatically that Napoleon is their long-awaited liberating messiah. This same ideology, expressed in the liberal, socialist, and social-democratic movements of the nineteenth century, succeeded in extending the suffrage to Jews, and in removing legal restrictions on their freedom of movement as well as their economic opportunities. In Eastern Europe, where liberalism of any kind made only a modest impression on anti-Semitic regimes, the commitment of many Jews to this ideology was correspondingly intense. While far from all European Jews situated themselves somewhere on the left of the political spectrum, a disproportionate number did so. In France and Germany and Italy there was a stratum of conservative and centrist Jewry, assimilated into the national cultures, but many of these Jews eventually converted or simply cast off any religious or ethnic identity.

It was from Continental Europe, and mainly from Central and Eastern Europe, that Jews emigrated to the United States. They brought with them, naturally, their political beliefs. Those political beliefs still dominate the thinking of most American Jews. A recent *Los Angeles Times* poll reveals that when Jews are asked about the qualities most important to their Jewish identity—(a) a commitment to social equality, (b) religious observance, or (c) support for Israel—the first, a commitment to social equality, turns out to be the most important. This is an odd finding, since an objective observer would see in the American Jewish condition today little reason why social equality should evoke such a passionate commitment. One might think that intermarriage rather than discrimination or exclusion should be regarded as having a greater bearing on "Jewish survival." But ideas can have a life of their own, and Jewish political attitudes in the 1980s have a more direct connection with Jewish political thinking in the 1880s than with current social, economic, or even political realities in the United States.

It must also be pointed out that Jewish immigrants, congregating in the major urban centers, found there a Democratic Party—usually dominated by the Irish, themselves earlier immigrants—that was hospitable to their aspirations, personal and ideological. Although the Democratic Party was by no means a left-wing party, its liberalism on issues of social reform and its commitment to "balanced tickets" on which Jews were actually (if not all that frequently) elected to office were sufficient to engender Jewish loyalties and establish a Jewish commitment. This was even the case for Orthodox Jews, who were largely apolitical and indifferent to contemporary ideologies (including Zionism). The Republican Party in those urban milieus was perceived, correctly, as dominated by Wasps (as we now call them) who were either anti-Semitic or, at the very least, inclined to discriminate socially and economically against Jews. Up to World War II, major corporations hired few Jews and the more affluent suburbs were "restricted" to non-Jews (and, it goes without saying, to nonblacks). The struggle for equality of "civil rights," led by the liberal wing of the Democratic Party, only reinforced the commitment of American Jews to an agenda of liberal reform.

What is puzzling, however, is the way in which the force of this commitment has survived the enactment of the liberal agenda in the postwar years. Even while social and economic discrimination against Jews has declined with a quite unforeseen rapidity, Jews are still haunted by the specter of anti-Semitism among traditional conservative sectors of the society. And even as Jews have become one of the most affluent and upwardly mobile of ethnic-religious groups, their political ideology has remained largely unaffected. To some degree, this can be explained by the fact that American blacks have not experienced anything like the same success, leading Jews to wonder about the security of their own achievement. To some degree, too, it has resulted from a justifiable skepticism regarding the Republican Party's willingness to accept as permanent the "civil rights revolution," a willingness diluted or subverted by the conservative dislike of governmental action in this field. But mainly the ideological loyalty of so many American Jews has been sustained and nourished by a historic change in their religious outlook, a change that reshaped the very conception of what it means to be a "good Jew."

This change goes back to the early decades of the nineteenth century and gathered momentum with time. To simplify considerably, it entailed a sharp shift in emphasis from the "rabbinic" elements in the Jewish tradition to the "prophetic" elements. One should not exaggerate the tension that traditionally prevailed between these two currents of Jewish religiosity. What today is called "normative Judaism" managed to strike a cautious and generally acceptable balance between them. After all, the high moralism of the biblical Prophets— compassion for the poor and unfortunate, the emphasis on universal peace as a specifically Jewish aspiration—was incorporated into rabbinical teachings, while the Prophets themselves insisted on the importance of observing traditional Jewish law. Prophetic moralism always or almost always stopped well short of antinomianism and messianic enthusiasm, while rabbinic legalism was always (or almost always) deferential to moral sensibilities. Jews prided themselves on being "more moral" than Christians, Muslims, or pagans, and, regardless of individual Jewish behavior, the Jewish religious tradition unquestionably put a greater stress on "good deeds" and "righteous living" than on faith or dogma.

Nevertheless, the tension was there and steps were taken to cope with it. There were undoubtedly incendiary possibilities in the declamations of the

Prophets, and prudence required that these be minimized. Even today, a student in the yeshiva in his early years never studies the Prophets in isolation from a study of the Pentateuch or the Talmud. And in the synagogue, the Prophets are read on the Sabbath only in the form of a commentary on the nonprophetic books of the Torah. Especially after the advent of Christianity, which can be seen as an antinomian and millenarian outburst within the Jewish prophetic tradition, it was a constant matter of concern to the rabbis that such "enthusiasm" be held in check by a more rigorous focus on lawful and orderly behavior.

After the French Revolution, however, what we today call "prophetic Judaism" acquired an ever-greater vitality and autonomy. This was part and parcel of the emerging messianic sensibility—in matters political, social, and economic—that the Revolution established throughout European society. An era of grand aspirations began. The Israeli historian, the late J. L. Talmon, opens his book *Political Messianism: The Romantic Phase* with the following sentences:

> The present inquiry is concerned with the expectation of universal regeneration which animated men and movements in the first half of the 19th century.
>
> No period before or after has experienced so luxurious a flowering of utopian schemes purporting to offer a coherent, complete, and final solution to the problem of social evil.

"Expectation of universal regeneration"—and in the foreseeable future, and to be achieved through political and social action! In this way, and in this period, did a secular version of Judeo-Christian messianism enter Western political thought and establish itself there as a rational option for reasonable persons. What made it seem both rational and reasonable was its apparent continuity with the theme of social, political, economic, and (perhaps above all) technological progress which had emerged so powerfully in the previous two centuries. Indeed, it seemed not only continuous with, but a plausible extension of, the idea of progress. Why should progress be so gradual, so intermittent even, so painfully slow? Why not, by deliberate action, hasten the progressive movement toward its predestined end, the universal regeneration of mankind?

Now, "hastening the end" had always been regarded by Jewish and Christian orthodoxy as a dangerous, heretical temptation, one that indigenous messianism made a permanent temptation, and therefore to be guarded against all the more vigilantly. But in a secular version, rooted not in religion but in science and the newly invented "social sciences," it escaped such vigilance. Traditional religious orthodoxy was neither confronted nor refuted by the new spirit of this new age, but was ignored and left to "wither away." In such a heightened, "progressive" perspective, capitalism—i.e., a society centered around a market economy—posed a problem for Jews. On this matter, the relation between Jews and capitalism, there has been a vast amount of intellectual confusion.

Judaism, as is generally and correctly recognized, is much more a "this-worldly" religion than Christianity. As a result, Jews have never been opposed to or contemptuous of business (or, for that matter, of sex) as a human activity. "Making a living" was always regarded as central to Jewish family life, and while Jewish law imposed some relatively mild inhibitions and prohibitions on commercial activity, there was never any sense of a conflict between the two. Becoming wealthy was similarly regarded as a legitimate, even admirable goal, so long as this wealth was used for benign (usually communal) purposes. But "business" in specific commercial markets is not "capitalism." Business is an activity; commerce is an activity; capitalism is an idea, an idea invented in the eighteenth century. Business proceeds, in one way or another, in all socioeconomic systems above the most primitive level. Capitalism is a prescription whereby business activity is incorporated into a market economy that is the major institution of civil society, an institution that is the source and guarantor of individual liberty.

It is the failure to distinguish between business activity by Jews and the capitalist idea that muddles the thinking and writing of Max Weber and Werner Sombart, and of some of our own contemporaries, who are perplexed by the fact that Jews do so well under capitalism while showing so little gratitude to the system. The fact that Jews, for various historical reasons, are adept at business, and the further fact that Judaism does little to frustrate business incentives, means that Jews always manage to do very well in a capitalist society. But it does not follow that Jewish affluence or Jewish prosperity brings with it Jewish contentment—peace of mind, peace of soul. In all existing capitalist societies, Jews have done and do extremely well for themselves. And in all existing societies, Jews, especially younger Jews, are profoundly uneasy about the legitimacy of their own success. The anti-Semitic fantasy in which Jews manage to be simultaneously wealthy capitalists and subversive radicals is but a paranoid inflation of a reality.

The only exceptions to this generalization are the strictly Orthodox Jews, who isolate themselves from modernity as a whole, and who continue to practice business in a capitalist society while being utterly indifferent to, even willfully ignorant of, the capitalist idea. For them, the religious community is the only authentic sociological reality. This makes them conservative by temperament and inclination, while remaining indifferent to modern conservative ideologies, modern liberal ideologies, or modern radical ideologies. Jews who are not strictly Orthodox, however, are fully implicated in modernity and its ideologies. For reasons already given, they are most likely to be attracted to that version of liberal ideology spawned by Continental radical-liberalism. This is most obviously the case for secularized Jews, who have been "liberated" from any formal attachment to the Jewish community, and who feel that adherence to such an ideology is an appropriate Jewish response to modernity. They find in the "secular humanism" of this ideology an adequate approximation of the ideals of the "prophetic Judaism" which emerged in the nineteenth century and has infused itself into all non-Orthodox versions of contemporary Judaism.

There really is such a thing as "secular humanism," just as there really is such a thing as "prophetic Judaism," and the connection between the two is deep and strong. Secular humanism, born of the Renaissance, is a form of atheism, one less interested in denying the existence of a divinity, either apart from or immanent in the cosmos, than in affirming the possibility of humanity's realizing its "full human potential" through the energetic application of high-minded (i.e., moralistic) intelligence. Prophetic Judaism, for its part, is a form of Jewish religiosity, of course, but a distinctly modern form, one less interested in God's word or Jewish law than in realizing, here on earth, a universalist version of the preaching of the Prophets.

Social and social-democratic movements are all inspired, officially or unofficially, by one version or another of secular humanism. Similarly, non-Orthodox Judaism today is, in varying degrees, inspired by, or infused by, the teaching of the Prophets rather than of the rabbis. In the case of Reform Judaism, such an inspiration was and remains its original *raison d'être*. In the case of Conservative Judaism, the prophetic teachings are allowed to dominate its secular involvements, even where there is substantial attachment to the law. And in the case of secular Jews, prophetic Judaism merges into secular humanism to create what can fairly be described as a peculiarly intense, Jewish, secular humanism.

It is this combination of secular historical experience and the religious mutation it provoked that accounts for the political predispositions of contemporary American Jews. And not only American Jews. Wherever European Jews (especially East European Jews) have settled, whether it be in Canada, Australia, South Africa, or Latin America, they have located themselves on the left-of-center of the political spectrum. This has most obviously and strikingly been the case in Israel, where shreds and tatters of the socialist tradition—and Israel, of course, was originally settled, for the most part, by socialist pioneers—still evoke a kind of pious loyalty, despite the obvious fact that the prevalence of socialist ideas is obstructing the growth of the Israeli economy and that such ideas have no relevance whatsoever to the realities that confront Israeli foreign policy.

Having said all this, however, one must add—perhaps, even, one must conclude—that this situation cannot endure for much longer. After two centuries, the socialist idea, in whatever version, is becoming more and more meaningless, more and more incomprehensible even to its advocates. In practically all countries with self-styled socialist regimes, the movement is away from socialism, in any traditional sense of the term. As concerns economics, the direction of this movement is toward a system in which self-interested economic activity in a freer market plays a greater role. As concerns politics, it is toward a system that is, ideologically, either left-wing authoritarian or right-wing authoritarian or some unstable combination of the two. The promise of a humanistic, democratic socialism, whether as an ideal to be realized or as a goal to be approached, is dissolving into the mists.

This leaves American Jews in a condition of what social psychologists call "cognitive dissonance." Their political loyalties become more desperate in proclamation, more unbelievable in fact. This is especially the case as the so-called Third World, where socialism is still a much-respected and often official doctrine, evolves toward socioeconomic-political systems that fall outside of any Western category and have in common mainly a hostility to Western liberal civilization, Western religious humanism, and Western secular humanism. It is this hostility that shapes the attitude of those countries toward Israel, perceived (correctly) as an outpost of Western civilization. More and more, a socialist, quasi-socialist, or left-liberal political outlook sympathetic to social democracy is becoming inconsistent with a concern, which American Jews overwhelmingly feel, for the survival of the state and nation of Israel. How long this condition of "cognitive dissonance" will continue, and where it will end, is not now foreseeable. Everything will depend on how the Western democracies themselves adapt to this new situation. What is certain, however, is that American Jews, even as they feel more and more "at home" in America (as they do), are going to find themselves among a much larger population of liberal Americans: the ideologically uprooted and dispossessed.

1988

Christmas, Christians,
and Jews

Once upon a time, long before the idea or phrase "sensitivity training" was born, the various religious groups in our heterogeneous society had developed a strategy for getting along with one another. It was a strategy based on civility and prudence. Since American society was then more provincial, more narrow-minded, than it is today, civility and prudence only worked up to a point. But I would maintain that they worked better than the current strategy, which by encouraging all of us to be perpetually "sensitive" to others, and especially sensitive to "militant" others, actually invites self-styled spokesmen for minorities to be aggressive, uncivil, and imprudent. Though religious discrimination has, thank goodness, declined sharply in the last fifty years, this decline is mainly visible at the individual level, the most important level, it ought to go without saying. What our liberals call "intergroup relations," however, relations at the public level, seem to be worsening, as the new version of "pluralism" feeds destructively upon itself. Eventually, one fears, there could be disagreeable repercussions on the individual level as well.

Jewish-Christian relations are a case in point, and this Christmas seems an appropriate time to ponder the issue. It is my strong impression that, while relations between Christians and Jews as individuals are far better today than ever before, tensions between the two religious communities are being exacerbated. It is not a matter of a "resurgent anti-Semitism," as some major Jewish organizations claim. Only within the black community is there evidence of any such resurgence, and since this phenomenon is as inexplicable as it is irrational, given the extraordinary Jewish commitment to the struggle for equality of civil rights, no one really has any idea of what to do about it. In any case, there is nothing even superficially Christian about black anti-Semitism, which is a peculiar, home-brewed racism that has little appeal to white Christians. What anti-Semitism still prevails in the larger society is primarily social, a reluctance to assimilate Jews into the social life and social activities of the non-Jewish community. Such discrimination has some nasty side effects at the occupational and professional level, though on the whole American Jews seem to manage to evade those effects. In any case, as a Jew who is not particularly interested in participating in such assimilation, I can live with it.

The kind of tension that is now building up between Jews and Christians has very little to do with traditional discrimination, and everything to do with efforts by liberals—among whom, I regret to say, Jews are both numerous and prominent—to establish a wall between religion and society, in the guise of maintaining the wall between church and state. The major Jewish organizations proceed from the correct proposition that legally and constitutionally we are not a Christian nation, to the absurd proposition that we are in no sense at all a Christian society. They are aware, of course, that the overwhelming majority of Americans are Christians, but insist that their religion be a totally private affair, one that finds no public expression and receives no public deference. Such insistence shows a lamentable ignorance of history, sociology, and psychology.

This ignorance is reflected in the quandary that these same Jewish organizations now find themselves in over developments in Israel. They really thought that one could have a Jewish state with a largely secular society inhabited by Jews? That the Jewish government of a Jewish state could blandly and resolutely ignore traditional, religious Jewish sensibilities? Since the original Zionist movements were largely secular and nationalist in their inspiration, many Israelis did once think along those lines. But, with the passage of time, this mode of thought has been chastened. No one in Israel today makes an issue of the fact that all food in the Israeli armed forces is kosher, though, in the nation's earlier days, this was a matter for some controversy. Other similar innovations have relentlessly occurred over the years. Today, in Israel—still theoretically that strange hybrid: a secular but Jewish state—there is no debate over the separation of church and state, only a debate over where one draws the line in the involvement of religion with both society and state. There is every bit as much religious toleration in Israel as in the United States, and Christians and Muslims are free to practice their religion without let or hindrance. But the Israeli government closes down on Yom Kippur, not on Christmas.

Now, the United States is not Israel. It is not, constitutionally or traditionally, a Christian state but a fully secular state. Moreover, the United States
is a pluralist society in a way that Israel is not, does not wish to be, and cannot be. (The "Law of Return" guarantees to Jews, and only Jews, the right to
come and live in Israel.) But the fact that Christmas is an official holiday
throughout the United States does indicate that the secular government of
this nation of Christians is at least minimally respectful of Christian sensibilities. I see nothing wrong with that, just as I see nothing wrong with the
public schools in New York City closing down on Yom Kippur. It is common sense and common prudence for a secular government not to put itself
unnecessarily at odds with the religious sensibilities of its citizenry. Diplomacy and tact is called for, not ruthless self-denial, which is what the American Civil Liberties Union calls for. Unfortunately, many Jews seem to think
that the extreme secularism of the ACLU is their best guarantee of religious,
social, and political equality. Since I believe that such extreme secularism is
contra naturam, except in a nation of atheists or agnostics, which the United
States is not, I also believe that the American Jewish community is misguided
in its now-dominant dogmatic view of how the relations between the two religions are to be structured.

The Jewish view, that religion ought to be an exclusively private affair with
no public involvement, is the understandable view of a religious minority with
long and vivid memories of official anti-Semitism, discrimination, and persecution. But the inescapable truth is that Jews are not going to be able to impose this view on the Christian majority of the United States. It is just too
extreme, so extreme that, even now, the major Jewish organizations stop short
of arguing against the status of Christmas as a national holiday, or school clos-
ings on Yom Kippur in some localities, or all sorts of other, traditional intru-
sions of religious expression and ritual into public life.

One reason American Jews were able to take seriously the prospect of a
near-total divorce between religion and society was the attitude of the major
Protestant organizations, whose liberal Protestantism was more keenly interested in social reform than in religious belief. Jews prefer Christians whose
Christianity is lukewarm and therefore, they feel, less likely to lead to Christian anti-Semitism of a kind our Jewish ancestors experienced for centuries in
Europe. This is perfectly understandable. But it is also a parochial perspective,
out of tune with current realities, and this for two reasons.

First, the anti-Semitism that has been so dangerous to Jews in this country,
and is still so dangerous today, is not Christian anti-Semitism. It is neo-pagan
anti-Semitism (Nazi and fascist), or Muslim fundamentalist anti-Semitism, or

Marxist anti-Semitism, or simply nationalist chauvinist anti-Semitism of a kind one now finds in Japan (of all places!) or Latin America. Our major Jewish organizations are oriented, almost hypnotically and surely atavistically, to the past rather than to the present or future. Secondly, it is ridiculous to think that liberal-modernist secular Protestant Christianity would remain forever "the wave of the future," and that never again would Christians want to be devout. Ever since World War II and the Holocaust, large numbers of American Jews have felt impelled to become "more Jewish," in one way or another. But the American Jewish community as a whole—always excluding the ultra-Orthodox, who are uninterested in Christians—was surprised to discover, was positively alarmed to discover, that something like a Christian revival was also occurring, primarily among the evangelical wing of Protestantism. So the Jewish organizations keep anxiously looking for signs of anti-Semitism among "born-again" Christians, exaggerate the few such expressions they do find, and wait for this phenomenon to pass. I don't think it will pass. I believe the secular era is fading, that Jews (at least those who remain Jews) will become more Jewish, Christians more Christian, Muslims more Muslim, Hindus more Hindu, etc.

American Jews are utterly unprepared for this new world, in which Christians wish to be more Christian without necessarily being anti-Semitic. They doubt the very possibility of this happening. I am willing to contemplate such a possibility. Which is why I refuse to get excited about a crèche being erected outside a town hall, or students in public schools singing Christmas carols or even putting on a Nativity play. In those communities that are predominantly Christian, this is to be anticipated, and Jews can live with it. Indeed we Jews always did live with it, in the America of my schooldays, before the courts became militant agents of secularism. To be sure, we lived more comfortably with it to the degree that our fellow Americans who were Christians exercised a suitable degree of tact and prudence. In my own school, our principal, confronting a student body that was perhaps one-half Jewish, would read from the Bible at assembly, but he would read only from the Psalms, the most purely interdenominational part of Scripture.

Tact and prudence: the recovery of these virtues, by both Jews and Christians, seems to me the key to decent relations between these two religious groups. I think it is foolish in the extreme for Jews even to appear to be anti-Christian, just as it would be wrong for Christians even to appear to be anti-Semitic. A lot of nice diplomacy is called for, but our religious leaders ought to be capable of that. This Christmas, as in all Christmases past and future, there will be no Christmas tree in my home. But I am not anti-Christian and see nothing wrong with the Christian majority erecting Christmas trees on public property. Indeed, I have what I regard as a theologically positive view of Christianity. Like the greatest Jewish theologian of this century, Franz Rosenzweig, I see Christianity as a sister religion to Judaism, as a form of "Judaism for the Gentiles." I can understand that some Christians might not think this theological view to be as positive as they would like, that they might even find it somewhat patronizing, just as I find somewhat patronizing the Christian view of Judaism as a necessary prelude to Christianity. But true theological difference of opinion ought not to impinge on the ability of the two faiths to live amicably together.

1988

Why Religion Is
Good for the Jews

If a religious community experiences a very low birth rate and a very high rate of intermarriage, 50 percent, what kind of future will it have? Obviously, not much of one. Yet the American Jewish community, which is experiencing both of these phenomena, seems to feel no anguish, only a growing anxiety. After all, a very low birth rate fits neatly into the upper-middle-class style of life which appeals to contemporary wives and husbands alike, and it is in this upper-middle class that Jews are ever more concentrated. And a high rate of intermarriage testifies to the ever-fuller acceptance of Jews by the non-Jewish community. Is that not what American Jews have always wanted? Is that not what America has always promised? How fortunate American Jews are to be living in such a wonderful country!

It really is a wonderful country, and they are truly fortunate to be a part of it. Never in the history of the Diaspora has there been anything comparable to the American experience. Never in Jewish history have Jews achieved, not mere toleration, but the full civic equality promised them by none less than George Washington himself. Along with this full civic equality there has also come an unparalleled degree of social equality. (These days, even Ivy League universities seem to feel they cannot do without Jewish presidents.) In short, America has so warmly embraced its Jews, and Jews have so enthusiastically responded to this embrace, that the American Jewish community may yet vanish, by osmosis, as it were. Is that what the community wants? And if not, what, if anything, can be done about it? Facing such questions, the major Jewish organizations are so skittish that one senses a positive relief and renewal on their part at the appearance of any new signs of old-fashioned anti-Semitism. That is a problem they are familiar with, and consider themselves expert in coping with.

A similar robustness characterized the reaction to a handful of purely theological statements made by some Christian fundamentalist preachers. These statements were to the effect that, when Jesus returns to the world, only Christians will qualify for redemption; Jews and other infidels need not apply. As it happens, Jewish theological teachings do not recognize the doctrine of a second coming of Jesus (or a first), so it is hard to see why Jews should take such offense at these statements. It is almost as if Jewish organizations, having fought (quite successfully) against Jewish exclusion from country clubs, now feel it necessary to take on the specter of discrimination in that Great Country Club in the Sky.

Still, even anti-Semitism cannot be counted on to restore a sense of purpose to the major Jewish institutions. The most blatant and vicious form of anti-Semitism in this country now emanates from the black community, and, incredibly, from black college students, black professors, and black preachers. This was not supposed to happen, and it has plunged Jewish organizations, with their predominantly liberal orientation, into a deep quandary of indecision. For several decades now, the official Jewish community has sincerely believed that it enjoys a strong alliance with black organizations. After all, Jewish money was always forthcoming to the Urban League, the NAACP, and the United Negro College Fund. And were it not for affirmative action, which the Jewish community has generally supported, many of today's black students would not even be in college, nor would their black professors be ensconced in their black studies departments.

So is today's black anti-Semitism another instance of the rule that no good deed goes unpunished? No, it is not. What we have here, rather, is a case of ideological folly reaping its unanticipated consequences. It is precisely because of the extensive Jewish involvement in black organizational life that black anti-Semitism is so virulent today. It is because Jewish officialdom has been a "patron" of blacks that a frustrated and racist black nationalism has turned against the Jewish community. The so-called black-Jewish alliance goes back to the early days of the struggle for black civil rights, a struggle in which Jews properly played a significant role, since civil rights is always a Jewish issue. The notion of an inherent alliance between the two communities survived the successful outcome of that struggle. Being liberal as well as Jewish, leaders of the Jewish community thought it natural that they should continue helping blacks achieve something like "real" (i.e., socioeconomic) equality.

Yet the liberal policies that were supposed to accomplish this goal have helped to create a black underclass and a demoralized black community.

Despite the fact that old-line "civil rights leaders" continue to demand more of the same, younger blacks, especially those drawn to one variety or another of black nationalism, are well aware of what welfare-state liberalism has done to their community. Black anti-Semitism today is a reaction to that liberal failure, and Jews, being so highly identified with liberalism, happen to make the most convenient target. Among black university students caught up in the revolt against welfare-state liberalism, the situation is coming more and more to resemble that of German university students in the 1930s. Their rebelliousness in the name of racial dignity and self-affirmation has a strong thuggish component, and is far closer to authentic fascism than anything we have seen since the 1930s. Since blacks make up only 11 percent of the population, they do not constitute any kind of real threat to American democracy. But the phenomenon of black anti-Semitism, which is a surrogate for black contempt and hatred for whites, and especially liberal whites, seems to have a ring of permanence. It is a passion that is even now reshaping the NAACP and the old-line black caucus in Congress, and it also marks a major turning point in American Jewish history, precisely because it so effectively challenges the historic commitment of American Jews to the ideal of a universalist, secular liberalism.

That triple loyalty—to Judaism, secularism, and liberalism—no longer seems as unproblematic as it once did. Indeed, the dissolution of the black-Jewish alliance, of whose very existence only a handful of blacks were ever aware, is a sign of the breakup of the larger liberal coalition, a coalition that is now mainly a Jewish illusion. True, labor unions with a substantial black membership—the teachers' unions, for instance, or the social workers' unions— can still be counted on to pass resolutions deploring anti-Semitism; but they are reluctant to pass a resolution denouncing Louis Farrakhan by name. And on the campuses, members of the newest Left, consisting of gays, lesbians, and radical feminists, are working to ally themselves with black "militancy" (notwithstanding the homophobia often associated with such militancy). About Jews and anti-Semitism they could not care less.

As the categories of "Left" and "Right" become hopelessly confused in postmodern politics, many people on the Left have begun to talk the language of fascism without knowing it, just as many black nationalists have unknowingly begun to act like fascists. Liberalism, bewildered by this new situation, is on the verge of a nervous breakdown. That leaves the major Jewish organizations, heavily populated by liberals, trapped in anachronistic modes of thinking. Some of these organizations already devote more attention to their liberal agenda than to their Jewish one. Thus, although the rate of abortion among Jewish women is far lower than in any other religious or ethnic group, a mass-membership organization like Hadassah has, in recent years, been more deeply engaged with the issue of abortion than with the issue of intermarriage. Or again, the leaders of some organizations find it easy to be for "choice," but find it more difficult to cope with promiscuity (aka "sexual activism") among their own children. Which is to say that, like liberalism itself, they are morally adrift. If two decades ago anyone had predicted that the major Jewish organizations would one day see nothing wrong with handing out condoms to students in junior high school, he would have been laughed out of court.

The one constant in this professional mind-set is the suspicion and fear of Christianity—and of conservatism. In both cases the suspicion and fear are based on atavistic European memories that have little relevance to the American Jewish condition. When it is pointed out that Christians in America today appear to be more interested in marrying Jews than in persecuting them, the rejoinder is quickly made that it is not those Christians who frighten Jews. It is the more devout ("orthodox") Christians, who keep talking about Jesus, and salvation, and even Armageddon. Such Christians, for the most part, do not want to marry Jews, a fact that in itself is taken as a symptom of potential anti-Semitism.

This brings us to the heart of the confusion with which we began. A plain and simple truth is that so long as Christians are willing and eager to marry Jews, and Jews to marry (secular) Christians, intermarriage will proceed apace. But another truth, not so plain and not so simple, is that while Jews are distressed by this situation, they are also flattered and reassured by it. One gets the impression that what many Jewish leaders want, ideally, is for Jews to remain Jewish, and to decline to marry the Christians who woo them, but not for Christians to be so Christian as to shy away from intermarriage with Jews. It is an impossible dream, reflecting the paradoxical situation in which American Jews find themselves today.

Meanwhile, the Jewish population as a proportion of the whole steadily declines. It is numbers that count, and Jewish numbers will count less and less. By the year 2000, just around the corner, the Mormon population, having tripled in the past two decades, will be greater than the Jewish population. As for the evangelical Christians, they increase steadily and will soon be the dominant force in American Christianity. By contrast, the "mainline" churches, steadfast in their social agenda and their own liberal-left commitments, continue to lose adherents; but they also continue to be the favorite churches of the institutional Jewish community, favorite because less aggressively Christian. Although there are signs of change in this area, as at least some Jewish organizations tentatively pursue an "opening" to the evangelicals, in general the Jewish-Christian liberal coalition is going down the path of the Jewish-black coalition, if for different reasons.

Or for some of the same reasons. Right now, for instance, some black preachers and educators, alarmed at the demoralization of black youth, are becoming enthusiastic advocates of prayer in the public schools. On this issue, as on many others, Jews find themselves increasingly isolated in their secular liberalism. They are isolated, too, in their Jewish universalism, a compound of grandiose moralism and messianic self-intoxication. Ever since the French Revolution, the "Jewish message" of universal justice in an ideal world has been interpreted as a political prescription for the real world. A secularized version of this message is the very heart and soul of Jewish liberalism. But the message now rings ever more hollow, as political messianism itself is drained of all credibility.

If ever there was a moment for Jews to turn inward, to think about their condition and their prospects in a more Christian America, that moment is now. In recent years, all the major Jewish organizations have quite suddenly decided that Jewish education is the solution to the problem of intermarriage. It is, if anything is. But what Jewish education means is itself a problem. Although more American Jews are sending their children to Jewish all-day schools, especially where the public schools are both unsafe and unfit for learning, the numbers are still too small to affect the overall picture. And in any case, most American Jews are not happy at the thought of parochial schools. They fear the taint of "ghettoization."

What happens in these schools is almost infinitely various. The Orthodox, of course, are a case apart; for most of them, the possibility of intermarriage is too remote to shape educational thinking. The more conservative of the Conservative schools work hard to teach Hebrew, to familiarize their students with the Jewish holidays and the more salient prayers, and to establish a sense of kinship with Jews everywhere, and especially in Israel. The Reform schools, a relatively recent phenomenon, emphasize a liberal social agenda accompanied by a smattering of Jewish learning. We do not yet know just how significant will be the impact of Jewish day schools, through the high school level, on the rate of intermarriage. Two separate studies done in 1993 conclude that Jewish education correlates positively with involvement in Jewish causes, and does act as a brake on intermarriage. But it is too early to tell. Anecdotal evidence suggests that many of the products of Jewish day schools quickly assimilate into the secular youth culture. When they go on to college, many, always excepting the Orthodox, may end up retaining only a vestigial connection with their Jewish heritage.

True, one can envisage a Jewish school system running right through the college years, and this might have a very marked effect. But that, too, is hardly a realistic prospect at the moment. It would be taken as suggesting a kind of voluntary resegregation, and segregation is what American Jews have fought against throughout their history. The official Jewish community would have to become a lot more "Jewish" than it is today for such a system of higher education to be allotted the resources it would need. Until that day dawns, relying solely on Jewish day schools to slow down the rate of intermarriage may be less than realistic. Still, as the only game in town, it is a move in the right direction.

The liberalism of the last two centuries liberated Jews from the ghetto and enlisted them as civic equals in Western society. The new challenge Jews will have to face is just how to live as equals in American society without committing demographic suicide. They can best confront this challenge by seeing it as an opportunity, not simply a problem. The opportunity is one for the American Jewish community to reestablish a Jewish core, a religious core, as a key to its identity. That is what many Christians today are seeking as our secular society continues to unravel, and there is every reason to think that Jews, willy-nilly, will be propelled in the same direction.

That does not mean that they will thereby instantaneously give up on their liberalism. So thoroughly does the liberal culture dominate attitudes in the Jewish community that even a turn inward, toward religion, may well become hostage, at least temporarily, to the liberal ethos. Thus, among rabbinical students at non-Orthodox seminaries in recent years, there has been a remarkable upswing in religious observance and a palpable move "rightward" in matters of ritual and liturgical practice. But this growing religious conservatism often goes hand in hand with a conventional liberal attitude about everything else, from racial politics to rock music to abortion, feminism, and homosexuality. It will be interesting to see whether the contradictions entailed in this adaptive maneuver can long survive.

In any event, being Jewish in a multiracial, multiethnic, and religiously pluralist society is the challenge of the hour. Or, to be more precise: the challenge is to find a way of incorporating the crucial religious dimension of "being Jewish" into American life.

1994

Taking Religious
Conservatives Seriously

The beginning of political wisdom in the 1990s is the recognition that liberalism today is at the end of its intellectual tether. The fact that it can win elections is irrelevant. Conservatives continued to win elections during "the liberal century" (1870–1970), but once in office they were unable to enact a sustained conservative agenda. The tide of public opinion was too strong against them. That tide has now turned. It is liberal administrations today, in all the Western democracies, that find themselves relatively impotent when in office. Just as conservative administrations used to nibble away at liberal reforms previously enacted, so liberals in office today do their share of nibbling at the occasional conservative reform that has taken hold. But more often, they find themselves nibbling away at the liberal reforms of their predecessors, reforms that threaten to bring about fiscal insolvency as well as political fragmentation.

The liberal consensus, as expressed in the media, is that, with the election of Bill Clinton, conservatism in America is in disarray, is groping for some center of equilibrium, and that only a "moderate" Republican coalition, one that disengages itself from the Religious Right, can create an American majority. This may be true in the shorter term, as defined by the next presidential election or two, but in the longer term it is false. The religious conservatives are already too numerous to be shunted aside, and their numbers are growing, as is their influence. They are going to be the very core of an emerging American conservatism. For the past century the rise of liberalism has been wedded to the rise of secularism in all areas of American life. In the decades ahead, the decline of secularism will signify the decline of liberalism as well. Already, on the far-left fringes of liberalism itself, artists and philosophers are welcoming the collapse of a "secular humanism" that they find sterile and oppressive. They can offer nothing to replace this liberal-secular humanism. But others can, and will. Today, it is the religious who have a sense that the wave of the future is moving in their direction.

The three pillars of modern conservatism are religion, nationalism, and economic growth. Of these, religion is easily the most important because it is the only power that, in the longer term, can shape people's characters and regulate motivation. In economics, secular incentives (i.e., materialist incentives) can be effective. But in the really troubled areas of modern life, where social policy is at work, the materialist incentives offered by the welfare state have given rise to a long train of calamities. Perverse economic incentives can encourage a corrupting dependency, and liberalism has, in the name of compassion, created a network of such perverse incentives. But it does not follow that modifying these incentives will have a dramatic effect. The reason is simple: it is not possible to motivate people to do the right thing, and avoid doing the wrong thing, unless they are told, from childhood on, what the right things and the wrong things are. This explains why so many of our newer immigrants, coming from traditional families, are able to ignore these tempting, corrupting incentives and instead move on to productive and law-abiding lives.

The most extraordinary social phenomenon of the liberal century has been the totally unexpected increase in criminality. The first obligation of government has always been to ensure the security of the person. Liberalism does not believe this; it represents "too punitive" a conception of the governmental mission. Instead, liberalism believes that if you diminish income inequalities and provide cradle-to-grave income security and ample medical care, then the criminal impulse will wither away. In the face of increasing criminality, therefore, liberalism responds with ever more fanciful and ever more desperate "therapeutic" programs, all of which are ineffectual.

As with crime, so with all the other social pathologies that now infest our liberal society and its welfare state. "The joy of sex" has been compromised by an infusion of sexual anxiety, as venereal diseases ranging from the noxious to the fatal proliferate. It has also produced a large and growing population of unwed mothers and their babies. The liberal answer to this disaster is either to deny that it is any kind of disaster—"just a new kind of family," the social workers chirp—or to create more programs of "sex education." But such secular, nonjudgmental education, an education bereft of moral guidance, has done much to create this problem in the first place.

Back in 1897, John Dewey defined the essence of the liberal credo: "The practical problem of modern society is the maintenance of the spiritual values of civilization, through the medium of the insight and decision of the individual." A noble idea but ultimately a self-contradictory one. You do not preserve spiritual values by turning them over to a rampant spiritual individualism. That experiment has been tried, and it has failed. But an admission of failure is not something we can expect. On the contrary: what we are witnessing is a prolonged spasm of liberal fanaticism, a redoubling of liberal effort as liberal program after liberal program fails. With each failure, the credibility of government is diminished and cynicism about politics increases. Does anyone really believe that the Clinton administration will significantly reduce, or that a second Bush administration would have significantly reduced, the budget deficit?

The plain truth is that if we are ever going to cope with the deficit, and the social programs that inflate it, we are going to have to begin with a very different view of human nature and human responsibility in relation to such issues as criminality, sexuality, welfare dependency, even medical insurance. Only to the degree that such a new, actually very old, way of looking at ourselves and our fellow citizens emerges can a public opinion be shaped that will candidly confront the fiscal crisis of the welfare state. Presidential calls for "sacrifice," meaning a willingness to pay higher taxes, are a liberal cop-out. Why don't we hear something about self-control and self-reliance? It's the traditional spiritual values that we as individuals need, not newly invented ones.

We hear it said frequently and with pseudo-solemnity that this fiscal crisis results from the people's demand for benefits that they are then unwilling to pay for. Were this so, the implication would be that these corrupt people are incapable of democratic self-government and need an elite to do the job for them. Liberals, despite their populist rhetoric, have been discreetly drawing this inference for many years now. Much of our overblown welfare state was created by liberal political entrepreneurs, not in response to an evident popular demand. Liberals may scornfully dismiss "supply-side" economics, but they are profoundly committed to "supply-side" politics, the politics of "unmet needs," a category that is constantly expanding. Also expanding, of course, are the official bureaucracies and the "helping" professions that cope with those "needs."

To counter the crisis that liberalism is provoking in our society, conservatism has to rediscover and reaffirm its attachment to its three traditional pillars of religion, nationalism, and economic growth. A reaffirmation of the goal of economic growth should not be difficult. It is becoming ever more widely appreciated that economic growth is crucially dependent on the ability of "economic activists" to invest and innovate. Just as political activists, spurred by political ambition, are at the heart of liberal public policy, so economic activists, spurred by economic ambition, are at the heart of conservative economic policy. It is they who promote the growth that pacifies egalitarian and redistributional appetites. There is still an influential segment of "old conservatives" who do not understand that a pro-entrepreneurial emphasis in economic policy is not simply a "pro-business" policy. But they are gradually fading away.

Similarly, an affirmation of the national spirit is practically inevitable, as the liberal internationalism that has defined American foreign policy since the days of Woodrow Wilson continues to unravel. The United States will surely want to, and will need to, remain an active world power, but this activity will not be within the confines prescribed by the United Nations or NATO or whatever. In this post–Cold War era, those organizations are on their way to becoming moribund. Nor are we about to engage in some kind of benign humanitarian imperialism—except in very special circumstances, decided case by case. A renascent nationalism will be accompanied by a renascent neo-realism in foreign policy. This is something that most conservatives have long wished for.

Coping with a religious revival, however, is something that conservatives and the Republican Party are not yet prepared for, and that the Democrats seem almost entirely uninterested in. Religious people always create problems, since their ardor tends to outrun the limits of politics in a constitutional democracy. But if American public life is to retain some semblance of civility, we had all better work hard at understanding these people. . . . In a sense, the influx of the religious conservatives into American politics is analogous to the influx of European immigrants into our urban centers between 1870 and 1914. Although the immigrants created many problems, the Democrats welcomed them while the Republicans shunned them. That was the origin of the "natural" Democratic majority. But the Democrats are very unlikely to welcome the religious conservatives in the foreseeable future. If the Republicans, too, keep them at arm's length instead of embracing them and shaping their political thinking, a third party and a restructuring of American politics are certain. One way or another, in the decades ahead they will not be denied.

1994

A Note on
Religious Tolerance

I am all in favor of Americans of a particular religion learning about other religions. On the other hand, I have little use for all these Christian-Jewish dialogues that are so popular nowadays. They are incredibly superficial—nothing more than self-gratifying celebrations, mainly by secularized Jews and secularized Christians, of mutual toleration. There is little learning and less understanding displayed on such amiable occasions, which are "successful" only to the degree that religious differences are thought to be of no great concern to well-meaning people. It is, in short, a liberal, enlightened, secular kind of tolerance, not an authentically religious kind of tolerance—that is to say, a tolerance that has religious roots as against secular roots.

Such an authentic tolerance is much to be desired in our world, where religious homogeneity among a nation's population is becoming ever scarcer. But a religious argument, as distinct from a secular argument, for religious toleration is, for a religion such as Christianity, exceedingly difficult to make. It would require a deep and painful reformation of traditional Christian beliefs, and one appreciates how reluctant any sincere Christian would be to engage in such an enterprise. Still, I do think it worthwhile to outline, in the abstract, what a religious belief in religious toleration would involve, even if one has little expectation of its actual emergence.

In this respect, a Jew is in a favored position, even a privileged position, to discuss the issues, because it is not (or at least should not be) a problem for him. Orthodox Judaism—which is to say, rabbinic Judaism—has affirmed religious toleration for some two thousand years now. It did so in the Talmud and in the form of a most ingenious (some would say far-fetched) commentary on the biblical narrative of Noah.

Noah, of course, was not a Jew. He was a biblical patriarch located midway between Adam and Abraham, with ten generations distance on each side. He was, we are told, a righteous man "in his generation" (a neat qualification) and was chosen by God to survive the Flood, along with the various species he collected in his Ark. The purpose of this survival was to permit him to engender a revived and uncorrupted (or less corrupted) humanity. As a reward, God promised there would be no more floods, and further entered into a covenant with Noah and his sons. The Bible gives us no details of this covenant—a covenant with humanity, not with Jews—but the rabbis, on their own, figured it out. The covenant contained the Noahide laws, which, if observed, enabled a community to obtain a redemptive share in the world to come. These laws consisted of six prohibitions: against idolatry, blasphemy, murder, sexual irregularities, theft, eating the flesh of a living animal—and, one positive commandment, the establishment of a legal system that enforced such laws (and perhaps others; that's not clear).

Later rabbis fiddled a bit with those seven laws, filling out the details so that the seven were easily multiplied. But the original seven have a specific standing in the Jewish tradition. It may be worth noting that the rabbis insisted that Jews had to observe, not only the Noahide laws, but all the laws and commandments, the Noahide laws alone being reserved for goyim. Later, more sophisticated rabbis debated among themselves whether these laws were revealed law or "natural law," but no conclusion was ever reached. The main point, for our purposes, is that these Noahide laws are overwhelmingly moral in substance, not theological, and that they obviously apply to all of humanity.* The important result is that religious toleration has rarely been a problem for Judaism. The existence of these Noahide laws also helps explain why Judaism has not been, for most of its history, a proselytizing religion.

Christianity is a very different kind of religion, far more intellectually complex—indeed, far more intellectually interesting, I must concede—because it has absorbed so much Greek neo-Platonism as well as a liberal sprinkling of gnosticism, in both belief and spirit. Judaism has had its theologians, of course, and sometimes advanced students within the Jewish academic world do study them, but they are marginal to the religion itself. This even includes a giant

---

*The prohibition against idolatry is certainly theological, but it is difficult to say how wide its scope is. Hinduism, for instance, certainly has the appearance of being an idolatrous religion, but several Hindu scholars have assured me that is a matter of popular superstition, not of theological understanding.

figure like Maimonides, who actually proposed a credo, a declaration of first theologian principles, but it never made its way into the prayer book. For Orthodox Jews, rabbinical commentaries are important. It is mainly some Conservative and Reform rabbis, plus secularized Jews of an intellectual bent, who take the trouble to read a Franz Rosenzweig or a Martin Buber, or even Maimonides' *Guide for the Perplexed*, a work that is, in contrast to his commentary on the Mishnah, too neo-Aristotelian for Orthodox tastes.

For Christianity, in contrast, religious doctrine has always played a central role. The history of the Catholic Church cannot be told without a focus on doctrinal controversies. And it was a set of doctrinal controversies that were at the origin of all Protestant denominations, as well as the inter-Christian religious wars of the seventeenth century. It is religious doctrine, not moral considerations, that shapes the Christian attitude toward other religions as well. How else could one explain the apparently unquenchable desire of Christians to convert Jews? There is no question of reforming Jewish behavior, which poses no problem for Christians. It's just having Jews do and say different things when they pray. To a Jew like myself, the attitude seems rather bizarre and the enterprise itself quite pointless. Jews believe that God listens to many voices, not just ours—why should Christians seek a monopoly of access?

Well, we know the explanation. Christians—believing Christians, anyway, as distinct from thoroughly secularized Christians—are convinced that only through Jesus Christ can the human race achieve salvation and obtain a share in the World to Come. They are persuaded that only a Christian life opens the doors to the sacred and holy, and they define this life in doctrinal terms, blandly ignoring the reality that there is hardly any difference, in moral and existential terms, between the kinds of lives that Jews and Christians lead.

To sum it up:

For Judaism, the moral behavior by believers in other religions trumps the official religious doctrines of those religions.

For Christians, the religious doctrines in the end trump moral behavior.

At this point, I can hear the inevitable accusation that I am avoiding the question of "truth," dodging the issue of whether Christianity is, as it claims to be, the highest truth. Yes, I am doing exactly that. The concept of "truth," I would insist, is best limited to things temporal and to those intellectual disciplines that limit themselves to the study of things temporal. It ought not be a theological concept; in that universe of thought it can contribute little but mischief. The core beliefs of all religions are matters of faith, not belief as to truth or falsity as these terms are used, for instance, in the sciences. Theology is a legitimate intellectual discipline, but it is not a science. Is the resurrection of Jesus Christ a fact that is either true or false? I believe that to be a misguided question. It is a matter of faith. Truth is born of reason, faith is born of revelation, and theology is the effort to reconcile the two as best it can. But theology proves nothing, though it may sometimes help persuade or even offer a dazzling insight. To insist that it does offer such proof gives rise to a moral mandate to convert humanity to a particular religion. Toleration can then be nothing more than a matter of prudence and expediency.

Religious wars over theological doctrine are one of the most absurd exhibitions of human passion. Theological relativism is a perfectly sensible idea, whereas moral relativism is indefensible in both theory and practice, violating as it does the very idea of a universal (or near-universal) "natural law." Today, the Christian religion finds itself shackled by an anachronistic concept of "truth" that is simultaneously temporal and super-temporal. In a world that is largely non-Christian, and seems determined to remain so, this is not a happy situation to be in.

And it can create problems for the Christian revival in our United States— a revival I applaud as a necessary corrective to postmodern paganism. The American tradition of religious toleration has always been more Noahide than Christian. One finds the roots of this tradition well expressed in George Washington's letter to the Jewish congregation in Newport, Rhode Island: "All [Americans] possess alike liberty of conscience and immunities of citizenship. It is now no more that toleration is spoken of, as if it was by the indulgence of one class of people that another enjoyed the exercise of their inherent natural rights. For happily, the government of the United States . . . requires only that those who live under its protection demean themselves as good citizens."

George Washington's own beliefs can probably be best described as those of a Deist of the Christian persuasion. Both Madison and Jefferson seemed to hold to pretty much the same view. Whether their doctrine of "inherent natural rights" has secular or religious or Christian roots one can leave to scholars to dispute. But the doctrine is unequivocal in its proposition that, in a society where economics is secular and politics is pluralist, morality, whatever its source, will always trump religious doctrine. And this proposition has long been firmly ratified by our Congress, our courts, and our public opinion. When the territory of Utah sought statehood, it was only the practice of polygamy that was seen as a problem to be resolved. No one bothered to read the Book of Mormon—which is perhaps as well—when considering statehood for Utah. And whenever the courts have to rule on whether or not a cult can be properly regarded as a religion, it is the moral behavior of its officials and members it examines, not its religious doctrines.

The famous "separation of church and state" is actually a separation of religious doctrines, not of religion-based morality, from state purview. This crucial distinction was overlooked by the six prominent professors of philosophy who wrote a brief to the Supreme Court supporting "assisted suicide" as "a profoundly religious act" and therefore protected by the First Amendment. This was a blatant exercise in hypocrisy which invokes religion only when convenient. But it was also a case of historical amnesia; they forgot the Mormons. In the United States, morality has always trumped religious acts since it trumps the doctrines on which those acts are based. This is at the core of what we have come to call our "civic religion."

This being so firmly the case, it would be nice if our Christian theologians made some serious effort to rethink, candidly, their doctrine of exclusivity when it comes to "truth" and redemption. I don't want to give undue emphasis to this matter, since their churches have already moved a long way toward harmony with the American reality. We hear more and more these days of "communities of faith" rather than "communities of believers," a not unimportant difference. And the Evangelical revival is more a moral movement than a religious one. The Catholic Church too, like a chess master, has gradually and quietly made a series of brilliant (if perplexing) moves in the direction of non-exclusivity, leaving the whole issue, as best as I can tell, in a theological muddle, which is often a sign that something healthy and fruitful is going on. But there is still a long way to go.

1998

On the Political
Stupidity of the Jews

The novelist Saul Bellow is fond of recalling a political incident from his youth. Saul, then an undergraduate at the University of Chicago, was, like so many of us in the 1930s, powerfully attracted to the ideologies of socialism, Marxism, Leninism, and Trotskyism, as well as to the idea of "the Revolution." He and a group of highly intellectual and like-minded fellow students would meet frequently at his aunt's apartment, which was located next to the university. The meetings lasted long into the night, as abstract points of Marxism and Leninism agitated and excited these young intellectuals. Saul's aunt, meanwhile, would try to slow things down by stuffing their mouths with tea and cakes. After the meetings broke up in the early hours of the morning, Saul's aunt would remark to him: "Your friends, they are so smart, so smart. But stupid!"

Of course, such hard-core adherence to Marxist or Leninist doctrines has declined with the years. But while the particular doctrines in question may have changed, the Jews, for the most part, have not. In Israel as well as in America, Jews to this day continue to combine an almost pathologically intense concern for politics with a seemingly equally intense inclination towards political foolishness, often crossing over into the realm of the politically suicidal. How is one to understand this very odd Jewish condition—the political stupidity of Jews?

It seems that the easiest explanation of this phenomenon is in terms of the actual political history of the Jewish people, a history which is for the most part one of political impotence. A people whose history is largely a story of powerlessness and victimization, or at least is felt to be such, is not likely to acquire the kinds of skills necessary for astute statesmanship. Neither the rabbinic nor the prophetic traditions can be of much assistance in this respect, since political thinking is inherently secular thinking, so that Jewish secular thinking about politics has traditionally focused on some splendid isolated incidents of resistance and rebellion, such as the wars of the Maccabees, and the resistance against Rome. But the memory of these incidents is hardly a sufficient basis on which to ground a real tradition of political wisdom that could teach contemporary Jews how to wield power and successfully defend Jewish interests. And the absence of such a tradition of political wisdom continues to haunt all Jewish politics, including the politics of Israeli Jews, despite the fact that they now have half a century of experience in self-government.

In fact, one of the most striking features of Israeli political discourse, when considered from the perspective of Anglo-American and European political thought, is how narrow and constricted it is. Public discourse in Israel is often superficially sophisticated, even trendy, but it lacks genuine historical echoes, historical tonalities. Echoes of references to the traditions of Western political thought, which are common in American and Western European journalism, are relatively absent in Israel. It is not any deficiency of scholarly knowledge—Israel does have some fine academics in disciplines such as political theory and philosophy—but the presence of such individuals does not begin to repair the deficiency of Israel's own political traditions. The main stream of Zionist political thought arose from the political thinking of nineteenth-century romantic nationalism in Central and Eastern Europe, and this is itself a movement whose shortcomings are plainly visible in Central and Eastern Europe today. In the Jewish state, as in Eastern Europe, an infusion of thought is needed from the outside; an infusion of thought, by which I mean the importation of genuine political wisdom, not just the imitation of whatever attitudes are prevailing in the West. In this regard, it is tremendously important to translate the classics of Western political conservatism into Hebrew for the benefit of Israeli readers. It is possible that the readership of these translations will be small, but only through a serious study of this tradition will it be possible for Israelis to begin to develop a genuine understanding of the function of a conservative politics in a healthy polity.

Given the historic attitude of the European Right toward Jews, it is natural that Jews in Israel should incline to ignore the conservative political thought of other countries, thinking almost automatically in terms drawn from the European Left. And Israeli political discourse, in fact, is drenched with left-wing attitudes and assumptions. It is so drenched, in fact, that even where the socialist agenda has been largely discredited, the socialist ethos remains as powerful as ever, successfully delegitimizing any serious effort to pursue a nonsocialist agenda. It is my experience that the majority of former socialists, in almost every country, remain opponents of capitalism. Socialism today is a political goal that dares not say its name, because socialism as a system has been discredited. But this does not mean that socialist societies stop being socialist. Instead, socialism takes refuge in a large variety of anticapitalist attitudes and policies, which simply go under other names, or under no name at all. It is this type of socialism that is visible in Israel today, as well as in England and France, and elsewhere. Israel is almost singularly bereft of the kind of clear presocialist or postsocialist thinking that would be most useful to its leaders and citizens.

Translating such thinking into accurate and readable Hebrew is essential. Translate and publish, and the readers will come eventually. I have seen this happen in the United States and in Britain, although it does require a tremendous amount of patience to see the process through, often more patience than we can imagine. Wrong ideas, once implanted in a young person's mind, become so plausible, so self-evident as it were, that change is hard. I remember a course I once taught at New York University on urban problems, in which we took up the issue of rent control. After a few weeks, the students had grasped what is apparent to most people who study the problem, that, except under emergency conditions, rent control is a bad idea in both theory and practice. Nevertheless, by the time the students took their examinations at the end of the term, it became clear that at least half the class had simply forgotten what they had learned about rent control; and once again, it seemed to them to be a perfectly good idea. It is a "progressive" illusion to think that, in the marketplace of ideas, truth will always win out over error. It is truth that needs help, while error usually manages to make its own way very nicely.

So in pursuing the path to political wisdom, one needs books to read, magazines and essays and articles to read. One has to be willing to work tirelessly to produce all these books and articles until the climate of opinion slowly changes. What I am describing is actually a formula for success devised by Lenin, which I still remember from my days as a young Trotskyist. First you publish a theoretical organ, then you proceed to books and pamphlets, and finally you publish a newspaper. Once you have a newspaper that can apply the theories developed in more sophisticated publications to day-to-day politics, you are in business.

This formula does not always work, of course, and one certainly cannot expect it to work if the ideas in question are poor ones. But one of the important virtues of the conservative political tradition is that, from a literary and intellectual point of view, it is really first-rate. And this is not merely a question of one's subjective preferences. The test of a great tradition is whether its perspective is sufficiently insightful to be of use long after it is first written, and the fact is that conservatives can continue to read and reread a good part of the literature in this tradition and profit from it. One should compare this to what happens to leftist political thinkers, who have their day and then disappear from sight. The risk of being progressive is that there is always some new version of "progress" which seeks to outgrow whatever was thought to be important by progressives a few years earlier.

Who, for example, reads Harold Laski today? When I was in college everyone read him. He was one of the world's leading political philosophers. He was a socialist and chairman of the British Labor Party, a very intelligent man who wrote endless volumes, and of course he was Jewish. He is simply not read anymore in political science courses in the United States or in England, and his books are out of print. Yet his successor at the London School of Economics, Michael Oakeshott, who was a conservative, was able to produce essays that are still being reprinted, still being quoted and still very readable, not only because his writing was so elegant, but because the ideas contained in them were of enduring value. This is the advantage the conservative has over thinkers on the Left writing on contemporary affairs. The conservative tends to think in permanent terms, so his ideas remain relevant.

The living presence of such a conservative tradition in Israel could contribute much, not only in changing the socialist atmosphere of the country. For example, it could move some to think in ways that might assist in bridging the divide between religious and secular Jews in Israel, which is one of the most vexing curses of Israeli politics. When I first started writing on conservatism, one of my major points was the need to reconcile Adam Smith with Edmund Burke—the economics of a free market with the political sociology of a conservative society. This contradiction between the two ways of thinking is a problem for American politics, since Smith's perspective frequently clashes with that of Burke within the Republican Party. It is obviously, and very dramatically, a problem for Israeli politics, where those who have an appreciation for the importance of freedom frequently have difficulty understanding the role played in a healthy society by tradition, and vice versa.

Yet oddly enough, Adam Smith and Edmund Burke were friends who admired each other's writings and, to the best of our knowledge, did not see them as being in conflict or fundamentally contradictory. Moreover, throughout the nineteenth century, conservatives in Great Britain had no problem regarding them with equal respect. How did they manage it? They managed it by being sensible and nondogmatic, and by understanding that ideas that are incompatible in the abstract can often coexist and complement one another in practice, so long as the imperial sweep of these grand theories is limited by political wisdom, which is itself distilled from popular common sense. In a way, this is the most conservative of all ideas, that there is such a thing as wisdom and that, in the end, it is of greater importance in determining good policy than any theory. It is this idea which, more than any other, is in need of affirmation in our time. We live in an age when wisdom is suspect in the eyes of what can only be understood as an overweening rationalism, and when what works in practice is inevitably regarded with suspicion until it is proved in theory.

The history of economic thought in the modern era is worthy of study precisely because it represents a largely successful effort to make rational sense of the workings of the free market, which had once appeared to be nothing but a seething cauldron of anarchic individual impulses, which could in no way be reconciled with what was good for a society. Today, one can come by an understanding of why a market economy is so beneficial to society without too great an effort; a careful reading of Adam Smith and Friedrich Hayek will do the job. But this understanding flies in the face of our initial intuitions on the subject, so the educational effort to retain our hold on this tradition of ideas has to be constantly renewed, year after year, generation after generation, or the profound insights contained in these books will simply be lost. And unless government and society work diligently to "internalize" what has been learned on this subject, transforming the abstract economic ideas involved into practical habits of the heart, the ability to make sound decisions in this realm will continually slip from our grasp. In other words, government and society must take steps—educational steps, legal steps—which are independent of the market, and which are necessary to make the market possible and profitable for all of society. The success involved in making a market economy work and prosper is a success of statesmanship, another conservative idea which is not rooted in ideology, but in experience. The statesman may pursue any policy, so long as it is derived from political wisdom concerning what has worked to protect and better society in the past, and so long as it continues to work well in the present. And statesmanship is something that both Israel and the United States are today noticeably lacking.

Now, if we have such a successful and refined political tradition in economic affairs, which leaves so much up to the initiative and decisions of the individual, why do we need religion? Doesn't liberty suffice to create the good society? Although there are certainly those who make this claim, the Western conservative tradition holds otherwise. According to conservative thought, a market economy cannot work except in a society comprised of people who are, in sufficient degree, bourgeois—that is, people who are orderly, law-abiding, and diligent, and who resolutely defer gratification, sexual as well as financial, so that, despite the freedom granted each individual, the future nonetheless continues to be nourished at the expense of the present. For people of this kind to lead lives of this kind, it seems to be the case that religion is indispensable. This appears to be a sociological truth. It is religion that reassures people that this world of ours is a home, not just a habitat, and that the tragedies and unfairness we all experience are features of a more benign, if not necessarily comprehensible, whole. It is religion that restrains the self-seeking hedonistic impulse so easily engendered by a successful market economy.

It is here that Edmund Burke makes such a decisive contribution to the political tradition of the West. Not that he was a particularly pious man (he was not a pious man) or a brilliant theologian (he was no kind of theologian). Burke's importance lies in the fact that he was a secular political theorist who could explain, to a critical mind, why a religious orthodoxy (like a political orthodoxy) can make intellectual sense. My wife, Professor Gertrude Himmelfarb, tells a pertinent story from a graduate course she taught on British political thought. In her class there was an Orthodox young woman, quiet and industrious. After several class sessions devoted to a close reading of Edmund Burke, this young woman approached my wife, and told her: "Now I know why I am Orthodox." What she meant was that she could now defend Orthodoxy in terms that made sense to the non-Orthodox, because she could now defend a strong deference to tradition which is the keystone of any orthodoxy in the language of rational secular discourse, which was the language in which Burke wrote.

It is the idea of tradition as a political concept which was central to the ideological debate between Edmund Burke and Thomas Paine, the latter being one of the best-known exponents of the French Revolution. It was Paine who declared: let the dead bury their dead. It was Burke, on the other hand, who argued that the dead should have the right of suffrage. We should in effect give them the vote in deciding on the ordering of our government and society because of the wisdom which we may gain from the ideas which they had derived from their experience.

Paine won this debate, unfortunately, which is why arguments based on tradition make so little headway with most young people today. There was a game I used to play with my own students in New York to try to assist them in understanding Burke's point. I would point out that in the United States, we have fifty states which are extremely different from one another in size, population, natural resources, per capita income, and so on. Yet despite these differences, each of these states has the same powers for dealing with such crucial matters as education, energy, transportation, and welfare within its borders. Moreover, each of these fifty states sends two members to the United States Senate. I would ask them whether this was reasonable. Of course, they did not think so, and in the blink of an eye they would begin redrawing the map of the United States, completely redesigning the country so that all the states were more equal in every possible respect. Only once they had thought about it did they begin to wonder whether this perfectly egalitarian scheme made practical sense. They realized that the people living in other regions had social, economic, and political attitudes which were not identical to those of New Yorkers, and that the new regions that they were inventing were not going to be homogeneous areas with a homogeneous population. And as they thought about this, they began to realize that at least some of the states represent local interests and points of view which would be silenced by their efforts to reach a kind of a pure rationalism in politics.

On the other hand, given the opportunity to study both Paine and Burke, there will always be some students who find Burke more persuasive. These include students who are subscribers to a religious tradition or are thinking vaguely of drawing closer to such a tradition. Burke is not usually thought of as a defender of Jews or Judaism, to which he seems to have given little thought. But it is interesting to read his remarks on what he called "prejudice"—by which he meant habit, custom, convention, tradition—with the Orthodox Jewish tradition in mind. According to Burke:

> We are afraid to put men to live and trade each on his own private stock of reason; because we suspect that this stock in each man is small and that the individuals would do better to avail themselves of the general bank and capital of nations, and of ages. Many of our men of speculation, instead of exploding general prejudices, employ their sagacity to discover the latent wisdom which prevails in them. If they find what they seek, and they seldom fail, they think it more wise to continue the prejudice, with the reason involved, than to cast away the coat of prejudice, and to leave nothing but the naked reason; because prejudice, with its reason, has a motive to give action . . . and an affection which will give it permanence. Prejudice is of ready application in the emergency; it previously engages the mind in a steady course of wisdom and virtue, and does not leave the man hesitating in the moment of decision, sceptical, puzzled and unresolved. Prejudice

renders a man's virtue his habit; and not a series of unconnected acts.
Through just prejudice, his duty becomes a part of his nature.

It is impossible to legitimize a conservative predisposition in politics, as
well as a conservative predisposition in religion, without having an authentic
respect for tradition. And this respect for tradition must be intellectually de-
fensible. For such a defense one turns to Burke who, when confronted by the
radical opposition to tradition which was the essence of the French Revolution,
became the first political theorist of the modern world to articulate a powerful defense of tradition.

But once deference to tradition has been rationally justified, it has to be
put into practice in society, and in government. And to do this, the innovative
market economy which characterizes contemporary democracy, and the conservative tradition, have to be adjusted to one another, a fact which was well
understood by the father of capitalist thought, Adam Smith. For unlike some
of today's free-market enthusiasts, Adam Smith was no radical economic individualist. He thought a state would be foolish to try to usurp the prerogatives
of the market, but he did not give these prerogatives a universal scope. He saw
an important role for the state in education, in taxation including redistribu-
tive taxation, and in certain forms of poor relief. It is impossible to say what his
attitudes would be regarding the affluent societies of our century, but he did,
after all, write a book, *The Theory of Moral Sentiments*, which placed a strong
emphasis on compassion as the natural bond between human beings, including human beings in a capitalistic market economy. So it is likely that, were he
alive, he would not wish to uproot the welfare state root and branch. And as
for Burke, while he emphasized the importance of the family and of the institutions of what we now call civil society, he also praised the properly ordered
state—whose propriety was visible in the respect it showed for the institution
of property—as a partner in the perfection of all things human. Nothing less
than that.

The possibility of reconciling conservative traditions of religion or morality with the freedom of a market economy is not only a matter of speculation.
It has formidable historical antecedents, which, even if they are unfamiliar to
many today, are nevertheless at the heart of the Anglo-American tradition of
free government. In the United States, between the founding of the republic
and World War II, approximately 175 years of conflict between the secular
market economy and a religious predisposition excited scarcely a tremor in
the body politic. One can find proof of this by consulting any major textbook
in American history published before 1945. A glance at the index may reveal

a few passing references to "church and state" relations, but nothing more. You look up "censorship" and you find no reference at all, although there was a great deal of censorship taking place. Over the last fifty years, the national issue which we now refer to as "religion in the public square" has engendered an entire library of legal arguments. But prior to 1945, it is clear that the issue could not have been that controversial, for the simple reason that there were hardly any legal rulings on the subject; there were virtually no Supreme Court decisions that addressed this issue.

The reason for this is an instructively practical one. Under the American federal system, issues such as school prayer, religious activities on public grounds, censorship of pornography—in short, the great majority of religious and moral issues—were adjudicated by political negotiations at the local level. These negotiations took into account the magnitude and intensity of public opinion on either side of an issue, and after some useful if sometimes painful experience, each community reached a *via media* that it could live with. In general, minority opinion was always respected, but majority opinion always received the greater deference. To reach such accepted norms in such a way that people could live together did not require a great deal of theorizing about absolute systems of universal rights; but what it did require was a great deal of inherited wisdom and common sense, on the part of the majority and on the part of the minority.

A few examples will suffice to make it clear what this meant in practice. When I went to elementary school in Brooklyn, we had an assembly once a week, which the principal of the school always began with a prayer. Now, the school was about one-half Jewish, with the rest of the students being Irish, Italian, or Anglo-Saxon Protestants. The principal was no fool, so he read a Psalm. The nice thing about the Psalms is that they are of Jewish origin, are part of the Christian Bible, but Jesus is not mentioned. So what Jew was going to object? Mind you, Jews these days do object to the reading of Psalms in public schools. But in those days, there were no Jews who would object to reading a Psalm, and no Christians who would object either. It was a commonsense solution to a problem; it worked for many, many decades.

Similarly, when I was young, there were burlesque shows, "topless" shows, we would call them, in New York, and Fiorello La Guardia, a very liberal and progressive mayor, decided that this was not good for the city. He did not want New York City to be known as a center for striptease shows, so he prohibited them. Just like that. The issue was taken to court, and the court ruled that La Guardia was the elected representative of the public, and if the public wanted things that way, it was their right. People who didn't like it could leave New

York City and move to Newark, where you could go to a burlesque show. There was no outraged public debate, no crisis, no book written on the subject. In the United States in that era, any community that wanted to order its public life in a certain way was permitted to do so. One's position had to be "within reason," but the point is that the range of issues which one could reasonably decide one way or another was considered to be quite broad, and open to a process of political trial and error. If Boston wanted to ban a book that had sex scenes in it, it did so. And then the booksellers in New York put up big signs in their store windows that said BANNED IN BOSTON, and this would be great for business. This might have been difficult to fit into some great universal system, but it took into account the traditions and feelings of these very different cities, and as a consequence, public life in both Boston and New York was conducted in a way that allowed most people in both cities to be happy.

In general, the political handling of controversial religious and moral issues in the United States prior to World War II was a triumph of reasoned experience over abstract dogmatism. Unfortunately, since around 1950, it is abstract dogmatism that has triumphed over reasoned experience in American public life. As everyone knows, this unwarranted and unfortunate reversal has provoked a constitutional crisis where there had never been one before. And much as I regret to say this, the sad fact is that American Jews have played a very important role, in some ways a crucial role, in creating this crisis.

It is a fairly extraordinary story when one stops to think about it. In the decades after World War II, as anti-Semitism declined precipitously, and as Jews moved massively into the mainstream of American life, the official Jewish organizations took advantage of these new circumstances to prosecute an aggressive campaign against any public recognition, however slight, of the fact that most Americans are Christian. It is not that the leaders of the Jewish organizations were antireligious. Most of the Jewish advocates of a secularized "public square" were themselves members of Jewish congregations. They believed, in all sincerity, that religion should be the private affair of the individual. Religion belonged in the home, in the church and synagogue, and nowhere else. And they believed in this despite the fact that no society in history has ever acceded to the complete privatization of a religion embraced by the overwhelming majority of its members.

The truth, of course, is that there is no way that religion can be obliterated from public life when 95 percent of the population is Christian. There is no way of preventing the Christian holidays, for instance, from spilling over into public life. But again, before World War II, there were practically no Jews who cared about such things. I went to a public school, where the children sang carols at Christmastime. Even among those Jews who sang them, I never knew a single one who was drawn to the practice of Christianity by them. Sometimes, the schools sponsored Nativity plays, and the response of the Jews was simply not to participate in them. There was no public "issue" until the American Civil Liberties Union, which is financed primarily by Jews, arrived on the scene with the discovery that Christmas carols and pageants were a violation of the Constitution. As a matter of fact, our Jewish population in the United States believed in this so passionately that when the Supreme Court, having been prodded by the ACLU, ruled it unconstitutional for the Ten Commandments to be displayed in a public school, the Jewish organizations found this ruling unobjectionable. People who wanted their children to know about the Ten Commandments could send their children to *heder*.

Since there was a powerful secularizing trend among American Christians after World War II, there was far less outrage over all this than one might have anticipated. The Jewish campaign against any suggestion that America was a Christian nation won one battle after another; eventually it made sufficient headway in the media and the legal profession, most importantly on the Supreme Court, that today there is widespread popular acceptance of the belief that this kind of secularism, which is tolerant of religion only so long as it is practiced privately and very discreetly, was indigenously and authoritatively "American," and had always been so. Of course, it has not always been so, and Americans have always thought of themselves as a Christian nation—one with a secular government, which was equally tolerant of all religions so long as they were congruent with traditional Judeo-Christian morality. But equal toleration under the law never meant perfect equality of status in fact. Christianity is not the legally established religion in the United States, but it is established informally. And in the past forty years, this informal establishment in American society has grown more secure, even as the legal position of religion in public life has been attenuated. In this respect, the United States differs markedly from the democracies of Western Europe, where religion continues steadily to decline and is regarded as an anachronism grudgingly tolerated. In the United States, religion is more popular today than it was in the 1960s, and its influence is growing, so the difference between the United States and Europe becomes more evident with every passing year. Europeans are baffled and a little frightened by the religious revival in America, while Americans take the continuing decline of religion in Europe as just another symptom of European decadence.

And even as the Christian revival in the United States gathers strength, the Jewish community is experiencing a modest religious revival of its own.

Alarmed by a rate of intermarriage approaching 50 percent, the money and energy that used to go into fighting anti-Semitism, or Israel Bonds, is now being channeled into Jewish education. Jewish day schools have become more popular, and the ritual in both Reform and Conservative synagogues has become more traditional. But this Jewish revival does not prevent American Jews from being intensely and automatically hostile to the concurrent Christian revival. It is fair to say that American Jews wish to be more Jewish while at the same time being frightened at the prospect of American Christians becoming more Christian. It is also fair to say that American Jews see nothing odd in this attitude. Intoxicated with their economic, political, and judicial success over the past half-century, American Jews seem to have no reluctance in expressing their vision of an ideal America: a country where Christians are purely nominal, if that, in their Christianity, while they want the Jews to remain a flourishing religious community. One can easily understand the attractiveness of this vision to Jews. What is less easy to understand is the chutzpah of American Jews in publicly embracing this dual vision. Such arrogance is, I would suggest, a peculiarly Jewish form of political stupidity.

For the time being, American Jews are getting away with this arrogance. Indeed, American Christians, and most especially the rising evangelical movements, are extraordinarily tolerant, if more than a little puzzled, by this novel Jewish posture. And the lack of any negative Christian reaction has only encouraged American Jews in the belief that they have discovered some kind of universally applicable formula for dealing with non-Jews. One can see this in the way many American Jews have taken to speaking about Israeli foreign policy in recent years. After all, why should getting along with believing Muslims be different from getting along with non-believing Christians? Many Jews honestly do not appreciate the difference, and therefore assume that if there is no peace in the Middle East, Israeli Jews must be doing something wrong.

But the political attitudes of American Jews have been shaped by something far deeper than their benign experience of life in Christian America in the last few decades. For what liberal American Jews, as well as liberal Israelis, have in common is nothing less than a deeply grounded utopian expectation that good "human relations" can replace political relations between other ethnic and religious groups, whether one faces these groups within the context of domestic American life or across the border in Israeli foreign affairs. At the end of World War II, the major American Jewish organizations, preparing to fight a possible upsurge in anti-Semitism (which never came), discovered a category of contemporary psychology called "conflict resolution," which they believed to be ideally suited to the problem they were facing; in fact, its great virtue was that it was ideally suited to their ideological predisposition. According to this branch of social science, ethnic, racial, or religious conflicts are the result of bias, prejudice, misunderstanding, or ignorance.

The vision of politics derived from this kind of social science can fairly be described as "therapeutic," as it assumes that ethnic, religious, or racial conflicts can be resolved by educational therapy that will uproot the psychological causes of the conflict. But ultimately it is just one more variant of the universal humanism which was the unofficial religion of the Enlightenment, to which Jews, lacking a realistic political tradition, were especially susceptible, and still are. In the United States, as well as in certain circles in Israel, such a universal humanism has acquired the status of a quintessentially Jewish belief. Whereas once upon a time it was not unreasonable to ask whether a given turn of events or policy was "good for the Jews," to ask that question in the United States today in Jewish circles is to invite a mixture of ridicule and indignation: ridicule at the retrograde parochialism of such an attitude; indignation at the suggestion that there is such a thing as a Jewish interest distinct from the interests of mankind as a whole. This is the reason that Jews, of all the religious and ethnic groups in the United States, are the most committed supporters of the United Nations. They may whine about the UN's unfriendliness toward Israel, but, despite considerable evidence to the contrary, prefer to think that this is a passing phenomenon; and like the ACLU, the United Nations Association floats on Jewish funding. The truth is that liberal Jews desperately need the United Nations, because it is their anchor in reality. The United Nations proves to them that their universal humanist ideals are not just daydreams, that they have a real existence in the world. The UN protects them from having to consider a reality of competition and painful political dilemmas and particularistic Jewish interests—which is to say, it protects them from thinking politically about foreign policy, something they have never done.

With the exception of a few quotations from the Prophets, there is nothing in the Jewish tradition that prepares Jews to think politically about foreign policy. It is not surprising, therefore, that Europe's Jews were so vulnerable to the universalist utopianism that characterized the Enlightenment, whose essence is the attempt to make do with abstract theories of universal rights and international laws in precisely those areas in which a people most desperately needs the practical experience of statesmanship and the political wisdom which at great length grows out of it. This political utopianism has left the Jews intellectually disarmed as they attempt to deal with the intractable foreign policy problems of an independent Jewish state, and charging down a blind alley in their search for constitutional arrangements that serve the Jewish interest in both the United States and Israel.

Before the daunting task of instilling a tradition of thinking politically among the Jews, there is little to be done other than to continue the work of education. Such work is very difficult, but it must be done if both Jews and Judaism are to survive. Those of us in the United States who have been involved in this enterprise for some years now are certainly encouraged to see a comparable enterprise under way in Israel. For our destinies are fused. American Jewry will not survive without Israel, and Israel cannot survive without the Jews of the United States. And neither community can survive without the development of a sound Jewish political tradition, which will teach us to think realistically about our politics, our economics, and our foreign relations.

1999

VIII

MEMOIRS

An Autobiographical
Memoir

Is there such a thing as a "neo" gene? I ask that question because, looking back over a lifetime of my opinions, I am struck by the fact that they all qualify as "neo." I have been a neo-Marxist, a neo-Trotskyist, a neo-socialist, a neoliberal, and finally a neoconservative. It seems that no ideology or philosophy has ever been able to encompass all of reality to my satisfaction. There was always a degree of detachment qualifying my commitment.

One "neo," however, has been permanent throughout my life, and it is probably at the root of all the others. I have been "neo-orthodox" in my religious views (though not in my religious observance). This is something of a puzzle to me, for my own religious background was not at all conducive to such a perspective. It is true that my parents' household in Brooklyn was Orthodox Jewish, but only in observance; belief seemed to have nothing to do with it. My father would go to synagogue only once a year, on the High Holidays; my mother never went, though she kept a strictly kosher household. We took notice of the other main Jewish holidays too, but we never "celebrated" them. I received absolutely no Jewish instruction at home, nor did my parents seem to care very much about my own observance. It is true that they dutifully sent me to an old-fashioned yeshiva—two afternoons a week and Sunday mornings—so that I could learn to read the prayer book and qualify for my bar mitzvah. There we also read the first five books of the Bible, translating from Hebrew into Yiddish, two languages I didn't know. (My parents spoke Yiddish to each other, but only English to the children.) I dutifully participated, learning to read the Hebrew and memorizing the Yiddish translations. Discipline was strict; if we misbehaved in any way, the rabbi would order us to stand up and then give us a stinging slap in the face. He also taught us to hate the *goyim* and to spit whenever we passed a church.

If ever there was a regimen that might have provoked rebelliousness, this was it. But though I obviously had not the faintest interest in my Jewish studies, I felt no impulse to rebel. I was duly bar-mitzvahed, making the conventional speech (in a memorized Yiddish) in which I thanked the rabbi and my parents for bringing me to this glorious day. I even continued to attend the yeshiva for at least six months afterwards, though I was not required to and my parents never encouraged me to. Then when I was sixteen my mother died of stomach cancer, and for the next six months I would get up at dawn, just when my father was setting off to work, and go to the synagogue to say the morning prayers, which included a prayer for one's recently deceased loved one. Again, my father never urged me to do this, and he himself seems never to have considered doing it. So why did I do it?

I don't know the answer to that. Though I took some adolescent pride in being a member of the "chosen people," I felt no passionate attachment to Judaism, or to Zionism, or even to the Jewish people. I had read nothing on any of these matters, and the only magazine that entered our house was *The New Masses*, to which my older sister, Lillian, subscribed as a consequence of attending City College at night. (She was an office worker during the day.) I did not think of myself as religious. On the other hand, one thing becomes clear in retrospect. There was something in me that made it impossible to become antireligious, or even nonreligious, though my subsequent intellectual commitments kept trying to steer me in that direction. I was born "theotropic," and not even my dismal experience of a decadent Orthodoxy could affect this basic predisposition.

Even while I was a young Trotskyist at City College, I was a dissident in this respect. I read Plato and was immediately persuaded that it made sense for a supra-sensible universe of ideas to exist. I read the King James Bible, and was immediately persuaded that the Book of Genesis was, in some nonliteral sense, true. Later in my college days I read Niebuhr, Tillich, and Maritain, along with Trotsky, Lenin, Rosa Luxemburg, et al., and found myself sympathetic to all of them. There were then no serious Jewish theologians available in English; it was not until after World War II that Buber, Rosenzweig, and Scholem began to be translated from the German. By that time, the Holocaust had touched my Jewish nerve and I was delighted to discover that there really could be an intellectual dimension to Judaism.

What impressed me most about the Christian theologians was their certainty, derived from the Bible, that the human condition placed inherent limitations on human possibility. Original sin was one way of saying this, and I had no problem with that doctrine, though how to reconcile it with my youthful utopian socialist hopes and beliefs was beyond me. In fact no reconciliation was possible, and the "neo" worm was already eating away at my socialist certitudes. It is interesting that the Jewish Prophets have never much interested me—their religious utopianism was too close to the political utopianism I was already becoming disenchanted with. I was more affected by the law-giving books of the Bible, and to this day I believe that this difference in emphasis will determine one's attitude toward traditional Orthodox Judaism as against modern reformed versions, which usually means "liberal" versions. Even as a socialist I had more respect for "tradition-bound" religion than for a modernized and liberalized one. This respect, however, did not necessarily extend to all traditional rituals and ways of behavior. I was a non-observant Jew, but not a nonreligious one. Hence the "neo" in my religious orientation.

For decades, and even now, some of my closest friends will occasionally wonder aloud whether I *really* believe in God's existence. My wife tells me that back in the 1950s, my revered teacher, Sidney Hook, took her aside on several occasions and asked her precisely that question. He, as a pragmatist and a rationalist, just didn't see how it was possible. The problem with that question, of course, is that "existence," in the normal usage of the term, is not a divine attribute. The mysterious term "being" is more appropriate. And a religious person doesn't "believe" in God, he has faith in God. One's relation to God is existential, not rationalist. As I learned later from a reading of Kant, pure reason will never get you beyond—pure reason. But the more you pray, the more likely you are to have faith. That is why children are taught to pray, rather than being instructed in "proofs" of God's "existence."

I have emphasized the importance of religion in my personal and intellectual development because, in my own writings, it is only on rare occasions evident. I am not a theologian, after all, though reading theology is one of my favorite relaxations. Other nonreligious thinkers, however, have had a more direct influence in shaping my mind. I have already mentioned Sidney Hook, whose writings revealed to me the power of logical, coherent analysis, something my formal education had neglected. He certainly helped me perceive the fallacies of Marxism, though, ironically, Hook always remained far more respectful of Marx, and of the socialist ideal, than I was. I sometimes think he taught me more than he intended. But that is the sign of a truly great teacher, which he was.

The two thinkers who had the greatest subsequent impact on my thinking were Lionel Trilling in the 1940s and Leo Strauss in the 1950s. Trilling was, in contemporary terms, a skeptical liberal, Strauss a skeptical conservative.

Trilling was an elegant and subtle literary critic, Strauss a powerful Germanic, super-subtle political philosopher. In both cases, their skepticism went to the very roots of modern liberalism and modern conservatism, respectively.

I still remember vividly first reading Trilling's essays in *Partisan Review*, later collected and published under the title *The Liberal Imagination*. They hit me with the force of a revelation. Though I had by then read widely in the modernist writers—D. H. Lawrence, T. S. Eliot, W. B. Yeats, Franz Kafka, Faulkner—it had simply never occurred to me that their vision was incompatible with the dominant socialist and liberal worldviews shared by all New York intellectuals, a group whom I regarded as a Sanhedrin of wisdom and sensibility. The "modern," it turned out, was not all of a piece; artistic sensibility and political reason were in conflict. To put it another way: the *metaphysics* of modern "avant-garde" art and the metaphysics of modern "progressive" politics were at odds with one another. Given my metaphysical bent, I took this very seriously indeed. No politics, I sensed, was viable if its own culture was radically subversive of it. The "neo" part of me was quickened and invigorated.

Trilling himself spent the rest of his life trying to reconcile "reactionary" modernism in literature with a secular liberalism. He was not a religious man, but, like Matthew Arnold whom he so much admired, his commitment to great literature was a kind of religious commitment. His "great books" had a biblical authority for him—the Bible, after all, was one of those great books. His Arnoldian liberalism kept him out of step with the "progressive" liberal community. After an early flirtation with the Left, the one certain thing about Lionel Trilling was that he was not a politically correct "progressive"—not in politics, not in education, not in cultural matters, not in manners and morals. At the same time, there existed no conservative intellectual body of thought worth noting, so that to the end Trilling remained a skeptical, out-of-step liberal, whom his students in later years would simply describe as "conservative." This lent a certain pathos to his life and thought, but it was a pathos that never came close to the pathetic. His luminous intelligence was as striking as ever as the years passed, and he coped with the disharmony of his condition by writing admiringly about Jane Austen and even Kipling instead of D. H. Lawrence or Kafka.

Leo Strauss—"Mr. Strauss," as his students called him, and still call him, posthumously—was from a different planet. A German-Jewish émigré who had been a student of medieval Jewish and Arabic philosophy, he was the quintessential philosopher, of a kind satirized in popular literature. Helpless in all practical matters, the author of very difficult and complex texts, studious and meditative, a rationalist who pressed reason to its ultimate limits, he was no kind of "intellectual," a class he held in, at best, tolerant contempt. (I would not be surprised if he had never read a line of Trilling's.) After several years at the New School in New York, he moved to the University of Chicago in 1949, where he became a most influential teacher. His students—those happy few who sat at his feet—became "Straussians," though they preferred to be known as "political theorists." (One such student was my dear friend, the late Martin Diamond, who helped me understand what Strauss was up to.) These students of Leo Strauss, in turn, have produced another generation of political theorists, many of whom have relocated to Washington, D.C., since the academic world of positivist "political science" has become ever more hostile to Strauss and "Straussians," even while his mode of thought has filtered down to an ever more numerous "happy few." This was understandable, since Strauss did not disguise his disgust for what his contemporaries called "political science."

Encountering Strauss's work produced the kind of intellectual shock that is a once-in-a-lifetime experience. He turned one's intellectual universe upside down. Suddenly, one realized that one had been looking at the history of Western political thought through the wrong end of the telescope. Instead of our looking down at them from the high vantage point of our more "advanced" era, he trained his students to look at modernity through the eyes of the "ancients" and the premoderns, accepting the premise that they were wiser and more insightful than we are. One read the premoderns, therefore, in order to understand them as they understood themselves, not to understand them better than they understood themselves. In addition, one read them in order to understand ourselves, products of the modern age, better than we are able to do on our own. In the battle between the "ancients" and the "moderns," he was on the side of the "ancients."

What made him so controversial within the academic community was his disbelief in the Enlightenment dogma that "the truth will make men free." He was an intellectual aristocrat who thought that the truth could make *some* minds free, but he was convinced that there was an inherent conflict between philosophic truth and the political order, and that the popularization and vulgarization of these truths might import unease, turmoil, and the release of popular passions hitherto held in check by tradition and religion, with utterly unpredictable, but mostly negative, consequences. Strauss was respectful of the common sense of the common man when this was guided by tradition, itself the heir to generations of practical wisdom when it came to the art of living a humane life. He was contemptuous of the modern demagogic idolatry of the common man.

Moreover, he was persuaded that the great philosophers prior to the Age of Reason, and many of the greatest poets, shared this point of view. As a result, they took the greatest care in their writing so as not, as the British would say, to "frighten the horses." To a greater or lesser degree, they had a prudential concern for the effects of their opinions, as well as for their own safety, this in an era when the secular and temporal authorities felt an obligation to suppress heterodoxy. And in most cases, especially where religion and political philosophy were concerned, they did subscribe to some heterodox views, simply by virtue of being rigorously thoughtful men. One therefore had to study, not read, their texts with a quasi-"talmudic" intensity and care, in order to distinguish between their "esoteric" and "exoteric" views. Nothing has enraged contemporary "enlightened" academic political scientists and political philosophers more than this approach to the "great books" of the premodern era. Our contemporaries do not study to learn so much as to read and express opinion.

Because Strauss believed, along with the "greats" he revered, that prudence was the greatest of practical virtues, he never allowed his aristocratic mode of thinking to determine, in any simple and linear way, his political opinions. Himself a victim of Nazism, he defended liberal democracy as the best alternative among modern political regimes, even while keeping it intellectually at a distance. He was no right-wing ideologue, as some of his critics have claimed, nor did he fit easily into contemporary conservative discourse. He did not, for instance, much admire Edmund Burke, a modern conservative icon, because he felt that Burke's emphasis on "prescription" as the basis of a social order was too parochially British, and too vulnerable to the modern insistence that we should, in the words of Tom Paine (echoed by Jefferson), "let the dead bury the dead." Modern populist conservatism, it goes without saying, was alien to him.

But one didn't study Strauss to discover ready-made political opinions. He opened modernity to serious, critical thought, of a kind that reveals Marxist and postmodern critiques to be, as they are, the paltry offshoots of modernism itself. In a sense, the premodern political philosophers served Strauss as the modern (or modernist) novelists and poets served Trilling, as a force for liberation from the contemporary progressive, liberal, or conventionally conservative outlook that prevails among our intellectual classes. Strauss, in conversation, once remarked that it was entirely proper for a young man to think Dostoyevsky was the greatest novelist, but it would be a sign of maturity when he later concluded it was Jane Austen who had the most legitimate claim to that place. Lionel Trilling, I think, would have agreed.

By the time I was twenty-two, my "intellectual formation" (as the French would say) was already beginning to take shape. The seeds of my future neoliberalism and neoconservatism had been sown, but any flowering had to come with writing, not merely reading and thinking. I wanted very much to be not only an "intellectual" but a "writer," and, with the arrogance of youth, I was convinced I could be one. An intellectual who didn't write struck me as only half an intellectual. But what kind of writer? Of that I had no idea. In college, I had written only term papers, which got me good grades but which, I, knew, revealed little by way of literary talent. There were, of course, the writers for *Partisan Review*—wonderful stylists like Dwight Macdonald and Mary McCarthy—but I sensed that they were not suitable models for me. They were out of my class, as it were. I recall a conversation I had with Saul Bellow, about a year later. I had then joined my wife in Chicago, where she was doing graduate work at the University of Chicago and where I was waiting to go into the army. Saul and I were friends and neighbors. He was just publishing his first novel, and I was writing occasional book reviews for *The New Leader*, at which my college friend Daniel Bell was an indulgent editor. I confided to Saul that I thought I had the potential to be a writer. He looked at me suspiciously and asked: "What kind of writer?" (Saul has always been convinced, as most novelists are, that the world does not need more than one novelist.) I thought for a moment and then said briskly, "Well, good enough to write for *The New Yorker*." He roared. At that time, we intellectuals did not think too much of that slick magazine.

What had given me even this degree of confidence was one of those strokes of luck that shape careers. In a bookshop that sold "remainders"—I think it was the Marboro Bookshop in Times Square—I picked up, for twenty-nine cents, a copy of John Crowe Ransom's *God Without Thunder*. I had never heard of Ransom but loved the title, since I, too, had little use for such a god. The book enchanted me, not so much for its theme, already familiar as well as congenial from my religious readings—by then I was into Charles Péguy and Léon Bloy—as for its style. That style was lucid, straightforward, unpretentious, but brightened with flashes of irony and wit. "That's the style for me," I thought, "I can do it!" Some months later, I submitted an unsolicited book review to *Kenyon Review*, which Ransom was then editing. I received a pleasant, handwritten rejection note, which strengthened my high opinion of him.

Another stroke of luck. At about the same time that I discovered John Crowe Ransom, I rediscovered W. H. Auden. To be sure, I had read his poems when they appeared in *Partisan Review*, had "appreciated" them, but I read them as a casual consumer of poetry, not as a writer reads, with an active in-

tellect. Learning to read in that new way I owed to Ransom, whose other writing I hastily searched out. There, he introduced me to the New Criticism. Applying myself to Cleanth Brooks, I. A. Richards, and others, I learned to read
poetry, really to read, as had never been possible for me before, simply because
no one had ever told me how to do it. And then I came across an older issue
of *Partisan Review*, where I found Auden's "September, 1939," whose opening
lines have echoed in my mind forever after:

> *I sit in one of the dives*
> *On Fifty-second Street*
> *Uncertain and afraid*
> *As the clever hopes expire*
> *Of a low, dishonest decade . . .*

I was certainly vulnerable to the sentiments and mood of this poem, but
what struck me forcefully was that phrase, "low, dishonest decade." What a
powerful use of ordinary words! "Clever hopes" is good too. Then I read
through all of Auden's longer poems, most of them in this edgy, conversational
style, savoring the language. They are uneven, of course, but a few wonderful
phrases can, for me, redeem an entire poem. In later years, I have had a similar experience with a few other poets (Eliot, Yeats, Larkin), but much of modern poetry, I confess, evokes no response within me. This is poetry written for
other poets, or for those engaged in the academic exegetical analysis of poems.
I take it on faith that Wallace Stevens is a major poet, but I cannot read him.
I once had the idea of compiling a brief anthology of poems for ambitious
young journalists who wished to write better, but nothing came of it. Instead,
I tell them to read Shakespeare's sonnets in their spare time—wasted advice, in
most cases.

I have mentioned the role of luck in the shaping of the mind, but it is clear
to me that my entire life has been one instance of good luck after another. My
relatively brief sojourn among the Trotskyists, for instance—I left before I was
twenty-two—was immensely fruitful, and not only because I witnessed, close
up, very sharp wits in ideological conflict. My becoming a Trotskyist, rather
than something else, was itself an accident. I knew nothing of radical politics
when I entered City College, but I did have two friends from Boys' High who
had accompanied me to college. We constituted a *troika* for the rest of our
lives—the late Harold Lubin, Earl Raab, and myself. Earl was an aesthete; he
had, in high school, introduced me to the short stories of James Joyce and
Thomas Mann. I was confused about my politics, so it devolved upon Hal

Lubin to explore the ideological terrain and report back to us what kind of radicals we should be. In later life, as it happens, both Earl and I remained politically involved, while Hal opted out and became a professor of literature. But at the time, he was more serious, more passionate, and more optimistic about "creating a better world" than we were. When he explained to us that the Trotskyist student group was the most interesting and least tarred with the sins of Stalinism—it was the first I had heard of such sins—we promptly followed him into the Trotskyist "movement," as we then called the dozen or so young men who sat around, reading and arguing about radical politics. Young men, because City College in those days was an all-male institution [only the night school was co-ed], with our sexual energies finding an outlet in either study or politics.

But the larger Trotskyist organization was, thank goodness, coed. Shortly after I was graduated from City College, I was assigned to attend meetings of a "branch" of young Trotskyists in Bensonhurst, in Brooklyn, at the opposite end of the borough where I lived. I dutifully attended the meetings, which were quite farcical since we were trying to recruit young blacks in the neighborhood, who were sensible enough not to take us seriously. But at these meetings I noticed a girl—she was eighteen, it turned out—who sat quietly at the other end of the small room. Her name was Gertrude Himmelfarb, but she was called "Bea." She had a trim figure and a strong, handsome face that radiated intelligence and sensibility. I noticed her for some weeks before approaching her and asking her out. In truth, I was already in love with her without even knowing her. She said "yes" quietly. And so we "went out," which is to say we went to the Saturday night movies—in cosmopolitan Manhattan rather than provincial Brooklyn—and saw only foreign movies since we were cultural snobs. After our first excursion, I already knew that this was the girl I wanted to marry. After the third or fourth movie, I finally asked her to marry me; perhaps because she was weary of subtitles, she said yes. Thus began what my friend Daniel Bell later described as "the best marriage of our generation," a judgment I have no quarrel with. We are about to celebrate our fifty-third wedding anniversary.

In retrospect, it is interesting that it never even crossed my mind to suggest a "love affair," or a "relationship," or whatever other connection young people experiment with these days. Many of the young Trotskyists were bohemian in their "lifestyles," but that was not for me. Trotskyist or no, radical socialist or no, I was bourgeois to the core. I sought no sexual adventures or experiments, but wanted a girl to love and marry. Bea was of a like mind. We even waited a year to get her parents' consent, a consent withheld on the grounds that they were not about to permit their lovely and brilliant daughter to marry a young man who was earning $13.89 a week as an apprentice machinist. But when the Japanese bombed Pearl Harbor, and my salary had reached $22 a week, they relented. We were married on January 18, 1942, when she was nineteen and I was just short of my twenty-second birthday.

With such a bourgeois character, one which I seem to have been born with, it is not surprising that, shortly before this twenty-second birthday, I (and Bea) had left the Trotskyists—in a state of pleasant and intellectually productive disaffection, but with no regrets. I had received an excellent political education of a special kind. I made several lifelong friends. And I had gained a lifelong wife. That is why I don't really mind when some journalist, even today, a half-century later, casually refers to me as an "ex-Trotskyist." I regard myself as lucky to have been a young Trotskyist, and I have not a single bitter memory. Even when Irving Howe "expelled" us for having had the ideological impudence to resign, I regarded it, and still do, as comic relief. Oddly enough, he never quite forgave me for leaving so many years before he did.

My subsequent army experience, as an infantryman in Western Europe, also had some significant, and on the whole benign, influences on me. I was shot at but not hit, and, in what military historians call "battles," did my share of shooting, though in the confusion I doubt that I ever hit anyone or anything. When V-E Day came and I was transported to Marseilles for shipment to the Far East, so as to help conquer Japan, the atom bomb was dropped and such shipments ceased. My wartime experience in Germany, however, did have the effect of dispelling any remnants of anti-authority sentiments (always weak, I now think) that were cluttering up my mind. My fellow soldiers were too easily inclined to loot, to rape, and to shoot prisoners of war. Only army vigilance kept them in check. At the same time, observing German women and young girls, living among the rubble and selling their bodies for a few packs of cigarettes, the currency of the day, rid me of any anti-German feelings which, as a Jew, might otherwise have been present in me. Even the subsequent revelation of the Holocaust could not make me feel differently about ordinary Germans. They, too, had suffered, more than most Americans realize. And I was not so convinced that the American soldiers I knew were a different breed of humanity from their German counterparts.

I spent about a year in Marseilles, and it was a kind of postgraduate sabbatical. Because I was a college graduate, I was assigned to headquarters, first in the library, where I pretended to understand the Dewey Decimal System, and then as chief company clerk. It was a small headquarters, a point of transshipment of American GIs going home, and I was assigned two young, intelligent prisoners of war who had been clerks in the German army. They were so much better than I in clerking that they were soon doing all the paperwork, leaving me to pursue my studies. My high school and college French stood me in good stead, needing only some refreshing to become usable. I spent my days reading French journals—*Les Temps Modernes*, *Critique*, *L'Esprit*, *Les Cahiers du Sud*, and others. I was especially fond of *Critique*, which gave excellent critical accounts of authors who were worth reading about but not worth reading. This went along with various philosophical-theological books by the likes of Jean Wahl, Rachel Bespaloff, and Lev Shestov, who made Kierkegaard's leap of faith seem like a modest hop. French intellectual life was then boiling over with a passionate interest in ideas. Existentialism was the rage, and I became quite knowledgeable about that depressing philosophy, without however being depressed by it since it was intellectually so exciting. I even read a novel by Simone de Beauvoir that set my teeth on edge, which may have been her existentialist intention. Enjoying anything, including existentialism itself, seemed to represent for existentialists some kind of spiritual transgression.

When I returned, once again a civilian, to the States, where Bea was finishing her graduate studies at the University of Chicago, I was immediately informed that another sabbatical was in prospect. Bea had received a fellowship to go to the University of Cambridge to work on the papers of Lord Acton, the subject of her thesis. But before we left, one small thing happened that was to be of considerable importance to me. Bea told me of this new magazine that had been born in my absence, a "serious" (i.e., quite highbrow) Jewish magazine called *Commentary*, which actually paid as much as $100 for a contribution. I read what issues were available and decided that there was no reason I should not be a contributor. So I sat down and quickly wrote a very short story about my encounter with a young Jewish survivor in a displaced persons camp outside Marseilles. To my delight and astonishment, they immediately accepted it and promptly paid as well. This last was not unimportant, because we had calculated that Bea's fellowship money and what she had saved from my army allotment would give us a budget of $12 a week in Cambridge. *Commentary*'s fee added another $1.50 a week. What I could not foresee at the time was that the *Commentary* connection was to play such a crucial part in my life.

We really need not have worried about our English budget, since there was nothing to buy in Cambridge. Food was still stringently rationed, and we mostly lived on fish and chips or cheese sandwiches. Rent was cheap too, for our furnished room with toilet upstairs and a sink in the backyard. But this was the year of the coal shortage and the Great Freeze, so we slept in our overcoats and poor Bea, who had developed chilblains, had to wear gloves when she worked on the Acton papers lest her bloody fingers stain them. Being young, we shrugged all this off. Cambridge was lovely, positively exotic to our eyes, and we were leading the kind of bookish life that suited us. I started writing again, pieces on English affairs for *The New Leader* and a couple of book reviews for *Commentary*. I also wrote a novel, in a style that was a bastard mixture of Saul Bellow and Jean Giraudoux, whose novels I was then enchanted by. Fortunately, I never tried to get it published and eventually incinerated it. I knew in my bones that I was not born to be a novelist. Indeed, had it been published it would have been a major disaster for me, since I then almost surely would have wasted some years (perhaps even a lifetime) doing something I was not really suited for.

We returned to New York in 1947 with a couple of hundred dollars in the bank and no visible prospects. Bea wanted to write her thesis, and I wanted a job that enabled me, in my spare time if necessary, to keep on writing. Once again, my luck held out. My brother-in-law, Milton Himmelfarb, then a researcher at the American Jewish Committee (which published *Commentary*), told me that he had heard that *Commentary* was looking for a couple of junior editors. I promptly applied and was thrilled to learn that I had been accepted. My salary was $3,600 a year, more than enough to allow us to rent a dark two-room apartment on Broadway and Ninety-sixth Street, immediately above a Bickford's cafeteria (now long since gone). The smells were awful, but the neighborhood was fine—at last we had our own apartment, and in the heart of Manhattan, no less! Interestingly, it never occurred to us to look for an apartment in Greenwich Village. Bohemia held no attractions for us, though we were then childless.

My colleagues at *Commentary* were an extraordinary group:

Elliot Cohen, the editor and founder, had edited *The Menorah Journal* at Columbia, to which his classmate Lionel Trilling contributed, and he then spent two decades in the bureaucratic wilderness of Jewish philanthropy. He was a thoroughly assimilated southern Jew whose interest was in Jews, not Judaism. He was very intelligent and wrote well, in a somewhat florid style. I liked and respected him, while he had a kind of fatherly affection for me.

Clement Greenberg, ten years older than I, was even then a prominent art critic. Clem, like Elliot, was interested in Jews (though not very interested) as distinct from Judaism. He wrote for *Partisan Review*, not for *Commentary*, and was our main link with the intellectual community around *PR*. Because he could read German, he became the editor for a brilliant group of German-Jewish émigré writers (most notably Hannah Arendt). Though he had a reputation as having a terrible temper, leading even to an occasional brawl, we

saw none of that. Toward his younger colleagues he was always genial, if distant. I recall vividly, for obvious reasons, his once offering to acquire for me a
large Jackson Pollock painting for $10,000. It was a friendly gesture, but I de-
clined. I didn't have $10,000, we didn't have space in our apartment for so
large a painting, and I didn't like (still don't like) "abstract expressionist" art.
That painting would today be worth millions. But, since I still don't like abstract expressionist art, I have never felt particularly regretful.

Robert Warshow was, for me, the most troubling of my colleagues. We
got along well enough—played poker together, that sort of thing—but he always made me feel uncomfortable. There was a hard, cold, almost affectless
streak in him, clothed in the purest rationalism. Like Elliot and Clem, his
interest in Jews was "ethnic," though, I always felt, as minimal as such an interest could be for an editor on a Jewish magazine. But he was a truly brilliant
writer, with a cool, chiseled, powerful style that suited his talent and personality perfectly. He would write in longhand, in pencil, on a yellow pad, in a
very large handwriting that permitted only six or seven lines a page, and when
he brought in his essays to be typed they were letter-perfect—no deletions, no
additions, not even a correction in punctuation. I have never seen anything
like it. It's as if every single word in the essay was preformed in his mind before
he sat down to write. Several of those essays, mainly on popular culture—and
there was very little serious writing about popular culture then—are deservedly
famous today.

Nathan Glazer, whom I had known at City College—he was a couple of
years behind me—became one of my closest friends and remains so to this
day. (He was later to succeed Daniel Bell as my co-editor of *The Public Interest*.) Intelligent, amiable, intellectually curious, he was a sociologist who was
skeptical of most of what then passed for sociology, and established a valuable
department, "The Study of Man," which summarized and criticized new
trends in the social sciences. He also had a more intense Jewish background
than Clem or Bob, and together we constituted the "Jewish" editors; I spe-
cialized in Jewish religious writing and he in the secular life of the Jewish community. We were also both more "political" than the others, having emerged
from the ideological hothouse of City College.

Richard Clurman, fresh from the University of Chicago, joined *Commentary* the same day I did. Bright and articulate, he was more interested in journalism than Judaism. We were not surprised when he left to work for *Time*
magazine, where he had a distinguished career.

My position at *Commentary* brought me to the margin of the world of *Partisan Review*, since the two magazines overlapped one another on the political

spectrum. Only on the margin, because the *PR* crowd was older than we were and far less bourgeois in what we now call their "lifestyle." Still, it was exciting to meet and get to know all these famous people I had been reading for the past ten years. My most vivid memory of our excursion into the world of *PR* occurred at a cocktails-and-buffet party at the apartment of William Phillips, the co-editor of the magazine. I had piled my plate with food and sat down in the middle of a couch, assuming Bea would join me there. Instead, what happened was this: Mary McCarthy sat down on my right, Hannah Arendt on my left, and then Diana Trilling pulled up a chair and sat directly opposite me. I was trapped, and I remember thinking, as I sank into a terrified paralysis of body and mind, that this was an event to remember. For the next hour, they argued about Freud and psychoanalysis while I sat there mute, not even touching my food lest eating seem like a rude intrusion into their high conversation. I kept wondering why my wife wasn't rescuing me, but she sat across the room eating and giggling. When the conversation finally broke up, I had not the faintest recollection of anything that had been said.

During my first years at *Commentary*, I wrote only on philosophy, religion, and occasionally on literature. My political views were what we would now call neoliberal, but I had no interest in expressing them. What brought me back into the world of political controversy was the extraordinary profusion of opinions sympathetic to, even apologetic for, the Stalinist regime in Russia among so many leading liberals. These opinions were dominant in *The Nation*, *The New Republic*, the *New York Times*, and Hollywood, so that anti-Stalinist liberals came to feel, as indeed they were, an isolated group within the larger intellectual community. Eventually, I was sufficiently irritated to write a short political piece.

The occasion was a book by Carey McWilliams, a leading "progressive" and a very stylish writer. We had actually published an article by him in *Commentary*, on how "social discrimination"—e.g., barring Jews from membership in country clubs—was part of a larger pattern of discrimination that sustained the hegemony of a ruling class. I did not like the piece because I did not see why any Jew should want to join a country club where Jews were not welcome. (In truth, at that time I didn't see the point of anyone belonging to a country club.) But Elliot, the editor, understood that this was an issue that did matter to those wealthy Jews who, as leaders of the American Jewish Committee, financed *Commentary*. He was quite right; the article evoked a chorus of appreciative approval from the AJC. Since relations between the AJC and *Commentary* were always under strain, our political posture being too anti-Communist for the more "mainline" liberal AJC members, this was no small matter.

McWilliams's book was a slick, prototypical exposition of this "mainline" liberalism, studded with a disingenuous rhetoric that cleverly wedded this liberalism, in the most natural way, with a discreet apologia for Stalinist fellow-traveling. My Trotskyist background, as well as my reading in literary criticism, made it easy for me to dissect his rhetoric and reveal its underlying purpose. To my astonishment, the review was enthusiastically received by people whose opinions I respected. I was astonished because political writing was so easy that I had no idea it was, as seemed to be the case, in scarce supply—at least so far as "our side" was concerned.

Well, one thing leads to another. Encouraged by the reception of that book review, I wrote what was to be the most controversial essay of my career. It was 1952, and McCarthyism was the issue of the day. The problem for liberal intellectuals was to define an attitude toward the civil liberties of Communists. (There was, so far as I was concerned, no problem in defining one's opposition to Senator McCarthy.) Most "mainline" liberals, many of them "fellow-travelers" in varying degrees, did not argue in favor of toleration of Communists as Communists, a perfectly acceptable opinion which I respected even if I didn't fully agree with it. They preferred to regard the question of whether anyone was or was not a Communist as an irrelevancy, since for them Communists were simply "progressives" who were more outspoken and militant than the rest of the breed. It was the disingenuousness, the hypocrisy, even the intellectual cowardice of such people that moved me to write my article in *Commentary*. In that article, I had a passing reference to Senator McCarthy as a "vulgar demagogue" who was making an impression on the American people because they knew him to be anti-Communist (as they were), whereas they knew no such thing about most of the leading spokesmen of the American liberal community. This was during the Korean War, a war in which as many American soldiers died as were later to die in Vietnam, and popular passions were high. And here were our leading liberals, many of whom were publicly suspicious of American motives in this war (though not of Communist motives), becoming passionate only in the defense of the civil liberties of American Communists, who openly supported the North Korean regime. My article dissected some of these leading liberal spokesmen, demonstrating that their ostensible concern for the civil liberties of Communists arose, more often than not, out of an ideological sympathy for Communists as "fellow progressives."

What a storm my article created! In truth, American liberals were so hysterical about McCarthy that they simply could not think straight about the issue I was addressing. My unforgivable sin, I subsequently realized, was in *not* being hysterical about McCarthy, whom I assumed to be a transient, ugly phenomenon with no political future. That I had no use for "witch-hunting" I assumed the readers of *Commentary* would take for granted. On the other hand, I did have the temerity to suggest that, while the American Communists had their civil rights under the Constitution, no American had a "right" to government employment, and the idea of "civil liberties" could not be stretched to give Communists, or even their loyal fellow-travelers, such a right. Nor did anyone's civil liberties make him immune to public opprobrium. The Communists, after all, were a totalitarian group hostile to our constitutional democracy. How we defined their civil liberties was a matter of prudence, not principle. After the experience of the Weimar Republic, this seemed to me a reasonable approach. Perhaps I didn't express these thoughts with the clarity they needed. But it would not have mattered, since most of my infuriated critics had an agenda of their own.

I survived the tumult and the shouting that article provoked because many prominent liberals thought that I had made a point worth making, one not at all offensive to an authentic liberalism which understood that there were indeed enemies on the left. The main effect was to define me publicly, for the first time, as a political writer with a voice of my own. The timing, as it happened, was not of the best. My situation at *Commentary*, after five wonderful years, had become intolerable. Elliot Cohen was in the process of having a nervous breakdown that would later cost him his life. I didn't understand the tragedy that was happening; all I knew was that his editorial interventions had become ever more capricious and arbitrary. As the managing editor, I found myself pinned between authors and editor, trying to negotiate acceptable solutions to the problems he was causing. Finally I felt so miserable that I had to resign. I came home and broke the news to Bea. She had news of her own. She was pregnant.

Job hunting was a new experience for me, and fortunately it did not last long. I applied for a position on *Fortune*, where a senior editor was an old friend of Elliot's who had become an acquaintance of mine. (He, too, had once been a Trotskyist!) He gently turned me down, essentially on the grounds that my kind of writing was too "highbrow" for them. Occasionally I wonder, with a shudder, what my life would have been like had they hired me.

It was Sidney Hook who came to my rescue, a practice he made a habit of doing for the rest of my life. Something called the American Committee for Cultural Freedom had recently been formed, associated with the Congress for Cultural Freedom in Paris. It was an organization of anti-Communist liberals with the mission of counterbalancing the pro-Communist liberals and *gauchistes* who were then so active in the intellectual worlds of the Western democracies, including our own. The position of executive director of the ACCF was then vacant, and Hook, who liked my political writing, campaigned successfully to get the job for me. Apparently I was acceptable even to those liberals on the Committee who thought my *Commentary* article had gone somewhat overboard.

The next ten months or so were tedium interspersed with crises. The tedium was the administrative chores, which I coped with easily enough. (I have always found administration a much-overrated skill.) The crises were internally generated by a heterogeneous group of intellectuals whose common cause turned out to be not quite common enough. There was a small group on the right, led by James Burnham, who if not pro-McCarthy was certainly anti-anti-McCarthy. There was a much larger group on the center-left, led by Arthur Schlesinger Jr. and Richard Rovere, who believed the Committee should be, above all, actively anti-McCarthy. Somewhere in the middle were a handful of very articulate people, led by Diana Trilling, who were unhappy with the ideological posture of the Congress in Paris, which was anti-Communist but which, in an effort to appeal to the anti-Communist Left, was not simply or belligerently pro-American. I mediated between these groups, not fully sharing the views of any in this respect—my guide was Sidney Hook, who was the Committee's moving spirit—but all such mediation could do was to put out one firestorm of controversy and prepare for the next. My only satisfaction was the organization of two public debates, the first (naturally) on the relation of religion to democracy (Paul Tillich versus Sidney Hook), the second on "containment" versus "liberation" in American foreign policy (Arthur Schlesinger versus James Burnham). They were very good debates, attended by some five hundred people, and the Committee actually made some money on them. In the end, however, the spirit of factionalism was bound to prevail, as it always does among intellectuals with ideological passions and little political common sense.

I was about at the end of my tether and tenure when Sidney, once again, came to the rescue. The Congress, he informed me, was interested in starting an English-language cultural-intellectual-political magazine in Paris to counteract the predominant influence of anti-American and often Communist fellow-traveling magazines in all the democracies, not only of Western Europe but in Asia as well. Would I like to be considered for the position of editor? That question answered itself. The prospect of editing such a magazine, in Paris no less, made my head spin with anticipation.

I had not, at that time, met anyone from the Congress, so some interviewing was in order. I flew to Paris—well, from there on it's something of a blur.

On either the first or second night Michael Josselson, the Congress's executive director, took me to dinner at the home of the ex-Communist novelist and critic Manès Sperber. I no longer recall who was there because after the appetizer of garlic-packed snails I passed out. (It turned out that I am allergic to garlic in large doses.) They laid me out on a dining room couch, Sperber fed me some pills, and they proceeded to an evening of fine food and animated conversation while I lay on that couch, regaining consciousness intermittently in order to throw up. For the rest of my trip I was violently sick. I do recall going to London with Mike to have lunch at the Savoy with the leaders of the British Committee for Cultural Freedom, among them Malcolm Muggeridge, T. R. Fyvel, George Lichtheim, and Fred Warburg, the publisher (Secker & Warburg, as it then was). I recall, while at the table rather than the "loo," their making a very strong pitch for locating the magazine in London—bereft of a good literary magazine since the death of Cyril Connolly's *Horizon*—and for making Stephen Spender (a member of the British Committee but then away teaching in Cincinnati) my co-editor. Mike found their case very persuasive, especially after Muggeridge offered to raise the money for Spender's salary. So did I, though I really would have preferred Paris. Anyway, I staggered home to inform my wife that we would be living in London after all. She, being as much an Anglophile as I was a Francophile, was happy to hear the news. A month or so later, I flew to London to find a place for us to live, to rent a temporary office, and to hire someone to help put out the magazine.

That was early in 1953, shortly before the Coronation. I had committed myself to a first issue in October—for an untitled magazine that wasn't even on a drawing board. I recall T. S. Matthews of *Time*, then in London ostensibly to fund some kind of highbrow British magazine, telling me that I was being wildly unrealistic. In the event, my magazine came out on schedule; his never did.

I rented a shabby two-room office and hired a secretary-assistant in the person of Margot Walmsley—a splendid woman, prematurely widowed, who stayed with the magazine until the bitter end, by which time she had become managing editor. (It also turned out that, on practically no money at all, she gave the liveliest cocktail parties at which all sorts of people showed up, some very interesting, some merely important.) The two of us put out our first issue. I solicited articles from my friends in the United States, Stephen, still in Cincinnati, wrote to his friends in London, we agreed on a title after much bickering, I found a printer and distributor, I designed a magazine modeled (with variations) on *Commentary*, and in the fall of 1953 the first issue did come out, as promised.

The history of *Encounter*, including the CIA connection, has by now been well told by Peter Coleman in *The Liberal Conspiracy*, and told less well by others, so I shall say little about it. I do feel compelled to say, however, that my relations with Stephen Spender were, against the odds, quite good, all things considered. After all, he was ten years older than I, infinitely more distinguished, and was far more sensitive to the opinions of British literary circles than I was. So there was always the possibility of friction, a possibility that was realized less often than I had feared. A poet, a man of letters, and a gentleman, Stephen was absolutely no kind of editor. I ran the magazine, he made major contributions to it. He brought W. H. Auden and Isaiah Berlin to *Encounter*, and the imprimatur that resulted was significant. He also solicited the most famous article ever printed in *Encounter*, Nancy Mitford's "U and Non-U," which provoked the popular press to a frenzy of "research" into the class-specific usages of the British vocabulary. This was not exactly the kind of article that our publishers in Paris had in mind for the magazine, and they, like all non-Brits, were mystified by the commotion it caused.

The 1950s were, despite Suez, the golden decade of England's postwar history, and we were lucky to be there then. The dollar was strong, and my modest salary, less so by British standards, went a long way. We lived in a succession of furnished houses and could even afford an *au pair* girl, which permitted Bea to continue her research and writing. Her biography of Lord Acton had already been published, to a laudatory review in the *Times Literary Supplement*, so she was of interest to the British in her own right. We made many friends, amid a host of acquaintances.

Very few of our friends and acquaintances came from Stephen's circle, the literary establishment. They were simply not my kind of people. There was never any serious intellectual or political talk at their parties, just malicious, witty, often brilliantly witty, gossip. I never felt more solemnly New York–Jewish than at one of these occasions, and never more bourgeois. They all seemed to have more money than we had, or at least lived more extravagantly and adventurously than we did. Many of them could fairly be called upper-class, but those who weren't affected upper-class mannerisms and modes of speech. As an American, I was to some degree outside the British class system, but only to a degree. The thought of attempting an entry never crossed my mind.

Our closest friends, almost inevitably, were older Jewish ex-radicals who were now on *Encounter*'s ideological wavelength and among whom we felt at home. These included Jane Degras, historian of the Comintern at the Royal Institute of International Affairs; T. R. Fyvel, who had been a close friend of George Orwell and who was now at the BBC; George Lichtheim, the fiercely independent neo-Marxist and anti-Communist; and Mark Abrams, who introduced opinion polling and market research to Britain. In addition, among the Labour MPs—the very first politicians I had ever met in the flesh—there was Woodrow Wyatt, now a prominent conservative journalist who sits in the House of Lords; Anthony Crosland, who was trying to redefine socialism in terms of simple social and economic equality, and who was fascinated by the "City College sociologists," especially my friends Daniel Bell and Seymour Martin Lipset; and Denis Healey, who transfixed the visiting Lionel Trilling at dinner one night with his knowledge of contemporary literature, leaving me to disabuse Trilling of the notion that all Members of Parliament were like Healey. The only conservative MP we were friendly with was Angus Maude, who should have been Prime Minister, but his fellow Tories thought him to be far too intelligent for that responsible position.

There were, however, conservatives not in Parliament with whom we established ties of friendship. They included Malcolm Muggeridge, then editor of *Punch* and the *enfant terrible* of British journalism, and Michael Oakeshott, who succeeded Harold Laski in his chair at the London School of Economics and who was already on his way to becoming one of the most distinguished conservative thinkers of this century. By marrying, as it were, Oakeshott to Muggeridge, three gifted young conservative journalists were born. They were Peregrine Worsthorne, Colin Welch, and Henry Fairlie, with all of whom we became fast friends. They had no counterparts in America at the time. And, of course, there was the steady stream of American visitors to enliven our days: Dan Bell, the Glazers, the Sidney Hooks, the Trillings, the Jason Epsteins, and numerous others.

In London, though our social life was politically ecumenical, my (and Bea's) evolving discontent with social democracy and liberalism continued. As an American and a co-editor of *Encounter*, I kept aloof from British politics—my writing for *Encounter* consisted of essays on Machiavelli, Tacitus, and the Marquis de Sade—but I found my conservative friends far more interesting than the others. I hadn't known any conservatives—as distinct from ex-radicals with budding right-wing opinions—in New York, and I was fascinated by the fact that they felt perfectly at ease with themselves as conservatives, neither apologetic nor unduly contentious. They were, after all, heirs to a long tradition of conservative politics and conservative thought in Britain, whereas there was no such tradition in the United States. Though in a distinct minority, they were accepted by society at large as having a legitimate place on the political spectrum. More than that, their claim to government could hardly be dismissed, with Winston Churchill still the overpowering figure that he was.

My discontent with social democracy *cum* liberalism had absolutely nothing to do with economics, of which I was perfectly ignorant. It did have to do with foreign policy, where I was, on general principles, a "realist" to the core, contemptuous of the Left's bland assumption that the class struggle was natural but that national or purely ideological conflicts were not. I was equally contemptuous of the Left's predisposition to see Communists as, in some sense, a wayward extremity of the Left, ultimately redeemable by therapeutic strategies. (My Trotskyist background stood me in good stead here.) The Cold War seemed to me not deplorable but inevitable. In contrast, the kind of liberal sentiments and thinking that went into the formation of the United Nations struck me as not at all inevitable and certainly deplorable. Even the so-called right-wing Labourites, who were friendly to *Encounter*, felt they had to be cautious in their anti-Communism, lest they appeared to be impugning their own socialist beliefs. For my own part, I found their socialist beliefs, especially the blind commitment to egalitarian politics across the board, ever more questionable. The prospect of the entire world evolving into a cheerless global Sweden, smug and unhappy, had no attraction for me.

Though we felt truly privileged passing these years in London, we had every intention of returning to America when the first opportunity presented itself. The longer we lived in Britain, the more American we felt. When our son, William, reached school age, we sent him to the French Lycée; we did not want him to return an imitation Brit. And when our daughter, Elizabeth, was born, we promptly registered her at the American embassy. I sensed that, though life in England could then be more pleasant, in so many ways, than coping with the tensions of American life, I also sensed that British politics and British culture were becoming ever more provincial. The United States, it was easy to foresee, was going to be the place where the action was, and, somewhat to my own surprise, I felt keenly that I wanted somehow to participate in that action. We had good friends in London who, as American expatriates, made very decent lives for themselves. But not for a moment did we have even the most fleeting idea of emulating them. Oddly enough, the sphere of action I had in mind for myself was domestic politics rather than foreign affairs. I intuited, rather than knew, that after the Eisenhower interregnum we were living through, American politics was going to become a lot more interesting.

The opportunity to return came as the result of an intervention in our lives of an old friend, Paul Jacobs, then a staff writer for *The Reporter*. The editor of that magazine—I think it was Theodore Draper—had just left, and the publisher and editor-in-chief, Max Ascoli, was seeking a replacement. Paul, then more sympathetic to *Encounter* than he was later to be, recommended me to

Max, who was intrigued enough to bring me to New York for an interview. I went with trepidation because editors of *The Reporter* seemed to come and go, and Max was reputed to be a difficult man to work with. The meeting went well. I liked him. He was an Italian antifascist émigré who had taught at the New School for Social Research in New York before marrying Marian Rosenwald, a very wealthy woman whose family had founded Sears, Roebuck. I was actually familiar with some academic articles he had written, which pleased him. He was also pleased by my European experience and my personal acquaintance with Raymond Aron, Ignazio Silone (who co-edited the Italian counterpart to *Encounter*), and Isaiah Berlin. He made me a generous offer and, eager to return home, I accepted. However things worked out, I reckoned, at least I would have some kind of head start in a career in the States.

We arrived in New York at the very end of 1958, rented a large, old apartment on Riverside Drive for $270 a month—Marian was shocked to learn that rents were so high—and quickly settled in. It did not take me long to learn that working with, in truth, under, Max Ascoli was as difficult as the reports would have it. He was kind, generous, and intelligent, but he was also egomaniacal, and sometimes tyrannical in behavior. He was also extremely snobbish. When I solicited and received a book review by George Steiner, then a young writer on the London *Economist*, Max was reluctant to publish it. But when he discovered that Steiner was the son of a well-known international banker, his attitude changed radically. We agreed that I was to be "reintroduced to America" by focusing at first on "the back of the book"—book reviews, the arts, cultural reportage—which seemed sensible enough. The trouble was that he wanted to keep me there. The political articles were his domain, over which he exercised a lordly sovereignty. Unfortunately, he was not really a good editor—his command of the English language left much to be desired—and in general he preferred second-rate contributors whose copy he could regard as raw material. Even more unfortunately, he regarded his long editorials, usually on the importance of NATO, as the magazine's centerpiece and very reason for being. Indeed, he bitterly resented any article that caused too much comment because it distracted attention from his editorials. He was always competing with his writers, and the only way he could win was to prefer the second-rate to anything better.

I first understood this clearly in the case of Daniel Patrick Moynihan. I was introduced to Pat, who was then teaching at Syracuse, by Bob Bingham, our managing editor, who had worked with Pat in the Democratic reform movement in New York City. He thought Pat might be a possible contributor, and so we had lunch. I was overwhelmed. Pat had enough wonderful ideas for articles to fill up his own magazine. We finally agreed that he would write a four-thousand-word piece on automobile safety, an issue he had worked on when he was an assistant to Governor Averell Harriman. I had high hopes, but they fell far short of the reality when, a little more than a week later, I received a ten-thousand-word article on automobile safety that was an editor's dream. I wanted to publish it *in toto* and feature it, but Max wouldn't have it. The article was cut to perhaps six thousand words, and when it attracted a lot of attention and won all sorts of prizes, Max was not at all happy. He soon made it clear that while he was willing to publish more Moynihan, it should not be too often and not at too great length.

I don't want to paint too bleak a picture. *The Reporter* was a better magazine than my own frustrating experience would suggest. It just wasn't a magazine where I could play a significant editorial role. The staff was friendly, and I liked them. My friendship with Pat Moynihan flourished, and there was also this young researcher, Meg Greenfield, in whom I had an ally in trying to enliven the magazine. But after one year, I felt trapped and decided to leave. Max was understanding and gracious, gave me a generous severance payment, and once again I was without employment.

I knew exactly what I wanted to do next—to write a book that would be a critical examination of the evolution of the American democracy, a kind of sequel to Tocqueville and Henry Adams. For three months I read furiously, took a large bundle of notes, and then realized it was all an exercise in futility. I was not a book writer. I did not have the patience and I lacked the necessary intellectual rigor to bring my ideas into some kind of consistent thesis. I learned a lot in those three months, and it stood me in good stead in the years to follow. But I needed a job, and, fortunately, soon found a congenial one. Through a mutual friend, I was introduced to Arthur Rosenthal, publisher and editor in chief at Basic Books, a small publishing house specializing in psychoanalytical works. Arthur wanted to expand the list to include the social sciences, and that was my mission, first on a part-time basis but in the course of the next ten years as executive vice president of the firm.

Arthur was a wonderful man to work for, and never in those ten years did we have a serious argument. I did what I was supposed to do, and I think I did it well. But it did not take me long to realize that though publishing was a business I could be passably good at, I lacked the kind of patience, passion, and commitment that is the mark of an authentic editor-publisher. Arthur had it; I didn't. I was exasperated by the fact that once you had wed a good idea to its potential author, it took two years at least for him to deliver a manuscript (often not the book you had had in mind in the first place), another year to get it edited and published, and then it might or might not sell for reasons which, so far as I could see, had little to do with its intrinsic merit or lack thereof. The cure for such exasperation was for me to do some writing on the side.

At that time, the Great Society was getting into full swing, and I found myself increasingly skeptical of the liberal ideas behind it and of the programs they spawned. I started to write occasional op-ed pieces for *The New Leader*, making the arguments in support of my skepticism; but, increasingly, I felt that something more was needed. Not surprisingly, that "something more" took shape in my mind as another magazine. The only existing conservative journal, the *National Review*, was not to our tastes—at that time insufficiently analytical and "intellectual," too stridently hostile to the course of American politics ever since 1932. I discussed these thoughts with my friend Dan Bell, then at Columbia, who shared my skepticism, though less from an ideological point of view than from that of a scrupulous social scientist. We even went around to a few wealthy individuals someone or other had put us in touch with, but they were immune to our enthusiasm.

It was not until the beginning of 1965 that a potential publisher appeared on the scene. At a dinner at Sidney Hook's, we found ourselves in the company of Warren and Anita Manshel. We had known Warren when, as a newly minted PhD from Harvard, he had come to work in Paris for the Congress for Cultural Freedom. There he had met and married Anita, the daughter of a very successful Wall Street investor. He was now himself on Wall Street, struggling with boredom because his heart belonged to politics. I mentioned the magazine idea, and he was interested. How much would it cost, he asked? I explained that, by my calculations, $10,000 could see us through the first year (i.e., four issues). The editors, Dan Bell and myself, would work *pro bono* (as they have ever since). He agreed to put up the money and became our publisher. Over time, in the following years, he invested much larger sums in what became *The Public Interest*, until such times as some foundations became interested in us.

I edited the magazine, the first issue of which came out in the fall of 1965, out of my office at Basic Books, with my secretary constituting the rest of the staff. For the first issues, I asked friends to contribute—Daniel Bell (my co-editor), Pat Moynihan, Nathan Glazer, James Q. Wilson, and others who I had reason to think were upset by the frothy ideological climate of the mid-1960s. One forgets just how frothy this climate was. The centerpiece of the War on Poverty was the sociological fantasy that if one gave political power to the poor, by sponsoring "community action," they would then lift themselves out of poverty at the expense of the rich and powerful. All of us at the core of

The Public Interest had grown up in lower-middle-class or working-class house-holds, unlike the academics who had authored the War on Poverty, and we knew that becoming politically militant was no way for poor people to lift themselves out of poverty. This, it seemed to us, was just a sociological echo of an older socialist idea that a "Great Society" could only come about as a consequence of class struggle.

There were many other such fantasies floating about at that time. One involved the threat and promise of "automation." We were, it seems, entering a "push-button" phase of human history, in which the economy would mechanically (or electronically) produce abundance, but in which no one would have steady work. What would all these people do? Thus arose the problem of "leisure" and how tens of millions of people, with time on their hands, could spend that time fruitfully. The Ford Foundation ran many conferences on this problem, and some very big books on "leisure" duly appeared. Lyndon Johnson even appointed a Commission on Automation. Fortunately, Dan Bell and the MIT economist Robert Solow became members, and they shaped the final report to suggest that things would never be as good or as bad as imagined. It was his experience on this Commission that persuaded Dan there was urgent need for a journal like *The Public Interest*, and Bob Solow contributed a piece on "automation" to our first issue.

I designed the magazine the way I had designed *Encounter*: by borrowing from the format of existing or previous magazines and changing things around a little. What was important was that, given our lack of staff, it should be as "idiot-proof" as possible. So the articles for the first issue came in, the printer delivered as promised, and there we were, with two thousand copies ready to be mailed to subscribers who had answered our ads as well as to a list of people who ought to have been interested. My secretary, Vivian Gornick, was an intelligent, pleasant young woman who had done graduate work in English literature. She had done the proofreading, dealt with the printer, and now she went down to the post office with a small truckload of copies to be mailed. But the post office refused to mail them; it turned out we had failed to get some necessary permits. Vivian came back in despair, and I was stumped. Then Vivian said that we should try again. It worked this time. Vivian simply sat on the loading dock, burst into tears, and the kindly older supervisor was so touched that he waived his objections. Shortly thereafter, Vivian wrote her first article for *The Village Voice*, which launched her career as a feminist—an increasingly radical feminist writer.

Though the founding of *The Public Interest* is generally seen in retrospect as the origin of "neoconservatism" (a term that had not yet been invented), the core group around the magazine still regarded themselves as liberal, if of a dissenting and revisionist bent. I was the most conservative of the lot, my British experience having exposed me to intelligent, thoughtful, and lively conservatives. But conservatism in the States at that moment was represented by the Goldwater campaign against the New Deal, with which none of us had any sympathy, and by *National Review*, which we regarded as too right-wing. The spectrum of opinion within our group was very narrow, with me slightly on the right, Dan Bell (ever loyal to his right-wing social-democratic background) on the left, and the rest somewhere in the middle. We considered ourselves to be realistic meliorists, skeptical of government programs that ignored history and experience in favor of then-fashionable left-wing ideas spawned by the academy. This was the original idea of the magazine, but events soon overtook us.

The major event of that period was the student rebellion and the rise of the counterculture, with its messianic expectations and its apocalyptic fears. It certainly took us by surprise, as it did just about everyone else. Suddenly we discovered that we had been cultural conservatives all along. This shock of recognition was to have profound consequences. We were bourgeois types, all of us, but by habit and instinct rather than reflection. Now we had to decide what we were for, and why. Cool criticism of the prevailing liberal-left orthodoxy was not enough at a time when liberalism itself was crumbling before the resurgent Left. Nor were we the only ones to experience this sea-change. The editor of *Commentary*, Norman Podhoretz, and most of the contributors to it, who had been moving left until 1965, now became our allies. As the New Left and the counterculture began to reshape liberalism, as can be seen by a perusal of the *New York Review of Books* and even *The New Yorker*, and, eventually, to reshape the Democratic Party, disenchanted liberals began to find themselves harboring all kinds of conservative instincts and ideas. Something like a "movement" took shape, with *The Public Interest* at (or near) the center. It never really was a movement, however, since no organizational efforts were made or even thought of. It would more fairly be described as a current of thought, represented by not more than a few dozen people who were rather more articulate and familiar with ideological controversy than most conservatives at the time. The political implications of this current of thought were gradually to reveal themselves under the pressure of events. One such key event was the nomination of Senator George McGovern as the Democratic candidate in 1972, which in effect sent us, most of us anyhow, a message that we were now off the liberal spectrum and that the Democratic Party no longer had room for the likes of us. Though none of us was a Republican, and few of us even knew any Republicans, our political landscape was in the process of being transformed.

One important agent in this transformation was the *Wall Street Journal*, a newspaper that, at the time, few American intellectuals had ever seen, much less read. But it turned out that a young conservative journalist in their Washington bureau, Robert Bartley, had been reading *The Public Interest* and sensed that something of interest to conservatives, a fresh wind, as it were, was happening. He rang me up for an interview and in May of 1972 his article about *The Public Interest*, "Irving Kristol and Friends," appeared. It was favorable almost (but not quite) to the point of embarrassment, and suddenly we had national exposure. A few years later, Bob was appointed editor of the editorial and op-ed pages, and I became a frequent contributor to those pages. More important, the editorials themselves began to reflect, in some degree, the mode of thinking to be found in *The Public Interest*—analytical, skeptical, and implicitly ideological in a way we did not ourselves at the time appreciate.

At that time, I had already left Basic Books to become a Luce Professor at New York University. (The appointment was largely due to vigorous lobbying by Sidney Hook.) I spent eighteen years as a professor there, as Luce Professor and then John M. Olin Professor, and enjoyed it immensely—lots of free time, long vacations, and if one can avoid entanglement with departmental or faculty politics (as I was able to do), a generally easy life. I also found teaching to be a useful exercise, because it forced me to seek more coherence in my thinking than I was accustomed to. The title of "professor" was desirable too, because otherwise I ran the danger of being labeled a "journalist." But it will not come as a surprise to NYU to learn that most of my energy and attention were focused on the "real world," of which academia these days is a creaking and reluctant part.

Washington, D.C., on the other hand, is very much in the real world, in the sense that what it does matters a lot even though what it thinks can often be extraterrestrial. At that time, when I had already marked my fiftieth birthday, I had been to Washington only once in my life, and that was a one-day visit while I was on home leave from *Encounter*. (The goal was to persuade Walter Lippmann to contribute an article to the magazine; he was friendly but unobliging.) I was still very much a New Yorker, still as much a free-floating intellectual as a serious "policy wonk" in my thinking. But Bill Baroody Sr., head of the American Enterprise Institute, a small conservative think tank in Washington, had been reading *The Public Interest* and the *Wall Street Journal* and sensed that something new and enlivening was occurring. He got in touch with me, offered me an honorary title of "associate fellow" (or some such thing), and a connection was established.

At that time, AEI was concerned solely with economics and a defense of the "free enterprise system." But Bill himself had a much broader range of interests, which included religion, political philosophy, and the social sciences generally. The emergence of a new group of "neoconservative" intellectuals—the term was invented, in a spirit of contempt for "renegades," by the socialist Michael Harrington—intrigued and excited him. He calmly ignored the fact that not a single one of us was at that time a Republican, a fact that caused much outrage among Goldwater conservatives who were the main financial support for AEI. In the course of the 1970s and '80s, Bill made a determined effort to recruit "neoconservatives" to AEI, and did in fact recruit, early on, Jeane Kirkpatrick, Michael Novak, Ben Wattenberg, as well as many others as the years proceeded. His task was facilitated by the appearance on the scene of a rejuvenated Bradley Foundation and John M. Olin Foundation, now staffed by younger men and women who had been exposed to, and influenced by, "neoconservative" thinking. Among them special note has to be made of Michael Joyce of Bradley, who turned out to be an accomplished neoconservative thinker in his own right.

This was all taking place during the Cold War—a war, it is often forgotten, that was not so cold for the United States, which lost over 100,000 soldiers killed in Korea and Vietnam. On the whole, though I wrote critically of the liberal illusions embedded in the thinking of our State Department and the foreign policy establishment—illusions about the nature of foreign affairs generally and of Communist intentions in particular—it was writing done with my left hand, as it were. The illusions were so simple-minded, and the whole controversy over foreign policy so intellectually unchallenging. (*The Public Interest* dealt only with domestic policy, as a consequence.) I had had an excellent education in communism at City College and in my Trotskyist youth group, and I knew that if you took Marxist-Leninist doctrine as seriously as the Soviet leadership did, the broad outline of an appropriate American foreign policy almost designed itself. To be a "hard-liner" vis-à-vis the Soviet Union or another Communist regime meant that you were likely to be right far more often than wrong. Only people who believed themselves so clever as to be able to outwit those odds could come up with original views on the Cold War. Unfortunately, our universities are well populated by such types. More unfortunately, some of them ended up micromanaging American policy in Vietnam, with disastrous results.

My intellectual perplexities in the 1970s began to focus rather on economics. Until that time I took it for granted that John Maynard Keynes had discovered the secret of the "boom-and-bust" cycle that seemed to characterize a market economy, and I assumed that astute fiscal management by the government could reconcile economic growth and economic equilibrium. This assumption certainly seemed validated by the postwar experience—until the 1970s, that is. Then we found ourselves confronting simultaneous inflation and depression, and no one seemed to be able to explain it, much less know what to do about it. I decided with the greatest reluctance that "neoconservatism" could not blandly leave the economy to the economists, and that I personally had to become economically literate. So I took a sabbatical leave from NYU in the academic year 1976–1977, and we moved to Washington, where I became a visiting fellow at AEI while Bea formed a similar relationship with the Woodrow Wilson Center.

The timing was most fortuitous. The Ford administration was winding down and, for the first time, I was able to see close up the basic political impotence of traditional conservatism, which lived off Democratic errors but had no governing philosophy of its own—at least none that could strike a popular nerve among the electorate. There were many fine people in the Ford administration, and by election time they were all defeatist, in the sense that they thought the Republican Party would be better off out of office than in it. Their party had reached the end of the road, the post–New Deal road, and was floundering in a blind alley.

A fair number of these people came to AEI, as a kind of temporary haven. The economists among them were useful for my purposes, since they could help me understand the economic literature, old and new, that I was assiduously studying. But the men I formed the closest ties with were three newly unemployed lawyers—Robert Bork, Antonin Scalia, and Laurence Silberman—who have remained close friends to this day. AEI had no lunchroom at that time, and so we "brown-bagged it" every day, munching on our hamburgers or sandwiches while talking about everything but law, for this would have excluded me from the conversation. Our main topics for discussion were religion (my permanent favorite) and economics, about which none of us knew as much as we would have liked. But it was clear to all of us that the Republican Party would have to become more than the party of a balanced budget if it was to be invigorated. As it happens, there was an apostle of a new conservative economics right at hand, also spending a year at AEI. He was Jude Wanniski, and something called "supply-side" economics was his theme. He became a frequent member of our little luncheon group.

I had known Jude, then an editorial writer for the *Wall Street Journal*, for a couple of years previously, and had been largely responsible for his getting the foundation grant that brought him to AEI to write his book on supply-side economics. Jude had tried very hard to indoctrinate me in the virtues of this new economics, with partial success. I was not certain of its economic merits but quickly saw its political possibilities. To refocus Republican conservative thought on the economics of growth rather than simply on the economics of stability seemed to me very promising. Republican economics was then in truth a dismal science, explaining to the populace, parent-like, why the good things in life that they wanted were all too expensive. In the course of my new studies in economics, I had become aware that this nay-saying economics originated with Ricardo and represented nothing less than a perversion of the optimistic economics of Adam Smith, an economic idea of capitalism I found far more congenial. It was Jude who introduced me to Jack Kemp, a young Congressman and a recent convert. It was Jack Kemp who, almost single-handed, converted Ronald Reagan to supply-side economics. Ideas do have consequences, but in mysterious ways.

Economists, most of them Keynesian or neo-Keynesian, have given supply-side economics a bad name. That is because, with its emphasis on microeconomic incentives and disincentives, supply-side economics calls into question the entire structure of macroeconomic analysis and forecasting developed since World War II. Since something like half the economists in the United States today are macroeconomists, in academia, industry, and government, they are understandably irked when someone comes along to suggest that their intellectual efforts, some of them technically brilliant, are largely in vain when it comes to "guiding" the economy or making short-term forecasts. Such forecasts are right only by accident; if it were otherwise, Wall Street would be an infallible mechanism for making all investors rich. The essential goal of supply-side economics is to keep increases in government spending below the historical rate of growth of the economy, avoid needless government regulations, and keep tax rates low so as to encourage investment and sustain growth. After that is done, particular circumstances will intervene in unpredictable ways, but the preconditions for enduring, long-term growth will exist.

Neo-Keynesian orthodoxy has persisted in claiming that supply-side economics was tried and failed during the Reagan years, during which the budget deficit ballooned alarmingly. This is a false accusation. To begin with, the Democratic Congress, in a political frenzy, enacted much larger tax cuts than President Reagan originally requested. Then, for the rest of the decade, the same Congress proceeded to make expenditures at a rate far above the rate of growth of the economy, so that even as government's revenues increased, as they did, despite the tax cuts, the deficit increased more rapidly. The reason these facts are either ignored or distorted is that liberal politicians, the liberal media, and a substantial segment of professional economists do not want to encourage people to think that the activities of government ought to be considerably more limited than they now are.

There is nothing wrong with supply-side economics, but there is often something wrong with people attracted to it. These people are all too likely to think that if you follow the correct economic prescriptions, the polity will bloom with social and political health as well as greater economic well-being. But there is a lot more necessary for a healthy society and a healthy polity than solid economic growth, as we have discovered in the post–World War II decades. Just as erroneous economic actions by government can wreck a society and a polity, so erroneous moral and political beliefs can accomplish the same end, more indirectly but just as effectively.

And here, I think, is where what we call "neoconservatism" has made its major contribution in these past two decades. By enlarging the conservative vision to include moral philosophy, political philosophy, and even religious thought, it helped make it more politically sensible as well as politically appealing. Supply-side economics, in one version or another, offered neoconservatism an economic approach that promised steady economic growth, a *sine qua non* for the survival of a modern democracy. Neoconservatism, for its part, has provided traditional conservatism with an intellectual dimension that goes beyond economics to reflections on the roots of social and cultural stability. If the Republican Party today is less interested in the business community than in the pursuit of the happiness of ordinary folk, and if, as I think is the case, this has made the party more acceptable and appealing to the average American, then I believe the work of neoconservative intellectuals has contributed much to this change.

In 1987, Bea and I made another major decision: to retire from our professorships, at the City University of New York and New York University, respectively, and move, along with *The Public Interest*, to Washington, D.C, where I would become a senior fellow at AEI. We were, and to a large extent remain, New Yorkers, but we found life in New York not only disagreeable in the details of daily living but boring as well. That our children and grandchildren were in D.C. was surely a large consideration, but I do believe we would have made the move anyhow. New York is the national center of the arts, the communications media, and finance, but if you are keenly interested in public policy, as we had gradually become, D.C. is the place to be, especially since public policy these days has its own cultural and intellectual aspects.

There were two other reasons behind the move. First, most of our New York friends in the academic and journalistic worlds had exited our lives, through either retirement or death, and we had little contact with the generation that replaced them. Second, we found ourselves more and more isolated politically, as a result of our shift toward conservatism. New York is a one-party town, where liberalism and the Democratic Party unite to establish a regnant orthodoxy. Conservatives are mainly found in the financial community, and their outlook tends to be narrow. We found ourselves more and more uncomfortable at dinner parties, where we were regarded as exotic curiosa. In Washington, there is no shortage of conservatives and Republicans, and of necessity there is a degree of comity between liberals and conservatives that is unknown to New York. Perhaps this situation will change, but it is my perception that while Washington is a pleasant place in which to live, New York has become ever more unpleasant. And while New York intellectual and cultural life becomes ever more parochial and sterile—witness what is happening to the *New York Times*, which used to be a national newspaper—Washington inches along toward greater hospitality toward the life of the mind. Or so it seems to me. So today we are "Washingtonians," joining a growing population of New York transplants.

Even before moving to Washington, however, I did have one final idea for a new magazine I would like to be involved in, one that was to be located in Washington. As I have noted, *The Public Interest* dealt only with domestic affairs. But as the Soviet regime showed signs of unraveling, it became clear to me that some kind of post–Cold War foreign policy would be needed. Such a policy would have to steer its own course between Wilsonian internationalist utopianism and a "pragmatism" that was little more than opportunism. In short, I foresaw a "neorealist" foreign policy journal that would complement the "neoconservatism" of *The Public Interest*. The idea for such a magazine took shape in the course of discussions with Owen Harries, an Australian political scientist, former Australian ambassador to UNESCO, now an American resident, and one of the wisest analysts of foreign policy. He was willing to be the editor of *The National Interest* (as it was to be called), while I would be merely the publisher, watching over the budget. The first issue appeared in the fall of 1985, and it is now, together with the long-established *Foreign Affairs*, the leading journal in its field.

Washington is not only the political center of the nation, but the government center as well. This is both good and bad. To see close up how government operates in both domestic and foreign affairs—how it must operate under the rule of law—is to appreciate how complex modern government is and how difficult it is to bring about political change. That's good, since to listen to the TV news or read the newspapers is to experience a radical simplification. What is bad is the natural tendency to get too closely involved in the problems of government and lose sight of the larger issues of politics, issues concerning what kind of country we want to be and what kind of lives we want to live in it.

In the past three decades, Washington has witnessed a surge of intellectual vitality. This is largely the result of the formation and growth of think tanks—conservative, liberal, and left-of-center. Washington's universities play only an ancillary role in this, since they are more teaching universities than research centers. And, it has to be said, the tendency among the think tanks is to focus on governmental activities, especially those affecting the economy. Still, with every passing year this focus is of necessity broadened to include such social issues as crime, illegitimacy, family problems, education, and other such matters that neoconservative social scientists have been especially prominent in highlighting. There is even a growing attention to cultural issues (e.g., the condition of the humanities and the arts). AEI, under Christopher DeMuth, exemplifies this wider focus. So it is far more possible than it used to be to lead a perfectly civilized life as well as an active life in Washington. And, of course, it is still the most gracious and beautiful city in the nation, which is why people hate to leave it. The recent modest decline in Washington's population is exclusively the result of middle-class black people moving to the suburbs.

So here I am and here we are. I conclude this memoir on my seventy-fifth birthday and a few days after our fifty-third wedding anniversary. Looking back, I am astonished how intellectually twinned Bea and I have been over the years, pursuing different subjects while thinking the same thoughts and reaching the same conclusions. And not only Bea and I but our children. An intellectual memoir like this necessarily shortchanges some of the most important and engrossing facts of life, such as children. I have been fortunate to have children, Bill and Liz, who are not only dear to me because they are my children, but who also happen to be gifted, interesting, and, even more remarkable, intellectually and politically congenial. And they, in turn, have managed to marry spouses who are equally gifted, interesting, and congenial. Susan Scheinberg Kristol is a classicist by training and a magnificent mother to her three children. And Liz, who still manages an occasional piece of sparkling criticism while caring for her two very young children, is married to Caleb Nelson, currently a law clerk for Clarence Thomas.

If I am, as is sometimes said of me, a cheerful conservative, it is because I have much to be cheerful about. So far at least, all of our family is right here with us in Washington. Bea has just published her tenth book, and only a cataclysm of some kind will slow her down. I, on the other hand, have definitely slowed down, simply because writing commentaries about current affairs interests me less. I am happy to leave such work to my son Bill, who is in any case the better political scientist. I find myself far more interested in the problems of American civilization, or even Western civilization, than in American politics as conventionally defined, and I am more intrigued by the problematical aspects of modernity itself than in our current social issues. One of these problematical aspects is the relation of our religious-moral traditions to the secular-rationalist culture that has been imposed upon them.

And where stands neoconservatism today? It is clear that what can fairly be described as the neoconservative impulse (or, at most, the neoconservative persuasion) was a generational phenomenon, and has now been pretty much absorbed into a larger, more comprehensive conservatism. My son and daughter and son-in-law and daughter-in-law, along with dozens of young "interns" who have worked at *The Public Interest* over the past thirty years, are now all conservatives without adjectival modification. They have, I should like to think, keener intellectual and cultural interests than was once common among conservatives. There are even "conservative intellectuals" today to whom the media pay attention, something that didn't exist fifty years ago.

So I deem the neoconservative enterprise to have been a success, to have brought elements that were needed to enliven American conservatism and help reshape American politics. But my personal opinion is hardly authoritative, and I am well aware that the unanticipated consequences of ideas and acts are often very different from what was originally intended. That, I would say, is the basic conservative axiom, and it applies to conservatives as well as liberals and radicals.

1995

Forty Good Years

Back in 1965, in New York, my old friend Daniel Bell, then a professor of sociology at Columbia University, and I, then vice president of the publishing firm Basic Books, were deeply troubled. The source of our discomfort was the mode of thought that was beginning to dominate political and social discourse in and outside of academia, an ideological mode that made nonsense of the existential reality of American life.

One of the most egregious examples of this ideological nonsense, popular among sociologists and dramatized by the press, was the idea that the way for the poor to escape from poverty was to organize to "fight city hall" and "gain power." This seemed plausible at a time when socialist and quasi-socialist ideas were still very much alive, prompting many to believe that the cure for poverty was political activism (relying upon the state) rather than economic activism (encouraging entrepreneurial energy in markets).

Both Dan and I had come from poor families, had gone through radical phases in our youth, and were appalled to discover that ideas we thought discredited had acquired a new lease on life. Dan, in those days, described himself as a democratic socialist (he still does, incidentally), while I was a somewhat skeptical liberal. We certainly thought there was a role for government in moving people out of poverty, a much larger role than conservatives thought appropriate. But we did not believe that political activism (aka "the class struggle") could deliver people from poverty.

Then there was the scholarly nonsense, promoted by the Ford Foundation and echoed by most of the other major foundations, that "automation" threatened to abolish people's jobs, while at the same time throwing them into a life of affluent leisure for which they were intellectually and morally unprepared. Obviously, these foundations, and the universities and media as well (the media by then being populated by college graduates), had a crucial role to play in rescuing the American people from this ghastly fate. The result was a plethora of conferences on the imminent problem of mass leisure, out of which emerged a plethora of big books.

Dan, who knew more economics than I did, was infuriated by the basic ignorance this episode revealed, an ignorance of how an economic system copes with innovation. I was astounded by the ease with which Marx's description of the idyllic life under socialism had been unwittingly transformed into a nightmare by persons mainly on the left. President Johnson lent credibility to the issue by appointing a Commission on Automation, which included Dan and a brilliant young MIT economist, Robert Solow. Together they helped write so sobering a report for the Commission that it succeeded in making the topic a deadly bore.

These were the kinds of issues that provoked the founding of *The Public Interest*. Financially, it was made possible by a $10,000 grant from a friend, Warren Manshel, who was promptly designated publisher, with Dan and myself serving as co-editors. The journal's first home (with the benign approval of another friend, the president of Basic Books) was my modest office at Basic Books, and the entire staff consisted of my secretary-assistant, Vivian Gornick, a talented young woman who was soon to launch her own career as a feminist and a writer for *The Village Voice*. Dan and I named the magazine, designed it, and printed (as I recall) some 1,200 copies of the first issue. For articles, we simply rang up friends and acquaintances whom we believed to be on our "wavelength." The first issue featured articles by Pat Moynihan, Robert Solow, Robert Nisbet, Jacques Barzun, Nathan Glazer, Martin Diamond, and Daniel Bell, among others. The second and third issues introduced such other notable contributors as James Q. Wilson, Earl Raab, Milton Friedman, and Peter Drucker—not all of them so very notable at the time.

We made one easy editorial decision at the outset: no discussion of foreign policy or foreign affairs. Vietnam was arousing a storm of controversy at the time, and we knew that our group had a wide spectrum of opinion on the issue. We did not want any of the space in our modest-sized quarterly to be swallowed up by Vietnam. The simplest solution was to ban foreign affairs and foreign policy from our pages.

We also made a financial decision: the co-editors would not be paid. Our reasoning, again, was simple. Because the subsidy to the magazine (with the increase of circulation it quickly went up to several tens of thousands of dollars a year) came from the pocket of a friend, we did not want to be in the position of taking his money for ourselves. This principle survived until today, despite significant changes in the magazine's circumstances. Among those changes were the renting of a sliver of office space in a nearby office building, losing Vivian Gornick to the world of journalism, and acquiring a new secretary-assistant, Rita Lazzaro, who spent the next eighteen years presiding admirably over our office. In 1987, we made what may have been the most significant change: moving to Washington.

After a few years, the increased recognition the magazine was receiving (alas, barely reflected in its circulation) attracted some conservative foundations. In one of my essays in the *Wall Street Journal*, I had urged such foundations to stop moaning about the welfare state, the "road to serfdom," the death of free enterprise by "statism," and the iniquities of the income tax, and address the realities of the conservative situation. I wrote this not as a "movement conservative" but as someone who thought it would be best for American democracy if conservatives would engage in a serious way the world as it existed, a world that in some respects was prospering, despite those fatal injuries the New Deal had presumably inflicted on it.

I struck a responsive chord. At least a few of those conservative foundations felt the desirability of breaking out of their self-imposed ghettos. First was the Smith Richardson Foundation, which consisted, in its entirety, of Randall Richardson, his secretary, and a large pot of money from his family fortune. Randy became a friend and supporter, and was soon followed by the Olin Foundation, headed for the last two decades by another friend and ally, James Piereson. Finally, there was the newly created Bradley Foundation under former Olin executive Michael Joyce, who became a tower of strength in the years ahead.

For the first seven years of its existence, *The Public Interest* was generally regarded (and regarded itself) as a moderately liberal journal. The editors and most of the contributors, after all, were registered Democrats. Pat Moynihan was in the Kennedy and Johnson administrations, and in 1968 I was on a Hubert Humphrey campaign task force. It was the election of 1972 that precipitated the first political divisions in our community. Daniel Bell could not bring himself to vote Republican and unenthusiastically endorsed George McGovern. About this time, he also stepped down as co-editor, to be replaced by another old friend, and, as it happened, Democrat, Nathan Glazer. I, on the other hand, repelled by McGovern's views on foreign policy, unenthusiastically endorsed Nixon's reelection. My Republican vote produced little shock waves in the New York intellectual community. It didn't take long, a year or two, for the socialist writer Michael Harrington to come up with the term "neoconservative" to describe a renegade liberal like myself. To the chagrin of some of my friends, I decided to accept that term; there was no point calling myself a liberal when no one else did. And I had to face the fact that voting for Richard Nixon was, in the university world and in the intellectual world generally, the equivalent of a Jew ostentatiously eating pork on Yom Kippur. It was an act of self-excommunication. In fact, some of my critics regarded it as especially heinous for a Jew to abandon the creed of liberalism. For them, neoconservatism was seen as a religious as well as a political heresy.

Some of my best friends and close associates at *The Public Interest* did not join me in that heresy. The magazine continued to shy away from anything resembling partisan politics and concentrated on revisionist social science. This was the original impulse behind the founding of the journal, and it continued to be the major, although never exclusive, focus of our editorial activity. It was, so to speak, the bread-and-butter of our offerings, suggesting new ways of looking at the problems of poverty, economic inequality, educational equality, sex education, gun control, and so on. We invited and published the findings of social research, however heterodox. We also enriched it with newer modes of economic analysis, thus giving it an additional claim to nonideological objectivity.

But we were never single-minded economists or social scientists. On the contrary, we soon discovered that behind the hard realities of economics and social science were the equally hard realities of morality, family, culture, and religion—the "habits of the mind" and "habits of the heart," as Tocqueville said, that determine the quality and character of a people. To the extent to which these factors, too, could be subject to social research and thoughtful social analysis, they gave our articles their distinctive character. In its last decade, the magazine had the good fortune to acquire, first as executive editor and then as the editor, Adam Wolfson, who brought with him a lively interest in and keen appreciation of just such subjects.

In my case, this mode of thought took the form of what came to be known as neoconservatism. I was then writing a monthly essay for the editorial page of the *Wall Street Journal*, and it was there that neoconservatism could be said to have been reared, if not born. I had no patience with the old conservatism that confronted the tides of history by shouting "Stop!" I could not summon up any admiration for Herbert Hoover or Alf Landon, and I did not regard Franklin D. Roosevelt as the devil incarnate. My political instincts were always inclined to the proactive rather than the reactive, to work with reality, not against it.

To inject some academic substance into my thinking about public policy, I took a sabbatical from New York University in 1976–1977 and spent a year at the American Enterprise Institute in Washington, studying economics primarily. It was there that I became disillusioned with conventional macroeconomics and sympathetic to what was called "supply-side" economics, an inelegant title for something I prefer to think of as the "economics of growth." It led me to publish in *The Public Interest* an article by Jude Wanniski arguing the case for supply-side economics, illustrated for the first time by the "Laffer curve." The world was not much impressed, but the *Wall Street Journal* was. Its editorial page now had as its editor a young Robert Bartley, who had already published in the *Journal* an article about our magazine, entitled "Irving Kristol and Friends." It was the *Journal* that went on to publicize supply-side economics, applying it to the issues of the day and creating something like a neoconservative economics. The crucial role of the *Journal* and of this new approach to economics can be seen even today by comparison with the European experience, where economic growth still suffers as the financial press remains captive to traditional "bankers' economics."

In foreign policy, *The Public Interest* continued to be mute. But I and many of our writers could express our views in *Commentary* (which, in turn, gave birth to the Committee for the Free World, headed by the then-retired politician Donald Rumsfeld). *Commentary* was the third of the publications that, along with the *Journal* and *The Public Interest*, constituted what the Russians call a *troika*, a team of three horses pulling a carriage. It is astonishing to think that the combined efforts of these three publications (two with very modest circulations) should have been so consequential, or so it would seem today, to judge by the extraordinary interest displayed throughout the world in neoconservatism.

The culture wars introduced yet another dimension in the neoconservative spectrum. In *The Public Interest*, those wars were fought mainly in the book review section. Here the journal found allies among liberals, in academia particularly, who were offended by the extravagances of the countercultural Left. The counterculture, for its part, moved steadily toward an aggressive secularism and an animus against religion, foreshadowing an ominous tension between the secular and the religious in American politics. Here, too, *The Public Interest* found itself on firm ground. It had always had a benign interest in religion, a secular interest in religion, one might say, deriving from traditional political and moral philosophy, which has been appreciative of religion as a social as well as a spiritual force.

Yet *The Public Interest*, it should be said, transcended any political ideology, or even any political "disposition." Inevitably, to be sure, my own political identity spilled over into the public perception of the magazine; there was no way I could erect what on Wall Street is known as a "Chinese wall" between my writings in other journals and this perception. But for many of its contributors and readers, and, not least, for its co-editors, first Dan Bell and then Nat Glazer, *The Public Interest* continued to have a non-ideological cast, in part because it continued to be focused largely on social research and social problems, and because it did so in a serious scholarly fashion. For these reasons and, I believe, because of its intellectual quality, it has been well received in a dominantly liberal academia, as well as in the media and in government circles. It has even, I venture to suggest, had an influence in shaping and reshaping the prevailing modes of discourse in the social sciences.

The past forty years, for its editors and contributors, as well as, I hope, for its readers, have been an exciting intellectual adventure. And there will be, no doubt, exciting times ahead for our successors as they cope with the extraordinary dilemmas posed by our new "brave new world." We can leave no better legacy for them than the spirit of goodwill and high spirits that has sustained us in that adventure.

2005

My "Public Interest"

I was, of course, immensely pleased to receive your invitation to a conference on *The Public Interest* [sponsored by the James Madison Program at Princeton University]. I am unable to attend, alas, though on second thought, perhaps it's just as well. That magazine no longer belongs to those who founded it, edited it, and wrote for it over its forty years' existence. It belongs to a subsequent generation who will make of it what they will. But the invitation provoked me to think anew about the magazine and my own relation to it. These thoughts are not memories so much as a reconstruction of my state of mind in the 1950s and 1960s, an account that, I must admit, is perhaps teleological as well as chronological.

I came to *The Public Interest* from a rather different background from my fellow editors, and with a vision that did not always fit comfortably with theirs. Fortunately, because *The Public Interest*, for good reasons, focused exclusively on domestic policy, this was only intermittently a source of mild irritation. In the 1950s we were living in London, where I was co-editing *Encounter* magazine. There, by the way, is another journal that deserves a conference of its own, though in London. But this won't happen because it would require the Brits to face up to the fact that, half a century ago, the CIA put out a better British magazine than the Brits have ever done since.

Anyway, I was happy to be in London—it was easy to be happy in London in those days, but I was also increasingly restless. Britain, and by extension Europe, had its charms, but it was clear that the United States, in all its gracelessness, was where the future of the West would be determined. Our NATO allies were turning in on themselves. This was accompanied by an increasing anti-Americanism, a recognition of the fact that we were pushing them into the world while their strong inclination was to stay at home and nurse the wounds that two world wars had inflicted. And as their national politics focused on one universal welfare program after another, the trivialization of European politics proceeded apace, regardless of which political party was in office. When it came to budgeting priorities, they were all social-democrats now. World War I had ended with the famous promise of returning soldiers to "a world fit for heroes." It is only a slight exaggeration to say that World War II ended with a commitment to "a world fit for victims."

I knew there was an important lesson for the United States in this development. There was clearly a growing American opinion that believed a European-type welfare state was the correct and inevitable model for the United States. Against this, there was a party on the right with a radical individualist ethos that opposed the very idea of a welfare state. As a child of the Great Depression, I found this attitude preposterous. Could there not be another option, a welfare state that could be reconciled with a world role for the United States? It was with this question in mind that, in 1958, I returned home.

In the 1960s, while pursuing a career in book publishing, I began to write an occasional brief column for *The New Leader*, a weekly magazine with a minuscule circulation to which I had contributed over the years. There was quite enough being written about Vietnam, so most of my columns concerned Lyndon Johnson's "War on Poverty" and were coolly critical of its strong ideological coloration, so reminiscent of European social-democracy. Not myself an economist or sociologist, I was in no position to argue my views in detail. I very much needed the company of like-minded scholars.

In 1965, through a series of circumstances that need not be recounted here, the stars became properly aligned so that my wish could become a reality. Dan Bell and I were able to start a new magazine devoted exclusively to domestic social and economic policy. We brazenly called it *The Public Interest*, and in our opening statement declared it to be non-ideological. We ourselves were rather unclear as to what we meant by that, but it soon became clear enough through the efforts of our contributors. It meant the proper, rigorous use of social-science methodology. In the feverish years of the 1960s, when what so often passed for social science was imbued with a sometimes apocalyptic, sometimes eschatological, but always political impulse, this very modest approach was refreshing. The result was a magazine with a distinctive tone that defined its identity for the next forty years. To critics who thought this tone was distinctly conservative, I am tempted to quote Margaret Thatcher: "The facts of life are conservative."

That our magazine was able to produce and publicize first-rate scholarly work reveals that the American academic community, ideological as it had become, nevertheless to some degree continued to respect old-fashioned academic standards. Will it last? That's not for me to say. What I can say is that my years at *The Public Interest* permitted me to observe how the idea of "national greatness" can be consistent with a welfare state that does not frustrate the spirit of enterprise and that does not instill risk-aversiveness as a universal virtue.

We have seen in the case of Europe how a social-democratic welfare state discourages population growth as well as economic growth, and suppresses the virtues traditionally associated with "manliness" in foreign policy. Europe is now paying a terrible price, to the point where it is in the process of losing its historic identity, because of the sovereignty it has accorded the social-democratic ethos over both domestic and foreign policy. That the two are inseparably intertwined has never been more convincingly demonstrated.

True, the American version of "national greatness" has recently run into some local difficulties out there in the Middle East, and I suppose that the idea itself will be muted for some time ahead. But I note that the American population has just reached 300 million, with 400 million pretty firmly projected for 2040. So my grandchildren will be living in a country with the world's third-largest population, the strongest economy, and the most powerful military establishment. Our critics may demand ever-greater humility from our ever-greater power; that would be a historic first were it ever to happen. So, for better or worse, "national greatness" is being thrust upon us.

I realize that my *Public Interest*, linking its work in economic and social policy to our national destiny as a world power, is a special interpretation that others will find questionable. But I trust that expanding the role of *The Public Interest* as I have done will surely not diminish its historic significance.

2006

IRVING KRISTOL BIBLIOGRAPHY

BOOKS

On the Democratic Idea in America. New York: Harper, 1972.
Two Cheers for Capitalism. New York: Basic Books, 1978.
Reflections of a Neoconservative: Looking Back, Looking Ahead. New York: Basic Books, 1983.
Neoconservatism: The Autobiography of an Idea. New York: Free Press, 1995.

EDITED COLLECTIONS

Encounters. Edited with Stephen Spender and Melvin Lasky. New York: Basic Books, 1963.
Confrontation: The Student Rebellion and the University. Edited with Daniel Bell. New York: Basic Books, 1969.
Capitalism Today. Edited with Daniel Bell. New York: Basic Books, 1970.
The American Commonwealth—1976. Edited with Nathan Glazer. New York: Basic Books, 1976.
The Americans: 1976—An Inquiry into Fundamental Concepts of Man Underlying Various U.S. Institutions. Edited with Paul Weaver. Lexington, Mass.: Lexington Books, 1976.
Crisis in Economic Theory. Edited with Daniel Bell. New York: Basic Books, 1981.

Note: An early version of this bibliography appears in *The Neoconservative Imagination: Essays in Honor of Irving Kristol,* edited by Christopher DeMuth and William Kristol (Washington, D.C.: AEI Press, 1995). An addendum was prepared (but not published) in 2005 by Neil Manning of the American Enterprise Institute. The present revised and expanded bibliography has been prepared with the assistance of Adam Wolfson, editor of *The Public Interest;* John Podhoretz, editor of *Commentary;* Myron Kolatch, editor of *The New Leader;* and Adam Paul of AEI. The last section, "Symposiums, Interviews, and Lectures," is incomplete, since Kristol left no vita or texts of his lectures. Reprinted items are abbreviated as follows: *Democratic Idea (On the Democratic Idea in America); Two Cheers (Two Cheers for Capitalism); Reflections (Reflections of a Neoconservative); Neoconservatism (Neoconservatism: The Autobiography of an Idea).*

ESSAYS

"Koestler: A Note on Confusion," *Politics*, May 1944.

"Adam and I" (story), *Commentary*, November 1946.

"The Myth of the Supra-Human Jew: A Theological Stigma," *Commentary*, September 1947.

"How Basic Is 'Basic Judaism'? A Comfortable Religion for an Uncomfortable World," *Commentary*, January 1948.

"What the Nazi Autopsies Show," *Commentary*, September 1948. Reprinted as "The Nature of Nazism" in *The Commentary Reader*, edited by Norman Podhoretz (New York: Atheneum, 1966).

"Who's Superstitious?" *Commentary*, November 1948.

"God and the Psychoanalysts," *Commentary*, November 1949. Reprinted in *Reflections*; *Neoconservatism*; and *Arguments and Doctrines: A Reader of Jewish Thinking in the Aftermath of the Holocaust*, edited by Arthur Allen Cohen (New York: Harper & Row, 1970).

"Love Affair: Psychoanalysts and Religion," *Time*, November 14, 1949.

"Einstein: The Passion of Pure Reason," *Commentary*, September 1950. Reprinted in *Reflections* and *Neoconservatism*.

"Is Jewish Humor Dead?" *Commentary*, November 1951. Reprinted in *Reflections*; *Neoconservatism*; and *Mid-Century: An Anthology of Jewish Life and Culture in Our Times*, edited by Harold U. Ribalow (New York: Beechhurst Press, 1955).

"'Civil Liberties,' 1952—A Study in Confusion," *Commentary*, March 1952.

"Ordeal by Mendacity," *Twentieth Century*, October 1952.

"Liberty and the Communists," *Partisan Review*, no. 4, 1952.

"After the Apocalypse," *Encounter*, October 1953.

"Men of Science—and Conscience," *Encounter*, October 1953.

"On 'Negative Liberalism,'" *Encounter*, January 1954; reply, *Encounter*, May 1954.

"The Simple and the True," *Encounter*, February 1954.

"Niccolò Machiavelli," *Encounter*, December 1954.

"Table Talk," *Encounter*, October 1955.

"Europe's Underground," *Encounter*, September 1956.

"Trivia and History," *Commentary*, December 1956.

"Bandung Powers: Danger Zone for U.S. Policy," *The New Republic*, January 14, 1957.

"The Shadow of the Marquis," *Encounter*, February 1957.

"A Mixed Bag," *Encounter*, June 1957.

"The Ideology of Economic Aid," *Yale Review,* June 1957.

"The Worst of Both Worlds," *Encounter,* October 1957.

"Class and Sociology: 'The Shadow of Marxism,'" *Commentary,* October 1957.

"Old Truths and the New Conservatism," *Yale Review,* May 1958.

" . . . And a Reply" (reply to Richard Wollheim, "One Man, One Vote"), *Encounter,* March 1960.

"Keeping Up with Ourselves," *Yale Review,* June 1960.

"High, Low, and Modern: Some Thoughts on Popular Culture and Popular Government," *Encounter,* August 1960.

"An Odd Lot," *Encounter,* December 1960.

"Machiavelli and the Profanation of Politics," in *The Logic of Personal Knowledge: Essays to Michael Polanyi on His Seventieth Birthday* (London: Routledge and Kegan Paul, 1961). Reprinted in *Reflections* and *Neoconservatism.*

"S. M. Levitas, 1894–1961," *The New Republic,* January 16, 1961.

"Dead-End Streets," *Encounter,* February 1961.

"Civil Disobedience in the Algerian War," *Yale Review,* May 1961.

"Explaining Ourselves," *Encounter,* May 1961.

"Deterrence," *Commentary,* July 1961.

"God and Politics in America," *Encounter,* August 1961.

"Of GE, TV, JFK, and USA," *Encounter,* September 1961.

"The Last Hundred Days," *The New Republic,* November 20, 1961.

"Social Sciences and Law," in *The Great Ideas Today,* edited by Robert M. Hutchins and Mortimer J. Adler (Chicago: Encyclopedia Britannica, 1962).

"The Drift of Things," *Encounter,* February 1962.

"No Special Relation," *Spectator,* October 5, 1962.

"Is the Welfare State Obsolete?" *Harper's,* June 1963.

"Why the Welfare State Doesn't Work," *Atlantic Monthly,* June 1963. Reprinted in *Reader's Digest,* November 1963.

"From the Land of the Free to the Big PX," *New York Times Magazine,* December 20, 1964.

"A Few Kind Words for Uncle Tom," *Harper's,* February 1965.

"The Twentieth Century Began in 1945," *New York Times Magazine,* May 2, 1965.

"Teaching In, Speaking Out: The Controversy over Vietnam," *Encounter,* August 1965.

"What Is the Public Interest?" (with Daniel Bell), *The Public Interest,* Fall 1965.

"What's Bugging the Students," *Atlantic Monthly*, November 1965.

"The Troublesome Intellectuals," *The Public Interest*, Winter 1965–1966.

"A New Isolationism?" *Encounter*, June 1966.

"New Left, New Right," *The Public Interest*, Summer 1966. Reprinted in *The Radical Left: The Abuse of Discontent*, edited by William Gerberding and Duane Smith (Boston: Houghton Mifflin, 1970).

"The Literary Intellectual," *Encounter*, August 1966.

"The Negro Today Is Like the Immigrant Yesterday," *New York Times Magazine*, September 11, 1966. Reprinted as "Today's Negroes: Better Off Than Yesterday's Immigrants?" in *U.S. News and World Report*, November 27, 1967; and as "The Negro and the City," in *A Nation of Cities*, edited by Robert Goldwin (New York: Rand McNally, 1968).

"It's Not a Bad Crisis to Live In," *New York Times Magazine*, January 22, 1967.

"Germany 1967," *Atlantic Monthly*, May 1967.

"American Intellectuals and Foreign Policy," *Foreign Affairs*, July 1967. Reprinted in *Democratic Idea*; *Neoconservatism*; and *The American Encounter: The United States and the Making of the Modern World*, edited by James F. Hoge Jr. and Fareed Zakaria (New York: Basic Books, 1997).

"The Underdeveloped Profession," *The Public Interest*, Winter 1967.

"The Malcontent Professors," *Fortune*, December 1967.

"Memoirs of a Cold Warrior," *New York Times Magazine*, February 11, 1968. Reprinted in *Reflections* and *Neoconservatism*.

"Decentralization for What?" *The Public Interest*, Spring 1968.

"We Can't Resign as 'Policeman of the World,'" *New York Times Magazine*, May 12, 1968.

"Why I Am for Humphrey," *The New Republic*, June 8, 1968.

"Our Shaken Foundations," *Fortune*, July 1968. Reprinted as "The Shaking of Foundations," in *Democratic Idea*.

"A Fellow Can Be Civilized, Though Executive," *Fortune*, September 1968.

"The Old Politics, the New Politics, the New, New Politics," *New York Times Magazine*, November 24, 1968. Reprinted as "The End of Liberalism?" in *Current*, January 1969.

"Ten Years in a Tunnel: Reflections on the 1930s," in *The Thirties: A Reconsideration in the Light of the American Political Tradition*, edited by Morton J. Frisch and Martin Diamond (DeKalb: Northern Illinois University Press, 1968).

"A Different Way to Restructure the University," *New York Times Magazine*, December 8, 1968; reply, January 5, 1969. Reprinted as "Toward a Restructuring of the University," in *Democratic Idea*.

"The New York Intellectuals: An Exchange" (with Irving Howe), *Commentary*, January 1969.

"The Crisis Behind the Welfare Crisis," *Fortune*, June 1969.

"Who Knows New York?" (with Paul Weaver), *The Public Interest*, Summer 1969.

"A Bad Idea Whose Time Has Come" (with Paul Weaver), *New York Times Magazine*, November 23, 1969.

"American Historians and the Democratic Idea," *American Scholar*, Winter 1969–1970. Reprinted in *Democratic Idea*; *Reflections*; and *Neoconservatism*.

"Writing About Trade Unions," *New York Times Book Review*, February 1, 1970; reply, March 1, 1970.

"What Business Is a University In?" *New York Times Magazine*, March 22, 1970; reply, April 19, 1970. Reprinted in *Current*, May 19, 1970.

"Urban Civilization and Its Discontents" (inaugural lecture as Henry R. Luce Professor of Urban Values at New York University, April 15, 1970), *Commentary*, July 1970. Reprinted in *Democratic Idea*; *Reflections*; and *Neoconservatism*.

"'When Virtue Loses All Her Loveliness'—Some Reflections on Capitalism and 'the Free Society,'" *The Public Interest*, Fall 1970; reply, Winter 1971. Reprinted in *Two Cheers*; *Democratic Idea*; and *The Essential Neoconservative Reader*, edited by Mark Gerson (Reading, Mass.: Addison-Wesley, 1996).

"Is the Urban Crisis Real?" *Commentary*, November 1970.

"Pornography, Obscenity, and Censorship," *New York Times Magazine*, March 28, 1971. Reprinted in *Democratic Idea*; *Reflections*; *The Essential Neoconservative Reader*; *The Neo-Con Reader*, edited by Irwin Stelzer (New York: Grove Press, 2004); as "Censorship: Where Do We Draw the Line?" in *Reader's Digest*, July 1975; and as "Is This What We Wanted?" in *The Case Against Pornography*, edited by David Holbrook (London: Tom Stacey Ltd., 1972).

"From Priorities to Goals," *The Public Interest*, Summer 1971.

"Welfare: The Best of Intentions, the Worst of Results," *Atlantic Monthly*, August 1971. Reprinted in *Neoconservatism*.

"A Foolish American Ism—Utopianism," *New York Times Magazine*, November 14, 1971. Reprinted as "Utopianism and American Politics," in *Democratic Idea*; and under original title in *A Public Philosophy Reader*, edited by Richard Bishirjian (New York: Arlington House, 1978).

"Capitalism and 'the Free Society,'" *The Public Interest*, Winter 1971.

"Of Populism and Taxes," *The Public Interest*, Summer 1972.

"Crisis for Journalism: The Missing Elite," in *Press, Politics, and Popular Government* (Washington, D.C.: American Enterprise Institute, 1972). Reprinted as "The New Demagogic Journalism," in *The Press and American Politics* (Washington, D.C.: Ethics and Public Policy, December 1978).

"An Urban Civilization Without Cities," *Horizon*, Autumn 1972. Reprinted as "America's Future Urbanization," in *Current*, November 1972; excerpted under original title in *Washington Post*, December 3, 1972.

"About Equality," *Commentary*, November 1972; reply, February 1973. Reprinted in *Two Cheers* and *Neoconservatism*.

"The American Revolution as a Successful Revolution" (lecture delivered at American Enterprise Institute, 1973), reprinted in *America's Continuing Revolution: An Act of Conservation* (Washington, D.C.: AEI, 1975). Reprinted in *Reflections*; *Neoconservatism*; *The American Revolution*; *Three Views* (New York: American Brands, 1975); *A Public Philosophy Reader*, edited by Richard Bishirjian (New York: Arlington House, 1978); and as "The Most Successful Revolution: The Leaders All Died in Bed," *American Heritage*, April 1974.

"Lag Found in Tempo of Reform," *New York Times*, January 8, 1973.

"Capitalism, Socialism, and Nihilism," *The Public Interest*, Spring 1973. Reprinted in *Two Cheers* and *Neoconservatism*.

"Utopianism, Ancient and Modern," *Imprimis*, April 1973. Reprinted in *Two Cheers*; *Neoconservatism*; and *The Alternative*, June-September 1974.

"The Need for a Philosophy of Education," in *The Idea of a Modern University*, edited by Sidney Hook, Paul Kurtz, and Miro Todorovich (New York: Prometheus Books, 1974).

"Republican Virtue versus Servile Institutions" (pamphlet of the Poynter Center at Indiana University–Bloomington), May 1974. Reprinted in *The Alternative*, February 1975.

"Who Stands for the Corporation?" *Forbes*, May 15, 1974. Reprinted in *Think*, May-June 1975.

"Taxes, Poverty, and Equality," *The Public Interest*, Fall 1974. Reprinted in *Two Cheers*.

"Thoughts on Reading About a Summer-Camp Cabin Covered with Garbage," *New York Times Magazine*, November 17, 1974.

"On Corporate Capitalism in America," *The Public Interest*, Fall 1975. Reprinted in *Two Cheers*; *Reflections*; and *Neoconservatism*.

"Libertarians and Bourgeois Freedoms," *National Review*, December 5, 1975.

"Moral and Ethical Development in a Democratic Society," in *Moral Development* (Princeton, N.J.: ETS, 1975).

"What Is a 'Neo-Conservative'?" *Newsweek*, January 19, 1976.

"Can Values Do the Job Moral Beliefs Used to Do? Namely Keep People Moral?" *Dividend* (journal of Graduate School of Business Administration, New York University), Spring 1976.

"*The Times*: An Exchange," *The Public Interest*, Spring 1976.

"Socialism: An Obituary for an Idea," *The Alternative*, October 1976. Reprinted in *Reflections*; *Neoconservatism*; and *The Future That Doesn't Work: Social Democracy's Failures in Britain*, edited by R. Emmett Tyrrell Jr. (New York: Doubleday, 1977; rev. ed., New York: University Press of America, 1983).

"Post-Watergate Morality: Too Good for Our Good?" *New York Times Magazine*, November 14, 1976. Reprinted in *Reader's Digest*, May 1977.

"Adam Smith and the Spirit of Capitalism," in *The Great Ideas Today*, edited by Robert Hutchins and Mortimer Adler (Chicago: Encyclopedia Britannica, 1976). Reprinted in *Reflections* and *Neoconservatism*.

"Memoirs of a Trotskyist," *New York Times Magazine*, January 23, 1977. Reprinted in *Reflections* and *Neoconservatism*.

"A Regulated Society?" *Regulation*, July 1977.

"In Memory of Martin Diamond," *The Alternative*, October 1977.

"Looking Back on Neoconservatism: Notes and Reflections," *American Spectator*, November 1977.

"The Measure of America," *Oklahoma Observer*, December 25, 1977.

"Thoughts on Equality and Egalitarians," in *Income Redistribution*, edited by Colin D. Campbell (Washington, D.C.: American Enterprise Institute, 1977).

"Sense and Nonsense in Urban Policy," *National Cities*, February 1978.

"The Spiritual Roots of Capitalism and Socialism," in *Capitalism and Socialism: A Theological Inquiry*, edited by Michael Novak (Washington, D.C.: American Enterprise Institute, 1979). Reprinted as "Christianity, Judaism, and Socialism," in *Reflections* and *Neoconservatism*.

"The Disaffection from Capitalism," in *Capitalism and Socialism: A Theological Inquiry*, edited by Michael Novak (Washington, D.C.: American Enterprise Institute, 1979).

"The Death of the Socialist Idea," *Saturday Evening Post*, March 1979.

"The Case for a Massive Tax Cut," *Reader's Digest*, April 1979.

"Does NATO Exist?" *Washington Quarterly*, Autumn 1979. Reprinted in *Reflections* and *Neoconservatism*.

"Confessions of a True, Self-Confessed—Perhaps the Only—Neoconservative," *Public Opinion*, October-November 1979. Reprinted in *Reflections*.

"What a Palestine Solution Won't Solve," *Washington Post*, October 25, 1979.

"The Adversary Culture of Intellectuals," *Encounter*, October 1979. Reprinted in *Reflections*; *Neoconservatism*; and *The Eighties: A Reader*, edited by Gilbert T. Sewall (Reading, Mass.: Addison-Wesley, 1997).

"Some Personal Reflections on Economic Well-being and Income Distribution," in *The American Economy in Transition*, edited by Martin Feldstein (Chicago: University of Chicago Press, 1980). Reprinted in *Reflections*.

"Rationalism in Economics," *The Public Interest* (special edition), 1980. Reprinted in *Reflections*.

"The Goal," *Encounter*, March 1980.

"Foundations and the Sin of Pride: The Myth of the Third Sector" (New York: Institute for Educational Affairs, 1980). Reprinted in *Giving Well, Doing Good: Readings for Thoughtful Philanthropists*, edited by Amy Kass (Bloomington: Indiana University Press, 2008).

"Ideology and Supply-Side Economics," *Commentary*, April 1981.

"A New Look at Capitalism," *National Review*, April 17, 1981.

"The Scandalous State of Human Rights," [London] *Times*, May 5, 1981.

"The 'Peace Process' Is Narrow," *Washington Post*, January 3, 1982.

"Muddled Thinking on the Middle East," *New York Times*, September 25, 1982.

"'No First Use' Requires a Conventional Buildup," in *The Apocalyptic Premise: Nuclear Arms Debated*, edited by Ernest W. Lefever and E. Stephen Hunt (Washington, D.C.: Ethics and Public Policy Committee, 1982).

"Israel and Palestine: 'Some Plain Truths,'" *Encounter*, September-October 1982.

"Charity and Business Shouldn't Mix," *New York Times*, October 17, 1982.

"The Only Way for Reagan," [London] *Times*, April 14, 1983.

"Soviet Intentions," *New York Times*, May 3, 1983.

"What's Wrong with NATO?" *New York Times Magazine*, September 25, 1983. Reprinted in *Current*, December 1983; and as "NATO Needs Shock Treatment," in *Reader's Digest*, February 1984.

"Life with Sid: A Memoir," in *Sidney Hook: Philosopher of Democracy and Humanism*, edited by Paul Kurtz (New York: Prometheus Books, 1983).

"The Political Dilemma of American Jews," *Commentary*, July 1984; reply, October 1984.

"A Rebirth of Capitalism," *Success!*, October 1984.

"Reflections of a Neoconservative," *Partisan Review*, no. 4, 1984. Reprinted in *Partisan Review: The Fiftieth Anniversary Edition*, edited by William Phillips (New York: Stein & Day, 1985).

"Sidney Hook: Humanist, Pragmatist, Democrat, American," in *Humanities* (Washington, D.C.: National Endowment for the Humanities, 1984).

"A Transatlantic 'Misunderstanding': The Case of Central America," *Encounter*, March 1985; reply, June 1985.

"Even in Israel, No Economic Miracles," *Quadrant*, April 1985.

"America's Doomed Mideast Policy," *New York Times*, August 11, 1985.

"Foreign Policy in an Age of Ideology," *The National Interest*, Fall 1985.

"Skepticism, Meliorism, and *The Public Interest*," *The Public Interest*, Fall 1985.

"Ideas Shape Every Generation," in *American Business and the Quest for Freedom* (Washington, D.C.: Ethics and Public Policy, February 1986).

"Abandon Your Lordships," [London] *Times*, August 26, 1986.

"Room for Darwin and the Bible," *New York Times*, September 30, 1986.

"On Economic Language," in *New York University Business* (New York: NYU Press, 1986).

"'Human Rights': The Hidden Agenda," *The National Interest*, Winter 1986–1987.

"Should U.S. Withdraw from NATO? The Case For," *San Francisco Chronicle*, April 8, 1987.

"Of Lords, Sirs, and Plain Misters: An Exchange Between Irving Kristol and Max Beloff," *Encounter*, June 1987.

"Don't Count Out Conservatism," *New York Times Magazine*, June 14, 1987.

"Ideological Subdivisions," *Public Opinion*, November-December 1987.

"The Spirit of '87," *The Public Interest*, Winter 1987.

"Not the Deficits," *Forbes*, December 14, 1987.

"War on Drugs? Then Get Serious and Use the Military," *Washington Post*, March 28, 1988.

"Liberally Applied, It's Not Voodoo," *Los Angeles Times*, April 4, 1988.

"Why I Left," *The New Republic*, April 11, 1988.

"The Conservatives Have Better Ideas," *New York Times*, October 30, 1988.

"Liberalism and American Jews," *Commentary*, October 1988; reply, January 1989. Reprinted as "The Liberal Tradition of American Jews," in *American Pluralism and the Jewish Community*, edited by Seymour Martin Lipset (New Brunswick, N.J.: Transaction, 1990).

"Christmas, Christians, and Jews," *National Review*, December 30, 1988.

"Forget Arms Control," *New York Times*, September 12, 1989.

"The Way We Were," *The National Interest*, Fall 1989. Reprinted in the *Wall Street Journal*, July 14, 1995.

"On the Character of American Political Order," in *The Promise of American Politics: Principles and Practice After Two Hundred Years*, edited by Robert Utley (New York: University Press of America, 1989).

"Second Thoughts: A Generational Perspective," in *Second Thoughts: Former Radicals Look Back at the Sixties*, edited by Peter Collier and David Horowitz (New York: Madison Books, 1989).

"There Is No Military Free Lunch," *New York Times*, February 2, 1990.

"Twelve Years and Out!" *Washington Post*, June 10, 1990. Reprinted in *American Legion*, February 1991.

"The Gulf: Born-Again Isolationists," *Washington Post*, August 22, 1990.

"Defining Our National Interest," *The National Interest*, Fall 1990. Reprinted as "Our National Interest: Ideas That Define Us," in *Current*, February 1991.

"The GOP Message: A State of Disunion," *New York Times*, January 27, 1991.

"Standing Room Only," *Times Literary Supplement*, July 16, 1991.

"The Future of American Jewry," *Commentary*, August 1991; reply, December 1991. Reprinted in *Neoconservatism*; and *American Jews and the Separationist Faith*, edited by David G. Dalin (Washington, D.C.: Ethics and Public Policy Center, 1993).

"A New Age of Faith?" *Wilson Quarterly*, Autumn 1991.

"The Capitalist Future" (Francis Boyer Lecture), American Enterprise Institute, December 4, 1991. Reprinted as "The Cultural Revolution and the Capitalist Future," in *Neoconservatism*; *Washington Times*, January 3, 1992; *The American Enterprise*, April 1992; and as "Economic Success, Spiritual Decline, the Capitalist Future," *Current*, June 1992.

Foreword to *Public Lives: Fifty Figures of Public Consequence* by Paul Greenberg (Washington, D.C.: Ethics and Public Policy Center, 1991).

"Vision of the Capitalist Future: Anti-Culture Threats from Within," *Washington Times*, January 3, 1992.

"Reply to William Buckley, 'In Search of Anti-Semitism,'" *National Review*, March 16, 1992.

"Secular Rationalism Has Been Unable to Produce a Compelling, Self-Justifying Moral Code," *Chronicle of Higher Education*, April 22, 1992.

"America's Mysterious Malaise," *Times Literary Supplement*, May 22, 1992.

"All That Jazz," *The National Interest*, Summer 1992.

Foreword to *Public Lives: Sixty Figures of Public Consequence* by Paul Greenberg (Washington, D.C.: Ethics and Public Policy Center, 1993).

"My Cold War," *The National Interest*, Spring 1993. Reprinted in *Neoconservatism*; and as "Why I Am Still Fighting My Cold War," [London] *Times*, April 8, 1993.

"Why Religion Is Good for the Jews," *Commentary*, August 1994; reply, November 1994.

"Countercultures," *Commentary*, December 1994. Reprinted in *Neoconservatism*.

"Taking Religious Conservatives Seriously" (foreword), in *Disciples and Democracy: Religious Conservatives and the Future of American Politics*, edited by Michael Cromartie (Grand Rapids, Mich.: Ethics and Public Policy Center/ William Eerdmans, 1994).

"The People's Revolution," *Washington Post*, February 17, 1995.

"Children, Hollywood, and Censorship," *The American Enterprise*, September-October 1995.

"American Conservatism, 1945–1995," *The Public Interest*, Fall 1995.

"The Vox Populi: Why Liberals Hate Talk Radio," *The American Enterprise*, March 1996.

"The Right Stuff," *Prospect*, October 1996.

"A Note on Religious Tolerance," *Conservative Judaism*, Summer 1998.

"On the Political Stupidity of the Jews," *Azure*, Autumn 1999.

"The Coming Clash of Welfare States," *American Outlook*, Winter 1999.

"A Democratic Statesman," *The Weekly Standard*, February 5, 2001.

"Is Technology a Threat to Society?" *The Public Interest*, Spring 2001. Excerpted in *The New Atlantis*, Summer 2005.

"The Neoconservative Persuasion: What It Was, and What It Is," *The Weekly Standard*, August 25, 2003. Reprinted in *The Neocon Reader*, edited by Irwin Stelzer (New York: Grove Press, 2004).

"Robert L. Bartley, 1937–2003," *The Weekly Standard*, December 22, 2003.

"It Wasn't Inevitable: Reagan's Military and Economic Policies Won the Cold War," *The Weekly Standard*, June 21, 2004.

"A Tory Revival Starts with a 10 Percent Tax Cut," [London] *Sunday Times*, March 29, 2005.

"Forty Good Years," *The Public Interest*, Spring 2005.

"My 'Public Interest,'" *The Weekly Standard*, December 18, 2006.

REVIEWS

"Auden: The Quality of Doubt" (by William Ferry), *Enquiry*, November 1942 (*The Double Man* by W. H. Auden).

"A Christian Experiment" (by William Ferry), *Enquiry*, January 1943 (*The Seed Beneath the Snow* by Ignazio Silone).

"Other People's Nerve" (by William Ferry), *Enquiry*, May 1943 (*Partisan Review*, January-February 1943 and March-April 1943).

"James Burnham's *The Machiavellians*" (by William Ferry), *Enquiry*, July 1943 (*The Machiavellians: Defenders of Freedom* by James Burnham).

"The Moral Critic," *Enquiry*, April 1944 (*E. M. Forster* by Lionel Trilling). Reprinted in *Lionel Trilling and the Critics: Opposing Selves*, edited by John Rodden (Lincoln: University of Nebraska Press, 1999).

Review of *Dangling Man* by Saul Bellow, *Politics*, June 1944.

"In Hillel's Steps," *Commentary*, February 1947 (*In Darkest Germany* by Victor Gollancz).

"Nightmare Come True," *Commentary*, October 1947 (*The Other Kingdom* by David Rousset, *Smoke over Birkenau* by Seweryna Szmaglewska, and *Beyond the Last Path* by Eugene Weinstock).

"Christian Theology and the Jews," *Commentary*, April 1948 (*Christianity and the Children of Israel* by A. Roy Eckardt).

"Boundaries of Belief," *Commentary*, March 1949 (*The Protestant Era* by Paul Tillich).

"The Slaughterbench of History," *Commentary*, July 1949 (*Faith and History* by Reinhold Niebuhr and *Meaning in History* by Karl Lowitz).

"Elegy for a Lost World," *Commentary*, May 1950 (*The Earth Is the Lord's* by Abraham Joshua Heschel).

"American Humanist," *Commentary*, November 1950 (*Classics and Commercials* and *The Little Blue Light* by Edmund Wilson).

"Flying off the Broomstick," *Commentary*, April 1951 (*Witch Hunt: The Revival of Heresy* by Carey McWilliams).

"In Power Begins Curiosity," *Partisan Review*, no. 3, 1952 (*The Irony of American History* by Reinhold Niebuhr).

"The Indefatigable Fabian," *New York Times Book Review*, August 24, 1952 (*Beatrice Webb's Diaries: 1912–1924*, edited by Margaret I. Cole).

"Two Varieties of Democracy," *Commentary*, September 1952 (*The Rise of Totalitarian Democracy* by J. L. Talmon).

"The Philosophers' Hidden Truth," *Commentary*, October 1952 (*Persecution and the Art of Writing* by Leo Strauss).

"The Web of Realism," *Commentary*, June 1954 (*The Web of Subversion: Underground Networks in the United States Government* by James Burnham).

"American Ghosts," *Encounter*, July 1954 (*The Adventures of Augie March* by Saul Bellow and *Brothers to Dragons* by R. D. Warner).

"The Judgment of Clio," *Encounter*, January 1955 (*Historical Inevitability* by Isaiah Berlin).

"The Family Way," *Encounter*, December 1955 (*Uncommon People* by Paul Bloomfield).

"America: Mystery and Mystifications," *Encounter*, January 1956 (*American Government* by Richard Pear, *History of the United States* by R. B. Nie and

J. E. Mopurgo, *The Great Experiment* by Frank Thistlethwaite, and *The Age of Reform: From Bryan to FDR* by Richard Hofstadter).

"Bridge and the Human Condition," *Encounter*, February 1956 (*Theory of Games as a Tool for the Moral Philosopher* by R. B. Braithwaite, *Aces All* by Guy Ramsey, and *Sorry Partner* by Paul Sterns).

"The College and the University," *Encounter*, March 1956 (*The Development of Academic Freedom in the United States* by Richard Hofstadter and Walter Metzger).

"The Heterodox Conformist," *Encounter*, April 1956 (*Socialism and the New Despotism* by R. H. S. Crossman).

" . . . And People Opening Veins in Baths," *Encounter*, May 1956 (*Tacitus on Imperial Rome*, translated by Michael Graves; and *Tiberius: A Study in Resentment* by Gregorio Maranon). Reprinted in *Encounters: An Anthology*, edited by Stephen Spender (New York: Basic Books, 1963).

"The Rock of Eden," *Encounter*, June 1956 (*The Dream of Success* by Kenneth S. Lynn, *The Man in the Grey Flannel Suit* by Sloan Wilson, and *The Exurbanites* by A. C. Spectorsky).

"A Philosophy for Little England," *Encounter*, July 1956 (*Philosophy, Politics, and the Soviet Union*, edited by Peter Laslett); reply, September 1956.

"Not One World," *Commentary*, August 1956 (*American Politics in a Revolutionary World* by Chester Bowles).

"Socialism Without Socialists," *Encounter*, August 1956 (*Twentieth-Century Socialism* by Socialist Union).

"Europe's Underground," *Encounter*, September 1956 (*Passion and Society* by Denis de Rougemont).

" . . . A Condition of Mere Nature," *Encounter*, October 1956 (*The Anglo-American Tradition in Foreign Affairs*, edited by Arnold Wolfers and Lawrence W. Martin).

"India to Us," *Encounter*, November 1956 (*Conversations with Mr. Nehru* by Tibor Mende).

"The New Forsyte Saga," *Encounter*, December 1956 (*How the Soviet System Works* by Raymond A. Bauer, et al., and *Russia Without Stalin* by Edward Crankshaw).

"Trivia and History," *Commentary*, December 1956 (*The Crucial Decade* by Eric F. Goldman).

"Vox Populi, Vox Dei?" *Encounter*, March 1957 (*Torment of Secrecy* by Edward Shils and *Freedom or Secrecy* by James Russell Wiggins).

"Politics, Sacred and Profane," *Encounter*, September 1957 (*Battle for the Mind* by William Sargent and *Captured in Tibet* by Robert Ford).

"The Essence of Capitalism," *Encounter*, November 1957 (*Polity and Economy* by Joseph Cropsey).

"I Dreamed I Stopped Traffic," *Encounter*, December 1957 (*The Hidden Persuaders* by Vance Packard).

"American Ambiguities," *Encounter*, January 1958 (*The Jacksonian Persuasion* by Marvin Meyers).

"On Boondoggling Democracy," *Commentary*, August 1958 (*The Affluent Society* by John Kenneth Galbraith).

"The Shadow of a War," *The Reporter*, February 5, 1959 (*Every War but One* by Eugene Kinkead).

"Guernica to Hiroshima," *The Reporter*, March 19, 1959 (*The Great Decision* by Michael Amrine).

"Toward Preemptive War?" *The Reporter*, May 14, 1959 (*War and the Soviet Union* by Herbert S. Dinerstein).

"The Conquistadors' Conscience," *The Reporter*, September 17, 1959 (*Aristotle and the American Indians* by Louis Hanke).

"Strange Gods on Capitol Hill," *The Reporter*, November 12, 1959 (*Advise and Consent* by Allen Drury).

"On the Burning Deck," *The Reporter*, November 26, 1959 (*Up from Liberalism* by William F. Buckley Jr.).

"The Masculine Mode," *Encounter*, December 1959 (*The Spare Chancellor: The Life of Walter Bagehot* by Alistar Buchan).

"D-a-v-y Da-v-y Crockett," *Commentary*, February 1960 (*Mark Twain and Southwestern Humor* by Kenneth S. Lynn).

"A Cool Sociological Eye," *The Reporter*, February 4, 1960 (*Political Man: The Social Basis of Politics* by Seymour Martin Lipset).

"Last of the Whigs," *Commentary*, April 1960 (*The Constitution of Liberty* by F. A. Hayek).

"Disagreeing on Fundamentals," *Encounter*, April 1960 (*America the Vincible* by Emmet John Hughes and *Beyond Survival* by Max Ways).

"A Treasure for the Future," *The New Republic*, July 10, 1961 (*Between Past and Future: Six Exercises in Political Thought* by Hannah Arendt).

"Democracy and Its Discontents," *Harper's*, September 1961 (review of eight books).

"The Idea of Mass Culture," *Yale Review*, February 1962 (*The Political Context of Sociology* by Leon Branson).

"Learning to Live with the NS&N," *Encounter*, August 1963 (*New Statesmanship* by Edward Hyams).

"The View from Miami," *Encounter*, November 1963 (*Great Britain or Little England?* by John Mander, *A State of England* by Anthony Hartley, and *The Outsiders: A Liberal View of Britain* by James Morris).

"Murder in New Jersey," *New York Review of Books*, April 16, 1964 (*Doe Day: The Antlerless Deer Controversy in New Jersey* by Paul Tillett).

"One Utopian, One Sensible Way to Reconcile State and Society," *Harper's*, March 1966 (*Freedom Through Power* by William Withers and *Reclaiming the American Dream* by Richard C. Cornuelle).

"The Don Comes Up Like Thunder," *Washington Post*, August 25, 1968 (*A Runaway World?* by Edmund Leach).

"Discipline as a Dirty Word," *Saturday Review*, June 1, 1974 (*Raising Children in a Difficult Time* by Benjamin Spock).

"The Feminist Attack on Smut," *The New Republic*, July 25, 1981 (*Pornography and Silence* by Susan Griffin).

"The Dubious Science," *The New Republic*, June 6, 1983 (*Dangerous Currents: The State of Economics* by Lester Thurow).

"Let Europe Be Europe," *New York Times Book Review*, June 10, 1984 (*Antipolitics* by George Konrad).

"The State of the Union," *The New Republic*, October 29, 1984 (*The Good News Is the Bad News Is Wrong* by Ben Wattenberg).

"A Choice of Blind Allies," *Times Literary Supplement*, November 23, 1984 (*Politics and the Pursuit of Happiness* by Ghita Ionescu).

"After New Models," *Times Literary Supplement*, December 6, 1985 (*The Trouble with America* by Michael Crozier).

"The New York Intellectuals," *Washington Times*, April 7, 1986 (*Prodigal Sons: The New York Intellectuals and Their World* by Alexander Bloom).

"What Every Soviet Leader Wants," *Fortune*, September 1986 (*The Soviet Paradox* by Seweyn Bialer).

"Wills' America: A 'Sophisticate' Takes Revenge," *Washington Times*, February 9, 1987 (*Reagan's America* by Garry Wills).

"Taking Political Things Personally," *Times Literary Supplement*, March 5, 1991 (*The American "Empire" and Other Studies of U.S. Foreign Policy in a Comparative Perspective* by Geir Lundestad; and *U.S. Foreign Policy in the 1990s*, edited by Greg Schmergel).

"Standing Room Only," *Times Literary Supplement*, July 12, 1991 (*American Citizenship: The Quest for Inclusion* by Judith Shklar).

"America's Mysterious Malaise," *Times Literary Supplement*, May 22, 1992.

"Liberties and Licenses," *Times Literary Supplement*, July 9, 1998 (*Freedom and Virtue: The Conservative/Libertarian Debate*, edited by George W. Carey).

THE NEW LEADER, 1946–1968

"Socialization and Trade Unions," November 2, 1946.

"British Labor Today," February 15, 1947.

"A Labor Minister's Life Is Not a Happy One," May 17, 1947.

"The Anti-Semitism of the Communists," May 24, 1947.

"Bevin and the Left-Wing Rebellion," June 14, 1947.

"Is Western Culture Anti-Semitic?" (review of *The Gentleman and the Jew* by Maurice Samuel), December 25, 1950.

"Koestler: One Who Survived," October 6, 1952.

"McGranery and Charlie Chaplin," November 24, 1952.

"Authors for 'Peace,'" December 22, 1952.

"Notes on Margate," October 24, 1955.

"Britain's Change of Life," October 21, 1957 (review of *They Are the British* by Drew Middleton).

"Thoughts on the Bomb," June 30, 1958.

"The Case for Intervention in Cuba," October 15, 1962.

"Big Government and Little Men," November 26, 1962.

"Of Newton Minow and Matthew Arnold," January 7, 1963.

"A Case of Uneven Development," February 18, 1963.

"The Politics of 'Stylish Frustration,'" April 1, 1963.

"Confessions of a Publisher," May 13, 1963.

"One Man, One Vote," June 24, 1963.

"Age of the Remittance-Man," August 5, 1963.

"Facing the Facts in Vietnam," September 30, 1963.

"My Friend, the Professor," November 11, 1963.

"Jobs and the Man," January 6, 1964.

"The Lower Fifth," February 17, 1964.

"Poverty and Pecksniff," March 30, 1964.

"Mythraking," May 11, 1964.

"The Metaphysics of Journalism," June 22, 1964.

"On Literary Politics," August 3, 1964.

"The Squares versus the Yahoos," September 14, 1964.

"Of Death and Politics," January 18, 1965.

"The Poverty of Equality," March 1, 1965.

"Of Copyrights and Commissars," April 12, 1965; reply, June 21, 1965.

"Where Has the Money Gone?" May 24, 1965.

"The Pauper Problem," December 5, 1966.

"Paying for Protection," December 2, 1968 (review of *Varieties of Police Behavior* by James Q. Wilson).

FORTUNE, 1967–1978 (REVIEWS)

"Professor Galbraith's New Industrial State," July 1967 (*The New Industrial State* by John Kenneth Galbraith).

"As Goes Demand, So Goes Invention," September 1967 (*Invention and Economic Growth* by Jacob Schmookler).

"Common Sense About the Urban Crisis," October 1967 (*Metropolitan Enigma* by U.S. Chamber of Commerce).

"Who's in Charge Here?" November 1967 (*The Power Structure* by Arnold Rose).

"Iron Mountain Lies Beyond Credibility Gap," January 1968 (*Report from Iron Mountain*, edited by Leonard Lewin).

"Men on the Move," March 1968 (*American Occupational Structure* by Otis Dudley Duncan).

"The Strange Death of Liberal Education," March 1968 (*Higher Education and Modern Democracy* by Robert Goldwin).

"Advice for Managers from a Florentine Consultant," April 1968 (*Management and Machiavelli* by Jay Anthony).

"The New Regulators," June 15, 1968 (*Report of the Secretary's Advisory Committee on Traffic* by U.S. Department of Health, Education, and Welfare).

"Why It's Hard to Be Nice to the New Left," August 1968 (*Permanent Poverty: An American Syndrome* by Ben Seligman and *Toward a Democratic Left* by Michael Harrington).

"The New Era of Innovation," February 1969 (*The Age of Discontinuity: Guidelines to Our Changing Society* by Peter Drucker).

"Bilious Sermon from a Hero of the Moral Elite," May 1, 1969 (*American Power and the New Mandarins* by Noam Chomsky).

"The Crisis Behind the Welfare Crisis," June 1969 (*Multi-Problem Dilemma* by G. E. Brown).

"The Improbable Guru of Surrealistic Politics," July 1969 (*An Essay on Liberation* by Herbert Marcuse).

"In Search of the Missing Social Indicator," August 1969 (*Toward a Social Report* by U.S. Department of Health, Education, and Welfare).

"Barbarians from Within," March 1970 (*Decline of Radicalism: Reflections on America Today* by Daniel Boorstin).

"Cities: A Tale of Two Classes," June 1970 (*The Unheavenly City* by Edward C. Banfield).

"The Young Are Trying to Tell Us Something About Scarsdale," August 1971 (*Movement Toward a New America* by Mitch Gooden).

"Does TV News Tell It Like It Is?" November 1971 (*News Twister* by Mitch Gooden).

"The Gang and the Establishment," April 1972 (*Our Gang and How It Prospers* by Richard W. Poston).

"IQ and a Professor's Nightmare," May 1973 (*IQ and the Meritocracy* by Richard J. Herrnstein).

"A College President Discusses America," April 1974 (*Blue-Collar Journey* by John R. Coleman).

"How Hiring Quotas Came to the Campuses," September 1974 (*Anti-Bias Regulations of the University: Faculty Problems and Their Solutions* by Richard A. Lester and *The Balancing Act* by George Roche).

"The High Cost of Equality," November 1975 (*Equality and Efficiency: The Big Trade-off* by Arthur Okun).

"Urban Utopias versus the Real World," July 1978 (*Urban Utopias in the Twentieth Century* by Robert Fisher).

WALL STREET JOURNAL, 1972–2000

"Why Jews Turn Conservative," September 14, 1972.

"The New Road for the Democrats," October 13, 1972.

"The Odd Distortions of TV News," November 16, 1972.

"Symbolic Policies and Liberal Reform," December 15, 1972.

"Is the American Worker 'Alienated'?" January 18, 1973.

"Convalescing from the Frantic '60s," February 16, 1973.

"The Misgivings of a Philanthropist," March 14, 1973.

"Social Reform: Gain and Losses," April 16, 1973. Reprinted in *Two Cheers* and *Neoconservatism*.

"The Nightmare of Watergate," May 17, 1973.

"What Comes Next After Watergate," June 14, 1973.

"The Frustrations of Affluence," July 20, 1973. Reprinted in *Two Cheers* and *Neoconservatism*.

"The Ironies of Neo-Isolationism," August 20, 1973.

"Vice and Virtue in Las Vegas," September 13, 1973. Reprinted as "Do We Want Legalized Betting?" in *Newsday*, October 4, 1973.

"Notes on the Yom Kippur War," October 18, 1973.

"NATO: The End of an Era," November 16, 1973.

"Where Have All the Gunboats Gone?" December 13, 1973.

"The Credibility of Corporations," January 17, 1974. Reprinted in *Two Cheers*.

"The Corporation and the Dinosaur," February 14, 1974. Reprinted in *Two Cheers*.

"The Corporation: A Last Word," March 14, 1974.

"The Meaning of Henry Kissinger," April 11, 1974.

"The Mugging of Con Ed," May 17, 1974.

"Inflation and the 'Dismal Science,'" June 13, 1974. Reprinted in *Two Cheers*.

"Horatio Alger and Profits," July 11, 1974. Reprinted in *Two Cheers*.

"The Shareholder Constituency," August 14, 1974. Reprinted in *Two Cheers*.

"The Inexorable Rise of the Executive," September 20, 1974.

"Political Pollution in Washington," October 17, 1974.

"Secrets of State," November 14, 1974.

"The Environmentalist Crusade," December 16, 1974. Reprinted in *Two Cheers*.

"Food, Famine, and Ideology," January 20, 1975. Reprinted as "Ideology and Food" in *Two Cheers*.

"The Politics of Appeasement," February 12, 1975.

"The War Against the Cities," March 13, 1975.

"Ethics and the Corporation," April 16, 1975. Reprinted in *Two Cheers*.

"Business and 'the New Class,'" May 19, 1975. Reprinted in *Two Cheers* and *Neoconservatism*.

"The Conservative Prospect," June 13, 1975.

"The 'New Cold War,'" July 17, 1975.

"Nuclear Disturbances," August 18, 1975.

"On Conservatism and Capitalism," September 11, 1975. Reprinted in *Two Cheers* and *Neoconservatism*.

"Some Doubts About 'De-Regulation,'" October 20, 1975. Reprinted in *Two Cheers*.

"The New Forgotten Man," November 13, 1975.

"New York Is a State of Mind," December 10, 1975.

"'The Stupid Party,'" January 15, 1976. Reprinted in *Two Cheers* and *Neoconservatism*.

"On 'Economic Education,'" February 18, 1976. Reprinted in *Two Cheers*.

"Henry Kissinger at a Dead End," March 10, 1976.

"Notes on the Spirit of '76," April 23, 1976.

"The Republican Future," May 14, 1976. Reprinted in *Two Cheers* and *Neoconservatism*.

"The Busing Crusade," June 17, 1976.

"The Poverty of Equality," July 12, 1976. Excerpted in *Current*, September 1976.

"What Is 'Social Justice'?" August 12, 1976. Reprinted in *Two Cheers* and *Neoconservatism*.

"Of Decadence and Tennis Flannels," September 21, 1976.

"Reforming the Welfare State," October 25, 1976. Reprinted in *Two Cheers*.

"Morality, Liberalism, and Foreign Policy," November 19, 1976. Reprinted in *Morality and Foreign Policy*, edited by Ernest Lefever (Washington, D.C.: Ethics and Public Policy Center, 1977).

"The Economic Consequences of Carter," December 22, 1976.

"The Hidden Costs of Regulation," January 2, 1977. Reprinted in *Two Cheers*.

"The OPEC Connection," February 2, 1977. Reprinted in *Two Cheers*.

"On Corporate Philanthropy," March 21, 1977. Reprinted in *Two Cheers*.

"Détente and 'Human Rights,'" April 15, 1977.

"Toward a 'New' Economics," May 9, 1977.

"The Foxes versus the Hedgehog," June 14, 1977.

"Summer Notes and Footnotes," July 18, 1977.

"On the Unfairness of Life," August 16, 1977.

"President Carter's Coming Crisis," September 19, 1977.

"A Three-Martini Recession?" October 18, 1977.

"The Myth of 'Business Confidence,'" November 14, 1977.

"Sense and Nonsense in Urban Policy," December 21, 1977.

"Pumping Air into a Balloon," January 13, 1978.

"Of Oil and the Dollar," February 16, 1978. Reprinted in *Society*, September-October 1978.

"The 'Human Rights' Muddle," March 20, 1978.

"The White House Virus," April 17, 1978.

"'Reforming' Corporate Governance," May 12, 1978.

"The Meaning of Proposition 13," June 28, 1978.

"People Who Are S-S-ST," July 24, 1978.

"Populist Remedy for Populist Abuses," August 10, 1978.

"Human Nature and Social Reform," September 18, 1978. Reprinted in *The Essential Neoconservative Reader*, edited by Mark Gerson (Reading, Mass.: Addison-Wesley, 1996).

"Understanding Trade Unionism," October 23, 1978.

"The Economics of Growth," November 16, 1978.

"The Wrong War on Inflation," December 22, 1978.

"Foreign Policy: End of an Era," January 18, 1979. Excerpted as "End of an Era," in *Current*, March 1979.

"No Cheers for the Profit Motive," February 20, 1979.
"Business Ethics and Economic Man," March 20, 1979. Reprinted in *Reflections*.
"Can Carter Reap a Windfall?" April 13, 1979.
"The 'New Class' Revisited," May 21, 1979.
"'Business' versus 'the Economy'?" June 26, 1979.
"Blame It on the People!" July 19, 1979.
"The Confusion over 'Inflation,'" August 22, 1979.
"NATO's Moment of Truth," September 24, 1979.
"Will 'Conservative' Economics Work?" October 22, 1979.
"The Worst Is Yet to Come," November 26, 1979.
"Mr. Carter and Iran," December 28, 1979.
"Our Foreign Policy Illusions," February 4, 1980.
"'Moral Dilemmas' in Foreign Policy," February 28, 1980. Reprinted in *Reflections*.
"The Panic over Inflation," April 1, 1980.
"The Trilateral Commission Factor," April 16, 1980.
"The Battle for Reagan's Soul," May 16, 1980.
"Two Economic Questions," June 26, 1980.
"The New Republican Party," July 17, 1980.
"The Quiet Death of the MAD Doctrine," August 15, 1980.
"Of Economics and 'Eco-Mania,'" September 19, 1980.
"Our Incoherent Foreign Policy," October 15, 1980. Reprinted in *Reflections*.
"The Shadow of '82," November 19, 1980.
"A Guide to Political Economy," December 19, 1980.
"False Principles and Incoherent Policies," January 13, 1981.
"A Letter to the Pentagon," February 20, 1981. Reprinted in *Reflections*.
"The Common Sense of 'Human Rights,'" April 8, 1981. Reprinted in *Reflections*.
"The Muddle in Foreign Policy," April 29, 1981.
"The Timerman Affair," May 29, 1981.
"NATO at a Dead End," July 15, 1981.
"The Trouble with Money," August 26, 1981.
"A Patch of Turbulence," September 25, 1981.
"Economic Policy: Trouble on the Supply Side," October 27, 1981.
"The Truth About Reaganomics," November 20, 1981.
"The Key Question: Who Owns the Future?" January 11, 1982. Reprinted in *Reflections*.
"The Focus Is on the Fed," February 12, 1982.
"Exorcising the Nuclear Nightmare," March 12, 1982. Reprinted in *Reflections*.

"Diplomacy versus Foreign Policy in the U.S.," April 15, 1982. Reprinted in *Reflections*.

"The Self-Destruction of the Republicans," May 13, 1982.

"Notes for a Dismal Spring," June 16, 1982.

"The Question of George Shultz," July 23, 1982.

"Reconstructing NATO: A New Role for Europe," August 12, 1982. Reprinted in *Current*, December 1982.

"Why Reagan's Plan Won't Work," September 10, 1982.

"The Big Question: Is Reagonomics Working?" October 14, 1982.

"The Succession—Understanding the Soviet Mafia," November 18, 1982. Reprinted as "Understanding the Soviet Mafia" in *Reflections*.

"The Emergence of Two Republican Parties," January 4, 1983. Reprinted in *Reflections* and *Neoconservatism*.

"The Reagan Administration Bottoms Out," February 17, 1983.

"What Choice Is There in Salvador?" April 4, 1983.

"Mideast Peace Is the Most Elusive Catch," May 10, 1983.

"Fed Policy: Compromises We Can Live With," June 27, 1983.

"Bar Pollsters from the White House," July 27, 1983.

"Put Not Your Faith in Economic Soothsayers," August 30, 1983.

"Running Like a Dry Creek?" October 6, 1983.

"Toward a Moral Foreign Policy," November 15, 1983.

"There'll Never Be a '1984,'" December 16, 1983.

"What Ever Happened to Common Sense?" January 17, 1984. Excerpted in *Reader's Digest*, February 1990.

"Try a Little Tenderness," February 29, 1984.

"Unhinging of the Liberal Democrat," March 29, 1984.

"'Fairness' and Income Equalizing," May 2, 1984.

"Our Four-Party System," June 15, 1984.

"Most Economists Ignore Reality," July 16, 1984.

"Dilemma of the Outside Director," September 11, 1984.

"Creative Coverage of Political News," October 11, 1984.

"The Honeymoon's Over, Mr. Reagan," November 15, 1984.

"An Automatic-Pilot Administration," December 14, 1984.

"Even in Israel, No Economic Miracles," January 25, 1985.

"A New Foreign-Policy Momentum," March 8, 1985.

"The Old World Needs a New Ideology," April 1, 1985.

"A White House in Search of Itself," May 13, 1985.

"International Law and International Lies," June 21, 1985.

"The New Populism: Not to Worry," July 25, 1985. Reprinted in *Neoconservatism*.

"Reviewing Reagan's Reviewers," September 11, 1985.

"An Economy Too Good to Be True?" October 2, 1985.

"Congressional Right Has It Wrong," November 18, 1985.

"Coping with an 'Evil Empire,'" December 17, 1985.

"Three Economic Notes for 1986," January 9, 1986.

"'Global Unilateralism' and 'Entangling Alliances,'" February 3, 1986.

"Now What for U.S. Client States?" March 3, 1986.

"Why a Debate over Contra Aid?" April 11, 1986.

"The David I Knew," May 9, 1986.

"American Universities in Exile," June 17, 1986.

"The Background to a Sluggish Economy," July 31, 1986.

"Schools Can Do This Much," September 8, 1986.

"The Force Is with Reagan," October 24, 1986.

"Why Did Reagan Do It?" December 17, 1986.

"The Missing Social Agenda," January 26, 1987.

"Economic Notes and Footnotes," March 2, 1987.

"NATO Edges Toward the Moment of Truth," April 14, 1987.

"The War of the Words," June 11, 1987.

"Nuclear NATO: A Moment of Truth," July 9, 1987.

"The New Liberal Isolationism," August 11, 1987.

"Ethics Anyone? Or Morals?" September 15, 1987.

"Look at 1962, Not 1929," October 28, 1987.

"Taking Glasnost Seriously," December 8, 1987.

"Foreign Policy Has Outlived Its Time," January 21, 1988.

"There's No 'Peace Process' in Mideast," February 19, 1988.

"The Reagan Revolution That Never Was," April 19, 1988.

"A Cure for Takeovers' Social Ills," May 13, 1988.

"The Bizarre Social Security Surplus," June 17, 1988.

"The Soviets' Albatross States," July 22, 1988.

"The Trouble with Republicans," August 22, 1988.

"The Question of Patriotism," September 16, 1988.

"Voodoo Economics or Voodoo Economists?" October 18, 1988.

"Bush Must Fight the GOP Energy Shortage," December 21, 1988.

"The War Against the Corporation," January 24, 1989.

"Cries of 'Racism' Cow Crime Fighters," February 28, 1989.

"A Smug NATO Is Letting Germany Secede," May 2, 1989.

"Some Kindergarten Remediation," June 22, 1989.

"Who Needs Peace in the Middle East?" July 21, 1989.

"End Game of the Welfare State," September 11, 1989.

"Education Reforms That Do and Don't Work," October 24, 1989.
"Sometimes It's Over Before It's Over," December 1, 1989.
"The Map of the World Has Changed," January 3, 1990.
"Conservatives' Greatest Enemy May Be the GOP," February 20, 1990.
"Bush Is Right About Lithuania," April 11, 1990.
"Inflation: Almost Never What It Seems," May 16, 1990.
"In Search of Our National Interest," June 7, 1990.
"It's Obscene but Is It Art?" August 7, 1990.
"Hoover, Nixon, Carter . . . Bush?" October 8, 1990.
"What Won, and What Lost, in 1990," November 16, 1990.
"The Challenge of a Political Reversal," December 17, 1990.
"After the War, What?" February 22, 1991.
"Tongue-Tied in Washington," April 15, 1991.
"The Conservatives Find a Leader," June 3, 1991.
"The Tragedy of 'Multiculturalism,'" July 31, 1991. Reprinted in *Neoconservatism*.
"The 1980s—Looking Beyond Reagan," September 11, 1991.
"How to Restructure Wall Street," November 1, 1991.
"Reflections on Love and Family," January 7, 1992. Reprinted in *Neoconservatism*.
"What Shall We Do with the NEA?" March 16, 1992.
"Men, Women, and Sex," May 12, 1992. Reprinted in *Neoconservatism*.
"'Peace Process' That Heads Nowhere," June 18, 1992.
"AIDS and False Innocence," August 6, 1992. Reprinted in *Neoconservatism*.
"'Family Values'—Not a Political Issue," December 7, 1992.
"The Coming 'Conservative Century,'" February 1, 1993. Reprinted in *Neoconservatism* and *Disciples and Democracy: Religious Conservatives and the Future of American Politics*, edited by Michael Cromartie (Washington, D.C.: Ethics and Public Policy Center, 1994).
"When It's Wrong to Be Right," March 24, 1993.
"Two Parties in Search of Direction," May 12, 1993.
"A Conservative Welfare State," June 14, 1993. Reprinted in *The Essential Neoconservative Reader*, edited by Mark Gerson (Reading, Mass.: Addison-Wesley, 1996); and *The Neocon Reader*, edited by Irwin Stelzer (New York: Grove, 2004).
"Clinton's Illusion—Spirit of the '60s," August 19, 1993.
"Too Clever by Half," October 12, 1993.
"From Perot to Buchanan," November 24, 1993.
"Russia's Destiny," February 11, 1994.
"The Inevitable Outcome of 'Outcomes,'" April 18, 1994.
"Sex, Violence, and Videotape," May 31, 1994.

"The Tragic Error of Affirmative Action," August 1, 1994.
"The New Face of American Politics," August 26, 1994. Reprinted in *Neo-conservatism.*
"Life Without Father," November 3, 1994. Reprinted in *Neoconservatism.*
"Who Now Cares About NATO?" February 6, 1995.
"America's 'Exceptional Conservatism,'" April 18, 1995. Reprinted in *Neo-conservatism.*
"Times of Transformation," June 13, 1995.
"The Way We Were," July 14, 1995.
"America Dreaming," August 13, 1995.
"Sex Trumps Gender," March 6, 1996.
"Age Before Politics," April 25, 1996.
"A Post-Wilsonian Foreign Policy," August 2, 1996.
"The Feminization of the Democrats," September 9, 1996.
"The Welfare State's Spiritual Crisis," February 3, 1997.
"The Emerging American Imperium," August 18, 1997.
"Conflicts That Can't Be Resolved," September 5, 1997.
"Income Inequality Without Class Conflict," December 18, 1997.
"Petrified Europe," February 2, 1998.
"Politics Reaches an Endpoint," July 29, 1998.
"The Two Welfare States," October 19, 2000.

SYMPOSIUMS, INTERVIEWS, AND LECTURES

"Letter to an American," *Yale Review,* Summer 1958.
"A Talk-In on Vietnam," *New York Times Magazine,* February 6, 1966 (symposium).
"Civil Disobedience Is Not Justified by Vietnam," *New York Times Magazine,* November 26, 1967 (symposium).
Interview with R. Emmett Tyrrell, *The Alternative,* August-September 1969.
"Urban America and the Democratic Idea," April 15, 1970 (inaugural lecture at New York University).
"What Are the Problems Facing an Urban Service-Centered Economy?" April 11, 1973 (lecture at New York City Council on Economic Education).
"The Relationship Between Jews and Revolutionary Forces," July 31–August 3, 1972 (conference at Van Leer Institute, Jerusalem; published in *Congress Bi-Weekly,* April 13, 1973).
"Coping with the Realities of the '70s," January 13–16, 1974 (lecture at the Super Market Institute, Bal Harbor, Fla.).

Interview with Robert Glasgow, *Psychology Today*, February 1974.

"Moral and Ethical Development in a Democratic Society" (lecture at the 1974 Educational Testing Service conference).

"World Perspective," February 15, 1975 (interview with *Boardroom Reports*).

"Is Technology a Threat to Liberal Society?" March 13–14, 1975 ("Science, Technology, and Modern Society" symposium of Polytechnic Institute of New York).

"America Now: A Failure of Nerve?" *Commentary*, July 1975 (symposium).

"What Is a Liberal—Who Is Conservative?" *Commentary*, September 1976 (symposium). Reprinted in *Professors, Politicians, and Public Policy*, edited by John Charles Daly (Washington, D.C.: American Enterprise Institute, 1977).

"How Equal Can We Be?" *Business and Society Review*, September 1977 (interview).

"Capitalism, Socialism, and Democracy," *Commentary*, April 1978 (symposium).

"Is America Moving Right? Ought It?" (conversation with Irving Kristol and Arthur Schlesinger Jr.), *Public Opinion*, September-October 1978. Reprinted in *Across the Board*, February 1979.

"Waste of Time," *Business and Society Review*, Summer 1979 (symposium on "Is Dishonesty Good for Business?").

"Where Do We Go from Here? Directions from Stage Right," *Public Opinion*, December 1980–January 1981 (symposium).

"William Baroody Sr., Recipient of the 1980 Boyer Award" (Washington, D.C.: American Enterprise Institute, 1981) (lecture).

"Neoconservative Guru to America's New Order," *MacLean's*, January 19, 1981 (discussion).

"A New Look at Capitalism," *National Review*, April 17, 1981 (symposium on *Wealth and Poverty* by George Gilder).

"If Conservatives Cannot Do It Now . . . ," *U.S. News and World Report*, July 20, 1981 (interview).

"Is Social Science a God That Failed?" *Public Opinion*, October-November 1981 (symposium).

Interview in *Reason*, January 1983.

"Should the United States Stay in NATO?" *Harper's*, January 1984 (symposium).

"Sex and God in American Politics: What Conservatives Really Think," *Policy Review*, Summer 1984 (symposium).

"Jewish Voters and the 'Politics of Compassion,'" *Commentary*, October 1984 (symposium).

"What's Going On Out There?" in *The State of the Nation: A Conference of the Committee for the Free World*, edited by Steven C. Munson (Washington, D.C.: University Press of America, 1985) (symposium).

"Why Europe Worries, and Why Washington Cares," *New York Times*, March 17, 1985 (symposium).

"Beyond Containment: The Future of U.S.-Soviet Relations," *Policy Review*, Winter 1985 (symposium).

"How Has the United States Met Its Major Challenges Since 1945?" *Commentary*, November 1985 (symposium).

"Who Should Succeed Reagan? Some Preliminary Thoughts," *Policy Review*, Summer 1986 (symposium).

"Should America Go It Alone?" *East-West Papers*, July 1986 (symposium).

"On the Reagan Presidency," *American Spectator*, October 1986 (symposium).

Contribution to "Scorpions in a Bottle: Dangerous Ideas About the United States and the Soviet Union," Hillsdale College, 1986 (symposium).

"The U.S. Needs the Will to Be a Winner," *Insight*, December 29, 1986–January 5, 1987 (symposium).

"Should America Quit NATO? *East-West Papers*, February 1987 (debate with Eugene V. Rostow). Reprinted in *San Francisco Chronicle*, April 8, 1987.

"American Jews and Israel," *Commentary*, February 1988 (symposium).

"The Reagan Doctrine and Beyond" (Washington, D.C.: American Enterprise Institute, 1988) (symposium), and "Freedom and Vigilance: Ronald Reagan" (Washington, D.C.: AEI, December 7, 1988) (symposium).

Our Country and Our Culture (New York: Orwell Press, 1989) (symposium of the Committee for the Free World).

"This Is the Place to Be!" *Washingtonian*, July 1989 (interview with Ken Adelman).

"The End of History and the Last Man" by Francis Fukuyama, *The National Interest*, Summer 1989 (symposium).

Does "the West" Still Exist? (New York: Orwell Press, 1990) (symposium of the Committee for the Free World).

"Books for Christmas," *American Spectator*, December 1990 (symposium).

Interview with Tom Bethell, *American Spectator*, December 1991.

"The National Prospect," *Commentary*, November 1995 (symposium).

"Taking His Measure: Five Historians Weigh Newt on the Scales of Time—and Against Other Leaders," *Time*, December 25, 1995–January 1, 1996.

"Will Future Americans Look Back at the 1996 Vote and Say 'Bingo'?" *The American Enterprise*, November-December 1996.

"Is There a Jewish Agenda for America?" *Reform Judaism*, Summer 1997 (symposium).

Arguing the World: The New York Intellectuals in Their Own Words, edited by Joseph Dorman (New York: Free Press, 2000) (TV interviews, 1998).

"There is No 'Third Sector,'" *Philanthropy*, November-December 1998 (interview).

"Censorship?" *The Weekly Standard*, August 23, 1999 (symposium).

"Why American Conservatism Is Exceptional," October 15, 2001 (lecture at American Enterprise Institute).

"Religion and Secularism," in *Religion and the American Future*, edited by Christopher DeMuth and Yuval Levin (Washington, D.C.: AEI Press, 2008) (symposium).

ACKNOWLEDGMENTS

The editor gratefully acknowledges permission to use articles from the following sources:

Reprinted from *Commentary*, 1947, 1948, 1952 (2), 1981, 1984, 1988, and 1994, with permission, all rights reserved: "The Myth of the Supra-Human Jew"; "How Basic Is 'Basic Judaism'?"; "'Civil Liberties,' 1952"; "The Philosophers' Hidden Truth"; "Ideology and Supply-Side Economics"; "The Political Dilemma of American Jews"; "Liberalism and American Jews"; and "Why Religion Is Good for the Jews."

Reprinted with permission from *The Weekly Standard*, 2003 and 2006: "The Neoconservative Persuasion" and "My 'Public Interest.'"

Reprinted with permission from *The National Interest*, 1986–1987: "'Human Rights': The Hidden Agenda."

Reprinted with permission: "Christmas, Christians, and Jews" © 1988 by National Review, Inc., 215 Lexington Avenue, New York, NY 10016.

Reprinted with permission of Michael Cromartie and the Ethics and Public Policy Center, from *Disciples and Democracy*, 1994: "Taking Religious Conservatives Seriously."

Reprinted from *Neoconservatism: The Autobiography of an Idea* (New York: Free Press), 1995, with permission, all rights reserved: "An Autobiographical Memoir."

Reprinted from *Prospect*, 1996: "The Right Stuff."

Reprinted with permission from *Conservative Judaism*, 1998: "A Note on Religious Tolerance."

Reprinted with permission from *Azure*, Autumn 1999: "On the Political Stupidity of the Jews."

Other articles for which the author holds permission rights originally appeared in various sources as follows:

Enquiry: "Auden: The Quality of Doubt"; "A Christian Experiment"; "Other People's Nerve"; "James Burnham's *The Machiavellians*"; and "The Moral Critic."
Encounter: "Niccolò Machiavelli"; " . . . And People Opening Veins in Baths"; "American Ambiguities"; and "High, Low, and Modern."
The Public Interest: "The Spirit of '87"; "American Conservatism: 1945–1995"; and "Forty Good Years."
Wall Street Journal: "The Ironies of Neo-Isolationism"; "Vice and Virtue in Las Vegas"; "Notes on the Yom Kippur War"; "Toward a 'New' Economics?"; "Human Nature and Social Reform"; "No Cheers for the Profit Motive"; "International Law and International Lies"; "It's Obscene but Is It Art?"; "The Way We Were"; "The Welfare State's Spiritual Crisis"; "Conflicts That Can't Be Resolved"; and "The Two Welfare States."
Yale Review: "Old Truths and the New Conservatism."
Atlantic Monthly: "What's Bugging the Students."
Indiana University Pointer Center pamphlet (speech): "Republican Virtue versus Servile Institutions."
Newsweek: "What Is a 'Neoconservative?'"
Institute for Educational Affairs: "Foundations and the Sin of Pride."
New York Times Magazine: "What's Wrong with NATO?"